Business Finance in Less Developed Capital Markets

Recent Titles in
Contributions in Economics and Economic History

Business Finance in Less Developed Capital Markets

Edited by
Klaus P. Fischer
and
George J. Papaioannou

Prepared under the auspices of Hofstra University

Contributions in Economics and Economic History,
Number 134

Greenwood Press
Westport, Connecticut • London

Library of Congress Cataloging-in-Publication Data

Business finance in less developed capital markets / edited by Klaus
    P. Fischer and George J. Papaioannou.
        p.   cm.—(Contributions in economics and economic history.
    ISSN 0084-9235 ; no. 134)
    "Prepared under the auspices of Hofstra University."
    "Papers and panel discussions presented in the International
Symposium on Business Finance in Less Developed Capital Markets,
held at Hofstra University, on September 22-23, 1988."—
    Includes bibliographical references and index.
    ISBN 0-313-27972-1 (alk. paper)
    1. Capital market—Developing countries—Congresses.
2. Corporations—Developing countries—Finance—Congresses.
I. Fischer, Klaus Peter, 1946-   . II. Papaioannou, George J.,
1947- . III. Hofstra University. IV. Series.
HG5993.B87   1992
 332'.041'091724—dc20   91-45574

British Library Cataloguing in Publication Data is available.

Library of Congress Catalog Card Number: 91-45574
ISBN: 0-313-27972-1
ISSN: 0084-9235

First published in 1992

Greenwood Press, 88 Post Road West, Westport, CT 06881
An imprint of Greenwood Publishing Group, Inc.

Printed in the United States of America

The paper used in this book complies with the
Permanent Paper Standard issued by the National
Information Standards Organization (Z39.48-1984).

10 9 8 7 6 5 4 3 2 1

Contents

Part II. Risk and Return in Securities Markets

Part III. Asset Management

Part IV. Credit and Financing Policy

Illustrations

FIGURES

TABLES

Introduction: Business Finance in Less Developed Capital Markets: An Emerging Field of Study

KLAUS P. FISCHER and
GEORGE J. PAPAIOANNOU

The chapters in this volume are based on papers and panel discussions presented in the International Symposium on Business Finance in Less Developed Capital Markets held at Hofstra University on September 22–23, 1988. The purpose of the symposium was to focus attention on theoretical and empirical issues pertaining to the application of financial decisions and policies by firms, financial institutions, and investors in the environment of less developed capital markets (LDCMs).[1]

The organization of the symposium was motivated by the relative lack of a well-developed body of literature that addresses finance issues germane to economies with less developed financial systems. The specific aim of the symposium was to promote research in this direction and to facilitate communication among researchers interested in the field.

The lack of literature specific to LDCMs may be explained by the fact that modern finance theory and its empirical testing grew primarily in the United States, which operates with a well-developed and well-functioning financial system. Based on the seminal work of Modigliani and Miller (1958), the basic tenet of modern finance theory is that the financial decisions of the firm should be evaluated by their wealth effects on the firm's securities; in turn, these wealth effects are the product of the valuation process that takes place in the capital markets where financial claims are traded. Thus a positive theory of finance has been developed in the context of the efficient capital markets (ECM) paradigm that describes the performance of the capital markets in the United States. In such a capital market setting, not only is the valuation process carried on outside of the firm, but the prices reflect all relevant information and therefore are unbiased estimates of true values.

Outside the United States and a few other industrialized countries (most notably Canada and the United Kingdom), financial systems do not conform to the ECM paradigm. Rather, they operate in an environment of limitations and distortions, the most serious of which are the following:

1. Financial repression in credit allocation and rates determination
2. Imbalances in the financial system, most commonly manifested in the predominance of indirect financing through credit institutions and weak securities markets
3. An inadequate menu of financial instruments to span the risk-return space
4. Socioeconomic factors and business practices and cultures that diminish or compromise the role of open capital markets as sources of capital and mechanisms for risk allocation

This implies that prices either are not existent or, if available, are biased by the distortions in the market. As a result, the applicability to these environments of the "external valuation" paradigm implicit in the Modigliani and Miller (1958) framework becomes questionable.

It must be noted that these symptoms are not associated exclusively with less developed economies. In various combinations, and with varying intensity, they are also characteristic of mature economies, as evidence with respect to capital controls in many Western European countries attests (at least prior to the onslaught of rapid financial deregulation and modernization in the 1980s).

Viewed from a developmental perspective, some financial systems are less developed by the nature of the stage they have reached on their way toward financial maturity, with the so-called emerging markets being a relevant example. Other financial systems, however, are less developed by virtue of endemic hindrances or deliberate policy choices. From a different viewpoint, financial development can be measured by the extent of completeness of financial institutions and market infrastructure, or its lack. Measures of completeness can refer to the organization of markets, the variety of financial claims, information disclosure and dissemination, and enforcement of financial contracts. The existence of national financial systems with diverse qualitative and quantitative differences and conforming to different levels of completeness raises an important question for the positive theory of finance, namely, what predictions one can make concerning the valuation process in different financial markets and the behavior of the firm under different capital market environments.

As an introduction to this volume, it is interesting to review the evolution of the academic interest on the subject of less developed capital markets, and its practical consequences. Following World War II, many industrialized countries, as well as less developed ones, ignored the development of robust financial systems. This can be attributed to the relatively lesser importance placed by early growth models on the role of financial markets as engines of economic growth. However, some significant empirical and theoretical developments shortly opened the debate on the role of financial deepening in economic development.[2] In particular, empirical work by Goldsmith (1969) provided evidence that there exists a link between economic development and financial structure. Systematic theoretical inquiry, begun by Gurley and Shaw (1955, 1960, 1967), modified contemporary monetary policy and its application as a tool of economic growth in order to fit the conditions found in economies with restricted credit policies and markets. Two more seminal academic contributions by Shaw (1973) and McKinnon (1973) helped solidify the importance of financial development to fostering growth. In other early academic works on the subject, Patrick (1966) and Wai and Patrick (1973) undertook insightful inquiries into the microeconomic aspects of financial markets in relation to the important question of how they contribute to financial capital mobilization and economic growth. These and other studies exerted significant influence on economic policy in several countries.

Despite their recommendations for elimination of restrictive credit policies and the promotion of financial deepening, these studies were not equally emphatic in suggesting the balanced development of market mechanisms for indirect as well as direct financing arrangements. On the contrary, most advocated the deepening of the money sector and the building of credit intermediaries before the development of full-fledged securities markets. In retrospect, it seems that the relative neglect of public stock and bond markets in most free-market economies was the manifestation of the influence of this failure to prescribe policies that favored the development of public markets.[3]

While issues of finance in less developed capital markets were dominated by economic growth and monetary policy prerogatives, academic interest on the finance aisle of the economic discipline was developing at a rather slow pace. Two factors contributed to this. First, finance as a scientific discipline came to being only in the late 1950s. Second, its theoretical tools were initially shaped to fit the efficient capital markets theory and its implication of firm value maximization.

A review of published articles in U.S. finance journals between 1960 and 1990 reveals that most of the studies on finance issues outside the United States referred to markets located in Europe and Japan. There were only sporadic cases of papers that dealt with finance issues in the LDCMs of the rest of the world. The preponderance of studies directed toward Europe and Japan seems to be a primary characteristic of the early phase of inquiry of a finance topic outside the United States. This can be attributed to the greater importance of these regions as financial centers compared to the less developed countries.

Another characteristic in the development of the literature concerning finance issues outside North America is the preoccupation of most studies with the major research questions that had been raised and debated in the United States. Thus early studies turned to the question of efficiency of securities markets in various industrialized and developing countries. The development and adoption in practice of modern portfolio theory gave further impetus to studies that investigated the opportunities for international portfolio diversification in capital markets outside the United States. On a parallel path, several studies addressed the question of the relevance of firm capital structure in various countries of Western Europe and Latin America. The obvious motivation of these studies was the ongoing debate on capital structure started by Modigliani and Miller in the late 1950s.

What is common in most of these studies is the firm grounding of their testable hypotheses and methodologies in the contemporary accepted finance theory and research in the United States. In most cases, the socioeconomic and institutional idiosyncrasies of the particular countries studied were ignored, and hence the basic research question was reduced to whether capital market and firm financial behavior in these countries mimicked that already documented in the United States. The consequence of this approach of inquiry has been the delayed emergence of a theory of finance for less developed capital markets.

Notwithstanding this epistemological deficiency, the literature on various international financial markets that fit the characterization of LDCMs has continued to expand. A wave of important developments occurred through the 1980s and contributed to this expansion of interest in LDCMs. Some of the most significant developments are the following. The securitization of corporate assets and sovereign debt as well as the need to tap foreign capital sources expanded the scope of interest outside the traditional world capital centers. The ascendancy of several countries of the Pacific Rim region toward mature economies with large capital surpluses and real investment opportunities enhanced the viability and importance of their securities markets and stimulated their upgrading. At the same time, investors, motivated by increased holdings of liquid assets, started to pursue bargains in securities markets outside the traditional financial centers of North America, Europe, and Japan. These developments necessitated the linkage of international markets in order to facilitate global portfolio management and led to the growing globalization of national financial systems. Furthermore, they highlighted the importance of securities markets for attracting foreign capital and generating additional economic activity. Finally, the movement toward free-market policies and away from financial repression and regulation mandated the development of equities and debt markets as part of the official economic priorities of many industrialized and developing countries. As a result of these developments, several European countries (e.g., France, West Germany, and others) have emerged with better-organized and more complete securities markets. More important, a promising new tier of securities markets, the so-called emerging markets, has established itself as a bona fide component of the international nexus of global finance.

Currently, the academic interest in LDCMs is manifested in the proliferation of journals attuned to finance issues in various international securities markets, international conferences on such topics, and more frequent presentations of papers in established finance conventions. Therefore it is fair to expect that the growing academic interest in LDCMs will lead to a more systematic and comprehensive study of business finance under market environments that incorporate the idiosyncrasies of LDCMs. Ideally, a complete theory of finance must also explain firm and investor behavior under the conditions of less developed capital markets.

Fortuitously enough, recent advances in modern financial theory seem to provide the foundations of a theory of finance that can explain a broad variety of phenomena in LDCMs. Such advances include the theories on agency costs, asymmetric information, and signaling. Interestingly, these new theoretical approaches, which grew out of the lack of satisfactory answers justified by the paradigms of firm-value maximization and efficient capital markets, seem to be useful tools to prod questions not foreign to firm financial behavior and capital market performance in LDCMs. It is indeed an open question whether future research will lead to a general theory of finance applicable to all capital markets or will lead to several finance theories, each one applicable to a different class of capital markets.

The chapters in this volume are organized into seven parts that cover some of the important areas in financial research. Thereby, we hope to provide some research leads in each of these areas as they apply to less developed capital markets. The first six parts deal with development of capital markets, risk and return in securities markets, asset management, credit and financing policies, the theory of the firm in LDCMs, and international capital and enterprise incentives. The final part consists of three commentaries on future research directions in the topic of business finance in less developed capital markets.

DEVELOPMENT OF CAPITAL MARKETS

The chapters in the first part address issues related to the development of capital markets. The authors consider innovations in capital markets from the point of view of emerging markets, such as venture capital and mutual funds. They also evaluate critically the current state and the development of capital markets in LDCM economies. One theme that persists through these chapters is the inadequacy of the formal (or orthodox) financial sector, including development banks, in providing funding commensurate to the growth opportunities of small- and medium-sized enterprises (SMEs), and the important role played by the informal sector in filling this gap. Although most of the discussions on informal markets appear in this part, the topic turns up in later chapters as well. The first two chapters could be considered primarily policy chapters. The third and fourth chapters are quite different in nature, one presenting a model of development of the financial system and the other reporting the development of mutual funds in Turkey.

The first chapter, by Richard Kitchen, investigates the suitability of venture capital for developing countries.[4] Kitchen examines the problems faced by SMEs in developing countries in obtaining financing, especially in those countries that lack functioning equities markets. The author also deals with the limitations of intermediated debt financing. Among the interesting contributions made by this chapter, we find a survey of established methods of SME financing and the role and functioning of informal-sector financing; a description of various forms of venture-capital financing; an account of some of the criteria used by venture capitalists in their search for suitable projects to finance; a discussion of the advantages of stock markets and their organizational form in financing SMEs; and finally and most importantly, a description of private and public venture-capital organizations established in various developing countries, including several that have been instituted with international cooperation.

The second chapter, by Ade Ojo, investigates in more depth the particular case of Nigeria, a case wholly representative of many other developing countries. Ojo critically evaluates both the conventional financial system, consisting of commercial and development banks, and the stock markets. The important role of the informal sector is discussed in some detail. The author presents interesting statistics about the relative share of SME financing provided by the form and informal sectors. An interesting highlight provided by the chapter is the regulation and functioning of the only existing second-tier stock market in the developing world, the Nigerian Second-Tier Securities Market.

P. C. Kumar and George Tsetsekos attempt to develop a theory of the link between security markets development and economic growth. The main line of argument of the chapter is that the development of the financial market takes place in five distinctive stages that are closely associated with specific phases of economic development. Among the points of interest associated with the development of the theory is a brief but comprehensive list of monetary, fiscal, and special incentive policies intended to promote the development of equities markets.

The fourth and last chapter in this part, by Yaman Asikoglu, Sevil Kutay, and I. Özer Ertuna, consists of an evaluation of the Turkish experience in developing mutual funds. The chapter is of interest also to countries beyond Turkey because it describes many of the problems found in most emerging markets when such financial innovations are undertaken. The chapter sharply criticizes several aspects of the regulatory framework established to develop these mutual funds. These criticisms are worth taking into consideration in every case in which similar financial market development objectives are undertaken.

RISK AND RETURN IN SECURITIES MARKETS

This part takes a more narrow focus on securities markets. Specifically, all the chapters present the results of tests of one form or another of market efficiency. The studies suggest that despite common preconceptions, these markets, generally speaking, do not seem to behave much differently from their developed brethren, the securities markets of the Western world, when they are subjected to tests using standard research methodologies. The problem is, of course, as the authors of the first chapter in this part pointedly assert, that a proponent of efficient capital markets always stands to win. We leave it up to the reader to investigate the details of this thought at the source. However, these studies, like many others done earlier, suggest the need for innovative approaches to evaluate the efficiency question.

In the first chapter, Cheng Few Lee, Gili Yen, and Chingfu Chang address the price behavior of common stocks around the Chinese New Year. Using data from 1975 to 1984, they find that it is possible to devise an abnormal-profit-making rule based solely on historical information. This implies that weak-form efficiency is rejected for the Taiwanese stock market.

The second chapter introduces an interesting line of thinking, which, we believe, could lead to a rich field of research in LDCM behavior. As a rule, LDCMs exist in small open economies that are much more sensitive to external shocks (events) than industrialized and well-developed economies. LDCM stock prices reflect domestic (and foreign) investors' perceptions of the impact of external shocks on the economy. Thus studying price behavior around specific events allows the researcher to make an empirical assessment of the economy's sensitivity to these shocks. Gili Yen and Philip Chang study the reaction of the Taiwanese stock market to trade talks with the United States. They find that the Taiwanese economy is highly sensitive to the trade-talk process. Unfortunately, they do not address the related and interesting question of the speed of price adjustment to changes in the publicly available information set.

The chapter by Antonio Zoratto Sanvicente and Everaldo Guedes Franca makes a rare attempt to test strong-form efficiency in a LDCM (namely, that of Brazil). The methodology used can be criticized (and the discussant does not spare the authors this pain). Nonetheless, this study provides a very interesting glimpse into the functioning of an institutional arrangement quite common in LDCMs. In Brazil, as in many other countries, mutual funds are managed by commercial banks. As a result, fund managers frequently hold "insider information" on the financial status of listed firms. If this is reflected in their investment strategy, mutual funds should outperform the market. This is exactly what Sanvicente and Franca find.[5] We hope to see more work that tests for the presence of information asymmetries among market participants, since such asymmetries arguably are one of the most critical problems of LDCMs.

Othman Yong, in the last chapter of this part, tests the weak-form efficiency of the Malaysian stock exchange. This is an improved evaluation of a quite extensively researched market. Yong arrives at the dead-end situation common for this type of study. Based on the autocorrelation structure of stock returns, weak-form efficiency can be rejected for some stocks. This, however, does not mean that the Malaysian market is not a "fair game." As the author correctly points out, whether this is the case can only be tested using filter rules. Interestingly, to the best of our knowledge, no filter-rule tests have been performed on LDCMs, despite the large number of studies that address the question of efficiency in these markets. The chapter concludes with a well-thought-out list of measures that, the author suggests, can improve the functioning of the Malaysian market. These improvement measures are also relevant and applicable to most other countries with LDCMs.

ASSET MANAGEMENT

This part focuses on the question of corporate asset management in economies with LDCMs. The chapter by Edgar Ortiz and Graciela Bueno starts with the assumption that imperfections in LDCMs invalidate many of the assumptions implicit in the use of asset-management tools commonly employed in industrialized countries. In particular, many of the market indicators that are useful for corporate financial decision making in industrialized countries are nonexistent or unreliable in LDCMs to discipline managers and guide decisions. The authors propose the use of goal programming as a suitable management tool and apply the model to Petroleos Mexicanos (Pemex)—a state-owned corporation—as a case study.

In the second chapter, Marjorie Stanley evaluates the validity of assumptions implicit in the most popular capital budgeting techniques when they are applied in a LDCM environment from the financial and ethical points of view. The evaluation is done from the viewpoint of the multinational corporation (MNC) as well as the domestic entrepreneur. The conclusions are too extensive to summarize in this brief introduction. However, the chapter underlines the absence of many of the market conditions necessary for the validity of accepted capital budgeting criteria in LDCM economies.

CREDIT AND FINANCING POLICIES

The chapters in the fourth part deal with the question of firm financing and investment and their relationship with economic policies of governments. Given the high level of government intervention and control and the volatility in macro-economic conditions characteristic of LDCM countries, this is indeed a very important issue. The three chapters presented in this part provide interesting insights on the response of business to changes in key economic variables, most of which are under the control of the government. This vein of research is crucial to understanding the linkage between government action (macroeconomic policy) and business response (microeconomic decision making). Fortunately, we are seeing an increasing interest in this field by researchers of the most diverse academic extractions.

The first chapter by James Tybout and Taeho Bark seeks to establish the relationship between macroeconomic policy variables and business performance with particular reference to growth and financing. Specifically, the model attempts to measure the relationship between interest rates, exchange rates, and aggregate demand conditions, on one side, and the firms' fixed assets, inventories, financial assets, and debt on the other. The model is applied to Uruguayan data. We agree with the discussant that the presentation of results is not very transparent. However, the study does present several important findings some of which are quite intuitive, but others of which are surprising. Two results are noteworthy because of our current lack of understanding of the issue: (1) the relationship between local currency fluctuations and firm performance and (2) the relationship between domestic interest rates and financing policies. Note in particular the parallel treatment of the "tablita" exchange regime in their chapter and in chapter 18.

In the second chapter, Mansoor Dailami models the interaction between optimal corporate capital structure and real investment decisions in the context of an economy with credit rationing, a controlled banking system, and an organized equities market. This is an interesting departure from similar models developed under assumptions of perfect capital markets and securitized markets for debt and equity. Perhaps more interesting than the somewhat comforting result presented in the conclusions, namely, that the Korean corporate sector benefitted from government investment incentives, are the comparative statics results of the theoretical model. We direct the reader to the section titled "Steady-State Equilibrium" for an interesting, and not too technical, discussion of the predictions generated by the model.

The last chapter in this section, by Uwe Corsepius, delves into the very important question of the relationship between formal and informal financial markets. The author suggests that changes in the formal financial sector may induce borrowers to shift from one market to the other, partly or totally offsetting the impact of the changes in the formal sector. This is a very interesting conclusion, critical to understanding the impact of governmental fiscal and monetary policies, and points the way toward a very rich field for future research.

THE THEORY OF THE FIRM IN LDCMs

This part, with only two chapters, addresses questions related to the development of a financial theory of the firm for LDCMs as well as issues involved in the financial management of the firm. The first chapter, by Stavros Thomadakis, introduces a set of ideas regarding corporate organization that may very well serve as one of the leading contributions to the topic of corporate finance in LDCMs. This chapter and the discussion by Lemma Senbet indeed open a fresh and very promising approach to understanding financial decision making in LDCMs and how the modern theory of financial contracting can be used to solve conflicts generated by the nature of LDCMs. First, Thomadakis makes a fundamental proposition that takes us away from the conventional reasoning in finance. In contrast to developed capital markets, in which the valuation of the firm is established from "outside" (the market), in LDCMs firm valuation is internalized. Second, Thomadakis provides some brilliant insights into the incentive structure to which entrepreneurs are subject in most LDCM countries. Many of the agency conflicts standard in the finance literature (e.g., shareholders versus managers) disappear, and new ones (e.g., owner versus noncapital stakeholders) appear. The most significant prediction generated by this line of argument is the formation of "enterprise groups" so common in many LDCM countries.

The second chapter, by V. N. Hukku, is an interesting and critical evaluation of the management practices of public (state-owned) enterprises in India. The critique covers a wide range of aspects of the firm's financial management, from financing practices to working capital management. Since public enterprises are quite common in many LDCM countries, the discussion presented therein is also of interest to researchers outside of India.

INTERNATIONAL CAPITAL AND ENTERPRISE INCENTIVES

The sixth part of the volume captures international issues from the point of view of the LDCM country and firm. We make a deliberate effort to avoid the conventional "MNC-bashing" practice as well as the "debt-crisis" analysis. The finance and economics literature provides plenty of both. Instead, we attempt to focus on the structure of incentives that the international financial environment imposes on both governments and business.

In the first chapter, Daniel Tzang evaluates within a game-theoretic framework the optimal contract form between local governments and multinational enterprises for oil exploration and extraction ventures. The final conclusion is that contract forms that ensure risk sharing between the parties and allow local government participation in petroleum operations appear to be optimal. In the process of completing the analysis, the author provides an interesting review of contractual forms most commonly used in oil exploration as well as their risk- and profit-sharing characteristics.

A methodologically similar analysis, but one focusing on debt negotiation, is presented by George Anayiotos in the second chapter of this part. Here the structure of incentives of a borrowing country is again systematically evaluated. One interesting conclusion of the analysis is that in the presence of sovereign risk and a high level of debt-service requirements, countries are subject to disincentives to invest and thus to lower economic growth.

The third chapter, by Graciana del Castillo, confronts us with the little-under-stood but crucial problem of exchange risk of foreign currency financing when exchange rates are controlled by the government. This is an instance of a massive political-risk exposure (which the author calls the "policy-risk factor" and explic-itly models as a function of fiscal imbalances) by domestic firms. The chapter builds the case around the experience of Uruguayan firms in the early 1980s when a controlled exchange-rate system called *la tablita* ("the table" of scheduled deval-uations) was in effect. Although generalizations are difficult to make, due to the particular set of circumstances that occurred in Uruguay, the chapter illustrates the strongly political nature of risk to which firms in LDCMs with a high level of government control are exposed.

RESEARCH DIRECTIONS

This final part includes commentaries on research directions for business finance in LDCMs made by three researchers, Edgar Ortiz, Lemma Senbet, and Vihang Errunza. All three commentaries clearly suggest that although academic interest has shifted to issues of finance in LDCMs, the task of starting to apply formal scientific analysis, as opposed to ad hoc theorizing, and understand the idiosyncrasies of LDCMs and the implications thereof for financial decision making lies ahead of us.

It is evident then that the contribution of the Symposium, and this volume of proceedings in particular, will be judged by the extent to which it succeeds to stimulate further formal research in the field of its theme, by presenting papers mostly written from the unique perspective of LDCMs.

NOTES

1. We acknowledge the influence of some of the chapters included in this volume on the ideas developed in this introduction.

2. See Fry (1987) and McKinnon (1976, 1989) for relevant reviews and contributions to this debate from an economic theory and policy viewpoint. Calamanti (1983) offers a more microfinance perspective on the importance of securities markets for economic growth.

3. Contrariwise, arguments in favor of the parallel promotion of direct and indirect financial markets can be found in Drake (1976), Cho (1986), and Papaioannou (1986). Calamanti (1983) has also contributed to this debate, but she sides with the early view in favor of credit intermediation.

4. Kitchen's chapter is appropriately the first, since he led the way in the development of the field with his book *Finance for the Developing Countries* (1986).

5. See also the chapter by Asikoglu, Kutay, and Ertuna in this volume. In their analysis of the Turkish mutual funds, they also find that most bank-managed funds outperformed the Istanbul Stock Exchange Index.

REFERENCES

Calamanti, Andrea. (1983). *The Securities Markets and Underdevelopment: The Stock Exchange in the Ivory Coast, Morocco, Tunisia.* Milan: Finafrica.

Cho, Yoon Je. (1986). "Inefficiencies from Financial Liberalization in the Absence of Well-functioning Equity Markets." *Journal of Money, Credit, and Banking* 18, no. 2 (May): 191–199.

Drake, P. J. (1976). "Securities Markets in Less-developed Countries." In *Finance in Developing Countries*, ed. P. C. I. Ayre. London: Frank Cass and Co.

Fry, Maxwell J. (1987). "Neo-Classical and Neo-Structuralist Models of Financial Development: Theories and Evidence." *Greek Economic Review* 9, no. 1: 1–37.

Goldsmith, Raymond W. (1969). *Financial Structure and Development.* New Haven, Conn., and London: Yale University Press.

Gurley, John G., and Edward S. Shaw. (1955). "Financial Aspects of Economic Development." *American Economic Review* 45 (September): 515–538.

———. (1960). *Money in a Theory of Finance.* Washington, D.C.: Brookings Institution.

———. (1967). "Financial Structure and Economic Development." *Economic Development and Cultural Change* 15 (April): 257–268.

Kitchen, Richard L. (1986). *Finance for the Developing Countries.* New York: John Wiley and Sons.

McKinnon, Ronald I. (1973). *Money and Capital in Economic Development.* Washington, D.C.: Brookings Institution.

———, ed. (1976). *Money and Finance in Economic Growth and Development: Essays in Honor of Edward S. Shaw.* New York and Basel: Marcel Dekker.

———. (1989). "Financial Liberalization and Economic Development: A Reassessment of Interest-Rate Policies in Asia and Latin America." *Greek Economic Review* 11, no. 1.

Modigliani, Franco, and Merton H. Miller. (1958). "The Cost of Capital, Corporation Finance, and the Theory of Investment." *American Economic Review* 48 (June): 261–297.

Papaioannou, George J. (1986). *The Development of Direct Financing in Greece* (in Greek). Athens: Centre of Planning and Economic Research (KEPE).

Patrick, Hugh. (1966). "Financial Development and Economic Growth in Underdeveloped Countries." *Economic Development and Cultural Change* 14, no. 2 (January): 174–189.

Shaw, Edward S. (1973). *Financial Deepening in Economic Development.* New York: Oxford University Press.

van Agtmael, Antoine W. (1984). *Emerging Securities Markets: Investment Banking Opportunities in the Developing World.* London: Euromoney Publications.

Wai, U Tan, and Hugh T. Patrick. (1973). "Stock and Bond Issues and Capital Markets in the Less Developed Countries." *IMF Staff Papers* 20, no. 2 (July): 264–272.

Part I

Development of Capital Markets

Proofs

as a rule, articles
& comments should
have the classifications
of Geographic Discriptors

Thanks!

GA G32   15-36
016 624

1

Venture Capital: Is It Appropriate for Developing Countries?

RICHARD KITCHEN

> Venture capital . . . unlikely people financing unlikely things
>
> Anonymous

A well-known writer on small-scale enterprises (SSEs) in developing countries, Malcolm Harper, expressed this view:

> Specialised venture capital or equity financing schemes, such as have been successful in the United States, are unlikely to be appropriate for the financial needs of small scale enterprises in developing countries. It is difficult enough for an unsophisticated entrepreneur to appreciate the differences between his own investment and any loan he may have received. The distinction between short and long term financing adds a further complication. The addition of outside equity and the associated need for incorporation, shared responsibility and dividends as opposed to drawings is unlikely to be manageable. (Harper 1984, pp. 60–61)

Two years later, I made an equally broad generalization, but with a rather more positive view of the possibilities of venture capital:

> For many developing countries we see considerable potential in the venture capital approach to SME (Small and Medium Enterprises) financing. The provision of equity, rather than loan, capital conforms to the principle that the higher the risk, the lower the debt to equity ratio should be. More important, it also enables suppliers of funds to share in the growth of successful companies which will offset the losses subsequent on financing the companies which fail. (Kitchen 1986, p. 293)

Such generalizations need more detailed consideration. The objective of this chapter is to examine the need for venture capital in developing countries and the conditions required for its successful implementation. The chapter will consider the financing of SMEs, the role and limitations of capital markets and existing methods of SME financing, and the role that venture capital might play. We will then discuss venture capital in industrialized countries and the embryo venture-capital sector in the developing countries and will conclude by assessing conditions needed for venture capital to succeed in developing countries.

CAPITAL MARKETS AND SMEs

Why does the financing of SMEs deserve special treatment relative to other businesses? In financial terms, the characteristic of SMEs is that they are relatively high-risk. Compared to larger businesses, smaller businesses possess shallow management, often with little experience and training; they are usually undiversified, one-product firms; they are sometimes new businesses, with little track record and poor financial recording; they may have a new, unproven product, or a product new to its country; they have little to offer by way of security to a lender; and they may be reluctant to raise outside equity capital for reasons of expense, loss of control, and increased disclosure requirements. These risks have been fully described by, for example, Anderson (1982) and also Levitsky (1983), quoted in Little (1987).

The degree of risk, as measured by the default rate of lending programs to small businesses in developing countries, varies considerably. Anderson (1982), for example, spoke of default rates varying from 10 percent to 60 percent or more. Little (1987), quoting Levitsky (1983) and Rangarajan (1980), concluded that "when loans have been made to very small and new enterprises by development banks, the default rate has been high—often catastrophically high."

Although the subject of this chapter embraces both small and medium enterprises, the problems of financing them are rather different. Medium enterprises will usually have a reasonable track record, significant fixed assets, and management with some experience. Few enterprises (unless they are subsidiaries of larger enterprises) start off at "medium" size; most have got there by growing from small enterprises. Medium enterprises, therefore, are likely to be able to attract financing from conventional sources more readily than small enterprises. The main difference is likely to be that medium enterprises generally require new finance in larger amounts than do small enterprises. The scale of financing may be a problem, particularly with equity financing, unless access to outside equity, for example through a stock-market listing, is available. As the problems of small-scale enterprises are likely to be more acute, this chapter is written particularly with them in mind. We will continue to speak of SMEs at times, but the reader should be aware that this is often a piece of convenient shorthand.

Capital markets provide debt and equity finance from external sources (as opposed to internal finance from the sponsors or from retained earnings). Capital markets may be divided into the formal (stock markets and bank and nonbank financial institutions) and the informal (friends, relatives, moneylenders, curb markets). The latter may be of more relevance to small businesses in developing countries, especially at the start-up stage.

For purposes of exposition, I will distinguish between the perfect capital market, "natural" imperfections, and government-induced imperfections.[1] The perfect capital market is competitive, possesses a wide range of instruments offering many different combinations of risk and expected return, and has perfect knowledge and foresight and no transaction costs. Natural imperfections include monopoly or cartel elements, imperfect knowledge and foresight, significant transaction costs, and significant gaps in the range of financial instruments and institutions in the market. Government-induced imperfections include controls on interest rates, controls on the direction of lending (for example, to specific sectors such as agriculture or SMEs), taxes and reserve requirements that drive a wedge between borrowing and lending rates, taxes on dividends, subsidies to various classes of borrowers and lenders, and direct controls or regulations that limit institutional activities and developments.

Even with a perfect capital market the availability of credit for small businesses is far from assured. First, the level of the risk perceived by the putative lender may be so high that the compensating return may be too high for the project to bear comfortably, which would increase the risk of failure still further. In formal terms, an increase in the interest rate will increase the expected net present value (NPV) of the loan up to an optimum point; beyond that point the expected NPV would fall. If the expected NPV at the optimum point is too low, the bank will not lend.

The capital market is imperfect and fragmented, to varying degrees, in all countries. Market imperfections may work in two ways: They may either favor small-business borrowers or discriminate against them. The general presumption is that the latter applies. However, comparisons tend to be made between the ways financial institutions actually treat small businesses and larger businesses, not between the actual treatment afforded to small businesses and the treatment they would receive under perfect capital markets. A priori, it is not possible to judge whether natural imperfections (or distortions) tend to favor or disfavor small businesses. It is quite possible that financial institutions make loans to small businesses that they would not make if their behavior accorded with the perfect capital market model.

A natural imperfection that does impinge significantly on SMEs, though, is that of transaction costs. The costs of loan investigation and administration are not proportional to the size of the loan and weight more heavily on smaller loans than on larger loans. The consequence is that in formal terms, the cost of the loan increases, making the expected NPV at the optimum rate of interest too low. The cost of loan investigation can be largely eliminated if the lender requests collateral instead of examining the use of the loan. However, many smaller businesses, and their owners, may be unable or unwilling to provide adequate collateral.

Government-induced imperfections may encourage or discourage SME financing. Financial repression through controlled interest rates and high bank-deposit requirements with the central bank will generally lead to credit rationing and the favoring of large, well-established borrowers with good track record and valuable collateral, and will therefore discriminate against smaller, younger, more innovative, and, essentially, riskier businesses (Kitchen, 1986).[2] On the other hand, the direction of lending to SMEs, the creation of special (and usually subsidized) arrangements for SME financing, and the provision of subsidized loans, subsidized loan-guarantee schemes, and subsidized industrial estates tend to favor SMEs.

Figure 1.1
The Lemon Gap

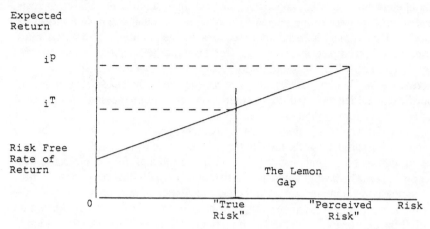

A systematic bias, though, may arise in SME financing because of the theory of the market for "lemons" (Akerlof 1970).[3] Because small businesses, especially in developing countries, are regarded as "high-risk," the level of risk associated with the riskiest small business tends to be applied to all small businesses. As a consequence, bad businesses tend to drive the good out of the financial markets, as the latter have to raise equity or debt on terms that exaggerate their risk. The gap between the true risk and the perceived risk of the financial markets may be termed the "lemon gap" (Figure 1.1). Only in cases where financiers are in a position to assess carefully the true risk of a small business can the cost of capital match the true risk; this may be the case with local moneylenders, but is seldom the case with formal financial institutions.

The case for subsidizing conventional small-business financing (whether credit schemes or venture capital) rests on the social desirability of eliminating the lemon gap. A subsidy would compensate for the failure of the market to identify the true risk of individual investments.

The specialized venture-capital fund (VCF) should itself go a considerable way toward eliminating the lemon gap, as VCFs depend for their success on careful assessment of risk. They therefore tend to compensate for the failure of conventional financial institutions. VCFs thereby fulfill a social function, but with high transaction costs (only 1 proposal out of 40 may be accepted, for example). Again, a case for subsidy may rest on compensation for these high costs.

Anderson and Khambata (1985) argued that in the case of debt markets, an efficient supply of finance for small industry requires the simultaneous liberalization of the level and structure of interest rates and the development of schemes for sharing the risks and administrative costs between the public and private sectors. They made the point that attention to one (interest rates) without the other (risk sharing, in particular) is unlikely to be successful from either a financial or an economic point of view. This implies that SME lending schemes should be subsidized, but Anderson and Khambata argued that this would be justified, as lending institutions would learn from experience to discriminate between potentially efficient and potentially inefficient investments: This externality justifies the subsidy, which can eventually be phased out. The externality only accrues in the long run, though, and seems as speculative as much of the high-risk lending it is intended to improve. Nonetheless, we accept their argument that the subsidy should not be provided through concessional interest rates, even though we would prefer to justify it on the grounds that in some sense SMEs may be more efficient and dynamic than larger enterprises.

The key to SME (or any other business) financing is the debt/equity ratio, or, more accurately, the ratio of debt to shareholders' funds, as retained earnings belong to shareholders and are a very common form of financing expansion investments. Under certain highly restrictive assumptions, Modigliani and Miller have shown that there is no optimum debt/equity ratio.[4] However, in practice, high capital gearing,[5] through the effect of fixed interest charges on fluctuating earnings, increases the risk of failure. There is, therefore, a limit on the extent to which lenders are prepared to see a debt/equity ratio rise. Given the rule of thumb that the assets in a "gone" concern will fetch only 50 percent of their book value, the cautious lender restricts the debt/equity ratio to 1:1. In many countries such a limit would be seen as being unduly conservative, and norms of 2:1 apply, for example, in India and Indonesia, and 3:1 in the Philippines (a few years go it was 5:1). Practice varies from country to country, depending on financing traditions, the availability of debt and equity, the perceived risk of the venture, and the ability of the entrepreneur to persuade people to put up equity or debt.

That being said, there is a ground rule that we can now lay down: The higher the risk of an enterprise, the higher the proportion of equity to debt should be. If we take volatility of trading profit as a measure of risk,[6] then a company with high gearing would increase its risk of failure because of the impact of the high and regular interest payments on its cash flow. If the risk of outright failure is perceived as being considerable, then lenders will not want to provide much debt. Rather, they may be more interested in sharing in the potentially high returns (which presumably are expected in view of the high failure risk) and will prefer to participate in the form of straight equity, convertible loan stock, or debt plus an equity option on terms defined at the outset.[7] Small businesses, especially start-ups, generally fall into one or another of the high-risk categories; they therefore require relatively low debt/equity ratios, which means that suitable equity or quasi-equity instruments need to be devised, or debt needs to be made attractive by some sweeteners (such as a partial guarantee or an option on equity). To the extent that equity is scarce (which it is in many developing countries), the suitable financing of small businesses becomes relatively more difficult compared with raising expansion capital for medium- or large-scale businesses.

ESTABLISHED METHODS OF SME FINANCING

In most countries the access of small businesses to external financing (external to the business, that is) is usually difficult. Bhatt (1978) and Nanjundan (1987) described the general practice of financing small businesses in developing countries. Start-up capital is provided almost entirely from personal savings, with some help from friends and relatives. As firms grow and become profitable, institutional credit, mainly from commercial banks, may provide working capital finance, but trade credits are equally important. The expansion of firms (except in Africa) tends to be financed by moneylenders, other informal credit markets, and retained earnings. Finally, the role of institutional finance and of special credit institutions, as well as of credit-guarantee schemes, becomes important in the upper ranges of small enterprises, that is, in medium-sized enterprises. "The bias of financial institutions towards units of larger size reflects a natural tendency to want to lend where costs are lower and risks less" (Nanjundan 1987).

SMEs in many countries are dependent on informal financial markets (IFMs) as a source of finance. Much has been written on IFMs in rural areas, where they provide predominantly small-farm finance (Bottomley 1975; Wai 1957, 1977; Adams 1980; Schaefer-Kehnert and Von Pischke 1986). However, comparatively little has been written on urban IFMs, which are more relevant to the financial needs of SMEs. One study of India (Timberg and Aiyar 1984) brought out a major difference between operators in IFMs and formal markets: Those in IFMs are much closer to their clients and potential clients, and through gossip and daily contact are much more aware of their activities than a formal banker would ever be. The important thing about these close relationships is that the IFM lenders know the risks they are exposed to. This enables them to discriminate between borrowers and reduce the risks that they face. This in turn permits a financial market to operate by removing the imperfections of lack of knowledge that pervade formal financial markets. In many ways, informal markets conform rather more closely to the perfect market ideal than do formal markets. Although interest rates charged in informal markets may appear high, these probably only reflect the risk and are well below the rates that would be charged by a formal lender with less knowledge and higher transaction costs—rates that make the existence of a market in formal loans to small businesses impossible.

Institutional arrangements for SME financing have been in place in many developing countries for many years. The best known include SME departments or funds established in development banks, the provision of finance for SMEs by international organizations such as the World Bank through lines of credit to development banks, and government credit-guarantee schemes to banks lending to SMEs with limited collateral. For example, in India the Deposit Insurance and Credit Guarantee Corporation guarantees loans to SMEs of up to 90 percent of the amount in default. Rao (1981) stated that "the flow of credit to small borrowers has been considerably facilitated by the small loan guarantee scheme." Guarantees have even been international; in The Gambia the UN Capital Development Fund guaranteed 75 percent of bank loans to SMEs that were made in cooperation with the Indigenous Business Advisory Service. Detailed accounts of conventional financing arrangements are given in Harper (1984) and Harper and de Jong (1986).

In some industrialized countries, notably the United States and the United Kingdom, bank-loan finance has been the traditional method of financing small businesses, after the owner's equity. As bank loans have tended to be only short or medium term, small businesses in the industrialized countries have until recently faced many of the same problems that SMEs in developing countries face.

In contrast to British and American practice, continental European banks have long been prepared to take equity positions in client companies and to take an active role in the direction of the companies. The practice dates back at least to 1822, when the Société Générale was established in Belgium to promote and invest in young companies. In France the well-known Crédit Mobilier was established in 1852. It raised money by accepting deposits and selling its own shares and by lending and investing its funds in the shares of client companies, often long-term industrial and infrastructure projects. It would then make a market in these shares when the time was ripe. The Crédit Mobilier is often considered to be the forerunner of the modern development bank and itself helped to establish similar universal banking in Germany, Austria, Spain, and the Netherlands. The fame and example of the Crédit Mobilier still survive; unfortunately, it was a higher risk taker than many of its successors and failed in 1867. Nonetheless, the practice of these early universal banks is still widely followed today, and the approach whereby the banks nurse their client companies from cradle to grave is much closer to the approach of a modern venture capitalist than is the conventional approach of British and American banks. However, banks are likely to take equity only in established businesses, rather than in start-up or young companies.

THE ROLE OF VENTURE CAPITAL

Venture capital, as its name suggests, is relatively high-risk capital. It generally involves the provision of equity or quasi-equity (such as convertible loan stock) capital to small and medium enterprises, in several cases business start-ups. It usually implies an involvement by the venture capitalist in the management of the client enterprises, which is the main feature distinguishing venture-capital funds from investment trusts. It has come to be associated, especially in the United States, with the financing of new and high-technology-based enterprises.[8] However, such enterprises are merely a special case of high-risk businesses, and it would be a mistake to associate venture capital exclusively with high-technology businesses.[9] What venture capitalists look for is growth potential; they are not looking for businesses that will remain small, but rather small businesses that will become large businesses.

As venture-capital finance involves the provision of equity, it is very suitable for higher-risk businesses. As it also involves a close relationship between the two parties, the venture capitalist can provide strategic, managerial, and technical advice to the company, which can strengthen the usually thin and hard-pressed management of smaller businesses and so reduce the investment risk. Moreover, the venture capitalist is usually involved for several years.

It is helpful to distinguish between different types of venture capital. The earlier stage (seed-corn capital) arises when an individual has a promising idea; the capital is put in to help the idea, and perhaps a prototype, to be developed. This usually involves relatively small amounts of very high-risk capital. The second stage is the start-up, when the idea has been developed to a point where it is ready for commercial production and marketing. As the product (but not its commercial potential) is now known, there is less risk involved. The third stage is expansion; by now the product has had some commercial success, and the management has had some experience of running the business; the risk is much reduced.

The provision of seed-corn capital is a specialized business, and while specialists do exist, they usually need to be complemented by other activities, as the volume of business (say £250,000 divided between ten firms) is generally small. Seed-corn funds are sometimes financed by larger, conventional VCFs, who are subsequently given first refusal to take over the more promising investments when further funds are needed. The provision of seed-corn capital is highly management-intensive, and the failure rate is high. On the other hand, by investing at an earlier stage than anyone else, the seed-corn fund can come in cheaper and obtain higher returns if the venture succeeds.

The provision of larger amounts of capital may be undertaken by a single firm, but the syndication of the investment is increasingly common. This involves spreading the investment and the risk between several venture-capital funds. On occasion, one fund may provide all the capital and subsequently place some of the equity among other investors. This is known as the "bought deal."

Venture capitalists, then, look for small or start-up businesses with the potential to grow beyond merely providing a lifetime income for their owners. The venture capitalist is prepared to risk his or her equity, but in return wants a full share of the future growth of the business, which sometimes can be spectacular. Therefore, a company unwilling to admit outside shareholders would not be of interest to a venture capitalist. VCFs reckon on perhaps three investments in ten being successful (spectacularly so, they hope), three being failures, and four that remain steady ("sleepers"). Their profits come from the successes. They will invest a second and third time to help to finance expansion of promising companies, but will tend not to invest a second time until companies have produced good growth. Essentially, VCFs are expected to revolve. However, a VCF will usually be willing to provide additional injections of capital to a promising firm as it grows and requires new funds for expansion.

Most small businesses are not suitable for venture-capital financing. Wall (1986) reported that in the United States it is common practice for the VCF to screen one hundred to two hundred proposals for each investment made.

Divestment possibilities are vital to VCFs. The best-known way is for the target company to obtain a stock-market quotation, thus giving the fund an opportunity to sell its stake. We shall discuss the importance of equity markets later. However, divestment by this route may be slow, partly because of the time required to obtain a listing, but also because the fund can usually sell its shareholding only gradually; otherwise it risks depressing the market. An alternative, which seems to be finding increasing favor, is to arrange a management buyout, a merger, a takeover, or a placing of the fund's equity. In this way the fund can sell its share stake much more quickly. However, the divestments of venture-capital funds require stock markets that offer the potential for flotation of the client company, an active over-the-counter (OTC) market, or an active acquisitions climate.

VENTURE CAPITAL IN INDUSTRIALIZED COUNTRIES

Space does not permit a detailed analysis of the growth of the venture-capital industry in industrialized countries. However, it is possible to come to a number of conclusions that are relevant to the establishment of venture capital in developing countries.

Table 1.1 shows the high variation in the importance of venture capital in industrialized countries. Only Ireland, the United Kingdom, the United States, and the Netherlands have substantial amounts of venture capital available. By contrast, the ratio of venture capital to gross national product (GNP) in Japan and Germany is low relative to that in other countries.

Table 1.2 shows that with the notable exception of the United States, venture capital has benefitted from incentives (in effect, subsidies) in most countries where it has developed significantly. In Japan and Germany, no incentives are provided. This suggests that the relationship of risk to expected return in venture capital is not attractive to investors, and that incentives may generally be intended to reduce risk or increase returns. Table 1.2 also shows that in many industrialized countries efforts have been made to increase share trading in smaller and younger companies, thus facilitating divestment by venture capitalists.

OECD (1986b), more specifically, gave three major reasons for the venture-capital boom in the United States:

- A very favorable attitude by the public at large toward entrepreneurship, failures as well as successes

- A very dynamic financial market illustrated by the existence of an efficient stock exchange, a tradition of company shares held by the public, and a competitive banking system

- Government intervention limited essentially to acting on the major framework conditions, including the individual taxation system

A recent assessment of the rapid growth of the United Kingdom's venture-capital industry (Mason 1987) gave the following explanation:

- The demonstration effect of the profitability of venture capital in the United States (e.g., the flotation of Apple Computer)

- The establishment of the Unlisted Securities Market and the Business Expansion Scheme

Table 1.1
Venture-Capital Pools

Country	Number of Venture-Capital Firms	Venture-Capital Pool[a] (Billions of ECUs)	Venture-Capital Pool/GNP[b] (UK = 100)
United States	530	21.2	49
United Kingdom	120	5.7	100
Japan	80	3.0	14
France	90	1.3	16
Canada	45	1.0	28
Netherlands	60	0.9	46
West Germany	30	0.6	9
Ireland	8	0.6	259
Italy	15	0.3	5
Belgium	10	0.2	16
Spain	27	0.2	10
Sweden	30	0.2	14
Denmark	19	0.2	23
Switzerland	15	0.1	6
Austria	3	0.02	0.1

Sources: Financial Times supplement "Venture Capital," December 4, 1987; and author's estimates.

[a]The pool is the total sum in European Currency Unit (ECU) equivalent, raised by venture-capital funds, accumulated over the years.
[b]Based on end 1986 GNP and exchange rates.

Table 1.2
Incentives to VCFs in Certain Countries

Country	Incentives	Capital Market Attractions
United States	Financing through government R&D expenditure	NASDAQ
United Kingdom	Business Expansion Scheme (BES) tax incentives to individuals	USM/Third Market
Japan	None	Second-tier market; OTC market
France	Tax concessions to start-up companies and to investors in registered Venture Capital Companies (VCCs); guarantees to investors in risky enterprises	Second Marché
Canada	Tax concessions on dividends and capital gains	None
Netherlands	Government regional finance; guarantee scheme; tax exemption on dividends	Parallel (second-tier) market
West Germany	None	None
Ireland	State financing; BES-type scheme	USM (linked to United Kingdom)
Italy	Tax concessions under consideration	None
Spain	Capital-gains tax concessions	None
Denmark	None	SME division of stock market
Sweden	State financing	OTC market for SMEs
Switzerland	None	None
Austria	Similar to United Kingdom	None
Australia	100 percent allowance on investments in licensed management and investment companies (VCCs)	Second-board markets

- The growth in the number of management buyouts, which has created a demand for equity finance

- The increased involvement of merchant banks providing venture capital to small, growing companies with a view to obtaining future fee-earning work from them

- The "bandwagon" mentality

Analyses of venture capital in other industrialized countries may be found in OECD (1986b), Wall (1986), and the *Financial Times* (1987).

VENTURE CAPITAL IN DEVELOPING COUNTRIES

Only in a handful of developing countries has any progress been made in establishing venture-capital companies.[10] The easy way to establish a venture-capital company is for development banks to set up independently managed specialized funds or subsidiaries, as the functions of development banks are generally very similar in principle to those of venture-capital companies. However, some may prefer to make smaller, higher-risk equity investments through a specialized subsidiary rather than through the mainstream development-bank activities. This route has been taken, for example, by the state-owned National Development Bank in Brazil, which has established a venture-capital subsidiary, BNDESPAR.

Specialized, independent venture-capital companies are few in developing countries, and several of those that do exist have been developed as joint ventures with the International Finance Corporation (IFC) since 1978, notably Sofinnova (Spain), VIBES (Philippines), Brasilpar (Brazil), IPS (Kenya), KDIC (Korea), and SEAVI (Southeast Asia). Although the IFC has helped with the development of these enterprises, its financial contribution has been limited, varying from 2 percent of the total initial capitalization in the case of VIBES to 8 percent in the case of Brasilpar. Details of the structure of these enterprises are given in OECD (1986a), but it is too early to make a full assessment of their performances. The main characteristic of these enterprises is their diversity.

It should not be thought, though, that participation of the IFC is a necessary condition for the successful establishment of venture-capital companies. Brazil has a number of other companies apart from those mentioned. Taiwan too has had venture-capital companies for some years, the Development Bank of Malaysia has a venture-capital scheme,[11] and Malaysia Ventures Bhd. (Bhd. stands for Limited Liability Company in Malai) is a private-sector VCF, set up in 1984. Korea is particularly noteworthy, with a number of companies having had their origins in the Korea Technology Advancement Corporation (KTAC) venture-capital group set up to invest in high-tech fields in 1974. KTAC was set up to commercialize research and development results from the Korea Advanced Institutes for Science and Technology (UNIDO 1987). The Korean Technology Development Corporation, the private-sector Korea Development Investment Corporation, and the Korea

Technology Finance Corporation also provide venture capital. The Asian Development Bank has made direct equity investments in the latter two (ADFIAP 1987), and the Deutsche Entwicklungsgesellschaft in KDIC. Venture capital is also developing in India. All the countries mentioned, significantly, have active stock markets.

Taiwan has attracted a number of foreign venture-capital firms as well as local ones since the initiation in 1983 of policies to encourage venture-capital growth. The government sees venture-capital investment as a means of encouraging the growth of a high-tech industry, thereby upgrading its industrial structure from reliance on traditional and labor-intensive manufacturing. It has invested in venture-capital funds through the development banks. However, progress to date has been slow, with a reluctance among Taiwan's entrepreneurs to take on outside and expensive equity. Moreover, the requirement that they should invest only in high-tech firms has made venture capitalists cautious. One interesting aspect has been the export of venture capital to small U.S. businesses, with a view to attracting them to invest in Taiwan when they want to expand. In this way, the funds hope to bring new technology to Taiwan.[12]

A significant aspect of venture financing in developing countries is the paucity of funds set up by development banks. These institutions do on occasion make equity investments, but they can hardly be considered to be entrepreneurial, venturesome institutions. India is a notable exception, as numerous state-owned development financing institutions provide venture capital, even seed capital. But Wall (1986) noted that some schemes have performed disappointingly, partly because of poor investment appraisal and lack of entrepreneurial spirit among technicians and managers. Islamic development banks, with their preference for providing equity rather than debt, also are exceptions, as is the Development Bank of Malaysia, which is something of a special case. The Industrial Finance Corporation of Thailand (IFCT) acts as a venture-capital organization, with investments in some 40 manufacturing enterprises. IFCT envisages stepping up its appraisal capacity to 300 projects per year. However, these cases seem to be among the few development banks with serious involvement in venture capital.

Commercial banks have been active in setting up VCFs. In Argentina, the S.A. Inversiones de Capital de Riesgo was set up in late 1986 by a leading bank, an insurance company, and two large diversified industrial holding companies. In 1986 the Philippines had 16 VCFs, all "closely affiliated to commercial banks" (Wall 1986). In India, Grindlays Bank has a VCF, and in Spain the Bank of Bilbao is a partner alongside IFC in Sofinova.

While a venture-capital sector may be desirable, it may be difficult to stimulate it. We take the view that governments and government-owned institutions are generally not a suitable base for venture-capital funds, although there may be exceptions. Civil servants and government employees are unlikely to possess the entrepreneurship, flexibility, and managerial skills needed in a venture-capital firm. This view is shared by Miller and Cote (1985), who stated that government-sponsored venture-capital funds "have a dismal record in first round financing."

But while direct public-sector involvement may not be desirable, governments have a crucial role to play in creating the right commercial, financial, and social environment for venture capital to be successful. Here we return to the discussion of capital markets in the first part of the chapter. In terms of finance, perhaps the most important thing government can do is to reduce financial market imperfections, both government-induced and "natural" imperfections. Ideally, venture-capital firms should be able to survive in financial markets on "level playing fields." Should a government feel that special encouragement should be given for the financing of SMEs (in our analogy, that venture-capital firms should be allowed to play downhill), then it may provide incentives.

More specifically, OECD (1986a) identified three areas where government action may be required. These are, in ascending order of difficulty, tax policy, divestment avenues, and attitudes toward risk. "In a general sense, governments and societies should not discourage an investor's ability to profit and accumulate wealth" (p. 32). We believe that care and skill are needed in developing tax incentives. What works in one country may not work in another. In particular, tax incentives may not be effective if the marginal tax rates are low. The question of avenues of divestment is important, and we take it up later in our discussion of securities markets.

Few developing countries provide specific incentives to VCFs. This is in marked contrast to industrialized countries, where incentives are frequently encountered. Moreover, several developing countries discriminate against VCFs, as their tax laws favor debt rather than equity. This applies, for example, where there is double taxation of dividends, or where there is no indexation of capital gains for tax purposes. Both these factors have been identified by Wall (1986) as acting as disincentives in Colombia, which has no VCFs. Brazil, on the other hand, provides tax concessions on both dividends and capital gains for venture-capital investment, and Korea gives exemption from capital-gains tax. In India, a third country where venture capital is well developed, the legislative and tax framework for VCFs is apparently unclear.

By far the most difficult environment to create is one of risk taking. Risk-averse individuals will not be attracted to high-risk/high-expected-return investments, whether physical or portfolio in nature. High-risk-taking investors are generally ambitious or hungry or gamblers, with perhaps a touch of all three. The attitudes are societal and not ones that governments can develop by decree. Exhortation and tax policies that give incentives may help, but do not guarantee the right attitudes.

EQUITY MARKETS

Equity markets provide important vehicles for divestment by VCFs, and their development is therefore important for the development of venture capital. We should note, though, that the share-price falls of 1988 exposed the vulnerability of equity-based methods of financing to stock-market movements. Alternative methods of divestment, such as mergers, acquisitions, private placements, and management buyouts may become increasingly popular.

In recent years equity markets have assisted the financing of SMEs in a number of ways. First, the development of second- and third-tier markets has allowed SMEs, including even some start-ups, direct access to funds. the expansion of over-the-counter (OTC) markets, notably the NASDAQ (National Association of Securities Dealers Automated Quotations) market in the United States, has performed the same function. Second, venture-capital funds hope to realize their capital gains by floating their client companies on stock markets (and, in some cases, by direct sale to other companies). Third, venture-capital companies sometimes issue their own shares on stock markets and use this route as a means to raise capital for investment. In the United Kingdom and France a number of venture-capital firms have gone public, in some cases at an early stage in their life. Fourth, novel methods of attracting direct investment by individuals in SMEs, such as the United Kingdom's Business Expansion Scheme, are underpinned by equity markets, especially second- and third-tier markets, because investors have a strong interest in being able to realize their investments after five years. A market quotation affords an important method of realization for individual investors.

Second- and Third-Tier Markets

In many countries the main stock markets have entry requirements of size of share issue and length and consistency of track record (such as five years profitability) that cut out flotation by many SMEs. Therefore, to enable such firms to raise equity capital, the United Kingdom, Japan, the Netherlands, France, and Denmark have introduced second-tier markets, in which the entry requirements are much less demanding and less costly. On the United Kingdom's Unlisted Securities Market (USM) and the French Second Marché only 10 percent of the share capital of a company need be sold, as against 25 percent on the main market. In Holland issues on the second market must be for a minimum of Fl 250,000, one-tenth of the requirement of the main market. The Unlisted Securities Market, established in 1980, can now be judged to be a substantial success. The rules are sufficiently flexible to admit even start-ups, and well over 500 companies have obtained USM listings, with some 75 moving up to a full listing. The Second Marché, which started in 1983, had attracted some 230 listings by the end of 1987.

The experience in the United Kingdom was that most businesses that obtained a USM listing were at the larger end of the SME scale, most having a market capitalization in excess of £1 million. This led the stock exchange to introduce a Third Market (which has since disappeared), starting in January 1987, for smaller companies, and with even easier listing requirements than those of the USM.[13] Third Market companies can, under certain circumstances, qualify for BES relief, whereas USM companies cannot. It is as yet too early to judge the effectiveness of the Third Market, but it has certainly not been a failure, even though it may not have fulfilled the more optimistic forecasts of the number of listings. About 30 companies were listed in 1987. It is of interest to note that the stock exchange established the Third Market as a direct competitor to the OTC market, which has not been a success in the United Kingdom.

Over-the-Counter (OTC) Markets

By far the largest OTC market in the world is the NASDAQ market in the United States. The number of companies traded is greater than on the New York Stock Exchange. Undoubtedly the availability of NASDAQ has been an important facility for venture-capital companies.

Elsewhere, OTC markets have not always been so successful. In the United Kingdom the OTC market is small (about 230 companies traded) and operated by a number of licensed dealers in securities. Its reputation has been tarnished by the dubious promotions and activities of some of the market makers, and the Stock Exchange is endeavoring to replace it with the Third Market, so far with limited success. The Swedish OTC market introduced in 1982, appears much more successful. Since then, 70 SMEs have been listed on the OTC market, and many others have applied; the capital raised by SMEs is about SKr 900 million (OECD 1986b).

Singapore established a new OTC second-tier market in January 1987, known as the Stock Exchange of Singapore Dealing and Automated Quotation System (SESDAQ). It provides a market for young, growing companies to raise equity capital when they do not meet the minimum qualifications for a main Stock Exchange of Singapore listing. SESDAQ has based its listing requirements broadly on those of the United Kingdom's USM and its trading arrangements on those of the U.S. NASDAQ, with trading by telephone on the basis of prices displayed on computer screens by competing market makers, similar also to London's Stock Exchange Automatic Quotations (SEAQ). To obtain a listing on SESDAQ, companies must have a paid-up capital of S$3 million (U.S. $2.0 million) and must offer at least 15 percent of the issued share capital to the public. Although SESDAQ is an OTC market in terms of trading practice, it is strictly regulated by the Stock Exchange of Singapore (Dinyar bin Framjee 1987).

The unfortunate events in the Kuwait OTC market in 1982 should serve as a salutary reminder that trading on unregulated markets can get out of hand. So far, it seems, this sort of excess has been avoided in Saudi Arabia's OTC market, but prima facie the case for bringing share trading into a more formal regulatory framework seems strong.

Securities Markets in Developing Countries

Should governments of developing countries encourage securities trading? In an earlier work (Kitchen 1986) I have analyzed the advantages and disadvantages and much of the available evidence.[14] Without going over the same ground again, my conclusion is still the same, that I am substantially in favor of encouraging stock markets in developing countries within a sound regulatory framework. Considerable detail of the operations of securities markets in several developing countries is given in van Agtmael (1984).

Of more importance to this study is the use of securities markets for SME financing. It is natural that organized stock exchanges should attract listings from the larger enterprises; indeed, it is doubtful if stock exchanges should encourage SME listings until the regulators and investors have acquired several years' experience of trading in the stocks of major companies. It would be unwise of the authorities to rush into the establishment of second- or third-tier markets that are designed for smaller, riskier businesses. If things do not go well, such stocks can easily give a stock market a bad name before the market becomes well established. Nonetheless, the provision of organized markets for smaller companies should be seen as a long-term aim of a stock exchange. To date, Nigeria is the only developing country with a second-tier market, although the idea has also been discussed in India.

In the meantime, this leaves an OTC market as the only possibility in many countries. As we have seen already, OTC markets, if we take a global view, have a mixed record. The objective, then, must be to try to capture the good points while excluding the bad. It seems that this can best be achieved by government approval and regulation of the market makers and by setting minimum qualifications for companies whose stocks are to be traded. Rules on disclosure of information and reporting should also be established. Singapore's SESDAQ may be worth examining in some detail, although it is very computer-intensive.

In many developing countries, development banks are the best-placed organizations to operate an OTC market. Indeed, they are often seen as the main alternative to an organized stock exchange. However, conflict of interest can arise when the development banks take shareholdings in client (or other) companies. Therefore, what appears to be the current practice in Saudi Arabia, that commercial banks (as well as brokers) are permitted to sell stocks, providing an informal OTC market, but are forbidden to buy and sell stocks for their own portfolios,[15] has much to recommend it. In spite of the practice in most of the major stock markets of combining the functions of jobber and broker into market makers, we prefer in principle to keep the functions separate to avoid conflict of interest. This is particularly important in countries where regulators may be inexperienced or weak. In small markets, or in stocks in which trading is thin, this may restrict the level of activity and lead to trading on a "matched-bargain" basis, but this is preferable to the risk of ruining the reputation of a market through undesirable practices, which will lead to distrust and avoidance of share buying by all but the cowboys and the gullible.

The encouragement of unit trusts and investment trusts (we prefer the latter),[16] with approval to invest a proportion of their portfolios in the shares of unquoted companies, can also help SME financing. Shares in investment trusts or units in unit trusts may be particularly convenient instruments for Islamic banks to offer in return for deposits.

The existence of a well-run securities market may encourage international flows of venture capital. Because of the need of venture capitalists to be in close contact with their client companies, the most likely vehicle for international spread is for a venture-capital company in, say, the United States or the United Kingdom to set up a subsidiary (wholly owned or joint venture) in a dealer's country.[17] The existence of a securities market would create prospects for offering shares in client companies for sale, and even for a sale of shares in the local venture-capital firm.

The trend in recent years toward large-scale international share trading has squeezed out small, regional stock exchanges within countries. In the United Kingdom all the regional stock exchanges had historically provided opportunities for medium-sized, local businesses to obtain a stock-market listing without the trouble and expense of a London Stock Exchange listing. However, in 1972 all the United Kingdom's stock exchanges were merged into the Stock Exchange, and regionalism almost disappeared. The United States and Canada still have regional stock exchanges, as do some third-world countries such as India and Nigeria, but improved communications tend to be a unifying force. Perhaps there is still room for regional stock markets, just as there is an evident need for second- and third-tier markets

CONCLUSIONS

It is important to recognize two types of measures to improve small-business financing: those that tend to reduce capital market imperfections and those that tend to discriminate positively toward SMEs. While improving the efficiency, competitiveness, and foresight of capital markets is in itself a worthwhile aim, measures that discriminate positively toward SMEs need to be justified on the grounds that SMEs deserve special encouragement. It is beyond the scope of this chapter to go into this question, but a full list of the reasons for favoring small industry is given in Nanjundan (1987). Little (1987) concluded more precisely:

To summarise, the prima facie case for policy interventions in favour of SSEs as a means of raising overall welfare in developing economies must rest on evidence that small units on average use factor inputs more productively than their larger counterparts, so that a shift of resources in favour of smaller units would yield a net increase in output as well as an increase in the demand for unskilled labour.

The first lesson from theoretical discussions is that SMEs require a sound equity base to provide financial stability. This may be provided by the owners or acquired gradually through retained earnings. However, outside equity is often needed, as the owner's resources may be small, opening the door for VCFs, but outside equity financing requires that owners of SMEs should be willing to accept it.

The provision of outside equity from the formal sector requires a set of financial institutions or mechanisms that is willing to provide equity. However, the provision of equity means taking rather more risk than does the provision of debt, and equity-based financing requires individuals and institutions who are willing to take the higher risk for a higher expected (but not assured) return. The VCF is ideally suited to play this role.

The second lesson is that the providers of venture capital appear to need incentives (see Table 1.2). As the OECD (1986b) remarked, "The Governments of almost all OECD countries supply some form of finance or financial assistance which would be used as a source of venture capital" (p. 39). It is likely that the same applies to developing countries.[18]

Third, it seems that an "enterprise culture" is needed to stimulate the supply of, and demand for, venture capital. The rapid growth in venture capital in the United Kingdom in the 1980s can be seen as a response to the encouragement of enterprise, combined with generous tax incentives.

Fourth, avenues for divestment are important. This would appear to limit VCFs to the more advanced developing countries with active equity markets. However, within these countries, it seems that VCFs can play an important role in SME financing and should be encouraged. VCFs should also find a niche in those Islamic countries that prefer equity to debt financing.

Finally, development banks have good opportunities to develop venture capital, either within their present framework or by setting up specialized subsidies. They should be encouraged to provide more equity capital.

NOTES

1. I do not use the term imperfection (or its alternative, distortion) in a pejorative sense. Indeed, many government-induced imperfections that are intended to ensure the stability and honesty of financial markets and institutions are to be welcomed.

2. A noneconomic obstacle to SME lending lies in the risk-averse attitudes of loan officers. In generally conservative financial institutions, a loan officer is likely to perceive that his career prospects are unlikely to be enhanced by taking on a number of high-risk loans. A further noneconomic obstacle to SME financing is that unprofessional lending practices, such as collusion and corruption, are encouraged by financial repression and credit rationing. Many authors, including Anderson and Khambata (1985), Lipton (1976), Howell (1980), and Von Pischke, Adams, and Donald (1983), have found that unprofessional practices lead to higher default rates, thereby increasing risk.

3. Akerlof (1970) is a foundation work on the market for higher-risk assets. It is also worth recalling the comment of Rothschild and Stiglitz (1976): "High-risk individuals cause an externality: the low-risk individuals are worse off than they would be in the absence of high-risk individuals."

4. The assumptions include a perfect capital market, no risk of failure, and no taxation. See Archer and D'Ambrosio (1983) for the main Modigliani and Miller articles.

5. Capital gearing (U.S. leverage) is the effect that the debt/equity ratio has on a company. The higher the gearing (i.e., the higher the debt/equity ratio), the higher the interest payments that a company has to make.

6. The volatility of earnings over time is usually measured by the standard deviation or variance in financial theory.

7. This statement presupposes a willingness on the part of the lender to take relatively high risks. A lender who is by inclination very risk-averse will not be interested in financing small businesses anyway.

8. However, venture capital is hardly a new concept, as is often believed. Queen Isabella of Spain provided venture capital for Columbus, and Shakespeare's Shylock was also a venture capitalist. So, too, were those who invested in the trading ventures from England and Holland, ventures that led to the formation of the large British and Dutch trading

companies. In recent times, the Bolton Committee (1971) used the term, and it was in contemporary usage in the United States well before then.

9. Contrary to common belief, only a small proportion of venture capital financing goes to high-tech industries. On the other hand, young, high-tech companies have depended considerably on venture capital. For an account of the role of venture capital in the electronics industry, see Young (1985).

10. Wall (1986) provided substantial descriptive material on risk capital (defined more broadly than venture capital) in Argentina, Brazil, Colombia, Greece, India, Indonesia, Kenya, Korea, Malaysia, Mexico, the Philippines, Portugal, Singapore, Spain, and Turkey. Not all of these countries have venture-capital funds yet. Several industrialized countries were also included in the survey.

11. The Development Bank of Malaysia (Bank Pembangunan Malaysia) set up a Venture Capital Loan Scheme in 1981 that provides "financial assistance in the form of soft loan, equity loan and equity participation to a project with the objective to get the project on, which in terms of quantum and evaluation criteria transcend normal banking risk" (Salim bin Dato Osman, n.d.).

12. See *Far Eastern Economic Review*, November 5, 1987, for further details.

13. For Third Market listings, there is no minimum proportion of equity that has to be in public hands; companies need only a one-year track record, as opposed to (normally) three years on the USM; there is no specific obligation to publish half-year figures; and listing requirements are less onerous, and therefore less expensive, than on the USM. ("Market for Gamblers," *Investors Chronicle*, January 23, 1987).

14. Briefly, the advantages of stock markets are the following:

- They provide firms a means of raising finance, both through primary issues and subsequent secondary issues (e.g., rights).
- They provide governments with an alternative way of issuing bonds and raising capital.
- They provide savers and investors an alternative market for their funds.
- They provide a spectrum of risks and returns.
- They provide a vehicle for indigenization and privatization of firms.
- They provide a means of attracting foreign portfolio investment.

The disadvantages are the following:

- They may increase the unequal distribution of wealth to an undesirable extent.
- They may encourage speculation that can be destabilizing.
- They may provide a vehicle for dishonest activity, such as market rigging.
- Because of the distorted nature of some developing economies, efficient financial markets can lead to a misallocation of resources.
- Inefficiency in the markets can nullify many of the advantages.

15. *Middle East*, May 1985.

16. Investment trusts are generally more transparent than unit trusts. Managers of the latter have all sorts of opportunities from abuse open to them, which act to the detriment of the unit holders. On the other hand, quoted investment trusts need a set of regulations to limit gearing and "pyramiding," which gave them such a bad reputation in the Wall Street crash of 1929. Venture-capital companies, incidentally, are really a form of investment trust, but play an active part in the direction of their client companies. They are not usually subject to investment trust regulations.

17. International diversification by VCDs to date has been limited, as managers appear to prefer to stay in the market they know. However, some U.S. companies have set up

subsidiaries in the United Kingdom and Europe, and two firms with United Kingdom stock-market listings (Biotechnology Investment Trust and Newmarket) have shifted their registered offices to the Bahamas, as they have considerable investments in the United States (and elsewhere).

18. It is arguable that the provision of equity, by taking risk, fulfills an important economic function that the provision of secured debt does not. Therefore, the risk-taking capitalist, despised in the traditional socialist lore, is performing a much more valuable function than the lending bank that obtains its reward for much less risk, in that it is a preferred, and usually secured, supplier of finance. This may justify the subsidy in the form of a tax concession.

REFERENCES

Adams, D. W. (1980). "Recent Performance of Rural Financial Markets." in *Borrowers and Lenders: Rural Financial Markets and Institutions in Developing Countries*, ed. J. Howell. London: Overseas Development Institute.

ADFIAP. (1987). *Newsletter*, Vol. 10, no. 2 (June).

Akerlof, G. (1970). "The Market for 'Lemons': Quality of Uncertainty and the Market Mechanism." *Quarterly Journal of Economics* 84: 488–500.

Anderson, D. (1982). "Small Industry in Developing Countries: A Discussion of Issues." *World Development* 10, no. 11: 913–948.

Anderson, D., and F. Khambata. (1985). "Financing Small Scale Industry and Agriculture in Developing Countries: The Merits and Limitations of 'Commercial' Policies." *Economic Development and Cultural Change* 33, no. 2: 349–372.

Archer, S. H., and C. A. D'Ambrosio, eds. (1983). *The Theory of Business Finance: A Book of Readings*. 3rd ed. New York and London: Macmillan.

Bhatt, V. V. (1978). *Interest Rate, Transaction Costs, and Financial Innovations*. Washington, D.C.: World Bank.

Bolton, J. E., Chairman. (1971). *Report of the Committee of Inquiry on Small Firms*. London: HMSO, Cmnd. 4811.

Bottomley, J. A. (1975). "Interest Rate Determination in Underdeveloped Rural Areas." *American Journal of Agricultural Economics* 57: 279–291.

Cary, L. (1985). *The Venture Capital Report: Guide to Venture Capital in the U.K.* Bristol: Venture Capital Report.

Dinyar bin Framjee. (1987). "Small Firms Join the Big League." *Singapore Business*, April.

Financial Times (1987). "Venture Capital (Special Survey)." December 4.

Harper, M. (1984). *Small Business in the Third World*. Chichester: John Wiley.

Harper, M., and M. F. de Jong, eds. (1986). *Financing Small Enterprises*. Proceedings of a seminar organized by the Netherlands Development Finance Company (FMO). London: Intermediate Technology Publications.

Howell, J., ed. (1980). *Borrowers and Lenders: Rural Financial Markets and Institutions in Developing Countries*. London: Overseas Development Institute.

Kitchen, R. L. (1986). *Finance for the Developing Countries*. Chichester: John Wiley.

Levitsky, J. (1983). "Assessment of Bank Small Scale Enterprise Lending." Washington, D.C.: World Bank Industry Department. Mimeo.

Lipton, M. (1976). "Agricultural Finance and Rural Credit in Poor Countries." *World Development* 4, no. 7: 543–553.

Little, I. M. D. (1987). "Small Manufacturing Enterprises in Developing Countries." *World Bank Economic Review* 1, no. 2: 203–235.

Mason, M. (1987). "Venture Capital in the United Kingdom: A Geographical Perspective." *National Westminster Bank Quarterly Review*, May, 47–49.

Miller, R., and M. Cote. (1985). "Growing the Next Silicon Valley." *Harvard Business Review*, July–August, 114–123.

"Much Venture, Little Gain." (1987). *Far Eastern Economic Review*, November 5, 81.

Nanjundan, S. (1987). "Small and Medium Enterprises: Some Basic Development Issues." *Industry and Development*, no. 20: 1–50.

OECD. (1986a). *Banks and Specialised Financial Intermediaries in Development*. Paris: OECD.

OECD. (1986b). *Venture Capital: Context, Development, and Policies*. Paris: OECD.

Rangarajan, C. (1980). *Innovations in Banking, The Indian Experience: Impact on Deposits and Credit*. Domestic Finance Studies 63. Washington, D.C.: World Bank.

Rao, J. C. (1981). *Financing of Manufacturing Enterprises in India*. Vienna: UNIDO.

Rothschild, M., and J. E. Stiglitz. (1976). "Equilibrium in Competitive Insurance Markets: An Essay on the Economics of Imperfect Information." *Quarterly Journal of Economics* 90: 629–650.

Salim bin Dato Osman. (n.d.). "The Malaysian Experience in SMI Development." *ADFIAP Journal of Development Finance*, no. 8: 121–137.

Schaefer-Kehnert, W., and J. D. Von Pischke. (1986). "Agricultural Credit Policy in Developing Countries." *Savings and Development* 10, no. 1: 5–30.

Timberg, T. A., and C. B. Aiyar. "Informal Credit Markets in India." *Economic Development and Cultural Change* 33, no. 1: 43–60.

UNIDO. (1987). *The Republic of Korea: Commercialization of R & D Results with Particular Reference to the Small and Medium Industry Sector*. UNIDO PPD.21. January 23. New York: United Nations.

van Agtmael, A. W. (1984). *Emerging Securities Markets*. London: Euromoney Publications.

Von Pischke, J. D., D. W. Adams, and G. Donald, eds. (1983). *Rural Financial Markets in Developing Countries*. Baltimore: Johns Hopkins University Press.

Wai, U Tun. (1957). "Interest Rates outside the Organised Money Markets of Underdeveloped Countries." *IMF Staff Papers* 6, no. 1: 80–142.

Wai, U Tun. (1977). "A Revisit to Interest Rates outside the Organised Money Markets of Underdeveloped Countries." *Banca Nazionale del Lavoro Quarterly Review*, no. 122: 291–312.

Wall, P. J. (1986). "Venture Capital Activities in Selected Countries, Another Look." Washington: International Finance Corporation. Mimeo.

World Bank. (1978). *Employment and Development of Small Enterprises*. Sector Policy Paper. Washington, D.C.: World Bank.

Young, G. (1985). *Venture Capital in High-Tech Companies: The Electronics Business in Perspective*. London: Frances Pinter.

p 15. **Discussant:** *Frank Tuzzolino*

This chapter by Richard Kitchen examines the virtually unexplored potential of venture-capital financing for developing countries. It is a particularly timely inquiry, given a debt crisis in less developed countries (LDCs), Mexican debt renegotiation, and other debt issues. The author develops a thorough and compelling case for the role of the venture-capital fund (VCF) in small and medium enterprises (SMEs) and cites the antecedents for the success of such initiatives.

An institutional perspective prevails throughout this chapter. The author's references to established methods of SME financing across the globe are both informative and comprehensive. I will therefore direct my discussion at some theoretical arguments one could also invoke in defense of venture capital for developing countries, and I will rely on agency theory and signaling for some insights.

Actually, the author provides us with a glimpse of theoretical scaffolding with his reference to a "lemon gap" (Akerlof 1970). A systematic bias may arise in SME financing due to the gap between the true risk and the perceived risk of a project. Thus informational asymmetries will exist; formal financial institutions are typically ill-equipped or unable to assess such risks and thereby will finance larger, lower-risk enterprises. This systematic bias has seriously distorted capital flows and to some extent has fueled the debt crisis in LDCs. As Rothschild and Stiglitz (1976) noted, an externality results and little bank-loan financing emerges for SMEs, given that such development is equated with higher-risk business, to which the venture capitalist is more ideally suited. Allow me to dispel some myths in this regard.

The fraction of equity retained in a project, labelled alpha in the classic Leland and Pyle (1977) framework, will attest to the quality of a venture. Therefore, the existence of VCFs in developing markets can serve as a signal of (potential) investment quality, thus reducing informational asymmetries and agency problems associated with more conventional financing arrangements for SMEs. In addition, SME financing need not be high-risk capital, a misconception leading to Gresham's law of ventures, if you will: Speculative projects (and their high default rates) drive out VCF initiatives.

In developing countries, low-tech projects abound, but financing does not. Production technology in many cases will be well understood by locals. VCFs would provide marketing and distributional and logistical technology in the development process. Informational asymmetries would be minimal. The venture capitalist, as an owner/manager, would serve as a monitoring mechanism and provide verification technology, thus reducing, if not eliminating, the disincentives and moral hazard associated with conventional debt arrangements. The case for VCFs in developing countries can thus be made, a fortiori, on agency-theoretic grounds.

As to capital market development in LDCs, and market failures thereof, I think we need to address direction of causality. The author rightfully claims that the existence of a well-run securities market may encourage international flows of venture capital. I think an argument could also be made for reverse causation (that is, that a flourishing venture-capital environment will spawn securities market development). The nature and direction of such causation needs some more serious attention. Indeed, the VCF could be instrumental in reducing market failure in host environments.

Let me provide an example. The recent Mexican debt renegotiation resulted in a menu of alternatives, including concessionary repayment options, additional lending, and debt/equity swaps. Only the latter can best be justified on theoretical grounds. A debt/equity-mix contract, that is, the provision of capital to developing countries under both debt and equity contractual arrangements, should reduce the risk-sharing inefficiencies and disincentive problems associated with such investment to date.

Again, the quality of aggregate investment would improve as principals acquired some equity participation in infrastructure projects. Agency problems and informational asymmetries, not to mention fraud and capital flight, would be greatly reduced. Monitoring is axiomatic to such a solution as well. It is not difficult to imagine the subsequent and rapid evolution of VCFs and an "enterprise" culture in Mexico, which in reality may be the only solution to Latin America's current plight of capital outflows, inflation, and underdevelopment.

I believe that any theories of capital market development and the role of VCFs should be framed with an eye toward existing and well-developed paradigms and/or models. Agency theory, transaction-costs models, signaling, and the life-cycle metaphor come readily to mind. The recent ascent of financial engineering solutions to agency problems and market imperfections, summarized by Finnerty (1988), also warrants some attention, particularly in this international context. To the extent that this chapter serves as a stimulus in such a direction, the academic and practitioner communities have much for which to be thankful. In summary, then, both from a rich institutional perspective provided by the author, as well as a theoretical lens proposed herein, the notion of venture capital in developing countries provides a fertile agenda for future research.

REFERENCES

Akerlof, G. (1970). "The Market for 'Lemons': Quality of Uncertainty and the Market Mechanism." *Quarterly Journal of Economics* 84: 488–500.

Finnerty, J. (1988). "Financial Engineering in Corporate Finance: An Overview," *Financial Management* 17, no. 4: 14–33.

Rothschild, M., and J. E. Stiglitz. (1976). "Equilibrium in Competitive Insurance Markets: An Essay on the Economics of Imperfect Information." *Quarterly Journal of Economics* 90: 629–650.

Ō / 6

2

Nigeria

Problems of Orthodox Formal Capital Markets in Developing Countries, with Particular Reference to Nigeria

G24

ADE T. OJO

In Nigeria and many other developing countries, the formal capital markets, which are essentially orthodox in nature, have proved grossly inadequate in financing business enterprises. These formal capital markets, broadly defined to include banks and other western-type financial institutions and markets, having been largely introduced by expatriates about a century ago, have some major adaptation problems that have made it quite difficult for them to cater to the financial needs of the bulk of indigenous business enterprises. Their operations in such a mal-adapted form are thus increasingly being criticized in these countries, particularly in Nigeria, where the president and other policymakers often criticize the formal financial institutions and markets as unhelpful in promoting economic development in the desired manner, making the large informal sectors lag far behind.

The formal financial institutions and markets have been functionally unable, or have not cared, to accommodate the financial needs of small borrowers—farmers, small and medium-sized enterprises, and consumers—which account for a majority of economic units. The vacuum thus created in the nation's finances had to be filled. Here the informal institutions and markets, about which we know very little, have evolved to meet, by and large, the requirements of the small, most indigenous enterprises in farming, petty trading, and other activities in many less developed economies.

In the view of the Committee on the Nigerian Financial System (Nigeria 1976), Nigeria had no financial system under the colonial era; what it had then was a set of financial arrangements within the financial system of the metropolitan country. The committee defined a financial system as the "congeries of financial institutions and arrangements which serve the needs of an economy." The service is rendered through (1) the provision of financial resources to meet the borrowing needs of individuals and households, enterprises, and governments; (2) the provision of facilities to collect and invest savings funds; and (3) the provision of a sound payments mechanism.

The major problem upon which this chapter is designed to focus attention is the urgency of the need and the difficulty of providing adequate financial assistance to the bulk of businesses—farming and small-scale enterprises—in less developed countries (LDCs). With particular reference to Nigeria, the chapter highlights the gaps in the financial system in an analysis of the problems of orthodox formal capital markets in financing business enterprises vis-à-vis the informal credit mechanisms.

THE STRUCTURE AND GAPS OF THE FINANCIAL SYSTEM

In Nigeria both the urban "modern" sector of finance and industry, on the one hand, and the rural or traditional sector, on the other hand, have various links, and any attempt to dichotomize them is only useful for the sake of analysis—the "informal," traditional or indigenous financial system and markets are not isolated as such from the "formal" or modern financial system and markets. For instance, there are some "deficit" and "surplus" economic units that operate in both sectors and markets; these serve to provide at least a tenuous link. The informal, traditional financial system has the same essential basic characteristics as the "modern" financial system, with the major exception being the fact that the institutions and transactions in the former are not formalized in any standard manner; but this does not mean that financial transactions in the informal capital market are unorganized or noninstitutional, as they are often taken to be. There are organized institutions in the informal financial system in Nigeria, and the system offers some avenues for regular savings and provides in simple form credit facilities, including some lender-of-last-resort facilities, for example, the moneylenders, as fully analyzed in Ojo (1976, chaps. 5 and 6).

The fact that the financial system has been inadequate to serve the development needs of the country has been quite obvious, as emphasized in the successive National Development Plans since independence, for example, in 1960, in the *1962–68 National Development Plan* (pp. 18–19), where the conservatism of the financial system was noted—a situation that remains virtually unchanged more than 30 years later. This inadequacy was shown as a gap in the Nigerian financial system in our earlier detailed study.[1] The financial gap exists not only on the side of the provision of finance but also in the availability of savings facilities. In our study of the gap, we analyzed fully the extent to which agricultural and small industrial enterprises that could productively utilize external finance have been unable to obtain such needed finance, either because of (1) an "information gap," which prevents them from knowing how and where to obtain this finance on acceptable terms, or (2) a genuine "availability of funds gap," which is due to the failure of financial institutions to appreciate the economic prospects and developmental role of these enterprises, or to the inability of supplying institutions, as hitherto oriented, to cater effectively to the needs of agriculture and small-scale industries. In examining the problem of obtaining finance at a reasonable cost, we further showed how the high price of finance could be a major factor in preventing promising enterprises from getting finance or inhibiting the performance of enterprises that secured external finance.

Another feature of the financial gap is concerned with the problems of getting the right type of finance at the appropriate time, in appropriate amount, and on satisfactory terms in a manner that would meet the demand of deficit economic units for external finance. We have shown that the risk obstacles to the financing of agriculture and small-scale enterprises in Nigeria (as well as in many other developing countries) are often exaggerated, partly because of a strict adherence to some anachronistic financial practices and partly because of the general lack of necessary information and ignorance of the most appropriate technique to adopt to minimize some risks inherent in such types of enterprises—a sort of "economic distance" caused by the capitalist imperfect knowledge of the economic potentials of the economic units concerned.

APPRAISAL OF PROVISION OF FINANCIAL SERVICES

Some common criticisms of bank operations in developing countries are briefly examined here:

1. Lack of delegation of authority to branch managers—this criticism seems to stem from the value that small businessmen appear to place on quick negotiation of finance.
2. Lack of understanding of local industries' needs, mainly because of the urban orientation of most bankers.
3. Personal guarantees and other forms of collateral securities that are not readily available. The fact that it is difficult to divorce small companies from the individuals associated with them makes the case for personal guarantees fairly strong, for this does ensure greater responsibility on the part of proprietors in the risks that they are prepared to take with borrowed money.

Financial Intermediation Role

In making an appraisal of the impact of the development of the financial system on the savings and investment process, a fundamental question is whether it brings forth higher savings than would be otherwise available. The financial institutions are expected to bring about an increase in the aggregate volume of real savings. In view of millions of naira invested in financial institutions outside the country by Nigerians, at least until recently, one might conclude that Nigerian financial institutions have not performed well in providing services in the three areas listed earlier. The institutions may not have been innovative enough in introducing new and more attractive financial assets to induce people to increase their rate of saving or to save their investable funds within the country. While demand deposits did not earn interest, time and savings deposits actually earned negative returns in real terms until recently. There was also the negative effect of the overvalued naira before the introduction of a new foreign exchange system in September 1986.

The quality of the services provided by the banks are shown, according to our study, to have been very poor—frustrating delays at the counters and long delays in making inquiries before opening accounts and obtaining other basic financial services. In most cases services are not provided in a convenient, cheap, and easily accessible manner. This does not make for the performance of the banks' financial intermediation role in the desired efficient manner and might even result in financial disintermediation with its attendant Shaw's "financial repression" consequences.[2] The special financing institutions like the Nigerian Industrial Development Bank (NIDB), Nigerian Agricultural and Cooperative Bank (NACB), and Nigerian Bank for Commerce and Industry (NBCI), probably by a deliberate act of omission, inefficiency, or sheer failure to grasp properly the main motive in setting them up, have left the gap they were established to fill as widely yawning as ever before, in much the same way as the indigenous banks have failed to fill the financial gap created by the ill-adapted operations of the former expatriate banks in the country.

Priority Lending Operations

Compliance with Sectoral Credit Guidelines

Banks' performances in respect of their compliance with the sectoral credit guidelines prescribed by the Central Bank of Nigeria (CBN) have been generally unsatisfactory over the years. According to the CBN in the 1986 Monetary Policy Circular no. 20, "Not only did commercial banks fail to meet the stipulated targets in 1985, but their performance represented a deterioration from the level achieved in 1984."

Financing Indigenous Enterprises

As regards the financing of indigenous enterprises, both categories of banks (development and commercial banks) were reported by the CBN to have defaulted in the previous years, having failed to reach the targets set for them in the CBN's Credit Guidelines, most especially in respect of loans to small-scale enterprises owned by Nigerians. As rightly remarked by the CBN, such unsatisfactory performance by the banks "militated against the important objective of encouraging the development of small scale enterprises as an essential spring-board for the promotion of rapid industrial growth."

In order to rectify this situation, each bank's minimum credit allocation to indigenous borrowers in 1982 was raised to 80 percent, and this level was retained in 1983. The share of this 80 percent that should be reserved exclusively for small-scale enterprises wholly owned by Nigerians was still maintained in 1988 to be not less than 16 percent, thus leaving 64 percent to other indigenous borrowers.

New Credit System to Help Small-Scale Investors

A demand that banking policies should be adapted to the nation's culture was made on June 24, 1986, by the governor of Nigeria's Ondo State while launching the state's "mass credit scheme for economic development." According to the governor, wholesale adoption of foreign banking policy by finance institutions had alienated the people. The mass credit scheme was designed to facilitate the access of small-scale investors to loans and to promote private enterprise in the state.

His contention, which we fully support, was that a banking practice built on the philosophy of the Western traditional banking system had not only been unhelpful to the people of the state, but had also continued to sustain a feature whereby investable rural credit continued to change hands outside the mainstream of banking practice through private thrift and credit organizations. "Until the banking institutions are able to enlighten the populace and establish the basis of confidence for pooling these circulative credits within the Nigerian rural communities, the relevance of the banks to the solution of Nigeria's development programmes will continue to be an illusion." He said that the new system, which is to operate under government guarantee, would ease the process of access to investment credit for small-scale investors, such as farmers, fishermen, traders, artisans, and industrialists who would not normally be covered under the traditional bank lending scheme.[3]

Thus, as regards the financial aspects of financing rural development, there is a need to devise better ways and more effective means to make financial facilities available to the often-neglected majority in the informal sector and rural areas of the country. There the sectors of major significance include (1) small-scale industrial enterprises and (2) agricultural enterprises.

Nigeria's existing financial system has been fashioned mainly on the Western type inherited from colonial times that fails to take cognizance of Nigeria's sociocultural background. The banks have thus found it difficult to adapt in a way that would make them useful in promoting the industrial advancement and economic development of the country. The techniques and style of operation are quite unsuitable to meet the financial requirements of the bulk of the people. The same could also be said of the capital markets developed in the country, which many wholly owned Nigerian indigenous enterprises have not found useful over the years. There is, therefore, a need to study Nigeria's indigenous savings and credit mechanisms to see how some features of these mechanisms could be incorporated into the existing banking system and the capital market. It is also necessary to see how the indigenous financing mechanisms could be improved upon to enhance their role in rural development.

THE STOCK MARKET AS A SOURCE OF
BUSINESS FINANCE

As in about 30 other developing countries, a stock exchange was created in Nigeria in 1961 in the great expectation that it could shape the financial system toward improving the allocation of capital resources as well as serve as an important source of business finance. As already argued in some previous studies, there are good reasons to believe that security markets in developing countries, in most cases, are neither efficient nor perfect. Once a stock market has been set up in a developing country, a consideration of its inefficiency is hardly seen as of much significance, since the general view now held is that the existence of such a market, efficient of inefficient, is better than no market at all. It is seen as a necessary part of the development of the Western-type capitalist financial system.

The desire for the stock market to significantly increase business finance for a growing number of Nigerian enterprises was impressively stated in the CBN *Annual Report* for the year ended March 31, 1960 (pp. 16, 19). The anticipated benefits from such a market have failed to materialize, and it has been recognized that after 30 years of stock-market nurturing and development in Nigeria, indigenous Nigerian enterprises that were expected to be beneficiaries could not in most cases readily utilize the rather exaggerated financial facilities of the market in its continuing transplanted egalitarian form. Although the market has been found useful by the authorities in Nigeria in the implementation of the indigenization programs of the 1970s and the ongoing privatization schemes, it has not yet been effective in meeting the aspiration of promoting the country's economic and industrial development.

The various problems facing the Nigerian Stock Exchange have remained virtually unchanged, as we had diagnosed early in the 1970s. "These problems are mainly those in respect of the limited supply of securities on the one hand, and generally weak and insufficient demand for them on the other. Both the demand and supply conditions reflect the underlying narrowness and other deficiencies in the functioning of the exchange."[4]

Although the stock exchange has been in existence for about 30 years now, a large percentage of potential investors and the business community can still hardly understand its operation and real benefits and thus cannot actively participate in its activities, with most stockbroking firms (about 80) operating in Lagos. The problems largely explain (1) why the Nigerian Stock Exchange, which started operations in 1961 with 4 securities, could boast of only 13 securities a decade later in 1971; and (2) why the sporadic growth in securities occasioned by the 1972 and 1977 NEPB Acts could not be sustained thereafter. The number of listed securities rose rather slowly from 148 securities in 1979 to 198 in 1987. The predominance of government stock is still as great as it has ever been, with well above 70 percent of the value of transactions relating to government securities.

Securities raised on the Nigerian Stock Exchange (NSE) comprised about 38 percent and 42 percent of total volume and value of new issues, respectively, in 1989. A total of 565,593,844 shares worth ₦682.7 million were raised through the exchange, while 994,926,803 shares valued at ₦944.9 million were raised outside the exchange.

Only 2 of the 138 new issues in 1989 were listed on the Second-Tier Securities Market (SSM), thus bringing to 10 the number of securities quoted on the SSM. Out of the 138 new issues in 1989, there were 73 on offer for subscription, 40 as rights issues, 12 as debenture stocks, 12 as preference shares, and one state government bond (Kaduna). Out of the 73 securities offered for subscription in 1989 (879,365,503 shares worth ₦715.2 million), a total of 558,064,543 shares worth ₦403.9 million were raised outside the NSE, while 321,300,960 shares valued at ₦311.3 million were raised through the facilities of the exchange.

The level of activity in the capital market has been boosted again since 1989 in terms of both the volume and the value of securities issued and traded. The increase has been due partly to the ongoing privatization program and partly to the sharp rise in bank lending rates. The rise in interest rates has induced the shift to equity financing by firms, while the sale of equity in government-owned companies under the privatization program has been increasing the volume and value of new issues.

Unlike in the previous years, rights issues have started to feature prominently since 1989 on the capital market. As noted by the CBN in its 1989 *Annual Report*, this has been due to their attractiveness in the mobilization of long-term funds in view of the scarcity of funds and the consequent high rates of interest in the money market. Thus in 1989 a total of 138 issues involving 1,560,520,647 shares valued at ₦1,627.7 million were raised in the primary market, compared with only 12 valued at ₦211 million in 1988. It should be noted that the bulk of the issues both in terms of volume (64 percent) and value (58 percent) were raised outside the stock exchange in 1989.

Apart from the fact that most of the basic problems of the stock market could be attributed to the present stage of economic and social developments in the country as well as the alien nature of the stock exchange and security market in our system, the NSE itself could improve its performance by being more innovative rather than clinging to old rigid rules and regulations. Other issues pertain to the costs of transactions in securities, the pricing of securities, and the listing requirements, which could be further looked into by the NSE.

The new-issue market does not always involve new shares, and not all capital raised there goes to purchase new fixed assets or to finance increases in production activities. Critics of the new-issue market therefore point to the small amounts of risk capital often raised. In many developing countries, an assessment of the role of a capital market is expected to place greater emphasis on the issue of new risk capital rather than on the exchange of existing equities, which is seen mainly as facilitating making profits from short-term speculative dealing. As shown earlier, the stock market is not the only market for securities. There are private placements, mostly of securities of unquoted companies. In addition, new funds can also be obtained through other financial channels, for example, by means of bank credit, presumably of short-term nature but often rolled over into medium-term loans. These other facilities for issuing and dealing in financial instruments and raising business finance—falling outside the restrictive scope of the stock market but within the broad financial market—constitute the major avenues for the provision of finance to the bulk of business enterprises, quoted and unquoted, private and public, medium and large sized. These extra-stock-market sources, which are the only avenues for the provision of institutional finance to small and medium-sized enterprises, have greater potential and will continue to constitute the most promising financial circuits, with further local adaptation by the financial intermediaries.

As fully analyzed in our study of the role of the Nigerian capital markets in 1974,[5] the securities market in the country (as in other developing countries) has not made and is unlikely to be capable to making in the foreseeable future any significant net contribution to funds supply for investment. The new funds raised on the market for the private sector, as a proportion of gross domestic product (GDP), are low, being in each year less than 10 percent. The largest proportion of funds raise to gross national product (GNP) was during the indigenization years of the 1970s, particularly in 1971, when ₦27 million (gross) was raised by companies, and in 1978, following the second indigenization decree, when the highest absolute amount of ₦90 million (gross) was raised by companies. This amount was small when compared with the amount of ₦113 million made available for industrial finance in 1978 by just one bank, Union Bank.

As shown in Ojo (1976, p. 26), the major reason for seeking public quotation in the 1970s was to offer shares to the public in a bid to comply with the requirements of the Nigerian Enterprises Promotion Decrees of 1972 and 1977, rather than for the purpose of raising additional funds. "In most cases shares held by proprietors and other former shareholders were offered to the public, and they did not, therefore, make available additional investment funds to increase the rate of capital formation." The stock exchange and securities markets are essentially suitable in a capitalist economic system with a strong private sector as a central part of the development strategy. Such a system has not been found as suitable for the Nigerian economy, which has been a "mixed" one in view of the major role of government in steering the development effort in the most desirable manner. Apart from the rather high costs, the disclosure and listing requirements of the NSE have been viewed as constituting one of the constraints against public quotation, especially by wholly owned Nigerian companies. There is no doubt that the listing requirements and the very strict manner in which the set standards of disclosure are monitored by the exchange are meant to provide the framework for the protection of shareholders and potential investors as well as ensuring confidence in the exchange. Nevertheless, there appears to be an urgent need to modify the listing and disclosure requirements, including a reduction in the cost of public issues, in the present attempt to make the stock market an attractive alternative source of business finance.

The Second-Tier Securities Market (SSM)

In an attempt to attract to the securities market indigenous Nigerian enterprises, most of which are of small and medium sizes, the Nigerian Stock Exchange launched in May 1985 the Second-Tier Securities Market (SSM). This is akin to the Unlisted Securities Market in the United Kingdom or the over-the-counter market in the United States. According to the information booklet published by the Nigerian Stock Exchange, *Understanding the Second-Tier Securities Market*, the SSM has the following trading features vis-à-vis the older first-tier market:

1. Trading in the SSM is less restricted than in the first-tier market.
2. Companies quoted on the SSM are under an obligation to maintain an informed market for their securities by entering into a formal relationship with the NSE.

3. Trading is subject to the normal dealing rules, that is, those existing for trading on the NSE.

In essence, the SSM operates in the same way as the first-tier market by providing a forum for the buying or selling of the shares of companies in the market. To this end, investors may directly instruct stockbrokers or banks to effect the transaction in the same way as for listed companies. Investors in the SSM are protected by the Nigerian Stock Exchange on the same terms as investors in listed securities.

Requirements for Admission into the SSM

The main requirements for admission into the SSM are stated by the NSE as follows:

1. Companies must be registered as Public Limited Companies under the provisions of the Companies Act.
2. Companies admitted into the SSM are expected to sign a "General Undertaking" with the NSE.
3. Companies must have no less than 100 shareholders.
4. Companies must submit the financial statements of their last three years in business to the NSE. Thereafter, companies must submit audited statements half-yearly and annually. The date of the last audited accounts must be no more than nine months before the date of application to the NSE.
5. At least 10 percent or ₦50,000 of the equity capital of companies admitted must be made available to the public, except in the case of an offer by introduction.
6. No shareholder may have, either directly or indirectly, more than 75 percent of the issued share capital of the company.
7. Companies admitted into the SSM are required to pay an annual fee of ₦2,000 each, apart from other costs, such as quotation, transaction, and advertising costs.

As can be noted from the brief review of the main features of the SSM, certain reductions in the requirements for securities listing and transactions have been effected. This will, no doubt, attract new indigenous Nigerian enterprises to the securities market. Apart from the initial high enthusiasm shown by some enterprises, most Nigerian enterprises are not yet convinced that the high costs and other listing and trading conditions have been reduced enough to justify resorting to participating in the securities markets. Our assessment of the role of the stock market as a very limited source of business finance in this chapter, therefore, remains the same, notwithstanding the rather partial remedial measures embodied in the Second-Tier Securities Market. The watered-down conditions have not proved attractive enough to most Nigerian small and medium-sized enterprises. Because the SSM has not been sufficiently adapted to the needs of the core indigenous enterprises, it has not been able to record the type of success attained by a similar second-tier market in the United Kingdom, the Unlisted Securities

Market (USM). Since its inception in 1980, the USM in the United Kingdom has been reported to have "successfully fulfilled the role of an organised equity market for small and medium-sized companies operating in growth areas." As reported in the *Midland Bank Review* (Spring 1987, pp. 11–12), the USM has improved access to equity capital for these companies and has reduced the cost to the companies of raising funds. By December 1986 a total of 529 companies had been admitted to the USM over the six-year period; new issues in 1986 amounted to £515 million, some £289 million of which was provided to new entrants, according to the *Midland Bank Review*.

Furthermore, the development of junior stock markets with less stringent listing requirements and lower issue costs has been undertaken to serve as a source of funds to close the equity gap. As reported in the *Midland Bank Review* (Spring 1987), entry to the USM, whose close counterpart in Nigeria is the SSM, has been relatively expensive for the smallest companies. Since the USM is thus not considered an appropriate vehicle for start-ups, the over-the-counter (OTC) market has specialized in younger companies.

THE ROLE OF THE INDIGENOUS INFORMAL CREDIT SYSTEM

As shown in our earlier study (1976), the indigenous informal credit system continues to play an important role in the Nigerian financial system, in that it looks after the credit needs of numerous small indigenous enterprises, artisans, and petty traders. Informal credit markets exist in a wide variety of forms in many developing economies like that of Nigeria. They are largely complementary to, but occasionally competitive in certain respects with, the formal banking system. These credit markets provide credit to businesses and people whom the formal banking system could not accommodate either because of explicit policy limitations or because the banks' requirements for borrowers are too onerous. The informal credit markets are better placed and structured and have demonstrated the possibility of accommodating new categories of clients and business in a more flexible and innovative manner than the formal credit markets. The improved operation of these markets will greatly enhance the provision of financial facilities in our model broadly based capital/financial market, which also accommodates rural and small indigenous enterprises, as already encouraged in India. For most deficit units (borrowers) in LDCs, the informal loan is the only possible source of credit, since these borrowers might be unable to provide the collateral to be considered for formal credit from banks. Even borrowers of standing at times find informal loans attractive because of the speed and/or secrecy with which they can be raised. There are several studies on the useful role of the informal credit markets in many other developing countries, including World Bank Staff (1979), Park (1976), Fernando (1986), Sadeque (1986), and the Sierra Leonean experience related by A. B. Taylor.

The relative importance of the major sources of finance available to farming enterprises in some areas in Nigeria covered by our survey in 1986 is shown as follows:

Table 2.1

Sources of Capital for Small Business in Nigeria

Sources of Finance	Number of Units Financed					
	Former Western State	Bendel State	Kwara State	Lagos State	Total	Percentages (%)
1. Owners savings (including esusu and use of club contributions)	13,273	2,709	1,023	4,156	21,161	96.41
2. Assisted by						
Banks	22	10	1	14	47	0.21
Government institutions	1	—	5	3	9	0.04
Local authorities	—	7	—	—	7	0.03
Cooperative societies	4	8	—	1	13	0.06
Relatives and friends	254	322	3	61	640	2.92
Money lenders	38	27	—	7	72	0.33
Total	13,592	3,083	1,032	4,242	21,949	100.00
Owners' Savings as % of Total	97.7	87.9	99.1	98.0	96.4	

Source: Ojo (1976 and 1985), table 6.2.

Sources of Finance for Farming Enterprises	Relative Importance (%)
1. Traditional/informal sources (e.g., esusu and family contributions)	51
2. Cooperative societies	31
3. Bank credit	18
4. Government sources	0
Total	100

As shown, the most important sources are the traditional or informal sources (51 percent), which include esusu or rotational group contributions and family contributions as well as moneylenders. Cooperative societies, which are next in relative importance with 31 percent, are also essentially an informal source. Bank credit was only 18 percent in terms of relative importance, and this was enjoyed mainly by the few large-scale farming enterprises, excluding over 90 percent of the small farming enterprises.

The relative importance of the main sources of capital for small businesses in Nigeria is shown in tables 2.1 and 2.2, from which it can be noted that nearly all the finance required by new business enterprises comes from informal financing sources, while the contribution of banks and other form sources in negligible or nil.

Table 2.2
Relative Importance of Sources of Capital for
Small Business in Nigeria

Sources	Start-up (%)	Growth (%)
Trade credit	30	35
Retained profits	—	32
Family assistance	29	—
Rotating credit contributions	25	3
Bank overdrafts	—	19
Personal savings	16	—
Leasing	—	4
Long-term loans	—	5
Hire purchase	—	1
Share Capital	—	1

It is only after the businesses have been established successfully and are in need of capital for growth that banks and other formal finance sources start to play some role, providing about one-quarter of the financial requirements of the business enterprises, as depicted in table 2.2. There is thus a need for suitably adapted financial institutions that could provide seed, risk, or venture capital for small and new businesses to supplement the limited start-up capital hitherto made available through the informal finance sources.[6]

It is important to note that the activities of the informal nonbank market finance are necessary to the balanced growth of the economy. These informal credit markets have demonstrated the possibility of accommodating new categories of clients and businesses. Only recently has the government seemed to become fully aware of this important role of the informal system, despite our recommendations on this as well as some suggestions on how to achieve improved operations of the system in our study more than a decade ago (1976). Some attempts are now being made by the government to get the informal contributors organized into cooperatives to make them perform better. The Peoples Bank and community banks now being set up are to assist the informal sector.

MEASURES TO DEVELOP A BROADLY BASED FINANCIAL SYSTEM

Some measures to develop a broadly based financial system that could provide more adequate financial facilities are briefly noted here:

1. Unit trusts that could be utilized by small investors and that could operate to increase the availability of venture capital in the domestic capital market should be encouraged to be set up. The trusts offer small investors a more practical alternative to share purchases.

2. Special institutions should be set up to provide financial and technical facilities to small industrial enterprises, for example, institutions specializing in medium- and long-term finance for indigenous firms, formed with official support and encouragement. In addition to provision of risk finance and venture capital, the institutions should be equipped to offer financial advice and consultancy services to the small firms.

3. In order to make the financing of many indigenous firms relatively more attractive to banks, the authorities could assist, inter alia, in setting up state-backed guarantee schemes for medium- and long-term bank loans to encourage banks to grant finance to small firms. An example would be guarantee arrangements through the CBN. The idea of an agricultural insurance scheme being floated forms an important aspect of our recommended package of measures.

4. The authorities should further consider the setting up of small-firm investment companies that qualify for special tax exemptions for the provision of equity finance for small firms.

5. Establish a rural development bank that operates mainly with funds mobilized from local sources and equity capital owned by the local people whom the institution should serve. The bank should offer full banking facilities taking deposits and granting loans mostly to agricultural and rural small industrial enterprises.[7]

CONCLUSION

We have attempted to highlight the major deficiencies in the functioning of the orthodox formal capital markets, mainly from the viewpoint of financing businesses and meeting the development needs of developing economies. This is not to say that the financial systems in these countries have not been developing, but rather that the development of most of their institutions has not been satisfactory and well adapted to suit local developmental needs.

In Nigeria, as well as in many other developing nations, the statement of the problem can be put this: The financial system has been of a "lame-duck" type that, although growing, has failed to satisfy the real developmental needs of the nation. We have considered in this chapter some required strategies and other measures that may be needed to rectify the defects as well as the need to further enhance the role of the informal capital markets.

For instance, an analysis of the banks' performance—the growth in deposits, loans and advances, investments, and profits—might easily make one conclude that they have been doing well generally. But where a consolidated evaluation of these institutions has been made, one would be hard put to conclude that the provision of their financial services (concentrated and in many cases duplicated in certain areas and sectors, to the neglect of the bulk of indigenous enterprises) augurs well for the country's real development needs. Such an unsatisfactory pattern of development justifies some form of state intervention to correct some of the anomalies, but such an intervention would only be useful where appropriate methods and a judicious approach are employed in bringing about the required well-adapted financial structure and orientation.

The so-called development banks are found to have failed in many respects to fill the gaps they were (or should have) primarily been set up to fill; such a gap-filling function was not performed by merely duplicating financial facilities to finance the same set of few enterprises being financed by commercial banks, that is, enterprises that could and did obtain the same facilities through other financial intermediaries. As emphasized in this chapter, the banks and other financial intermediaries in Nigeria should devise new ways of extending financial facilities to the hitherto-neglected sectors rather than justifying why this should never be done at all.

A consideration of what small businesses expect of their bankers and other financiers clearly explains why they have found traditional informal institutions more accommodating and useful than Nigeria's bankers in fulfilling their expectations. As highlighted by Bolton (1978), small businesses expect a friendly and understanding response to their needs and problems from their financier. They expected the financier to get a feel of their business by going to see it, thus gaining an insight and a basis for a more effective judgment of their case than can be obtained from reading sophisticated reports. As shown in this chapter, their expectations have been largely unfulfilled in Nigeria and many other LDCs.

The promotion of our suggested new breed of financial institutions, facilitating accommodation of the financial requirements of new and larger categories of indigenous clients and businesses, would ensure in a better manner the balanced growth of the economy, rural and urban, and of small, medium, and large-scale enterprises. In essence, the suggested package of measures would bring forth a much broader financial system that can more effectively harness investable funds for investment in a wider range of enterprises than in the case of the existing, very narrowly structured financial system.

NOTES

1. Ojo (1974), chaps. 7 and 8. See also Ojo (1976), chaps. 5 and 6.
2. Shaw (1973), chap. 4.
3. For three detailed accounts of the poor performances of banking services to customers by bank employees, see Abiola Irele, "What Are Banks For?" The *Guardian*, October 15, 1986, p. 9.
4. Ojo (1976), p. 28.
5. Ojo (1974), chap. 4.
6. See Ojo (1974, 1976), Ojo and Adewunmi (1982), and Okigbo (1983) for further analyses of some inadequacies of the Nigerian financial system.
7. See Ojo (1974, 1976) for details on this recommendation. Also, see Nikoi (1986) for an interesting experience in developing a rural bank for a cocoa-farming community in Ghana.

REFERENCES

Alile, H. I. (1984). "A Comparative Analysis of Capital Markets Development in the Less Developed Countries." Mimeo.

Bolton, J. E. (1978). "The Financial Needs of the Small Firm." In *The Banks and Small Businesses*, ed. the Institute of Bankers, Cambridge Seminar, UK, 1978).

Fernando, Edgar. (1986). "Informal Credit and Savings Organizations in Sri Lanka: The Chetu System." *Savings and Development, Quarterly Review*, no. 3: 253–263.

Nigeria, Federal Republic of. (1976). *Report of the Committee on the Nigerian Financial System* (Chairman: Dr. P. N. C. Okigbo). Lagos, December.

———. *Federal Military Government's Views on the Committee on the Nigerian Financial System*. Lagos: Federal Ministry of Information.

Nikoi, Gloria. (1986). "Rural Banking on the Rise." *Development Forum*, March: 5–10.

Ojo, Ade T. (1976 and 1985). *The Nigerian Financial System*. Cardiff: University of Wales Press.

Ojo, J. A. T. (1974). "Financial Sector and Economic Development, with Special Reference to the Nigerian Capital Markets." Ph.D. thesis, University of Wales.

Ojo, Ade T., and Wole Adewunmi. (1982). *Banking and Finance in Nigeria: A Study of the Role of Banking and Financial Institutions and Markets in a Developing Economy*. Leighton Buzzard, U.K.: Graham Burn Publisher.

Okigbo, Pius. (1983). "Reforming the Banking System for the 1990's." Lecture delivered at the Nigerian Institute of Bankers.

Osaze, B. E. (1981). "Financing Small Rapid Growth Firms." Ph.D. thesis, University of Bath.

Park, Yung Chul. (1976). *The Unorganized Financial Sector in Korea, 1945–75*. Studies in Domestic Finance no. 28. World Bank, Washington, D.C., November.

Sadeque, Syed. (1986). "The Rural Financial Market and the Grameen Bank Project in Bangladesh: An Experiment in Involving Rural Poor and Women in Institutional Credit Operations." *Savings and Development, Quarterly Review,* no. 2: 181–196.

Shaw, Edward S. (1973). *Financial Deepening in Economic Development*. London: Oxford University Press.

Taylor, A. B. *Money and Banking in Sierra Leone*. Finafrica and Cariplo Monographs on the Credit Markets of Africa Series, no. 15. Milan, Italy: A. Giuffre Publisher.

World Bank. (1979). "Informal Credit Markets in India." Report on a Study at the Public and Private Finance Division of the World Bank, prepared by the Development Policy Staff, August.

3

Securities Market Development and Economic Growth

P. C. KUMAR and GEORGE TSETSEKOS

The financial-sector–economic-growth nexus has not yet gained wide currency among academicians and policymakers. However, consequent to the works of Goldsmith (1958, 1969, 1983), McKinnon (1973), and Shaw (1973), it is generally accepted that financial-structure development is a necessary condition for economic growth. The objective of this chapter is to develop a theory of securities market development and economic growth. Its thrust is that beyond a certain stage of growth, financial intermediation is more efficient, paralleled by resource-allocation efficiencies, with securities markets than with banks. Mutually reinforcing feedback effects between securities markets and the real economy exist that propel the latter to higher levels of growth. Undoubtedly, there are costs associated with securities market development, but when the costs are considered jointly with the benefits produced, securities markets are more efficient. However, it should be stressed that securities market development should be considered only at a particular phase in the development sequence. At any other phase, the costs are likely to outweigh the benefits.

The first section of the chapter provides a historical perspective and a literature review. The second section presents a discussion of substitutes and complements in the financial structure. The theory of securities market development and economic growth is presented in the third section. The final section presents some concluding remarks.

FINANCIAL-STRUCTURE DEVELOPMENT AND
ECONOMIC GROWTH: HISTORICAL PERSPECTIVE
AND LITERATURE REVIEW

The financial-development–economic-growth nexus has not been accorded prominence in the literature either in economics or in finance. The classical Harrod model analyzes the nature of equilibrium between planned savings and investment in a growing economy. However, it does not incorporate incentives to enhance savings or the financial intermediation process by which savings are transferred from surplus units to deficit units. The neoclassical growth model ignores the financial component. Among the neo-Keynesian approaches, Kaldor (e.g., 1955), in the same vein as Harrod, introduced a savings function but with no reference to the intermediation process. On the other hand, the theory of finance has largely developed along micro considerations, with little or no explicit analysis of the larger implications for real economic growth.

The literature in economics does acknowledge the association between financial and monetary phenomena in economic growth and development. Much of this has developed along the lines of responses to the classical question in monetary economics whether money really does matter rather than the explicit role of financial institutions and markets. In a cross-sectional study of 57 countries, Kuznets (1971) showed that the share of the agricultural sector in gross domestic product is inversely correlated with per capita GDP. The share of the industrial sector, including transportation and communication, is closely and positively associated with per capita product. The share of the service sector is positively but weakly correlated with per capita product, but the share of banking, insurance, and real estate increases in a dramatic manner as the focus is shifted from low-income to higher-income countries.

Much of the modern interest in financial structure and financial intermediation has been generated by Goldsmith's seminal work (1958), which reported that the activity of intermediaries, as measured by their share in national assets, in tangible assets, and in all claims, showed a substantial increase in the United States from 1860 to 1952. Similarly, Goldsmith (1969) found that the ratio of financial institutions' assets to gross national product rose substantially from 1860 to 1963 in both developed and less developed countries, including Argentina, India, Japan, Great Britain, and the United States. The number of households with savings accounts, the number with life insurance policies, and the number with stock ownership as percentages of the population were consistently low for the developing countries relative to the developed countries. Goldsmith (1983) focused on trends in investment and saving, development of money, banking and other financial institutions, and methods of financing households, business, and government in a comparative study of Japan, India, and the United States in the period between 1850 and 1975. The financial interrelations ratio, which measures the size of the financial superstructure by the ratio of financial to tangible assets, had the lowest level and rate of increase in India.

McKinnon (1973) developed a growth model providing a description of the institutional structure available in developing countries with a justification for holding money. He assumed that investment is lumpy, not perfectly divisible, and that no borrowing is available, thus rendering the accumulation of money necessary prior to investment. McKinnon argued that if no money is available, working capital will be held in the form of physical assets. When money is available, it can be substituted for physical assets, thus freeing resources for more productive purposes. This use of money is called the "conduit effect." To the extent that paper money is used to replace physical goods in working balances, monetary accumulation is a complement to physical-asset accumulation. After all the physical working balances have been replaced by paper money, any further monetary accumulation will be an alternative to physical accumulation. Thus, McKinnon argued, there is an optimal size of the monetary system that maximizes growth.

Shaw (1973) rejected the preceding analysis and argued that money, consisting of currency or bank deposits, should not be considered wealth. Money is debt—currency represents the debt of the central bank, while demand deposits form a part of the debt of commercial banks. In the aggregate balance sheet of the economy, these assets and liabilities neutralize each other. For example, the liabilities of the central bank (currency) cancel out assets (cash) of individuals; liabilities of commercial banks (deposits) cancel out the same deposits held as assets by individuals. Money is not wealth, and its accumulation is not a substitute for the accumulation of physical capital. In Shaw's view, money is only one of many outputs produced by the overall financial system. These outputs of the financial system serve as intermediate inputs to the production process. Producing more of these inputs will enhance the growth of real output. In developing countries, government intervention in the financial system had "repressed" its size and development and inadvertently economic growth as well. Thus the financial services in many developing countries are relatively small in the sense that they are less than optimal.

In extending Shaw's analysis, Long (1983) enumerated the services provided by the financial system:

1. Provision of a medium of exchange
2. Mobilization and allocation of capital
3. Transformation and distribution of risk
4. Transformation of the size of financial transactions
5. Transformation of maturities, that is, offering savers the short-term liquid deposits they prefer and at the same time providing borrowers longer-term loans better matched to the cash flows generated by their investment
6. Provision of professional management, including the advantages related to scale economies in the collection and analysis of information
7. Risk reduction through diversification
8. Stabilization of economic fluctuation through financial policies

Both McKinnon (1973) and Shaw (1973) argued that the financial systems in many developing countries are below their optimal size and ascribed the principal cause of their economic underdevelopment to this reason. Long (1983) identified possible reasons for the undersized financial structure as being infant-industry problems, externalities, and inappropriate government policies in developing countries.

SUBSTITUTES AND COMPLEMENTS IN
FINANCIAL STRUCTURE

The Scope for Substitutes and Complements

Banking institutions and securities markets constitute alternate channels of financial intermediation.[1] They may be competitive, which suggests substitution possibilities, or complementary to each other. Government policies influence their respective roles and the degree of their interrelationship. In most countries, banks provide short-term loans purely for working capital needs. In other situations, they have been encouraged to accept term risks as well.

When banks borrow in the short term through the acceptance of deposits and lend in the long term, they are in competition with securities markets and as such constitute alternatives to these markets. On the other hand, if banks borrow in the long term through the issuance of bonds or negotiable certificates of deposits and lend in the long term, so that the maturity structures of their assets and liabilities are balanced, they are complements to the securities markets. In such case, securities markets are the principal sources of funds for banks, and in turn banks are major suppliers of securities to such markets.

Traditionally, banks tend to lend in the short term, as their liabilities are mostly in the form of deposits on demand. By contrast, securities markets mostly offer transactions in long-term securities. The extent to which banks depart from their roles is largely influenced by government policies. Governments promote the supply of long-term finance by the banking sector through the following measures:

1. Reducing the liquidity risk of banks lending in the long term while simultaneously borrowing in the short term
2. Directly subsidizing long-term lending by banks
3. Indirectly subsidizing banks by subjecting them to less costly supervision and regulation
4. Encouraging debt finance over equity finance

In the first instance, if the liquidity risk associated with lending in the short term and borrowing in the long term is reduced, then the related risk premium, measured as the differential between the lending and borrowing rate, can be partly reduced. Banks can undercut securities markets by providing long-term finance at lower interest rates. Banks are considered crucial to economic policy, while the same consideration is not extended to securities markets. The reduction of liquidity risk of the banks by the government is accomplished by (1) providing rediscount facilities, (2) "salvaging" ailing banks, and (3) providing deposit insurance.

Central banks provide commercial banks with some degree of liquidity in the event of major deposit withdrawals. Further, as a general practice, central banks arrange "aid" for commercial banks in a liquidity bind rather than permit a run on the deposits. Finally, in a number of countries, the government guarantees the repayment of deposits up to a limited amount.[2] In contrast, government assistance to securities markets is mostly nonexistent or available only to a limited extent.

The scope for substitution between banks and long-term securities markets is limited primarily to the market for debt finance. As they do not purchase corporate equity on their own account, banks are not generally substitutes for the equity markets. With government encouragement and subsidization, banks tend to offer long-term debt financing at cheaper rates than those prevailing in the securities markets. Further, the availability of low-cost debt finance causes a shift in the preferences of the users toward debt rather than equity financing. Of course, excessive reliance on debt finance increases the prospects of financial risk. Equity finance is limited to private placements and retained earnings. Hence resource allocation is not as efficient as that obtained in a competitive securities market.

The social costs associated with excessive government support for the banks and the social benefits accruing to a competitive securities market, more frequently than not, go unrecognized. Interest on bank deposits in many countries is free of tax. The social costs of this subsidy, as well as its provision of liquidity to banks that lend long on short-term deposits, are not taken into account. On the other hand, an efficient and competitive securities market generates a wealth of data and analytical information for the market participants. The social benefits of this service usually pass unnoticed.

In some countries, banks function as securities market institutions, either by providing broker-dealer services and trust and investment management services, or through separate entities owned and controlled by bank holding companies. The degree of involvement of banks in such securities market activities is a major policy issue and involves the following considerations:

1. Conflicts of interest
2. Specialization and entrepreneurship
3. Concentration of economic power

The argument of conflict of interest arises on the grounds that if banks operate as underwriters or brokers, they may well persuade firms to accept the method of financing most convenient to the banks rather than to the client firm. When banks act as managers of trust funds, it is argued that they can buy equity positions in firms to influence their banking decisions. If banks can act as broker-dealers and trust managers, they can use their influence as lenders to persuade corporations to grant them underwriting business. While there is nothing to prevent banks from being able to perform the specialization and entrepreneurial function, securities market institutions have traditionally developed communications systems and market-making skills needed to supply liquidity for long-term securities. Finally, involvement in the supply of all sources of finance to corporations endows banks with an inordinate degree of influence to control corporations. On the other hand, arguments extended in favor of banks engaging in securities market operations are as follows. Economies of scale allow banks to conduct securities market operations more efficiently than independent institutions. This is made possible by their extensive branch networks, which allow for more efficient securities distribution.

Second, banks in their credit-granting functions develop efficient evaluation procedures, which are useful in their trust functions. Finally, as major financial institutions win the confidence of depositors, banks can attract and manage trust funds. In the ultimate analysis, scope for domination of financial markets by banks does exist. It is for the government to evaluate the social costs of such bank monopolies and to decide on the separation of the banking and securities market functions.

Securities Markets: Supply-leading or Demand-following?

Wai and Patrick (1973) identified the principal issue in the financing of economic development as the extent to which governments should aid the development of capital markets. The authors questioned whether the capital markets should develop in response to the demand for their services, that is, whether they should be demand-following, or whether the governments should subsidize the creation and operations of the capital markets in advance of the anticipated demand, that is, whether markets should be supply-leading. Improving the supply of the factors of production, enhancing their quality, and combining them efficiently are important in promoting growth. The causal chain extends from financial variables to real variables to the growth of output and employment. This causal chain is distorted by market imperfections that are more prevalent in developing than in developed economies. Thus imperfections exist in capital and money markets, foreign exchange and trade, government revenues and expenditures, and labor markets, as well as in markets for stocks and bonds. Whereas Shaw (1973) attributed the underdeveloped state of developing countries to the less-than-optimal size of the financial services provided, Wai and Patrick (1973) identified market imperfections as being the underlying cause.

TOWARD A THEORY OF SECURITIES MARKET
DEVELOPMENT AND ECONOMIC GROWTH

A general theory relating securities market development to a sequential process of economic development is described in the following paragraphs.

The Stages of Economic Development

Economic development may be conceptualized as an evolutionary process progressing in distinct stages.[3] Initially, the economy is characterized by a traditional society with low productivity, with consumption at subsistence levels. In the second stage, assets expand with productivity improvements to promote the emergence of a dominant sector, such as agriculture. Further increases in the proportion of savings and investment to national income promote the development of other leading sectors in manufacturing and agriculture together with the proliferation of social and political institutions. Thus in the third stage the growth of the economy is poised to increase dramatically (Rostow's [1960] "takeoff stage"). Higher growth with the development of new leading sectors in manufacturing industry and services and further increases in the share of investment in national income drive the economy toward maturity. Technology and export development have major roles in the fourth stage as the economy drives toward maturity. The final stage is characterized by additional leading sectors in consumer goods and services, all of which are heavily technology-intensive (see figure 3.1).

The Corresponding Phases of Financial-Sector Development

The conceptual foundation of the theory is predicated on the notion that financial-sector development is a necessary condition for economic growth. While other factors, such as investment, manufacturing activity, export development, absorption of technology, and human-capital and institutional development, are undoubtedly necessary, the financial sector is the vital catalyst that activates the interrelationships among them. Specifically, the theory posits that development of a subset of the financial sector, namely, the securities market, is necessary for the economy to progress to the fourth and final stages of economic growth.

The traditional society is characterized by the total absence of the financial sector. In this barter economy, all savings are held in the form of real output, with participants being exposed to the resulting risks. With the emergence of the dominant sector in the second stage, the economy becomes monetized and better organized. A banking subsector is started, but as it is still in its infancy, it is

Figure 3.1

Securities Market Development and Economic Growth

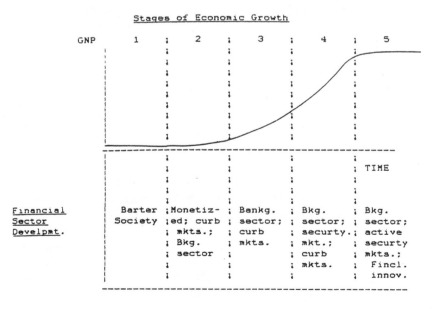

accompanied by an informal but active curb market. In the third stage, as savings and investment increase and social and political institutions proliferate, the banking subsector gets better organized, but activity in the curb markets increases. With the development of new leading sectors and demand for even higher levels of investment in the fourth stage, the banking subsector and curb markets continue to grow. However, efficiency of financial intermediation through them leaves scope for improvement, and securities markets providing for the trading of claims issued by economic entities are developed. As development of securities markets progresses, the activities of the informal curb markets diminish. In the final stage, the banking subsector matures with reduced growth, and activities in the secondary securities markets increase dramatically. Financial innovation in the form of derivative financial instruments based on contingent claims lend dynamism to the securities markets. The curb markets virtually disappear at this stage.

In the last two stages, securities markets develop and grow. This is closely paralleled by the growth in the economy. As the securities markets intermediate in the financial sector more efficiently, the allocation of investment in the real economy improves and output increases further. In turn, this creates new demand for intermediation services from the securities markets with the concomitant increased growth in the economy. Thus there are mutually reinforcing feedback effects between the real output growth and increased securities market activities (see figure 3.1).

Some Caveats, Issues, and Observations

Financial Repression

McKinnon (1973) and Shaw (1973) have actively preached against financial repression in developing economies and have promoted the beneficial effects of financial liberalization. Financial repression implies administered ceilings on interest rates, consequent to which the supply of funds for investment is restricted, curb markets flourish, and the economy generally stagnates. If interest rates are permitted to find their own levels, they lead to increased savings and greater efficiency of capital allocation. Cho (1986) argued that in addition to the problems of restricted interest rates and lack of competition among banks, there are two other major constraints in developing countries. The first is imperfect information, which can be a significant barrier to efficient credit allocation even when banks are free of interest-rate ceilings. The second is the oligopolized and cartelized banking structure found in most developing countries. Liberalization of the banking system from interest-rate ceilings and other government interventions will not be adequate to achieve full allocation efficiency. Banks supply debt contracts, and in the presence of asymmetric information, there exist the adverse-selection and moral-hazard effects. Consequently, there may be borrowers who are potentially productive but unable to obtain loans due to the problem of adverse selection. On the other hand, equity contracts traded in securities markets are free from this effect when the same degree of imperfect information exists. It is therefore suggested that substantial development of the equity market is a necessary condition for complete financial liberalization.

Policy Measures to Promote Securities Markets

First, interest-rate ceilings, as mentioned in the foregoing discussion, stifle the development of securities markets. Higher interest rates on bank lending encourage corporate borrowers to seek equity finance as an alternative. Any increase in the demand for securities by individual savers or institutions will depend on their risk-adjusted return.

Second, special incentives may be offered to corporations to issue shares and debentures. This strategy has been attempted in some European countries and Brazil with some measure of success.[4] Consideration may be given to the policy of requiring foreign corporations to issue some local equity. Measures of privatization, which have gained current popularity, can contribute to the development of securities markets as the public sector divests itself of ownership.

Third, fiscal policy measures may be employed to foster the growth of equity markets. Some measures adopted in Brazil with great success are as follows: (1) treating substantial proportions of the share purchase price as tax-deductible expenses; (2) provisions for partial exemption of share dividends from personal income taxes; (3) concessional tax rates for shareholders of corporations with widely dispersed shareholdings; and (4) provisions for individuals and corporations to offset tax liabilities against shareholdings of special mutual funds.[5]

Finally, adequate regulation of securities markets is essential to protect the interests of investors and promote growth of these markets. The regulation should ensure full disclosure and widespread dissemination of information to all market participants.

Costs of Promoting Securities Markets

Some of the costs associated with the promotion of securities markets are explicit and others are implicit. The infrastructure for securities market development includes the legal framework and necessary regulations; the financial network, comprising banks, clearing houses, and so on; and communications facilities. Given the technology-intensive nature of modern markets, the latter are absolutely essential. It is for this reason that securities market development is advocated in the fourth stage. In an earlier stage, the economy cannot sustain the investment in necessary infrastructure. At the same time, the economies of scale that justify this investment are absent.

Second, subsidization of the participants in securities markets is bound to run counter to the goal of equitable income distribution. By the same token, substitution of securities markets by bank financing will not ameliorate this problem, as bank credit is made available to a restricted clientele.

Finally, the opportunity costs of providing government assistance for the growth of securities markets need to be weighed against the costs of intervention elsewhere. These include, inter alia, the administrative and compliance costs of interest-rate controls and other forms of capital market repression.

CONCLUSION

This chapter describes a theory of securities market development to promote economic growth. Financial-structure development is seen to be a necessary condition for economic growth. Specifically, the development of securities markets is seem to be necessary for the economy to progress to its final growth stages. The reinforcing feedback effects between the securities markets and the real economy propel the latter to higher growth levels.

Undoubtedly there are costs of promoting securities markets, but the overall benefits are believed to outweigh the costs. While the theory in its entirety does not yield a testable hypothesis, the final two stages do permit empirical verification. At the very minimum, it is possible to test whether the characteristics of securities markets in developed and developing nations are sufficiently distinct to differentiate between them.

NOTES

1. A broad definition of capital markets includes the entire organized financial system, covering commercial banks and all other financial intermediaries as well as short-term and long-term primary and nonmonetary financial claims. A definition at the intermediate level includes all organized markets and institutions dealing in long-term instruments only, such as equities, bonds, term loans, mortgages, time and savings deposits, and so on. The narrowest definition includes organized markets dealing in stocks, bonds, and convertibles, using the services of brokers and dealers. For further details, see Wai and Patrick (1973).

2. For example, in the United States, deposits up to $100,000 with commercial banks are insured by the Federal Deposit Insurance Corporation (FDIC).

3. Much of the following description draws heavily from Rostow's (1960) celebrated "stages of growth" concept.

4. See Drake (1977), p. 84.

5. Ibid., p. 85.

REFERENCES

Cho, Y. J. (1986). "Inefficiencies from Financial Liberalization in the Absence of Well-functioning Equity Markets." *Journal of Money, Credit, and Banking* 18, no. 2: 191–199.

Drake, P. J. (1977). "Securities Markets in Less-developed Countries." *Journal of Development Studies* 2 (January): 73–91.

Goldsmith, R. W. (1958). *Financial Intermediaries in the American Economy Since 1900.* Princeton, N.J.: Princeton University Press.

———. (1969). *Financial Structure and Development.* New Haven, Conn.: Yale University Press.

———. (1983). *The Financial Development of India, Japan, and the United States.* New Haven, Conn.: Yale University Press.

Kaldor, N. (1955). "Alternative Theories of Distribution." *Review of Economic Studies* 23: 83–100.

Kuznets, Simon S. (1971). *Economic Growth of Nations: Total Output and Production Structure.* Cambridge, Mass.: Harvard University Press.

Long, M. (1983). "A Note on Economic Theory and Economic Development." In *Rural Financial Markets in Developing Countries,* ed. J. D. Von Pischke, D. W. Adams, and G. Donald. Baltimore: Johns Hopkins University Press.

McKinnon, R. I. (1973). *Money and Capital in Economic Development.* Washington, D.C.: Brookings Institution.

Rostow, Walt W. (1960). *The Process of Economic Growth.* Oxford: Clarendon Press.

Shaw, E. S. (1973). *Financial Deepening in Economic Development.* New York: Oxford University Press.

Wai, U. T., and H. T. Patrick. (1973). "Stock and Bond Issues and Capital Markets in Less Developed Countries." *IMF Staff Papers* 20: 264–272.

ρ ऽऽ¦ **Discussant:** *Asmo P. Palasvirta*

Kumar and Tsetsekos use an evolutionary approach to the analysis of capital market development in less developed countries (LDCs). The authors conduct their analysis in the context of thinking in terms of stages of market development. This is a very productive and underutilized approach to the analysis of LDC financial market development.

In their analysis, they discuss the initial states in the ultimate development of a financial sector, that is, a monetary economy in which the primary instruments created are bank instruments, which by definition are short-term instruments. They look forward toward the development of the economy from a reliance for capital needs on a banking system that by its structure is more oriented to short-term investment objectives to the creation of efficient financial markets in which the instruments are longer term. I can only agree with this analysis.

My confusion is with their conclusion. They observe that financial-structure development is a necessary condition for economic growth, which it is. But they conclude that government must provide direct intervention in order to promote development from the monetary economy into the financial economy. The confusion lies in the fact that in many instances of developmental economics of LDCs, the government is the problem and thus cannot be part of the solution until structural changes occur in the way in which these governments operate.

For example, I am unconvinced that this is a demand problem; that is, I think that there is substantial demand for investment securities in LDC economies. Fischer, Ortiz and Palasvirta (1991) made the argument that investors in LDCs would prefer to invest in their own markets, but find large disincentives to do this with respect to the level of political risk that is inherent within the local economy. Thus the political-risk characteristics of an economy lead investors to hedge by diversifying into securities that are not domestically supplied.

Consequently, domestic investors with relatively substantial wealth find ways to export capital to diversify political risk internationally into countries having relatively less political risk. Domestic investors with relatively modest wealth diversify political risk by diversifying into black-market-acquired foreign exchange. Although both of these methods of diversification of political risk have very high transactions costs, domestic investors endure such costs because no domestic instruments exist that provide the same diversification benefits.

Disincentives for development of domestic supplies of investment instruments exist not because there is underregulation, but because there is overregulation. Often overregulation is in the form of direct programs by the government to redistribute wealth within the LDC economy. Regulatory wealth-redistribution policies, in and of themselves, are not a problem, but the high probability that political forces will contrive within the medium term to drastically change any current redistributive rule is a problem. We have observed successive changes in redistributive rules occurring a number of times to favor yet another element in the economy. Under such conditions, owners of wealth, in order to insulate most of their wealth from redistributive risk, hold it in forms that are difficult for the domestic regulator to target.

Kumar and Tsetsekos observe that commercial banks exist as the main conduits of domestic capital flows. This is so not only because the regulator needs them to promote his or her redistribution schemes, but also because individuals need liquidity for their domestic market transactions. However, individuals in an economy will hold a suboptimal level of liquidity balances in the banking system. Because of the cost, generally through inflation, of holding liquidity balances in the bank, much domestic liquidity is kept in alternative forms that are not very efficient. For example, liquidity often is held in the form of inventories of goods, because goods are hedges against inflationary pressures.

Securities markets are not as pliable to government manipulation for redistributive purposes, so it is not surprising the LDC governments have not promoted them. I think that the theory of securities market development needs to address these types of issues. Kumar and Tsetsekos emphasize the ways in which government can promote this development, but do not address the fact that it is not particularly in the government's interest to do so.

Current investment instruments used by individuals in LDCs are sought for the purpose of hedging against the domestic political risk. Consequently, I do not think that the kinds of regulatory efforts suggested by Kumar and Tsetsekos will be sufficient. It is the high probability of further changes in government wealth-redistribution policies that leads to current investment behavior. The only way that the domestic economy will be able to tap the full wealth of domestic investors is for the government to create continuity in regulation. This problem is not addressed by the current chapter.

REFERENCE

Fischer, K. P., E. Ortiz, and A. P. Palasvirta. (1991). "The Industrial 'Group' and Risk Management in Imperfect Capital Markets." In D. Dimon and R. Sarathy, eds. *Management and Economic Growth Prospects in Latin America and the Caribbean.* San Diego: University of San Diego.

4

Mutual Funds in Developing Capital Markets: A Critical Evaluation of the Turkish Experience

YAMAN ASIKOGLU, SEVIL KUTAY, and I. ÖZER ERTUNA

Changes in the forms and delivery modes of financial services offered by commercial banks and other nonbank financial intermediaries have taken place at an unprecedented pace during the last several decades in developed Western financial markets. The development and growth of investment companies and mutual funds as intermediaries in this highly innovative environment took place during the postwar period, especially in the 1960s. Serving as media through which individual investors acquire a stake in bonds and stocks, investment companies have had a great influence on investor habits and the securities markets.

A growing number of developing countries are restructuring their economies to increase the operational and allocational efficiency of their capital markets. Joining this group, Turkey, as part of its far-reaching structural reforms toward liberalization and stabilization, started rapid changes in the role and workings of its capital markets and financial system. The emergence of different forms of intermediation and new financial instruments and institutions demands a well-orchestrated and carefully monitored mechanism to ensure the optimal contribution of each upsurging component to the smooth functioning of the overall system.

In this chapter we will present a critical evaluation of the Turkish experience with a developing economy undergoing some fundamental structural changes in its financial sector, emphasizing the role of newly established financial institutions, specifically the mutual funds. Our purpose in analyzing the Turkish case is twofold. First, we believe that the issues raised should provide a useful input for future efforts in the same direction by other developing economies. Second, since Turkey is still undergoing its structural adjustment program, both market participants and the regulators could benefit from our critical evaluations and warnings. We believe that mutual funds, as one of the newcomers to the system, will play a pioneering role and contribute in many ways to the development of efficient and healthy capital markets in Turkey if the regulators facilitate their functioning by taking the necessary steps in time.

The first section of this chapter will present the background information about financial markets in Turkey. The second section will discuss the current issues in the country's capital markets and the role of mutual funds toward their resolution. The critical evaluation of the Turkish experience and some policy recommendations with respect to mutual funds will be summarized in the third section for both the short and long runs. The final section will conclude the analysis with suggested future extensions in this area, some of which are already under way by the authors.

THE BACKGROUND AND STRUCTURE OF FINANCIAL MARKETS IN TURKEY

In this section we present a brief overview of the financial markets and institutions in Turkey, emphasizing the developments that have been taking place in the post-1980 period. A comprehensive analysis of these developments is beyond the scope of this chapter, and the interested reader is referred to Cosan and Ersel (1986), Ersel and Sak (1987), Ertuna (1987a, 1987b), and Inselbag and Gultekin (1988) for more detailed treatment. Our limited objective is to provide a background against which the contribution of mutual funds to the Turkish financial system can be discussed.

In 1980 Turkey launched a stabilization and liberalization program in order to bring about a solution to the dual problems of high inflation and an unsustainable external deficit. In addition to introducing short-run policy measures to deal with these problems, the new economic program also started a process of structural change with the objective of fostering greater reliance on market forces. Restructuring the financial system occupied a high priority in the new program since operational and allocational efficiencies of financial markets are key to the performance of a development strategy based on the market mechanism.

The Pre-1980 Period

The characteristics and problems of the financial structure to which mutual funds have been introduced are the legacy of the way economic development of the country was financed in the pre-1980 period. During the 1960s and most of the 1970s Turkey followed an inward-looking, strongly growth-oriented development strategy led by both public- and private-sector investments. The former were financed primarily through monetizing budget deficit and through issuing low-yield government bonds that were absorbed mainly into the portfolios of public pension funds whose asset choice is restricted (through legislation) to government securities and bank deposits. The dominant form of financing private-sector investments has been commercial bank loans. Until 1980 deposit and loan rates were controlled and kept at artificially low levels by the authorities. Resulting negative real interest rates in an inflationary environment and the close ties of corporations with the banking system caused debt financing, rather than equity financing, to be preferred by firms, with bank loans being the single most important item in corporate liability structure. On the demand side, negative real interest rates led investors to shift away from financial securities into nonfinancial assets such as real estate, gold, and durable consumer goods.

With no significant competition from other financial institutions, commercial banks dominated the financial system. This, in turn, gave rise to very high intermediation costs reflected in high spreads between deposit and credit rates, on the one hand, and across loan rates with different maturities, on the other.

Excessive use of debt financing in the form of bank loans hindered the development of primary markets in corporate securities (common stock and corporate bonds) and removed, at the same time, the need for institutions and services related to security issuing, such as underwriting activities and rating agencies. The underdeveloped nature of the primary markets had its adverse effects on the secondary markets: The tiny volume of outstanding common-stock shares did not generate sufficient trading activity for the development of stock exchanges. The fact that government bonds have been redeemable at par and that most of the corporate bonds were sold to be repurchased at predetermined prices eliminated the need for a secondary market in debt securities. The absence of active secondary markets and hence the limited liquidity of securities, in turn, reinforced the factors hindering the growth of primary markets.

Finally, the simple nature of financial decisions in this essentially "bank-deposit–bank-loan" financial economy did not warrant the establishment of institutions and services such as investment counselling, professional portfolio management, independent information-gathering organizations, and external auditing practices. Consequently, Turkey did not build up the necessary infrastructure for financial information gathering and evaluation, which proved to be critical in the 1980s when the policymakers launched a series of financial reforms that substantially increased the complexity of financial decisions.

Recent Reforms and Developments

Beginning in 1980, a series of financial reforms have been undertaken with the objective of reducing the State's involvement in the financial system, increasing the level of private savings and achieving a more efficient allocation of funds raised in the financial markets. Owing to the weight of the banking system in the financial structure of the economy, the first set of measures was directed at this sector. In order to stop financial disintermediation caused by negative real interest rates, the ceilings on deposit rates and on non-preferential credit rates were eliminated in 1980. Regulations regarding the determination of interest rates changed several times due to difficulties which emerged in the process of deregulating the banking industry. Since 1984, deposit ceilings have been set and periodically revised by the Central Bank. On the lending side, commercial banks are allowed to set non-preferential rates. Overall, the new measures have been successful in maintaining positive real interest rates and in channeling a substantial amount of funds from non-financial assets into the financial sector in the form of bank deposits.

Simultaneously with the deregulation of interest rates, an unofficial and unregulated money market has emerged. Institutions called "bankers" (essentially money brokers) collected large amounts of funds from investors offering interest rates significantly higher than the rates offered by banks. They managed to do so by the wholesale purchasing of commercial bank certificates of deposit and corporate bonds at a discount and retailing them to the public at "par" with their own repurchase guarantees. As the brokers could not easily employ these funds to earn returns greater than the promised interest payments, the majority of them failed in December 1980. The resulting financial crisis, commonly referred to as "bankers' crisis," not only strained the liquidity position of the banking system, but also had profound and lasting adverse effects on the public's confidence in financial markets. Furthermore, the crisis highlighted the role of an information generation process and of public education in orderly functioning of financial markets, underlining the urgent need for credit rating agencies, investment counselling and independent auditing practices.

The authorities reacted to the financial crisis by taking regulatory measures for both the banking system and capital markets. As to the former, the 1982 bylaw which was later replaced by the 1985 Banking Law, introduced, among other things, provisions regarding deposit insurance, the capital structure of banks, standardized accounting system, and auditing and reporting standards. The main institutional developments and regulations in the capital markets were the enactment of the Capital Market Law (CML) in 1981, establishment of the Capital Market Board (CMB) in 1982, and reorganization of the Istanbul Stock Exchange (ISE) in 1986. The CMB is the main regulatory agency responsible for regulating and supervising the primary and secondary capital markets. It has been authorized to set the necessary regulations for the issuance of securities, to give permission with respect to all public offerings of the private sector securities, to regulate all institutions in the securities markets, and to introduce new regulations regarding the capital markets.

Another important feature of the post-1980 financial system is the development, in 1986, of an official and regulated money market which consists of interbank money market transactions in domestic currency and open market operations of the Central Bank. The rapid growth of this market has indicated that, in the context of the Turkish financial system, money market instruments and institutions have a better chance of development compared to their counterparts in capital markets.

Changes in the pattern of financing the government deficit have exerted important effects on restructuring the Turkish financial system. In line with the authorities' desire to reduce inflation through monetary controls, there has been a shift away from monetizing the deficit into financing it, through issuing public sector securities. As part of this new direction, the public sector started and so far has led the process of financial innovation by introducing new securities with attractive yield and maturity structures (T-bills and Revenue Sharing Certificates) and by reissuing the known ones (government bonds) at more attractive conditions. Presently, six-month treasury bills and (short-term) one-year government bonds are the main instruments being used in financing the deficit. Revenue sharing certificates (RSC) enable the holder to participate in the revenue of public utilities and are available in Turkish lira denominated or foreign exchange indexed forms.

New types of securities have been introduced in the corporate securities market as well. In 1986, Development Banks were given the permission to issue short-term debt instruments in the form of Bank Bonds and Bank Guaranteed Bonds, and in 1987, corporations were allowed to issue commercial paper (referred to as "finance bonds").[1] Finally, special finance houses, established after 1984, started issuing Profit Loss Sharing Certificates (PLSC).

CURRENT ISSUES IN THE TURKISH FINANCIAL SYSTEM AND THE POTENTIAL CONTRIBUTION OF MUTUAL FUNDS TOWARD THEIR SOLUTION

Despite the positive effects of new developments and regulations in the post-1980 period, the financial system still faces serious obstacles that constrain its growth from both the supply and demand sides of the financial markets. In this section we briefly overview the most pressing obstacles and discuss the potential role of mutual funds in overcoming these issues.

Inflation and Financial Markets

Persistently high levels of inflation severely limit the external financing alternatives for corporations. As in the case of developed countries, equity investment in Turkey has failed to be an effective hedge against inflation, leading to negative and highly volatile real returns. On the other hand, during the 1980s time deposits and government securities consistently yielded positive real returns. Consequently, bank deposits (especially time deposits) have been the most popular investment medium where savings have been kept in the post-1980 period.[2] An inflationary environment adversely affects the use of debt financing as well since corporate bonds are subject to a minimum two-year maturity condition, which is much longer than the planning horizon of investors. The disappearance after 1980 of attractive short-term bank lending practices at negative real rates left corporations with an acute financing problem, which started manifesting itself through widespread bankruptcies in the early 1980s. Allowing corporations to issue commercial paper in 1986 was a welcome development, but the effective and optimal utilization of this financial instrument by both deficit and saving units of the economic required (and still does) the establishment of efficiently functioning money markets and institutions specializing in producing and processing information for these markets.

Lack of Competition among Financial Institutions

Despite the recent structural changes, commercial banks still retain their dominant position in the financial system. Unlike their counterparts in developed capital markets, private and public pension funds and insurance companies in Turkey remain passive, with no effective contribution toward making the environment more competitive for banks. This is due to the fact that either the operations of these nonbank institutions are constrained by legislation, or some of these institutions are controlled by banks. Public pension funds are allowed to invest only in domestic bank deposits and public-sector securities. Asset selection of private pension funds, most of which are established by banks, is not restricted by legislation, but portfolios of these institutions are composed mainly of deposits and shares of the affiliated bank's participations. The Turkish insurance industry, being premature and weak particularly in life-insurance-related services, has not played, and still is not playing, any significant role in financial markets. Government bonds, shares representing the participations of banks, and shares of holding companies that control these insurance firms make up the major part of their portfolio. Facing no significant competition in their financial operations, banks carry out the intermediation services at extremely high costs, and this, besides keeping the system from reaching a reasonable degree of operating efficiency, also aggravates the financing burden of corporations for which bank loans constitute the major form of external financing.

Excessive Financial Leverage and Narrow Equity Base of Corporations

Corporations are still highly leveraged despite the fall in leverage ratios in recent years. Moreover, the share of bank loans within the overall liability structure has increased in spite of the high real costs of borrowing.[3] This reflects the increased dependence of corporations on the banking system and, in turn, renders both banks and corporations highly vulnerable to monetary developments such as changes in inflation and interest rates. Correction of this problem calls for creation of conditions and media conducive to direct financing by going public (bonds and stock issues) instead of through bank-negotiated financing (bank loans).

Furthermore, several factors on both the demand and supply sides of the stock market have led to a very narrow equity base and relatively thin equity markets. Favorable tax treatment of debt financing and the availability of bank loans at negative real rates until 1980 removed the incentives for financing and raising funds through equity instruments on the supply side. Lack of a reliable information-generation and dissemination process and the absence of liquidity and marketability due to thin secondary stock markets are the main demand-side obstacles for the growth of equity markets. Inducing the family-owned corporations to go public and privatizing the state economic enterprises are the two commonly discussed, viable, shorter-run, alternative solutions for further development of equity markets.

The Dominant Role of the Public-Sector Issues in Securities Markets and Crowding Out of the Private Sector

Debt instruments dominate the Turkish securities market, and public-sector issues constitute the overwhelming share of both primary and secondary markets in Turkey.[4] More than the magnitude of the government's fund-raising as the primary deficit unit in financial markets, what is distressing is its intervention in the process of interest-rate determination, which, in turn, distorts the risk-return relationship in the market. Riskless government securities are tax exempt and offer higher returns than risky corporate debt instruments. Corporate securities are not tax exempt and are subject to interest-rate ceilings (a 1.3 multiple of the rate applied to time deposits). As a result, corporate securities are not given the opportunity to offer yields high enough to compensate investors for differential tax treatment and higher risk. Even if interest ceilings are removed, the financing problem of corporations cannot be fully resolved under the present system unless inflation is brought under control and the government securities offer relatively lower real after-tax returns. In order to compete with government securities, corporations will have to undertake high-risk projects that in turn will increase the overall risk level, decrease the overall quality of productive investments (i.e., suboptimal investments) in the economy, and hinder the demand for corporate debt securities. This adverse effect is unavoidable within the current structure of Turkish capital markets, which lack internal efficiency with respect to information due to imperfect and asymmetrically distributed information in the economy. Given the inability of investors to differentiate the high-profit corporations from those that mimic them, unless a separating equilibrium can be achieved so that high-risk and low-risk firms can be distinguished, the existence of the former makes the latter worse off and can lead to market failures.[5]

Absence of Financial Services and Lack of Investors' Knowledge of and Confidence in Financial Markets

The bankers' crisis revealed how much the average investor is vulnerable to being misled and deceived due to lack of knowledge and education about the workings of the financial system, as well as his or her lack of information as to the quality and functioning of the components of the system. In the absence of an adequate financial information-generation, processing, and evaluation industry, this translates into lack of confidence in risky financial securities, which naturally explains the popularity of government securities and bank deposits among individual investors. Educating the public and increasing its confidence in corporate securities, which was damaged and lost after the bankers' crisis, is key to the development of financial markets.

In light of the preceding discussion, one immediate issue facing the Turkish financial system is the removal of demand- and supply-side obstacles impeding direct financing activities of corporations. The solution to this problem requires measures effective in both the short and long runs, and our contention is that mutual funds should, and will, have important contributions in both time horizons. The critical ingredients in this solution would be the investors' understanding of the actual risk level associated with publicly issued corporate securities (commercial paper, bonds, and stocks); their ability to measure and determine whether the current rates of return reflect this appropriate risk level; their ability to compare risk-return trade-offs across different securities; and their understanding of the opportunity to diversify through mutual funds. This way the corporates (a commonly used term for corporate securities) can be perceived as alternative investment media, offering attractive yields and terms (when and if they do) commensurate with their risk level as compared to the securities issued by the government and commercial banks.

Potential Contribution of Mutual Funds in Turkey

Short-run Contributions of Mutual Funds

In the current inflationary environment and short-term investment horizon, in the immediate-term the financing of corporations should be shifted away from bank loans into money market instruments. This will help corporations to reduce cost of intermediation through commercial banks and help the private sector, in general, to change its passive role (as far as raising funds in the financial markets is concerned) into a more aggressive and competitive one. The positive role of mutual funds in this process can be outlined as follows:

1. Mutual funds will purchase money market instruments like commercial paper in large denominations and sell them to the public in small denominations in the form of participation certificates. By so doing they lower the flotation and transaction costs associated with the issuance of these securities. The ability of investors to redeem the mutual funds' participation certificates on demand (in the case of open-end funds) will provide liquidity to the money market investments and hence lower the required return of investors.

2. By combining a variety of instruments (commercial paper, government securities, etc.) issued by different participants with different risk classes into a diversified portfolio, mutual funds will be able to reduce the perceived riskiness and hence financing cost of individual money market instruments.

3. Indirect ownership of financial securities through mutual funds will benefit from a screening mechanism by professional portfolio managers. This will lower the required return of investors and help establish a separating equilibrium in which low risk firms use commercial paper held by mutual funds and high risk firms use bank loans at higher cost. This, in turn, will reduce inefficiencies due to asymmetric information about firm quality.

4. Mutual funds will provide an opportunity to corporations to compete with the public sector in the process of financial innovation. New private sector securities responding to changing market conditions can be designed and issued with higher liquidity and less risk through the direct involvement of mutual funds.

5. Competition by mutual funds is expected to lower commercial banks' intermediation costs and hence increase the operational efficiency of financial markets. This development will be particularly relevant for those firms which are dependent on bank financing as they do not meet the requirements of the CMB to issue commercial paper.

6. One of the most important contributions of mutual funds would be a fostering of public confidence in financial markets through creating a safer and more professional financial environment and through their direct contribution to public education. Development of mutual funds will positively affect the establishment of a sound financial infrastructure by increasing the demand for a variety of financial services provided by other institutions such as rating agencies, independent auditing companies and information gathering agencies.

7. Finally, mutual funds will diversify the overall risk in financial markets by separating the risk of the corporate sector from that of the banking system through weakening the strong interdependence between the two components of the financial system.

Longer-run Contributions of Mutual Funds

Two other interconnected problems of the Turkish financial system can be tackled within a longer time horizon. These are the excessive financial leverage of corporations and the narrow base of equity ownership. Contributions of mutual funds in having healthier debt-equity ratios and broader ownership of equity capital can be outlined as follows:

1. Professional management services in "packaging" the financial claims of various economic units into portfolios as well as information acquisition and processing services offered by mutual funds will lower the perceived risk associated with stock ownership.

2. Portfolio diversification by mutual funds across different equity and debt issues will lead to lower risk compared to direct stock ownership by small investors. This factor will be particularly valuable in the inflationary environment of Turkey. Liquidity and marketability of mutual fund certificates as compared to individual equity issues can be another factor promoting the demand for equity through indirect ownership.

3. Mutual funds can be effectively used in inducing family owned corporations to go public. Fiscal incentives to this end can be more easily implemented for indirect ownership through funds. Some examples to encourage investment in new equity would be: the favorable tax treatment of investment income derived from investing in equity funds; direct exclusion (from taxes) of a major portion of the fund income coming from investment in securities of the companies opening to the public for the first time; as well as additional incentives to encourage these privately held corporations to issue public securities for the first time, such as income tax exclusions.

4. By similar reasoning, mutual funds can contribute to privatization of state-owned enterprises. For example, public demand for shares of privatized institutions can be increased through fiscal incentives directed to mutual funds investing in these securities. Management problems of privatized enterprises (due to possible broad ownership across a large number of small investors holding the stocks directly) can be overcome by giving the ownership base, and therefore managerial responsibility, to mutual funds (rather than to the large number of small investors as would be the case in the absence of mutual funds).

5. Mutual funds could also have positive effects on the area of international finance. First, they can play a role in arranging market solutions to Turkey's external debt issue, such as debt-equity swaps. Second, mutual funds can help attract foreign direct investment by lowering the perceived riskiness of investing in Turkish securities, and with the professional outlook they bring along to investment and financial management in the country.

CRITICAL EVALUATION OF MUTUAL FUNDS IN TURKEY
AND SOME POLICY RECOMMENDATIONS

The objective of this section is to survey the regulatory and organizational aspects of mutual funds in Turkey and to critically review the current experience with mutual funds. We approach the problem by asking the following questions: Would the existing structure of mutual funds enable these institutions to fulfill their expected role in the development of the Turkish financial markets? What sort of modifications and/or improvements are necessary in the regulatory and organizational structure of these funds so that they can better undertake the tasks they have set forth? Again we will distinguish and discuss both short- and longer-run considerations in our analysis.

Regulatory Aspects of Mutual Funds

Regulations regarding mutual funds were set by the 1981 CML, which defined three types of nonbank financial institutions: underwriters, investment trusts, and mutual funds. Investment trusts are joint-stock companies established to manage portfolios formed with the funds obtained from shareholders in return for share certificates. Mutual funds differ from investment trusts in two important aspects: (1) only commercial banks are authorized to establish mutual funds, and (2) instead of stock certificates, a mutual fund issues participation certificates in return for the money raised from the public. No investment trust has been founded yet, and the first mutual fund was established in July 1987. The six-year lag between the legislation of the CML and the establishment of the first mutual fund was mainly because banks considered these funds to be competitors to their deposit accounts. As of August 1988 there were 17 mutual funds in operation, and 10 others have obtained permission from the CMB to be established (see table 4.1).

In order to establish a mutual fund, the founding bank prepares a "fund statute" and applies to the CMB for approval. The statute should contain information regarding the following: total value for the fund, management rules, the principles concerning the choice of securities and the dispersion of risk, principles governing the sale and repurchase of the participation certificates, the rules regarding the evaluation of the securities included in the fund's portfolio, the determination of the fund's profits and their distribution to the participants, the management and service fees to be charged by the founding bank, the duration of the fund, conditions for joining and leaving the fund, and provisions related to the liquidation of the fund. Once the permission of the CMB is obtained, the founding bank extends a cash advance to the mutual fund in the amount of the fund's total assets. The fund uses this advance to construct its portfolio. When the participation certificates are sold to the public, the fund returns the advance to the bank together with the accrued interest. Assets of the mutual fund are separated from those of the founding bank, but the fund has no separate legal identity. A bank can set up more than one mutual fund, but the size of these funds is limited by the bank's paid-up capital plus

Table 4.1
Mutual Funds in Turkey

Operating Funds	Number of Funds	Total Assets (Millions/Lira)	Date of Issue
1. Isbank	1	10,000	13.7.1987
2. Interfon 1	1	5,000	19.8.1987
3. Iktisat 1	1	5,000	16.9.1987
4. Garanti	1	5,000	22.10.1987
5. Yapi Kredi 1	1	10,000	2.11.1987
6. Esbank	1	5,000	16.11.1987
7. Interfon 2	1	5,000	14.12.1987
8. Iktisat 2	1	5,000	9.2.1988
9. Yapi Kredi 2	1	7,000	7.3.1988
10. Yapi Kredi 3	1	1,000	7.3.1988
11. Yapi Kredi 4	1	5,000	7.3.1988
12. Yapi Kredi 5	1	10,000	7.3.1988
13. Yapi Kredi 6	1	5,000	7.3.1988
14. Vakiffon	1	5,000	9.5.1988
15. Disbank	1	3,000	30.6.1988
16. Tutunbank	1	3,000	4.7.1988
17. Chemical Mitsui	1	2,000	15.7.1988
Total	17	91,000	

Funds Internal Statutes of Which Have Been Approved

	Number of Funds	Total Assets (Millions/Lira)	
1. Ziraat Bankasi	1	10,000	
2. Pamukbank	1	5,000	
3. Adabank	1	2,200	
4. Interfon	2	10,000	
5. Koc-Amerikan	1	2,000	
6. Finansbank	1	2,000	
7. T. Emlak Bankasi	1	5,000	
8. Egebank	1	5,000	
9. Iktisat 3	1	5,000	
10. Desiyab	1	5,000	
Total	11	51,200	

reserves. In striking contrast to the regulatory framework of mutual funds in the United States, in Turkey the same legal entity exercises all the essential functions of a mutual fund: Establishment, portfolio management, custody of assets, and evaluation of the value of the fund are all to be undertaken by the founding bank.

The mutual funds in Turkey can be described as semi-closed-end. Investors can redeem their participation certificates anytime, as they can from the open-end investment companies. However, the total assets of the mutual fund are fixed. Once all the participation certificates are sold, the fund cannot issue new ones but can only resell the redeemed certificates. It should be noted that the size of the fund can be decreased through redemptions, although it cannot be increased by new sales. The participation certificates are valued based on current prices of the securities in the fund's portfolio. The redemption value of one certificate is found by dividing the current value of total fund assets by the total number of certificates.

The regulatory framework imposes certain constraints on the portfolio selection of the mutual funds. For example, article 41 of the CML states that the fund cannot invest more than 25 percent of its assets in a single firm's capital, it cannot buy more than 10 percent of a single firm's total capital or voting rights, and the total number of shares issued by the founding bank's participations cannot exceed 20 percent of the fund's assets. Furthermore, the statute of each fund is required to specify minimum portfolio weight for cash and highly liquid assets and maximum weights for common stocks (subject to the limits provided in article 41 of the CML), public-sector securities, revenue-sharing certificates, and private-sector securities other than common stocks.

Portfolio Selection of Mutual Funds

Due to short experience with mutual funds (MFs), as of August 1988 the largest data set for any mutual fund consisted of 13 monthly observations. Hence our analyses and conclusions should be interpreted carefully. Table 4.2 displays the portfolio weights of alternative assets in individual mutual funds' portfolios. For expositional convenience, securities are divided into two categories: public-sector securities and private-sector securities. The former group includes government bonds, treasury bills, revenue-sharing certificates, and the foreign-currency-indexed RSCs. The latter group is composed of corporate bonds, commercial paper, common stocks, and cash and deposits. As table 4.2 reveals (for the period July 1987 through July 1988), the portfolio composition of MFs has changed considerably over their short lives with respect to private- versus public-sector holdings and across individual securities within each group. The funds investing heavily in public-sector securities include Yapi Kredi 5 (YK 5), Yapi Kredi 4 (YK 4), Vakiflar Bank (Vakiffon), Disbank, and Isbank; those investing heavily in private-sector securities include Yapi Kredi 2 (YK 2), Yapi Kredi 6 (YK 6), Iktisat 1, Iktisat 2, Interfon 2, Garanti, and Esbank (see columns 8 and 9 in table 4.3).

Within public-sector securities there has been a shift from bonds to T-bills, and within private-sector securities corporate bonds showed a substantial increase during the last two months of our sample. Among public-sector securities for almost all of the funds T-bills appear to be the preferred instrument, with the exception of Isbank and Esbank, for which government bonds dominate this category. RSCs, in general, have been in demand by only a small subset of funds. These certificates, both regular and indexed ones, appear in significant amounts only in the portfolios of Isbank (both types), Iktisat 1 (significant in indexed RSCs), Vakiffon (both), Esbank (indexed ones only), and YK 1 (regular ones only).

Table 4.2 also reveals the fact that all of these funds except YK 3 (which is primarily a common-stock fund) have a negligible amount of investment in common stocks within the private-sector category. When we compare the corporate bonds (CB) and commercial paper (CP), it is observed that the former are by far the more preferred security. Only Interfon 1, YK 1, Interfon 2, YK 3 (though the share of CP went to zero in July 1988), and Disbank exhibit a more balanced investment in CBs and CPs (although CBs still dominate CPs).

When we analyze the individual funds over time, some, such as YK 1, Esbank, YK 2, and Vakiffon, show relatively stable portfolio structure, while others, such as Interfon 1, Garanti, YK 6, and Iktisat 2, have changed their portfolio composition quite often since their first establishment. For Isbank fund, although initially the weight of government securities was around 60 to 70 percent, their proportion started to decline and fell below 50 percent after May 1988. Interfon 1 has a rather stable investment profile, with about 40 percent weight in public- and 60 percent in private-sector securities (except for the first two months of its operations, where the preference was just the opposite). Within public-sector securities, although T-bills dominate, there was a shift from bills to bonds starting in April 1988. The substantial share of both CBs and CPs also remains stable over time. Iktisat 1 invests heavily in the private sector, with the major portion being in corporate bonds. Investment in public-sector securities is confined mainly to indexed bonds and RSCs. the fund's investment strategy exhibits a great deal of stability.

While Garanti fund started out with a balanced preference for public- and private-sector securities, there has been a significant shift toward CBs. Besides this general shift, there has been substantial volatility in the weights of government and corporate bonds.

YK 1 and Esbank have rather stable portfolio compositions, with about 30 percent in the public sector and 70 percent in the private sector for the former and 40 percent in the public sector and 60 percent in the private sector for the latter. Similarly, the portfolio activities of Iktisat 2 (with more than 80 percent invested in the private sector, specifically in corporate bonds), YK 2 (with more than 95 percent in private-sector bonds and only T-bills in the public sector), and YK 5 (with over 95 percent in T-bills and below 5 percent in CBs) also exhibit quite a stable trend.

Interfon 2 exhibits a moderately stable investment policy with a recent shift toward T-bills. Although YK 3 exhibits quite a stable breakdown between the public (slightly over 60 percent) and private (below 40 percent) sectors, within each category there has been a substantial shift in holdings, from T-bills to indexed bonds in the public group and from CBs to common stocks in the private group. It must be emphasized that YK 3 is the fund with the largest common-stock holdings.

Table 4.2
Portfolio Composition of Mutual Funds

	Public-Sector Securities						Private-Sector Securities				
	Gov't Bond	T-Bill	RSC	F.C. Ind. Bond	F.C. Ind. RSC	Total	Corp. Bond	Comm. Paper	Common Stock	Cash/ Deposit	Total
Is Bankasi											
Sample Mean	35.41	6.93	10.53	0.00	8.45	61.33	33.34	0.39	1.17	1.78	38.67
Sta. Dev.	13.34	6.38	1.37	0.00	2.03	7.19	7.09	0.54	3.22	1.61	7.19
Interfon 1											
Sample Mean	3.35	38.15	0.00	2.12	0.00	43.62	37.14	19.03	0.17	0.03	56.38
Sta. Dev.	5.32	6.71	0.00	5.04	0.00	8.11	6.85	3.88	0.16	0.03	8.11
Iktisat 1											
Sample Mean	0.71	0.91	0.88	7.99	14.95	25.44	70.46	0.00	3.03	1.07	74.56
Sta. Dev.	0.95	1.34	1.24	2.70	5.84	5.87	10.50	0.00	7.53	0.85	5.87
Garanti											
Sample Mean	0.00	13.11	0.00	18.26	0.10	31.47	67.07	0.00	0.87	0.59	68.54
Sta. Dev.	0.00	11.50	0.00	1.33	0.29	10.42	11.09	0.00	1.27	0.53	10.42
Yapi Kredi 1											
Sample Mean	0.00	10.52	13.89	5.44	0.00	29.85	57.84	10.82	1.12	0.37	70.15
Sta. Dev.	0.00	0.89	1.24	0.11	0.00	0.35	1.84	0.84	1.59	0.36	0.35
Esbank											
Sample Mean	11.23	6.87	0.00	2.36	16.19	36.65	61.40	1.63	0.01	0.30	63.35
Sta. Dev.	6.70	6.50	0.00	3.34	4.37	2.39	2.56	0.58	0.03	0.38	2.39
Interfon 2											
Sample Mean	0.99	23.23	0.00	0.00	0.00	24.10	53.24	16.08	0.00	0.40	70.64
Sta. Dev.	1.66	9.18	0.00	0.00	0.00	9.40	6.53	6.82	0.00	0.46	7.91

Iktisat 2											
Sample Mean	0.00	5.43	2.67	4.93	3.98	17.00	79.72	0.00	0.33	1.70	81.06
Sta. Dev.	0.00	3.15	2.02	2.43	2.59	3.57	3.50	0.00	0.37	1.12	4.06
Yapi Kredi 2											
Sample Mean	0.00	4.26	0.00	0.00	0.00	4.26	95.73	0.01	0.00	0.00	95.74
Sta. Dev.	0.00	0.67	0.00	0.00	0.00	0.67	0.67	0.02	0.00	0.00	0.67
Yapi Kredi 3											
Sample Mean	0.00	50.61	0.00	11.18	0.00	61.79	10.81	4.43	22.90	0.07	38.21
Sta. Dev.	0.00	19.37	0.00	22.36	0.00	3.54	4.14	2.86	3.37	0.05	3.54
Yapi Kredi 4											
Sample Mean	0.00	68.05	0.00	18.31	0.00	86.37	13.63	0.00	0.00	0.00	13.63
Sta. Dev.	0.00	8.83	0.00	6.38	0.00	6.23	6.25	0.00	0.00	0.00	6.25
Yapi Kredi 5											
Sample Mean	0.00	96.44	0.00	0.00	0.00	96.44	3.54	0.00	0.00	0.02	3.56
Sta. Dev.	0.00	1.12	0.00	0.00	0.00	1.12	1.13	0.00	0.00	0.01	1.12
Yapi Kredi 6											
Sample Mean	0.00	15.55	3.10	5.30	0.03	23.98	74.77	1.24	0.00	0.01	76.02
Sta. Dev.	0.00	6.08	0.22	0.06	0.06	6.11	6.79	0.74	0.00	0.01	6.11
Vakiffon											
Sample Mean	10.37	22.88	24.03	0.00	22.65	79.94	18.32	0.00	1.60	0.14	20.06
Sta. Dev.	2.03	5.83	0.96	0.00	5.30	0.47	0.66	0.00	0.20	0.08	0.47
Disbank											
Sample Mean	0.00	65.81	0.00	0.00	0.00	65.81	23.67	10.53	0.00	0.00	34.20
Sta. Dev.	0.00	2.70	0.00	0.00	0.00	2.70	2.37	0.33	0.00	0.00	2.70

Table 4.3
Performance Ranking of Mutual Funds

	Wkly Rate of Return (%)		Performance Index			Mean		Share of Pub. Sec.	
	Sample Mean	Standard Deviation	P.I.	Rank	Rank (MF Only)	Rank	Rank (MF Only)	Share (%)	Rank
Isbank	0.942	0.441	0.594	11	10	6	4	61.33	6
Intfon 1	0.878	0.253	0.783	9	8	14	11	43.62	7
Iktisat 1	0.904	0.444	0.504	13	12	11	8	25.44	11
Garanti	0.931	0.369	0.680	10	9	7	5	31.47	9
YK 1	0.917	0.218	1.084	2	1	9	6	29.85	10
Esbank	1.070	0.452	0.862	5	4	2	1	36.63	8
Interfon 2	0.981	0.366	0.822	8	7	4	2	24.10	12
Iktisat 2	0.896	0.257	0.836	6	5	12	9	17.00	14
YK 2	0.906	0.209	1.082	3	2	10	7	4.26	15
YK 3	0.102	1.253	-0.462	21	15	23	15	61.79	5
YK 4	0.786	0.324	0.326	14	13	18	13	86.37	2
YK 5	0.843	0.300	0.542	12	11	15	12	96.44	1
YK 6	0.884	0.218	0.931	4	3	13	10	23.98	13
Vakiffon	0.953	0.328	0.830	7	6	5	3	79.94	3
Kisbank	0.688	0.479	0.015	19	14	19	14	65.81	4
ISEI Index	1.893	11.898	0.102	15		1			
Time Dep. (1 MO.)	0.530	0.080	-1.873	23		22			

Time Dep. (3 MO.)	0.622	0.064	-0.912	22	21
Time Dep. (6 MO.)	0.680	0.086	0.000	20	20
Time Dep. (1 YEAR)	0.835	0.108	1.428	1	16
DM/TL	0.999	5.984	0.053	17	3
$/TL	0.811	2.762	0.047	18	17
Gold	0.921	2.854	0.064	16	8

Consequently, parallel to changes in the Istanbul Stock Exchange, the management of YK 3 appears to actively manage its portfolio.

YK 4 has exhibited a steady increase in private-sector holdings, with all invested in CBs. Within the public sector, there has been a shift between T-bills and indexed bonds in several instances. In the YK 6 fund there has been a steady shift from T-bills into private-sector corporate bonds, with more than 70 percent of the portfolio invested in CBs. Vakiffon generally maintains approximately 20 percent in private-sector and 80 percent in public-sector securities, experiencing substitution from indexed RSCs to T-bills within the public-sector category. Since Disbank has only two observations, Chemical Mitsui has only one, and Tutunbank has none, it is hard to make meaningful comparisons for these funds.

Based on these observations, the mutual funds can be broadly classified into three groups according to the degree of stability in their investment policy in the long run. Interfon 1, Iktisat 1, YK 1, Esbank, Iktisat 2, YK 2, YK 5, and Vakiffon have exhibited relatively more stable investment strategies, whereas Interfon 2, YK 4, and YK 6 have been moderately stable, and Isbank, Garanti, and YK 3 have followed more volatile portfolio management.

Regression Results for Mutual-Fund Returns and Performance

As discussed in the preceding section, the MFs have followed considerably different policies regarding the composition of their portfolios. We attempted to inquire whether or not there is a statistical relationship between the asset choice of MFs and their realized returns. The analysis was carried out in two stages. First, a set of cross-sectional regressions was run using the sample means returns of 15 mutual funds and the sample means of several alternative indicators of their portfolio compositions. No significant relation was found between mean returns and (1) the proportion of assets invested in public versus private securities, (2) the share of government bonds, (3) the share of T-bills, and (4) the share of commercial paper.

A positive and relatively more significant relationship was found between mean returns and the average weight given to corporate bonds. Although the limited size of our sample (15 funds) makes it difficult to reach stronger conclusions, it can be argued that investment in corporate bonds has favorably influenced the returns of mutual funds.

At the second stage of our analysis we used pooled time-series and cross-sectional regressions to investigate the relationship between MF portfolio composition and the rate of return on these funds. For this purpose a monthly data set was used. First, we regressed monthly returns against a constant and a set of six portfolio shares: government bonds, T-bills, corporate bonds, commercial paper, common stocks, and RSCs. This revealed that only common stocks and T-bills significantly influenced the returns, both in negative direction. Second, we regressed returns against different portfolio shares taken one at a time. Significant negative relationships were found between returns and T-bills and common stocks. Corporate bonds positively and significantly influenced the MFs' returns. No significant relationship was found between returns and other investments. These results give support to the argument of Sak and Süngü (1988) and Soydemir and Akyuz (1988) that the underdeveloped nature of the CB market had strong implications for the performance of MFs. As indicated in these studies, commercial banks price the CBs that they underwrite and transfer them to the MFs that they manage. Consequently, "The fund managers tend to adjust their rates of return through bond operations instead of managing their securities portfolio."[6] The negative influence of stock investment on mutual-fund returns is indicative of the difficulties in managing stock portfolios in a thin market that has exhibited substantial price volatility since July 1987. Taken together, these two results explain the significant increase in the share of CBs and the decline in that of common stocks in the mutual-fund portfolios.

Performance Evaluation

In this section we attempt to evaluate the performance of mutual funds using the sample means and standard deviations of their weekly rates of return together with the means and standard deviations of the rates of return on several alternative investments: the Istanbul Stock Exchange Index (ISEI), time deposits with different maturities, deutsche marks, U.S. dollars, and gold. We first ranked the MFs and other investments (relative to six-month time deposits) according to a measure similar to Sharpe's reward-to-variability (performance-index) ratio. Our ratio measures the excess mean return over the six-month deposit rate per unit of standard deviation.

Columns 4 and 5 of table 4.3 rank MFs and other investments together, and MFs only, respectively. Concentrating only on MFs, we observe that YK 1, YK 2, and YK 6 are the top three in the ranking, whereas YK 3, Disbank, and YK 4 are the last three in the ranking. We also rank the mutual funds according to their mean returns and compare this ranking with the previous one in order to draw inferences about the success of MFs in generating extra returns by taking additional risk. The comparison reveals that although Isbank and Interfon 2 have a high ranking according to the mean return, their ranking deteriorates according to the risk-adjusted (standardized) method of ranking. Conversely, although YK 1 and YK 2 have lower ranking according to the mean return, they attain a higher ranking according to our performance index.

Performance of MFs can also be compared with that of other investment alternatives. According to the performance index, with the exceptions of YK 3 and Disbank, MFs have yielded superior results than investing in deutsche marks, U.S. dollars, and gold. It should be noted that although deutsche marks and gold have relatively high ranking according to mean return, their ranking deteriorates significantly when their risk is also taken into account.

The risk-return relationship for the MFs is plotted in figures 4.1 and 4.2.[7] It is observed that the existing MFs provide a wide range of opportunities for investors in terms of return and risk. Therefore, it is possible to combine different MFs into

Figure 4.1
Risk versus Return for Mutual Funds, Including YK 3

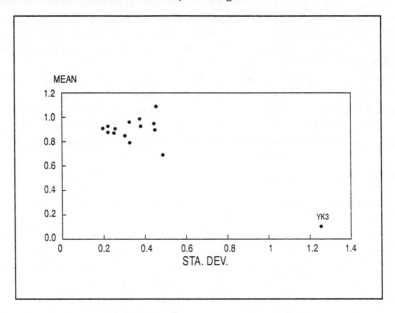

Figure 4.2
Risk versus Return for Mutual Funds, Excluding YK 3

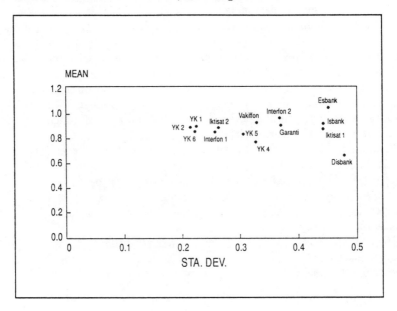

a portfolio to obtain desired levels of risk and return. Second, some of the funds dominate the others according to the mean-variance efficiency criterion. For example, YK 1 is superior to YK 6 and Interfon 2 to Garanti, as they yield higher returns at the same or lower level of risk. By combining the MFs in different proportions, an efficient set can be generated that would exclude some of the funds, including YK 6, Interfon 1, YK 5, and Disbank. Finally, we should emphasize that the risk-return frontier is not as smoothly curved in the mean–standard-deviation space as it is traditionally represented to be. This has the important implication that the optimal portfolio would be invariant to the risk-free rate for a wide range of changes in the riskless rate. The importance of this testable proposition derives from the difficulties involved in choosing the appropriate riskless asset in a less developed capital market. Hence constructing the optimal portfolio independently of the riskless asset eliminates an important analytical issue from the problem of portfolio selection.

Mutual Funds before and after the February 4, 1988, Measures

On February 4, 1988, the Central Bank of Turkey took a series of measures, including increasing liquidity and reserve requirements, that led to a general rise in interest rates in both primary and secondary markets. It is argued that after February banks transferred to the MFs some of the unsold corporate bonds and commercial papers that they had underwritten originally with less attractive rates. It is also observed from the evolution of the portfolio composition of MFs that there has been a more active management since February 1988.

In this section we examine whether the performance of MFs changed after the February 4 measures. For this purpose we repeat our performance rankings in two subsamples corresponding to pre- and post-February form. As table 4.4 displays, the average weekly returns of all MFs but Esbank rose after February. Furthermore, the mean weekly return of the seven MFs that existed before this date increased from 0.915 to 0.972 percent, while their standard deviation decreased from 0.331 to 0.321. However, the average return of all MFs, including the ones that were established after February, decreased to 0.857 percent and their standard deviation increased to 0.374. These results indicate that the MFs that had a longer history could maintain or improve their performance after February, whereas performance of the MFs as a group deteriorated due to the less favorable performance of the newly established ones. Despite this, MFs, with the exception of YK 3, have continued to outperform investment in deutsche marks, U.S. dollars, and gold. Rankings of all fifteen MFs after February and for the entire sample period exhibit considerable stability. YK 1, YK 2, and YK 6 advanced in ranking ahead of others, while there was no significant change in the relative ranking of the remaining funds.

The risk-return frontier of mutual funds in the two subsamples are displayed in figures 4.3, 4.4, and 4.5. For the seven funds that existed before February, the frontier shifted up, maintaining its positive slope, and differences across funds got smaller (see figures 4.3 and 4.4). However, the frontier for all MFs exhibited greater divergences across funds and tended to slope downward (see figure 4.5).

Table 4.4
Pre- and Post-February 1988 Performance Ranking of Mutual Funds

	(–Feb.) Wkly Rate of Return (%)		(Feb. +) Wkly Rate of Return (%)		PERFORMANCE INDEX (–FEB.)			PERFORMANCE INDEX (FEB. +)				
	Sample Mean	Standard Deviation	Sample Mean	Standard Deviation	P.I.	Rank (7 MF)	Rank (7 MF & Others)	P.I.	Rank (7 MF)	Rank (7 MF & Others)	Rank (MF Only)	Rank
Isbank	0.872	0.318	1.001	0.515	0.791	6	6	0.373	6	6	8	8
Intfon 1	0.787	0.085	0.951	0.312	1.950	1	1	0.459	5	5	6	6
Iktisat 1	0.819	0.627	0.976	0.144	0.315	7	8	1.165	1	1	1	1
Garanti	0.875	0.234	0.965	0.427	1.064	4	4	0.367	7	7	9	9
YK 1	0.916	0.249	0.918	0.201	1.184	3	3	0.544	4	4	4	4
Esbank	1.319	0.659	0.960	0.252	1.058	5	5	0.602	2	2	2	2
Intfon 2	0.818	0.147	1.034	0.398	1.338	2	2	0.565	3	3	3	3
Iktisat 2			0.896	0.257				0.339			11	11
YK 2			0.906	0.209				0.469			5	5
YK 3			0.102	1.253				-0.564			15	19
YK 4			0.786	0.324				-0.069			13	13
YK 5			0.843	0.300				0.115			12	12
YK 6			0.884	0.218				0.345			10	10
Vakiffon			0.953	0.328				0.440			7	7
Disbank			0.688	0.479				-0.252			14	15
ISEI Index	-0.973	10.924	-1.618	6.228	-0.146		11	-0.390		10		17
DM/TL	1.929	4.127	0.050	1.660	0.317		7	-0.457		11		18
$/TL	1.685	4.747	0.373	1.411	0.224		9	-0.309		9		16
Gold	1.463	4.113	0.359	2.352	0.205		10	-0.191		8		14

90

Figure 4.3
Risk versus Return for Mutual Funds (Pre-February 1988 Sample Period, Seven Existing Funds)

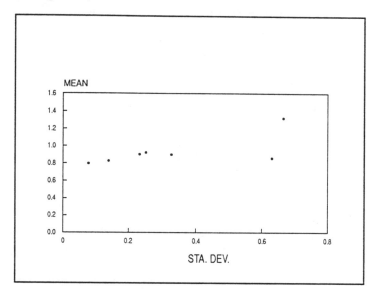

Figure 4.4
Risk versus Return for Mutual Funds (Post-February 1988 Sample Period, Seven Funds That Existed before February 1988)

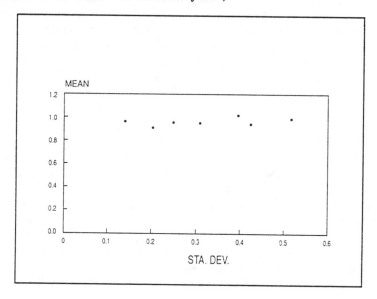

Figure 4.5
**Risk versus Return for Mutual Funds (Post-February 1988 Sample Period,
All Fifteen Existing Funds)**

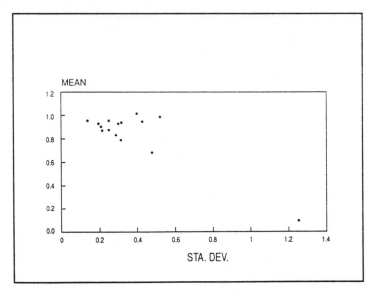

Critical Evaluation

On the basis of the regulatory framework outlined earlier and the preliminary data on the performance of mutual funds, we reach several conclusions regarding the functions of mutual funds in Turkish financial markets. First, the fact that only banks are authorized to establish mutual funds is not consistent with the expectation that mutual funds can introduce competition among financial institutions. The monopoly of banks in this respect can be justified on the grounds that for the time being, banks are the most developed and trustworthy financial institutions in Turkey. Agreeing with this position only in the short run, we suggest that other institutions like insurance companies and brokerage houses should also be given authority to establish mutual funds.

Second, given the present circumstances and the existing mutual-fund–bank interconnection, special care must be given to certain issues. Most important, the management, custody, and evaluation functions should be separated and performed by different institutions. The CML includes provisions directed toward preventing potential "moral-hazard" issues arising from the banks' involvement with mutual funds. In particular, portfolio choice of funds is restricted, and it is stated that funds' assets cannot be mortgaged or used as collateral by banks. However, as highlighted by Süngü (1987), there is still considerable scope for banks to use the funds' assets to their own advantage. We recommend that efforts should be directed toward introducing competition between financial institutions in establishing mutual funds, rather than concentrating on strengthening the regulatory framework under the present monopoly of banks.

Third, the choice between closed-end funds and open-end funds involves a trade-off in the case of Turkey. Mutual funds in Turkey are required to repurchase their participation certificates. Since evaluation of funds' assets and pricing of the certificates are done by banks, rather than by independent agencies, it might be argued that closed-end funds would be more appropriate, with the additional advantage of increasing the trading activity in the secondary markets.[8] However, the thinness of secondary markets and hence excessive volatility of prices and the opportunity for speculative behavior in these markets should also be considered in reaching a balanced conclusion. Given the existing semi-closed-end nature of the mutual funds, the recommended action is the separation of the evaluation function from banks.

Fourth, the equity of a commercial bank puts an upper limit to the size of the mutual funds that it can establish. This provision can be defended on the grounds of protecting investors. However, it limits the growth of the mutual-fund industry and gives an advantageous position to the large banks. We believe that more effective protection of investors would lie in making the establishment and management of mutual funds more competitive.

Fifth, portfolio characteristics of mutual funds indicate that even the existing small number of funds provides a large variety of investment alternatives and diversification opportunities to individual investors. As expected, money market instruments dominate the portfolios of mutual funds. Greater weight given to the private-sector securities in most of these funds supports the expectation that mutual funds would positively contribute to financing of corporations. However, for the time being, commercial paper does not command a significant share. Incentive measures should be considered to encourage mutual funds' investment in high-grade commercial paper.

Sixth, in line with our earlier discussion, common stocks represent negligible shares of the investments of mutual funds. Longer-run contributions of mutual funds should not be disregarded, and efforts must be spent on encouraging greater participation of mutual funds in equity markets. Fiscal incentives to this effect should be considered simultaneously with efforts to privatize public enterprises, to encourage private corporations to go public, and to increase the trading activity in the secondary equity markets. We also recommend the provision of scope for specialization among mutual funds such as money market funds equity funds, public-sector funds, and different industry funds such as utility-industry funds, mining-industry funds (in case public enterprises are privatized), and so on. Recognizing the difficulties facing the development of equity funds in an inflationary environment, we suggest that fiscal incentives be provided for these funds at the early stages of their development.

Finally, although it is hard to quantitatively evaluate the contribution of mutual funds in increasing the public's education and confidence in financial markets, we believe that so far the experience has been positive. Mutual funds provide an invaluable opportunity to reinstate public confidence. In this respect we strongly agree that this opportunity should be used very carefully. Potential problem areas in the regulatory framework as highlighted in this chapter should be corrected at once, and business practices risking the safety of financial markets should not be tolerated.

CONCLUSION

In this chapter we have attempted a critical evaluation of the Turkish experience with mutual funds. Due to the short history of these institutions in Turkey, we primarily focused on raising several issues and pointing out the potential problem areas. Although several statistical tests were carried out to substantiate the discussions, we were limited by the insufficient amount of data gathered to date.

Our investigation of Turkish mutual funds will continue as we enlarge our data base on their performance. Among the issues we will look at in the future will be whether the increased level of activities on the part of mutual funds affects (and decreases) the spread between the deposit and lending rates of banks and the spread across different maturities; what the determinants are of mutual funds' portfolio choices in Turkey; how the regulations and policy changes affect their performance; and whether the overall level of activity in the financial markets changed after the emergence of mutual funds. Furthermore, we are in the process of measuring the performance of existing mutual funds using more refined and reliable evaluation techniques. Besides analyzing the mutual funds, another interesting line of study for Turkish capital markets would be a separate investigation of other financial institutions such as savings and loan associations, credit unions, life insurance companies, and rating agencies for their feasibility and desirability within the Turkish financial system and for their contribution to the efficiency of these markets along with the investment funds.

NOTES

We would like to express our thanks to Dr. Hasan Ersel, Mr. Enver Capci, Mr. Güven Sak, and Ms. Sevtap Süngü for extended discussions and for the data they provided. S. Kutay acknowledges a research and travel grant from the School of Business Associates Program and the Office of Research Services at Queen's University. Y. Asikoglu acknowledges support from the Schwaeger Fund of the City College of New York. All three authors would like to express their appreciation to Osman Sari for his invaluable research assistance. Material from this chapter was also presented in a paper at the European Finance Association Conference in Istanbul, Turkey, September 1–3, 1988.

1. Bank bonds are issued by development and investment banks and are considered to be promissory notes arranged by the banks while carrying the title of the debtor. Bank-guaranteed bonds, on the other hand, are issued to the public by corporations under the banks' guarantee and require the companies to maintain certain credit arrangements with the bank, plus the permission of the Capital Market Board.

2. See Cosan and Ersel (1986) for a detailed analysis of household portfolio composition of financial asset holdings in Turkey.

3. See Ersel and Sak (1986) for the financial structure of corporations in Turkey.

4. In 1985 total debt instruments accounted for 92.7 percent of the new issues and 70 percent of already-outstanding securities. Public-sector securities amounted to 91.1 percent of new issues and 65.61 percent of outstanding securities.

5. See Rothschild and Stiglitz (1976) for a discussion of pooling and the separating equilibrium.

6. Sak and Süngü (1988), p. 20.

7. Figure 4.2 excludes the YK 3 fund, which appears to be an outlier in figure 4.1.

8. See Ertuna (1987a) and Tinic (1986) on this issue.

REFERENCES

Cosan, F. M., and H. Ersel. (1986). "Turkish Financial System: Its Evolution and Performance—1980–1986." In *Inflation and Capital Markets*, 26–65. Proceedings of the OECD-CMB Conference held in Abant-Bolu, Turkey, August.

Dougall, H. E., and J. E. Gaumnitz. (1975). *Capital Markets and Institutions*. Englewood Cliffs, N.J.: Prentice-Hall.

Ersel, H., and G. Sak. (1986). "The Financial Structure of the Corporation Subject to CMB Supervision." In *Inflation and Capital Markets*, 89–139. Proceedings of the OECD-CMB Conference held in Abant-Bolu, Turkey, August.

———. (1987). "Public Borrowing and the Development of Financial Markets in Turkey." Paper presented at the OECD-CMB Conference on the Interrelations between Money and Capital Markets, Bursa, Turkey, August.

Ertuna, I. Ö. (1987a). "Recent Developments and Regulations in Turkish Capital Markets." Bogazici University, Istanbul. Mimeo.

———. (1987b). *Turkiye'de Mali Piyasalar: Sorunlar ve Cozumler*. Istanbul Chamber of Commerce, Publication no. 1987-6.

Inselbag, I., and N. B. Gultekin. (1988). "Financial Markets in Turkey." In *Liberalization and the Turkish Economy*, ed. T. Nas and M. Odekon. Westport, Conn.: Greenwood Press.

Rothschild, M., and J. E. Stiglitz. (1976). "Equilibrium in Competitive Insurance Markets: An Essay on the Economics of Imperfect Information." *Quarterly Journal of Economics* 91 (November): 629–650.

Sak, G., and S. Süngü. (1988). "Turkish Experience in Mutual Funds." Paper presented at the OECD-CMB Conference, Ankara, Turkey, June.

Sharpe, W. F. (1985). *Investments*. 3rd ed. Englewood Cliffs, N.J.: Prentice-Hall.

Soydemir, S., and A. Akyuz. (1988). "Issues Related to the Management and Performance of Mutual Funds in Turkey." Paper presented at the OECD-CMB Conference, Ankara, Turkey, June.

Süngü, S. (1987). "Genel Olarak Yatirim Fonlari ve Turkiye'deki Uygulama." Research Department, Publication no.. AGD/8716, Capital Market Board, Ankara, Turkey, December.

Tinic, S. M. (1986). "An Introduction to Investment Companies and Some Observations on the Feasibility of Organizing Mutual Funds in Turkey." Unpublished paper, University of Texas, Austin, May.

Discussant: Demir Yener

Of late, investor interest in country-based funds has proliferated. These funds are preferred mainly by the small investors. The growing popularity of the global investment funds is likely to continue as the emerging securities markets integrate further with the larger, more liquid, established markets. In this regard, a window of opportunity exists for holders of country mutual funds as equity participants in the rapidly expanding economies of the emerging countries. Turkey has success-fully positioned itself during the past decade as a fast-growing economy with a vibrant stock market. This chapter is a critical evaluation of past developments leading to the current phase in the development of Turkish capital markets and addresses capital-formation issues through mutual funds as an alternate way to raise equity capital.

The emergence of new financial intermediaries alongside the established com-mercial banking system is vital to the development of a healthy equity market in Turkey. In order for well-functioning, efficient capital markets to exist, there is a need for a more liberal and unrestricted financial information system in which all securities, including the mutual funds, can develop.

The existence of efficient capital markets requires a standardized financial reporting system as well as the free flow of information about corporations. After many years of debate, a public accounting system similar to the one in the United States was developed in Turkey. Since 1985 investors have been able to obtain financial information freely and at a reasonable cost.

Efforts to ensure the development of capital markets in Turkey began with the introduction of an ambitious program of economic development using five-year economic plans during the 1960s. Planned economic development continued throughout the 1970s. Generous tax, financial, and other types of incentives to industries providing import substitution or export orientation fueled the rapid growth of manufacturing firms.

During the planned economic expansion period, a popular trend in the manu-facturing sector was to group the operating firms around a system of holding companies in order to maintain control and yet be able to finance and sustain growth using the low cost of capital through a combination of bank loans and bond debt with a relatively small amount of equity funds. The holding-company mechanism allowed access to preferential debt financing from commercial banks at conve-niently low interest rates regulated by the government. Another advantage of this system was that it allowed the holding company to use the equity collateral created by revaluing the shares of an operating company to obtain new financing from the capital markets for itself while it maintained full control of the subsidiaries which were still considered to be publicly owned.

Many of the holding companies set up during the periods of artificially low cost of capital during the 1970s ran into financial difficulties because of the lack of a real equity base when the government lifted the interest-rate subsidies in the early 1980s. This also led to the disastrous collapse of many "banker" firms that were basically speculators trading in debt securities of these institutions. As a natural consequence of this crisis, there was a total loss of investor confidence in the markets.

Financial reforms that have been accomplished since 1985 ensure reduction of government intervention and aim to improve the functioning of the capital markets. As a result of the new improvements, and following the "bankers" experience, financial markets in Turkey operate with much more scrutiny and caution than before under the watchful eye of the Capital Market Board and the newly reorganized Istanbul Stock Exchange.

Under the new regime, a new money market has been developed in addition to the introduction of new financial products and instruments for the securities exchange. One of these financial instruments is the mutual fund, which offers a diversified investment opportunity in corporate securities to the interested, but shy individual investor who is seeking low risk securities prices. The diversified mutual fund comes at a time when external financing through the capital markets has long been limited due to the persistently high inflation levels. Mutual funds enable the issuing commercial banking institution to raise equity funds for the underlying firm with less reliance on its demand deposits. In Turkey, banking institutions constitute the largest outside source of capital other than the stock market for many corporations.

Commercial banking is the most established type of financial institution in Turkey. As it did in the past, bank financing at the present time dominates over securities market financing. As the firms grow in relative size, their need for funds will eventually exceed the lending capacity of many of the banking institutions and force them to find other, more innovative ways of financing their growth. This will help reduce the heavy reliance of corporations on bank financing and increase efficient allocation of funds and public confidence in publicly traded securities.

The chapter stresses the importance of mutual funds in the development of capital markets in Turkey. It asserts that the use of mutual funds will facilitate financing for corporations, increase the public confidence in investing in the securities markets, and increase competition among institutions to offer more financial alternatives. While I agree with most of the general issues, I see a need for improvement in the following areas: First, there is a need for free dissemination of financial information. If mutual funds are to reduce investor reluctance to invest in equities due to the perception that they are too speculative, much has to be done in order to increase the flow of information about the publicly owned companies to the public. This flow at this time is still difficult to attain due to the still-evolving nature of certified public accounting practices.

Second, thin trading volume is a problem. Currently, the liquidity of the Turkish capital market is low because of inadequate trading volume and the length of time required for order clearance, which sometimes reaches a couple of days, contributing to the limited liquidity of the market. Additionally, the number of existing stocks available in the market for investment does not yet reach one hundred. Market efficiency will only be possible if volume is increased and the market is kept liquid with a large variety of stocks available for trading.

Third, there is a need for a governing body that insures against loss of investors' funds. This kind of organization is necessary to prevent the disastrous experience of the early 1980 from repeating itself. The existence of a regulatory body such as the Capital Market Board is an improvement over the past, but an insurance institution would be needed to cover for small investors' investments.

Fourth, if only the commercial banks are allowed to issue the mutual funds, how could the corporations have a better bargaining position against the banking sector for their financing needs? Through their participations in these firms, the banks would already have total financial control, limiting the ownership base to a few investors. I would like to see this issue addressed.

In discussing some of the new developments in the Turkish financial markets, the authors indicate the popularity of short-term government instruments as well as the public-utility and public-economic-enterprise share offerings. This condition is typical in countries where uncertainties of the market lead to reduced time horizons or the desire to invest only in the perceived high-quality investments. This is also true for the Turkish markets, where investors will be safer by staying liquid in the money markets.

One of the major obstacles hindering the healthier development of the financial markets lies in the inflationary nature of the Turkish economy. The prevailing persistently high inflation rates limit investors' time horizons and necessitate a shorter or intermediate investment time horizon, thereby increasing interest for CDs, commercial paper and treasury bills, notes, and bonds, which offer more attractive yields.

The emphasis on debt financing in corporate capital structure continues to be an issue in Turkey. This high degree of leverage may generate disturbing results for equity investors in the event of a slowdown in the global economic trends. Despite the attractiveness mutual funds may offer in the form of diversification, under the given economic and investment climate in Turkey, investors may view this instrument as being as speculative as the straight equity investments.

For the long term, mutual funds will provide a good investment opportunity for Turkish or international investors seeking diversification. For this to become possible, capital markets must become more liquid and the proportion of equity investment relative to bonds must increase; the funds must be allocated internationally into a diversified portfolio of securities; and there must be a reduction of the national debt through debt swaps in the international markets. This requires convertibility of the local currency, the Turkish lira, and opening of the stock markets to foreign investors by allowing them free access, as well as repatriation of dividends, interest income, and capital gains to the investors' country of origin. At this juncture, this sort of change is beginning to take place in the capital markets in Turkey as a result of the government policies.

Part II

Risk and Return
in Securities Markets

5   Taiwan

The Chinese New Year, Common-Stock Purchasing, and Cumulative Raw Returns: Is Taiwan's Stock Market Informationally Efficient?

CHENG FEW LEE, GILI YEN,
and CHINGFU CHANG

RESEARCH OBJECTIVES

Following Fama, Fisher, Jensen, and Roll's (1969) pioneering study, researchers have widely used event studies to examine market efficiency. Studies in the early 1970s pointed to the confirmation of market efficiency (Fama 1976). However, a few years later, more and more evidence against market efficiency was reported (Jensen 1978). It is no surprise that a rapidly growing literature has addressed this unresolved issue.

In view of the fact that a unanimous opinion on market efficiency has yet to be formed, this chapter first proposes an improved testing methodology and then provides some empirical evidence bearing on this unresolved issue. Specifically, this study proposes market suspension around the Chinese Lunar New Year as an event to be used to study market efficiency. Since both financial and real transactions come to a halt during this period, most will agree that the festival constitutes a purely nominal event. Hence the quagmire of judging whether a chosen event is "truly" or "seemingly" nominal can be avoided. When annual data for the Taiwan stock market from the period 1975 to 1984 are analyzed, it is found that in most years shrewd investors could beat the market by purchasing common shares in advent of the New Year and selling them off some time after the stock market reopened.

This chapter is divided into five sections. In addition to this introductory section that describes the research and objectives of the present study, the remaining portion of the chapter is organized as follows. The second section describes the proposed refined methodology. The third section conducts empirical analysis. Discussion and interpretation of the empirical findings are presented in the fourth section. The fifth section concludes the chapter.

A REFINED METHODOLOGY

A fundamental problem with previous event studies is that they have used events that might not be entirely nominal, such as stock dividends/splits or dividends/ earnings announcements. When there are no associated price movements, one can argue that this is the expected result since an efficient capital market should be unresponsive to a nominal event containing no information. However, if price movements do occur, then one can still legitimately claim that the efficient capital market hypothesis cannot be rejected since the events chosen were "seemingly" nominal rather than "truly" nominal. In other words, what appears at first to be nominal might actually exert real effects. In this way the efficient capital market theory can never be rejected.

To turn the hypothesis of (semistrong) information efficiency into a refutable one, we propose to examine stock-price movements around the Chinese Lunar New Year festival, a period of about six days during which both "real" and "financial" transactions are virtually suspended.[1] Given the suspension of economic activity in this period and the fact that the New Year is an entirely predictable event, the festival has no information content and is therefore purely nominal. As a result, a clear-cut test of the efficient capital market theory can be pursued.

RESEARCH DESIGN

As indicated earlier, we test market efficiency by examining whether investors can earn excess profits by buying stocks before the arrival of the Chinese Lunar New Year and selling them off later. To carry out the proposed test, we follow a three-step procedure: First, determine sample firms as well as sample years; second, select an appropriate profitability indicator; finally, specify the base and the observation periods in the days around the New Year.

In order to minimize sampling error, all companies listed on the stock market from 1975 to 1984 were adopted as the sample firms. This ten-year period was also chosen as the sample period for stock-price data. The period is long enough to give a sufficient data base for conclusions about market efficiency. During this ten-year period, three years—1977, 1982, and 1983—were ruled out. In 1977 and 1982 the stock-price index nosedived on the 14th and the 19th day, respectively before the arrival of the New Year. In contrast, there was a strong and continuous rise in stock prices in 1983 during the weeks before the New Year. Consequently, we were forced to abandon these three years since there was no effective way to evaluate the independent effect on stock prices arising from the trading suspension around the New Year.

Several methods are available for calculating profitability. In the present study it is inappropriate to adopt methods designed for a specific portfolio, such as market-adjusted returns (e.g., Brown and Warner 1983), since the New Year exerts a marketwide influence. In addition, no adjustment for risk is necessary since we are interested in returns of identical stocks.[2] All things considered, we decided to

Table 5.1

Cumulative Raw Returns for the Period 1975–1984

D	1975	1976	1978	1979	1980	1981	1984
1	8.38	5.40	9.46	4.24	2.05	1.47	6.87
	(6.0*)	(6.3*)	(7.6*)	(8.2*)	(3.4*)	(3.2*)	(10.6*)
2	8.53	8.61	11.95	6.31	1.72	1.55	8.14
	(5.2*)	(8.8*)	(8.3*)	(11.4*)	(2.6*)	(3.5*)	(11.9*)
3	9.72	8.25	11.91	4.53	3.05	2.13	8.47
	(5.6*)	(6.9*)	(7.5*)	(9.0*)	(4.6*)	(4.4*)	(11.5*)
4	14.99	5.50	9.32	2.58	2.88	3.83	9.52
	(8.2*)	(5.1*)	(6.6*)	(5.1*)	(4.8*)	(7.0*)	(11.8*)
5	16.28	2.53	6.79	6.12	2.42	5.40	12.07
	(8.8*)	(2.6*)	(5.1*)	(10.8*)	(3.5*)	(10.3*)	(12.6*)
6	15.93	1.99	8.05	5.23	3.32	6.80	12.51
	(7.8*)	(2.1*)	(5.1*)·(8.0*)		(4.2*)	(11.1*)	(11.9*)
7	15.49	3.57	6.53	2.49	3.44	6.63	9.77
	(7.6*)	(3.2*)	(4.3*)	(4.0*)	(4.1*)	(10.1*)	(10.3*)
8	11.40	2.79	4.29	0.67	5.75	7.95	11.38
	(5.8*)	(2.6*)	(3.0*)	(1.1)	(6.6*)	(11.1*)	(12.9*)
9	11.89	4.49	6.44	1.26	6.98	8.19	11.15
	(5.7*)	(3.7*)	(3.9*)	(2.2)	(8.7*)	(11.2*)	(13.3*)
10	12.89	3.71	8.35	1.88	7.49	7.93	9.12
	(6.0*)	(3.0*)	(4.7*)	(3.3*)	(8.2*)	(9.5*)	(12.5*)
11	9.33	4.86	8.43	0.93	10.82	7.60	8.06
	(4.5*)	(3.5*)	(4.6*)	(1.7)	(10.7*)	(8.9*)	(12.4*)
12	9.73	5.27	8.48	2.08	11.99	10.13	9.62
	(4.6*)	(3.7*)	(4.4*)	(4.0*)	(11.4*)	(10.0*)	(13.1*)
13	8.28	4.83	10.18	2.63	13.05	11.96	11.16
	(3.9*)	(3.6*)	(5.1*)	(5.1*)	(10.5*)	(9.9*)	(13.4*)
14	7.99	5.34	10.23	1.03	13.44	10.12	12.04
	(3.5*)	(4.0*)	(4.9*)	(2.0)	(9.4*)	(8.9*)	(14.0*)
15	10.34	5.59	8.68	-0.54	13.81	11.11	11.50
	(4.8*)	(4.2*)	(4.6*)	(-1.1)	(10.1*)	(9.7*)	(13.2*)
16	12.68	4.98	8.43	-0.69	13.17	9.01	11.26
	(6.1*)	(3.9*)	(4.4*)	(-1.3)	(9.7*)	(8.5*)	(12.6*)
17	11.60	2.11	9.02	-0.48	12.68	8.96	11.27
	(5.8*)	(1.8)	(4.3*)	(-0.9)	(9.9*)	(8.6*)	(12.1*)
18	9.83	2.51	9.82	1.25	11.12	8.76	13.25
	(5.0*)	(1.9)	(4.7*)	(2.4*)	(8.6*)	(8.5*)	(13.0*)
19	12.38	2.97	10.00	1.98	12.07	8.24	13.92
	(6.3*)	(2.1*)	(5.0*)	(3.7*)	(8.9*)	(7.6*)	(13.0*)
20	10.23	3.91	8.17	3.29	8.73	7.67	12.35
	(5.3*)	(2.7*)	(4.4*)	(5.9*)	(7.0*)	(7.1*)	(11.3*)
21	10.24	4.43	8.27	4.06	8.77	7.78	8.64
	(5.5*)	(2.8*)	(4.3*)	(7.4*)	(6.8*)	(6.8*)	(8.5*)
22	7.77	3.70	5.56	4.74	7.51	8.51	8.71
	(4.3*)	(2.2*)	(3.1*)	(8.4*)	(5.7*)	(7.1*)	(8.9*)
23	7.96	2.01	5.69	3.63	6.94	7.64	9.19
	(4.4*)	(1.1)	(3.2*)	(6.5*)	(5.2*)	(6.2*)	(8.5*)
24	6.88	2.43	5.38	1.54	4.41	7.08	8.91
	(3.9*)	(1.3)	(3.1*)	(0.7)	(3.2*)	(5.8*)	(8.3*)
25	9.59	5.54	4.63	2.59	3.71	6.43	7.09
	(5.2*)	(3.1*)	(2.6*)	(4.6*)	(2.8*)	(5.4*)	(6.9*)
26	8.33	5.29	5.54	1.78	5.44	5.86	5.28
	(4.6*)	(2.9*)	(2.9*)	(3.0*)	(3.9*)	(4.8*)	(5.1*)
27	7.98	5.34	6.97	2.03	4.88	6.32	8.40
	(4.4*)	(2.7*)	(3.7*)	(3.2*)	(3.8*)	(5.4*)	(7.7*)
28	8.64	7.04	6.97	3.14	3.74	7.36	7.79
	(4.7*)	(3.4*)	(4.0*)	(5.0*)	(3.2*)	(6.2*)	(6.8*)
29	7.70	9.79	7.67	2.85	2.14	5.93	9.79
	(4.2*)	(4.6*)	(4.3*)	(4.4*)	(1.8)	(5.3*)	(8.1*)
30	8.53	10.13	8.39	2.90	4.09	3.68	10.64
	(4.6*)	(4.4*)	(4.6*)	(4.2*)	(3.3*)	(3.5*)	(8.5*)

Legends:
1. D represents the $\underline{D}$th transaction date after the restoration of the market.
2. H_0: CR4=0; H_1: CR4>0. $z(\alpha=.01)=2.237$; $t(\alpha=.01)=2.492$.
3. z- or t-statistics are in parenthese.
4. *z- or t-statistic is significant at 1% level of significance.

use daily raw returns as the profitability indicator.[3] Cumulative raw returns (CRR) can be accordingly defined.[4]

A preliminary analysis made on historical price indices of the Taiwan Stock Exchange revealed that stock prices around the Chinese Lunar New Year moved upward in almost every year pending market suspension and continued to rise after the resumption of transactions. Therefore, our study shows that the beginning of the adjustment took place in advance of the arrival of the event, whereas the ending of the adjustment lagged behind the announcement of the event.

We arbitrarily used the period of the 15th day to the 6th day prior to Lunar New Year's eve as the base period to take care of possible information leakage. Two considerations were involved in choosing the observation period. On the one hand, most will agree that stock-price adjustments to newly released information can hardly occur simultaneously no matter how efficient the capital market is. Consequently, too short an observation period would lead to incomplete adjustment. On the other hand, an extended observation period enhances the possibility of incorrectly capturing information associated with other events. Given these factors, we decided to use stock prices over a 30-day period after the restoration of the market.

DISCUSSION OF EMPIRICAL RESULTS

From the results reported in table 5.1, we can clearly see that the pattern of cumulative raw returns is in line with our a priori expectations. However, a z-test was applied to examine whether or not these cumulative raw returns are statistically significantly different from zero.[5] Although we cannot reject the null hypothesis that CRR = 0 in four cases in the year 1976 and eight cases in 1979, the cumulative raw returns ran high in both years. At the 1 percent level of significance there is only one z-value falling in the acceptance area for 1980. As for 1975, 1978, 1981, and 1984, the null hypothesis can always be rejected at the 1 percent level of significance. All told, the evidence shows a high degree of conformity and suggests that a profit-making trading rule exists.

We resist the temptation to explain away the anomaly reported in this study for two closely related reasons. First ex post explanations that arise in light of empirical findings are more often than not ad hoc. Second, the emphasis on searching for specific explanatory variables per se may well misdirect future research efforts. At this stage, searching for a better way of testing market efficiency is our primary concern. If this study, together with the rapidly growing literature, helps stimulate researchers to conduct further research in this area, then it will have already served its purpose.

CONCLUSION

The mounting evidence against market efficiency has motivated the authors to search for a refined methodology and to provide empirical evidence bearing on this controversial issue. By analyzing daily stock-price movements around the Chinese Lunar New Year—a public event—it was found that a profit-making rule existed over an extended period (1975–84). The authors therefore conclude that Taiwan's stock market does not satisfy semistrong information efficiency.

NOTES

The authors are indebted to Lee K. Benham, Lawrence R. Klein, and numerous individuals for comments and/or encouragement. Stylistic advice generously provided by Dann Isbell and R. Harbaugh is gratefully acknowledged.

1. In 1975 and 1978 the suspension lasted for seven days owing to the presence of Sunday during the interval under examination.

2. As Copeland and Weston pointed out, "Because each security is compared with itself, there is no need to adjust for risk" (1983, p. 304).

3. In formal terms, raw returns of the jth stock earned on date t, $R_{j,t}$, can be defined as follows:

$$R_{j,t} = \frac{P_{j,t} - P_{j,t-1}}{P_{j,0}},$$

where

$t =$ the tth trading date after the reopening of the market,

$P_{j,t} =$ the closing price of the jth stock on date t, and

$P_{j,0} =$ arithmetic mean of the closing price of the jth stock over the base period.

4. Based on the profitability formula defined in note 3, cumulative raw returns, $CRR_{j,t}$, can be defined as follows:

$$CRR_{j,t} = \sum_{t=1}^{\tau} R_{j,t},$$

where $1 \leq \tau \leq 30$.

5. The sample size of 1975 was somewhat smaller than that of other years, so a t-statistic instead of a z-value was computed.

REFERENCES

Brown, S. J., and J. B. Warner. (1985). "Measuring Security Pricing Performance." *Journal of Financial Economics* 14: 3–31.

Copeland, T. E., and J. F. Weston. (1983). *Financial Theory and Corporate Policy*. Reading, Mass.: Addison-Wesley.

Fama, E. F. (1976). *Foundations of Finance*. New York: Basic Books.

Fama, E. F., L. Fisher, M. C. Jensen, and R. Roll. (1969). "The Adjustment of Stock Prices to New Information." *International Economic Review*, February, 1–21.

Jensen, M. C. (1978). "Some Anomalous Evidence Regarding Market Efficiency." *Journal of Financial Economics* (June/September): 95–101.

p 101 ? ## Discussant: Hugh Haworth

Professors Lee, Yen, and Chang have prepared a very stimulating study of the turn-of-the-year effect of the Taiwanese stock market. This study adds measurably to the literature examining the anomalies to the efficient market hypothesis. The authors examine the semistrong form of the efficient market hypothesis by investigating stock-price movements around the Chinese Lunar New Year. They report that during this time both "real" and "financial" transactions do not occur in the Taiwan market. Based on longitudinal data from 1975 to 1984, they find that a profit-making rule seems to exist. They feel that their findings cast doubt on the efficacy of the hypothesis of semistrong efficiency, at least when it is applied to thin markets such as Taiwan's. They find that investors, by buying stocks before the arrival of the New Year and selling them later, earned discernible profits.

It is important to put their analysis in perspective. A nominal addition to the authors' literature review would help. Rozeff and Kinney (1976) found seasonal patterns in an equal-weighted index of New York Stock Exchange (NYSE) prices over the period 1904–74. Specifically, the average monthly return in January over these seven decades was about 3.5 percent, while other months averaged about 0.5 percent. Banz (1981) found that small firms have higher returns than was consistent with their riskiness. Keim (1983) showed that the small-firm effect and the January effect may be the same thing: The January effect appeared only in samples that gave equal weight to small and large firms as opposed to samples that weighed firms by value. The high returns in January were not observed in an index that was composed only of large firms, like the Dow Jones Industrial Average (Lakonishok and Smidt 1986).

Reinganum (1983) clarified the situation further by pointing out that the January returns were higher for small firms whose prices had declined the previous year, and the excess returns in the first five days were not observed for small "winners." Roll (1983) found evidence consistent with Reinganum's. He reported that stocks with negative returns over the previous year have higher returns in January.

The turn-of-the-year effect is special in other ways. DeBondt and Thaler (1985) found that the firms that had been the biggest winners or losers over a five-year period subsequently had excess returns in the opposite direction. That is, the previous big winners had negative excess returns, and the losers had positive excess returns. The excess returns, especially for the losers, were concentrated in January.

There are probably several separate factors affecting prices around year's end. Not all are limited to small firms. In most markets January marks the beginning and ending of several potentially important financial and informational events. January is the start of the tax year for investors and the beginning of the tax and accounting year for most firms. Preliminary announcements of the previous calendar year's accounting earnings are made. Thus, at least for those firms with year-end fiscal closings, the month of January marks a period of increased uncertainty and anticipation due to the impending release of important information.

There is a tendency for prices of all firms regardless of size, to rise on the last trading day of the year (Lakonishok and Smidt 1984). In volume and frequency of trading, there is a very active market toward the end of the year for small companies. This is consistent with the tax-loss hypothesis. (By contrast, there is a decline in trading volume for large firms between Christmas and New Year's.) The most active day for small firms is the last day of the year. Trading in January for small companies continues at a very active rate. Although not quite as great as in late December, it is substantially greater than in October and November.

For small firms, small trading volume and large bid-ask spreads militate against big profit opportunities. None of the anomalies seem to offer enormous opportunities for private investors (with normal transaction costs). Some traders do face zero transaction costs, and investors who now buy in January could buy in December.

INTERNATIONAL EVIDENCE

Of special interest with regard to this chapter is the turn-of-the-year effect in various countries. Gultekin and Gultekin (1983) looked at the seasonal pattern in 16 countries and found that turn-of-the-year returns were exceptionally large in 15 of them. They found large mean returns around the turn of the tax year as predicted by the tax-loss hypothesis. Their findings did not rule out a tax-induced TOYE in most countries except Australia. Since the authors used value-weighted indices from the different countries, their returns cannot be explained by a size-related anomaly.

Berges, McConnell, and Schlarbaum (1984) found a TOYE (turn-of-the-year effect) in Canada similar to that reported in the U.S. markets. They found a significant January effect, and the effect was more pronounced for smaller firms. They concluded that it was possible that the tax-loss-selling-pressure hypothesis explains abnormally high returns for small firms in Canada, as was concluded by Roll and Reinganum for U.S. securities.

The international evidence suggests that while taxes seem relevant to the TOYE, they are not the entire explanation. First, the TOYE is observed in Japan, where no capital-gain tax or loss offsets exist (Kato and Schallheim 1985). Second, Canada had no capital-gains tax before 1972, yet it had a TOYE before 1972 (Berges, McConnell, and Schlarbaum 1984). This may have been caused by the heavy involvement of U.S. investors in the Canadian market.

Interestingly, the tax effect exists even when it does not occur at the end of the year. Great Britain and Australia have such effects, even thought their tax years begin on April 1 and July 1, respectively. Returns are high in April for Great Britain and high in July for Australia.

REFLECTIONS

Since there are several competing hypotheses on the turn-of-the-year effect, it would be very interesting if the authors considered testing those most applicable to the Taiwan context. Many of the empirical tests for inefficiencies associated with the year-end effect have looked at the returns in all the months of the year. This is an area that the authors may want to pursue. It gives a clear indication as to how unusual the returns may be in the month of January.

The authors excluded three years from their observations: 1977, 1982, and 1983. They noted that for 1977 and 1982 prices nosedived prior to the arrival of the New Year, on the 14th day and the 19th day, respectively. For 1983 stock prices rose continuously over the period before the New Year. Though this, on the face of it, may appear to be a problem, it does not seem to be a reason to eliminate the observations.

Many studies examining trading rules net out retail customers' round-trip transaction costs to see if such programs are profitable. In most markets, though, floor traders and institutions can trade much more cheaply than retail customers. In fact, others could be considered low-cost investors also: (1) those rebalancing their portfolios, (2) those with new funds available for commitment to the market, and (3) those liquidating positions for reasons like capital disbursement. To have a true test of the proposition, the lowest trading costs should be applied since they will definitely have an impact at the margin. Consequently, the authors' conclusion regarding significance of the discovered anomaly would be bolstered by using a lower, relevant set of transaction costs.

In the study most of the years examined had a progressively increasing price movement in the base ("control") period as well as in the test period. Since statistics on the cumulative excess returns (CERs) are not present for the base periods, it is difficult to say whether there may be a problem. Nevertheless, it might be appropriate to move the base period back further so it ends even 10 or 15 days before the start of the test period. This could eliminate the unexpected upward movement of CERs in the base period and avoid picking up some of the early turn-of-the-year effects.

The authors eliminated the stocks that had dividend distributions in the period under examination. This is a wise precaution when there are plenty of observations. With the limited number of companies available, though, it may be worth the while to examine these stocks to see if there is a run-up in prices preceding the announcement of dividend distributions. If so, they could not be used in the announcement occurs within the base or test period.

Several studies on the TOYE have used monthly data. The authors were right in going with the daily prices to test their hypothesis. Yet they lost about 30 percent of their observations to infrequent trading. They could use weekly data to recover some of their observations and still have a valid test.

AGREEMENT

The authors are correct in stating that there are problems with accepting an absolute form of market efficiency as representing the norm. Milgrom and Stokey (1982) showed that rational agents with asymmetric information will not offer to trade securities based on naive interpretations of their private information. Instead, rational investors will want to buy or sell securities to provide for large expenditures or to adjust risk exposure. However, it is clear that only a small percentage of stock-market trades can be explained in this way. The majority of trades appear to reflect belief on the part of each investor that he or she can outwit his or her competitors, which is inconsistent with assumptions of market efficiency.

Efficient market theory attributes asset-price changes to information about fundamentals. Returns should be explainable ex post by such fundamentals. A study by Roll (1984) cast doubts on this. He asserted that weather information that should be the dominant influence on orange-juice futures' prices explained empirically only a small fraction of the variation in such prices.

In addition, Roll (1986) interpreted stock-price declines that typically follow takeovers as validating the pretakeover valuation of the firm on the part of the large majority of investors and invalidating the "excessive" run-up before the takeover, which can be attributed in part to acquirers overpaying because of "hubris." This is not consistent with the efficient market theory because there should be no systematic pattern of price declines following such events when there is such publicity involved in the total process.

REFERENCES

Banz, Rolf. (1981). "The Relationship between Return and Market Value of Common Stocks." *Journal of Financial Economics* 9, no. 1 (March): 3–18.

Berges, Angel, John J. McConnell, and Gary G. Schlarbaum. (1984). "The Turn-of-the-Year in Canada." *Journal of Finance* 39, no. 1 (March): 185–192.

DeBondt, Werner, F. M., and Richard Thaler. (1985). "Does the Stock Market Overreact?" *Journal of Finance* 40, no. 3 (July): 793–805.

French, Kenneth. (1980). "Stock Returns and the Weekend Effect." *Journal of Financial Economics* 8, no. 1 (March): 55–69.

French, Kenneth, and Richard Roll. (1986). "Stock Return Variances: The Arrival of Information and the Reaction of Traders." *Journal of Financial Economics* 17, no. 1 (September): 5–26.

Gultekin, Mustafa N., and N. Bulent Gultekin. (1983). "Stock Market Seasonality: International Evidence." *Journal of Financial Economics* 12: 469–481.

Jaffe, Jeffrey, and Randolph Westerfield. (1985). "The Week-End Effect in Common Stock Returns: The International Evidence." *Journal of Finance* 40, no. 2 (June): 433–454.

Kato, Kiyoshi, and James S. Shallheim. (1985). "Season and Size Anomalies in the Japanese Stock Market." *Journal of Financial and Quantitative Analysis* 20: 243–260.

Keim, Donald B. (1983). "Size-related Anomalies and Stock Return Seasonality." *Journal of Financial Economics* 12, no. 1: 13–32.

Lakonishok, Josef, and Seymour Smidt. (1984). "Volume and Turn-of-the-Year Behavior." *Journal of Financial Economics* 13, no. 3 (September): 435–455.

Milgrom, Paul, and Nancy Stokey. (1982). "Information, Trade, and Common Knowledge." *Journal of Economic Theory* 90, no. 1 (February): 166–175.

Reinganum, Marc. (1983). "The Anomalous Stock Market Behavior of Small Firms in January: Empirical Tests for Tax-Loss Selling Effects." *Journal of Financial Economics* 12, no. 10 (June): 89–104.

Roll, Richard. (1984) "Orange Juice and Weather." *American Economic Review* 74, no. 5 (December): 861–880.

———. (1983). "On Computing Mean Returns and the Small Firm Premium." *Journal of Financial Economics* 12: 371–386.

———. (1986). "The Hubris Hypothesis of Corporate Takeovers." *Journal of Business* 59, no. 2 (April: 197–216.

Rozeff, Michael S., and William R. Kinney. (1976). "Capital Market Seasonality: The Case of stock Returns." *Journal of Financial Economics* 3: 379–402.

6

Reactions of the Taiwanese Stock Market to Trade Talks with the United States

GILI YEN and PHILIP CHANG

ISSUE AND OBJECTIVE

The trade surplus of Taiwan with the United States has been constantly increasing over the last 20 years. Table 6.1 shows the trade flows between these two countries during the period from 1966 to 1986. The United States has also been Taiwan's predominant foreign market. Table 6.2 shows the major Taiwanese commodities exported to the U.S. market. Note the importance of textiles. Concerned about the trade imbalance, the United States first initiated trade talks with Taiwan in 1978. Since then, trade talks between the two countries have become an annual event. In addition, there have been a number of talks targeted at specific industries, in particular, the textile industry. The goal of the U.S. side is to trim its huge deficits by limiting Taiwanese exports and by persuading Taiwan to open up its markets to American businesses.

Because of the extreme importance of the U.S. market to the Taiwanese economy, the trade talks conducted between the governments of the United States and the Republic of China are expected to exert a substantial impact on that economy. The purpose of this chapter is to examine empirically this impact by observing the reaction of Taiwan's stock market to the Sino-American trade talks that took place during the period from October 1, 1981, to September 30, 1986. News of developments in the trade talks is classified into the mutually exclusive categories of "good," "bad," and "indeterminate," reflecting the probable effects of the developments on Taiwan's stock market.

The balance of the chapter is organized as follows. The first section reviews previous studies. The second section illustrates the empirical methodology. The third section describes the collection and classification of the sample. Findings are presented and discussed in the fourth section. The fifth section concludes the chapter.

Table 6.1

Trade between Taiwan and the United States, 1966–1986

(Amounts in Thousand of U.S. Dollars)

	Imports	Exports	Balance
1966	166,335	115,885	−50,450
1967	247,302	167,815	−79,487
1968	239,494	278,194	38,700
1969	291,752	399,047	107,295
1970	363,839	564,174	200,335
1971	408,159	859,200	451,041
1972	543,424	1,251,317	707,893
1973	952,533	1,677,106	724,573
1974	1,679,905	2,036,638	356,733
1975	1,652,129	1,822,737	170,608
1976	1,797,540	3,038,699	1,241,159
1977	1,963,852	3,636,253	1,672,398
1978	2,376,063	5,010,378	2,634,315
1979	3,380,797	5,652,243	2,271,446
1980	4,673,486	6,760,300	2,086,814
1981	4,765,671	8,158,392	3,392,721
1982	4,563,255	8,757,795	4,194,540
1983	4,646,443	11,333,712	6,687,269
1984	5,041,643	14,867,709	9,826,066
1985	4,746,274	14,772,990	10,026,716
1986	5,415,788	18,994,694	13,578,906

Source: Taiwan Statistical Data Book, Council for Economic Planning
and Development, Executive Yuan, 1987.

Table 6.2
Major Taiwanese Export Items to the United States
(Amounts in Thousands of U. S. Dollars)

Item	1977	1978	1979	1980	1981	1982	1983	1984	1985	1986
Total	3,636,253	5,010,378	5,652,243	6,760,300	8,158,392	8,757,795	11,333,712	14,867,709	14,772,990	18,994,694
Canned food	58,871	57,991	60,778	70,936	40,811	46,327	55,209	69,547	56,146	58,582
Sugar	7,862	7,648	3,723	—	—	15,647	13,383	13,763	9,475	7,158
Textile products	893,104	1,162,222	1,171,675	1,506,735	1,524,828	1,661,054	1,909,500	2,520,629	2,344,850	2,696,869
Plywood	100,683	172,623	189,560	135,693	140,026	113,052	165,211	142,703	108,167	120,478
Metal manufactures	151,226	265,274	341,107	400,523	558,772	579,210	871,334	1,152,945	1,196,110	1,574,468
Plastic articles	385,383	520,820	595,693	790,553	926,271	883,032	1,139,878	1,580,481	1,767,533	2,310,213
Rubber products	51,030	58,657	76,253	98,385						
Toys and games	88,505	132,062	169,042	202,452	262,776	291,660	358,602	472,395	393,928	453,940
Others	1,899,589	2,633,081	3,044,412	3,555,023	4,704,908	5,167,813	6,820,595	8,915,246	8,896,781	11,772,986

Source: Taiwan Statistical Data Book, Council for Economic Planning and Development, Executive Yuan, 1987.

113

A BRIEF REVIEW OF EARLIER STUDIES

There are many studies that classify the information content of chosen events and then examine their influences by observing the reaction of the stock market. Ball and Brown (1968) investigated the informational content of accounting numbers. Based on the difference between actual and expected incomes, the authors classified information contained in the earnings announcement into "good" and "bad," calculated the abnormal performance index (API) for the period, and examined the relationship between information of different kinds and API. The authors found that accounting numbers did contain valuable information in the sense that they were associated with abnormal fluctuations in stock prices.

Niederhoffer (1971) examined the relationship between global events and U.S. stock prices. Associating the information classified "good" or "bad" with the magnitude as well as direction of the rate of change in the stock-price index, the author found that stock prices tended to fluctuate in tune with information in the expected direction. Although fluctuations were concentrated on the very day of the major event or one day following it, a full adjustment required as long as five days.

Yu (1974) used a method similar to that of Niederhoffer (1971) to study the impact of major events on Taiwan's stock market. The author found that the probability of observing significant fluctuation on the first trading day after the arrival of a major event was higher than it would be on ordinary trading days. The duration of these fluctuations, however, seldom exceeded three days. The author also noted that Taiwan's stock market was more sensitive in response to events regarding foreign affairs, finance, and economic conditions as compared with other types of events.

Palmon and Schneller (1980) examined the changes in security-related news (SRN) in the neighborhood of abnormal price movements (APMs). APMs were classified into "positive" and "negative," and SRN was classified as "good" or "bad." The relationships between APMs and SRN was then studied. The authors found that SRN led to abnormal changes in stock prices.

Cosset and Rianderie (1985) studied the reaction of the foreign exchange market to the announcement of changes in the business environment. The authors classified political information into "favorable" and "unfavorable," calculated abnormal foreign exchange returns around the event date, and used both a sign test and the Wilcoxon rank coefficient to examine the relationships between the two variables just mentioned. It was found that political news did contain valuable information.

Yen (1987) studied the impact of the mandatory pension plan on the market value of listed companies in Taiwan. The author classified information regarding the mandatory pension system into "good" and "bad" and found that pension-related news exerted little influence, if any, on the market value of listed companies. A possible explanation is that a large number of the listed companies had already set up pension plans on their own initiative much earlier than required by the Labor Standards Law.

Yen and Lin (1991) studied the impact of political events on Hong Kong's stock market. The authors classified information regarding the negotiations between the

United Kingdom and mainland China on the future status of Hong Kong into "good" and "bad" and calculated the rate of change of the daily Hang-Seng stock index. Using the sign test to determine the relationship of the variability, the authors found that political information exerted a substantial impact on Hong Kong's stock market.

RESEARCH METHODOLOGY

Most studies reviewed in the previous section called for a classification of the information into "good" and "bad" categories, to be followed by a calculation of the associated changes in price of individual stocks or stock-market indices. The relationship between them was examined accordingly.

Since the purpose of this chapter is to examine the impact of trade-talk events on the entire stock market, a formula for calculating the rate of change in the stock-price index is used. This formula similar to that adopted in Bradley (1980), can be stated as

$$ER_t = \frac{P_t - P_b}{P_b} \, ,$$

where

$ER_t =$ rate of change of the stock-price index on day t;

$P_t =$ stock-price index on day t;

$P_b =$ stock-price index on the base day.

With respect to choosing the base period, preliminary analysis of the data indicated that Taiwan's stock market usually begins to react to trade talks—if such reaction occurs at all—on the very first day of or one day immediately after the announcement.[1] Under such circumstances, if no information leakage occurs, the stock-price index on the date of announcement or one day earlier is a natural choice for the base index. The choice of the date of announcement, however, has two apparent shortcomings. First, if the adjustment begins on the day of the announcement, we are mistakenly adopting a biased base index, which in turn will result in a biased estimate of the effect triggered by the event. Second, in several cases, the stock market happened to have been closed on the date of announcement. For these two reasons, we decided to adopt the day prior to the date of announcement as our base day. The index used for the base day is the Value-Weighted Stock Price Index compiled by the Taiwan Stock Exchange.

As for the observation period, it is extremely difficult, if not totally impossible, to find a period of proper length suitable for all trade talks. For this reason, we decided to observe the index on the very first day of the news release only. In other words, as in several previous studies, we rely on a sign test to ascertain whether or not a systematic relationship exists between the release of trade-talk-related news and the movement in the stock-price index.

The final step is to associate the trade talks with the stock-price indices. When the stock-price index goes up (down) with "good" ("bad") news, a positive correlation is said to exist. Otherwise, a negative correlation is said to exist.

DATA SOURCES AND SAMPLE

In order to conduct empirical tests, trade-talk information and other relevant information for the period from October 1, 1981, through September 30, 1986, was collected from the following sources:

1. Information on the trade talks was collected from *Economic Daily, Commercial Times, Central Daily, China Times, United Daily, Youth Daily, Taiwan Daily, Hsinsheng News, Minsu Evening News,* and *Dahwa Evening News.*
2. Major events other than the trade talks were retrieved from the weekly column "Stock Market Weekly" as reported in the *Commercial Times.*[2]
3. Data on the stock-price index and textile index for the period from October 1981 through December 1985 were taken from "Securities Statistics" (April 1986). As for the period from January 1986 through October 1986, indices were compiled from the "Daily Securities Prices" as reported in the *Economic Daily.*

Through careful reading, 263 Sino-American bilateral trade talks reported during the period from October 1, 1981, to September 30, 1986, were retrieved from the various newspapers mentioned. When two events occurred within two days, the latter event was merged into the earlier one since their effects could hardly be separated. Additionally, although arbitrariness to a certain degree was inevitable, we tried our best to reduce bias by observing the following three rules: (1) When an even contained both "good" and "bad" news, it was labelled as "indeterminate." (2) We viewed trade talks over intangible property rights as beneficial to the listed firms, the reason being that unlisted firms as compared with listed firms are engaged more frequently in rights-infringing activities. (3) When a definitive judgment could not be reached on an event per se, references were made to previous related items.[3] Through this procedure 163 events were obtained. Five events among the 163 were further eliminated because the stock market was closed on the base day. Therefore, 158 events were used in the study. According to their information contents, these events were further classified into 27 good, 105 bad, and 26 indeterminate events.

EMPIRICAL ANALYSIS

Reaction of the Stock Market without Controlling for Other Events

Among the 132 good or bad events, 82, or more than 60 percent, exhibited positive correlation. It appears that performance of the stock market is related to the information contents of the trade talks. To test the relationship statistically, the following hypotheses were established:

H_0: The stock-price index is not affected by the good (bad) information contents of events of the trade talks. Operationally speaking, the authors assume that the probability that the index goes up (down) with good (bad) news is 0.5.

H_1: The stock-price index is affected by the good (bad) information contents. Put in a different way, the probability that the index goes up (down) with good (bad) news is greater than 0.5.[4]

If the statistic Z is used to perform the sign test, the null hypothesis that the stock-price index is not affected by the trade talks can be rejected at the .05 level of significance.[5] It appears that the market tends to go up (down) with good (bad) trade-talk news.

Reaction of the Stock Market after Considering Confounding events

As trade talks with the United States are not necessarily the only events that would have affected stock prices, we should be able to obtain a more accurate assessment if confounding events are taken into account. Events other than trade talks that might have influenced the stock market were compiled from the column "Stock Market Weekly" of the *Commercial Times*. To control for the impacts arising from other events, trade-talk events that were recognized along with other events in the "Stock Market Weekly" were eliminated. After this deletion, there were 87 trade-talk events left.

Based on the nature of the information and the stock-market reaction, a positive association was found for 57 events out of the remaining 87 events. Through use of the sign test, the null hypothesis that the stock-price index is not affected by the trade talks is again rejected at the .05 significance level.[6]

Reactions of the Textile Stocks to Textile-specific Talks

Textile products have been a major Taiwanese export to the United States for years. They constituted 19 percent of Taiwan's total exports to the United States in 1981. In the same year, the United States purchased 33 percent of the total textile products exported by Taiwan. In 1986 these two statistics were 14 percent and 37 percent, respectively. It is not surprising, then, that textiles have been prominent on the agendas of trade talks. In fact, textiles are the most frequently discussed item. Among the 132 trade talks, 54 were related to textiles.

To examine the impact of trade talks on textile stocks, the Textile Stock Price Index was used. Two additional tests were executed in a method similar to that used in the two previous tests. We first examined in the third test the impact of the 54 textile-related talks. We then moved to examine in the fourth test the impact of textile-related talks after confounding events were controlled. There were 45 events left after the confounding events were taken into account.

In the third test, we found 35 positive correlations between the Textile Stock Price Index and the information contents out of 57 events. The null hypothesis that the textile stocks are not affected by textile trade talks can be rejected at the .05 significance level. In the fourth test, we found 28 positive correlations among the remaining 45 events. Again, the null hypothesis is rejected at the .10 significance level.[7]

SUMMARY AND CONCLUSION

This chapter examines the impact of the Sino-American trade talks on Taiwan's stock market. Based on the nature of information contents news on trade talks was classified into "good," "bad," and "indeterminate" categories. The relationship between the nature of the news and the reaction of the stock market was then empirically examined.

In all four empirical tests, it was found that the stock-price index tended to move in tune with the informational content of the trade talks. We therefore conclude that the Sino-American trade talks do exert a noticeable influence on Taiwan's stock market.

NOTES

The authors are indebted to Mahendra R. Gujarathi and Eva C. Yen for their helpful comments and C. Y. Tsai for his valuable assistance. Stylistic advice provided by R. Harbaugh is gratefully acknowledged.

1. This is the third type of stock-price reactions as classified by Hillmer and Yu (1979).

2. The column in question was used for the following three reasons:

1. This weekly column covered the entire five-year period of the study.
2. It was written by the same columnist, Chen Tai. The viewpoints expressed should be more consistent than those in a column contributed by several reporters.
3. Most important, there were countless events that might have influenced the stock prices. To make this study feasible, the reports and analysis written by the same columnist had to be relied upon.

3. At this juncture, let us call to readers' attention the comments made by our discussant, Mahendra Gujarathi, concerning the classification of the sample and the method used to estimate the impact of trade talks. Although, as Gujarathi correctly points out, the present study is quite similar to the voluminous body of research done in accounting and finance on the relationship between an event and the security-price movements, three things deserve special mention. First, it is hoped that readers can be convinced that the classification is not as arbitrary as it might first appear since the classification is systematically done on the basis of the three screens mentioned in the text. Moreover, before classifying any trade talk, we made reference to previous events whenever such need arose. The issue of prior expectation, if not totally eliminated, has therefore been partially taken care of. Finally, we cannot agree with Gujarathi's remark that "the good/bad categorization is apparently faulty in the study; how can you explain 105 bad (and only 27 good) events in a period during which the trade surplus for Taiwan went up from $0.4 billion to $13.5 billion?" In this chapter we examine the stock-price movements in the vicinity of a chosen event, which, needless to say, are largely independent of the trendy change in the stock market.

4. In the current study, it is assumed in the null hypothesis that the probability that the index goes up (down) with good (bad) news is 0.5. If it went up more frequently, as was

usually the case during the sample years, then since there was a larger number of cases of bad news than of good news on trade talks, the statistical relationship would be even stronger than presently claimed.

5. The Z value is calculated with the following formula:

$$Z = \frac{X - np}{\sqrt{np(1 - p)}},$$

where

n = total number of events,

X = number of positive correlations, and

p = 0.5.

The calculated Z value is 2.872, $Z = \dfrac{82 - (132 \times 0.5)}{\sqrt{132 \times 0.5 \times 0.5}} = 2.785$, greater than $Z_{0.05} = 1.645$.

6. $Z = 2.895$, greater than $Z_{0.05} = 1.645$.

7. For the third test, $Z = 1.722$, greater than $Z_{0.05} = 1.645$; for the fourth test, $Z = 1.640$, greater than $Z_{0.10} = 1.282$.

REFERENCES

Ball, R., and P. Brown. (1968). "An Empirical Evaluation of Accounting Income Numbers." *Journal of Accounting Research*, Autumn, 159–178.

Bradley, J. (1980). "Interfirm Tender Offers and the Market for Corporate Control." *Journal of Business* 53, no. 4: 345–376.

Copeland, T. E., and J. F. Weston. (1983). *Financial Theory and Corporate Policy*. Reading, Mass.: Addison-Wesley.

Cosset, Jean-Claude, and Bruno Doutriaux de la Rianderie. (1985). "Political Risk and Foreign Exchange Rates: An Efficient Markets Approach." *Journal of International Business Studies*, Fall, 21–55.

Fama, E. F., L. Fisher, M. C. Jensen, and R. Roll. (1969). "The Adjustment of Stock Prices to New Information." *International Economic Review*, February, 1–21.

Hillmer, S. C., and P. L. Yu. (1979). "The Market Speed of Adjustment to New Information." *Journal of Financial Economics* 7 (December): 321–345.

Lin, C. P. (1971). "Information Contents in the Financial Statements of Public Companies in Taiwan." Master's thesis, National Taiwan University, Taipei, June (in Chinese).

Lin, Y. T. (1985). *Modern Investments: Institution, Theory, and Practice* (in Chinese). 3rd ed. Taipei: San-Min Publishing.

Niederhoffer, V. (1971). "The Analysis of World Events and Stock Prices." *Journal of Business* 44, no. 2 (April): 193–219.

Palmon, D., and M. I. Schneller. (1980). "The Relationship between Securities Abnormal Price Movements and Wall Street Journal News." *Journal of Banking and Finance* 4: 235–247.

Scholes, M. S. (1972). "The Market for Securities: Substitution versus Price Pressure and the Effects of Information on Share Prices." *Journal of Business* (April): 179–211.

Yen, Gili. (1987). "Mandatory Pension Plan and Market Value of the Firm—An Exploratory Study." In *Proceedings of the 1987 Conference on Economic Development and Social Welfare in Taiwan*, 605–654. Taipei, Taiwan, Republic of China: Institute of Economics, Academia Sinica.

Yen, Gili, and T. Y. Lin. (1991). "Impacts of Political Events on Hong Kong Stock Markets: The Case of the Political Negotiation between Mainland China and the U.K." Mimeographed.

Yu, R. T. (1974). "Impacts of Major Events on Taiwanese Stock Prices" (in Chinese). Master's thesis, National Cheng-chi University, Taipei, June.

G14

121 - 23

pUl ' **Discussant: Mahendra R. Gujarathi**

This study is another in the voluminous body of research done in accounting and finance on the relationship between an event and the security-price movements. This study is, however, different in two respects: (1) It studies the relationship of an event to the changes in the prices of the market as a whole rather than the individual security-price movements. (2) The setting is a market where efficiency has been proved only in a weak form. The chapter by Lee, Yen, and Chang alludes to this.

The chapter is interesting. Any study on the Taiwanese market is of interest because of the huge trade imbalance the United States has with Taiwan, and also because of the skyrocketing securities prices Taiwan has recently experienced. The methodology is the standard one: isolating an event and investigating the behavior of prices in the vicinity of that event. The conclusion, to me at least, was obvious. In a market where only the weak form of capital market efficiency is accepted, trade-talk news would have an effect on the market, and that is what the authors found. My substantive comments on the chapter are summarized in the following paragraphs.

A necessary condition for a valid characterization of news as good or bad is the frame of reference of prior expectations. A security's price performance can only be considered "abnormal" relative to a particular benchmark. Even in an individual security's situation it is difficult to decide whether the even is good or bad. The event always has to be examined in the light of expectations the market had about it. A good event might receive a cold shoulder because it was not as good as the market had expected it to be. In their classification of the news (good, bad, or indeterminate), the authors have relied entirely on their judgment. At the minimum, they could have presented the news to a number of security analysts and based the categorization of good/bad on their responses. Also, aren't there shades of good and bad? Was it possible to given a five- or seven-point scale to analysts to get their categorization? The good/bad categorization is apparently faulty in this study; how can you explain 105 bad (and only 27 good) events in a period during which the trade surplus for Taiwan went up from $3.4 billion to $13.6 billion?

The authors' use of the market index one day prior to the announcement date as the base index is problematic, to say the least. The authors have assumed that the reaction starts on the very day of the announcement or one day after the announcement. It is entirely possible that the market had the information from the U.S. media or at least had an expectation about such information built into the market index for a few days prior to the announcement. Taking a single day's index as the base is also likely to make the returns volatile. Instead, an average index for a few days before the announcement would have been a better proxy for the market expectation.

The choice of the ending date of the observation period is also inappropriate. It is more than likely, especially in a market that is efficient only in a weak form, that the adjustment to stock prices is not complete on the day of the announcement itself.

Even in the developed stock markets of the West, several events trigger market response that is abnormal for several days following the day of announcement. The use of only the announcement day as the observation period is thus erroneous.

If the authors have relied upon the sign test to examine the association between the trade talks and market movements, nothing is gained by computing the return (i.e., the rate of change). This information has not been used since all that has been tested is the correlation between the sign of the change in the market index and the good/bad nature of the trade-talk news. A valuable opportunity is missed in the process. If the rates of change in the index were used in conjunction with a longer observation period, the authors would have been able to derive some interesting conclusions about the time the market takes to return to normalcy. A conclusion on these lines would have shed light on the efficiency or lack of efficiency of the Taiwanese market.

The authors do not state the reason for the selection of their sample period of 1981 through 1986. It would have been more interesting to do the study starting in 1978 when the United States first initiated trade talks with Taiwan. The longer sample period would have enabled the authors to examine the response to the trade talks in the initial years in comparison with the later years. The authors have chosen to study the impact of trade talks on the textile stocks separately, but there is another Taiwanese industry that is quite important. In each year of the sample period 1981–86, the plastic and rubber products together constituted more than 10 percent of Taiwan's exports to the United States. It would have been interesting to study the reaction of the plastic and rubber stocks to trade talks.

The authors' attempt to eliminate the impact of confounding events is well taken. However, the subjective nature of the analysis in this section makes one wonder about the validity of the results.

An important question is how long the effect of the news lasts. If you assume it to last for several days, it is necessary to make sure that there is no other event occurring in the vicinity. This is a serious limitation of the study. For example, there is a bad event on January 10, 1982, a good event on January 13, 1982, and a bad event on January 17, 1982, and another good event on January 21, 1982. When the events are so close together, drawing any meaningful conclusions becomes rather difficult.

As for the methodology, I have a question. Does the market return include a dividend component? Noninclusion of a dividend component can introduce a significant error in the computation of returns. In many of the market indices of third-world countries, the stock-price indices and dividend-yield indices are built separately, and it is not known how to put the two together. There have been some studies in this direction that the authors need to consider.

Finally, the study is not well motivated. It references works that are dated, and the two recent references are in Chinese. In a market where only the weak form of efficiency is proven, isn't it to be expected that the market will respond to the talks with the major trade partner like the United States? What are the implications of the study? Do the results say something more about the efficiency of the Taiwanese market that has not been said by the prior research studies? Some elaboration on the motivation of the study and reference to the recent work done in the United States would help enhance the usefulness of the chapter.

G12
G23
G16
Brazil

125-33

7

Mutual-Fund Performance in the Brazilian Stock Market, 1984–1985

ANTONIO ZORATTO SANVICENTE and EVERALDO GUEDES FRANCA

This chapter reports the results of applying an "ex post characteristic curve methodology" (Sharpe 1981) to evaluate the performance of mutual funds in the Brazilian stock market. More specifically, we have attempted to establish whether certain institutional investors possess superior "security-selection" and "market-timing" abilities. This study is especially important for two main reasons. First, the comparatively limited availability of information on assets traded on Brazilian stock exchanges could make for a less-than-efficient market, conferring cost advantages to larger, institutional investors vis-à-vis smaller, individual investors. Second, it is part of Brazilian stock-market folklore (as elsewhere) that success in that market is possible only when one possesses access to inside information, and that institutions, thanks to their privileged access to the managements of listed firms, do possess that access. In Brazil mutual funds are usually de facto divisions of larger banking conglomerates, with all possible kinds of financial dealings with business firms with listed securities. Thus they are more likely to have access to information that is not available to other investors.

The chapter is organized as follows: In the first section we present a brief outline of the relevant literature, with emphasis on previous attempts at measuring mutual-fund performance in Brazil. Little attention is given to the literature developed in the United States, since that literature is well known. The second section outlines the methodology as well as the tests used. The third section describes the data and gives a short outline of the state of the Brazilian mutual-fund industry in the period covered by the study, that is, 1984 and 1985. In the fourth section we present and discuss the results.

RELEVANT LITERATURE

The use of relative-to-market measures and the consideration of portfolio risk in examinations of mutual-fund performance can be traced to Sharpe (1966), Treynor (1965), and Jensen (1968). It is based on the idea that there exists a benchmark, passive strategy of operating "according to the averages," which involves constructing a diversified portfolio to mimic the market for risky assets. Alternatively, and assuming identical operating-cost schedules, active mutual-fund management would involve (1) finding and buying (or selling short) undervalued (overvalued) securities, and/or (2) anticipating the movements of the entire market with appropriate shifts in portfolio composition. These concepts are summarized in Sharpe's (1981) equation (18-1) and represent a joint test for superior stock selection and superior market timing. This model was also used in a study of the performance of 57 mutual funds in the United States during the 1953–62 period (Sharpe and Sosin 1974).

In Brazil there have been three attempts at measuring mutual-fund performance: Brito and Neves (1984), Contador (1975), and Vital (1973). Vital (1973) examined the 1968–72 period and found an inferior mutual-fund performance. This result was obtained by comparing the performance of ten mutual funds and four "tax-incentive-based funds" against the IBV (Indice da Bolsa de Valores, that is, the Rio Stock Exchange Index). The author described the method used as an "ex post characteristic line," but since excess returns (returns on a portfolio minus returns on a proxy for a risk-free asset) were not computed, it actually involved estimating market-model parameters. Also, since semiannual data were used, the number of observations for each fund was very small, ranging from only four to at most eight data points per fund.

Contador (1975) studied the 1971–74 period and also obtained evidence of inferior mutual-fund performance. Again, the methodology involved estimating market-model parameters, but in this case the number of observations was more adequate, since weekly data were used. Thirty mutual funds were included in the sample. An attempt was made at measuring "market-timing" ability by employing a regression model with a leading value for the rate of return on the market. No evidence of market-timing ability was found, based on the results of this test.

Brito and Neves (1984) examined the period January 1977 to June 1981. They used monthly data and tested mutual-fund performance with the use of an "ex post characteristic line," that is,

$$R_{p,t} = a_p + b_p R_{m,t} + u_{p,t}, \tag{7.1}$$

where returns were measured in relation to the rates of Brazilian Treasury Bills with 30 days to maturity. Brito and Neves examined the performance of two types of funds: the so-called "mutual funds," or regular stock funds, and "tax-incentive-based funds," called "fundos 157" after the decree that created them in the 1960s. The entire period was divided into two subperiods to evaluate the consistency of performance. Thirty-four regular funds and 32 "fundos 157" were included in their sample. A nonparametric rank correlation test indicated that performance in the subperiods was not consistently superior or inferior. However, one of the more interesting findings was simply reported and not discussed at any significant length. It had to do with their finding of negative alphas (the estimate of the a_p coefficient in equation (7.1) above for all 66 funds in the sample (no standard errors were given for their estimates of that coefficient). In terms of ex post characteristic lines, that would indicate inferior performance by a substantial portion of the mutual-fund industry in Brazil. In addition, with very few exceptions, the fund-portfolio betas were less than unity. This result is not surprising since the industry is regulated and is required to make a minimum investment in treasury securities and/or is not allowed to invest all funds into common or preferred stocks.

METHODOLOGY AND TESTS

As mentioned earlier, our test is based on an "ex post characteristic curve," as proposed in Sharpe (1981) and Sharpe and Sosin (1974):

$$R_{p,t} = a_p + b_p R_{m,t} + c_p (R_{m,t})^2 + u_{p,t}, \qquad (7.2)$$

where R_p and R_m, as in Brito and Neves (1984), are, respectively, excess returns on the portfolio of mutual fund p and a proxy for the market portfolio m, computed after subtracting the rate of return on a treasury security. Given equation (7.2), a_p is a measure of the ability of the management of fund p to spot and purchase or short-sell mispriced securities, b_p indicates the beta of the fund's portfolio in the period, and C_p denotes the fund's ability to forecast the movements of the market. Therefore, for each fund p, we have tried to answer the following questions:

1. Are the estimated values of the a_p coefficient significantly different from zero and positive, looking at the years 1984 and 1985 as different subperiods? That is, is there evidence of superior security selection?

2. Are the estimated values of the c_p coefficient significantly different from zero and positive, again looking at the data for each of the two years? That is, is there evidence of superior market-timing ability?

3. Are the resulting rankings of funds by each of the two coefficients significantly and positively correlated when one compares the two years in our study? That is, is that performance consistent?

4. Are there significant changes in each fund's performance from 1984 to 1985?

In particular, for answering the fourth question, we used the following dummy-variable regression model:

$$R_{p,t} = a_p + a'_{p,t} + b_p R_{m,t} + b'_{p,t} + c_p (R_{m,t})^2 + c'_{p,t} + u_{p,t}, \qquad (7.3)$$

where $a'_{p,t} = 0$ for 1984, 1 for 1985,

$b'_{p,t} = 0$ for 1984, $R_{m,t}$ for 1985, and

$c'_{p,t} = 0$ for 1984, $(R_{m,t})^2$ for 1985.

DATA

As already indicated, the study covers the 1984–85 period. Daily data are used, and for a significant reason. In Brito and Neves (1984) there was a concern with the finding of superior or inferior performance in terms of whether return relative to risk and alpha had been consistent; hence the use of nonparametric correlation tests on rankings in the two subperiods—the January 1977 to June 1981 period was divided into two halves. Clearly, the idea is that superior or inferior portfolio managers or policies, if they exist, should produce systematically superior or inferior performance. However, the longer the period covered, the less likely it becomes that a manager or policy would be maintained, particularly if the funds themselves do not know and/or use appropriate evaluation techniques to identify those successful managers and/or policies that should be retained. Therefore, we opted for using daily data and studying fund performance over a shorter period (two years). While the likelihood of changes of managers or policies is certainly not eliminated, it may be reduced.

Daily data on the value of mutual-fund shares were collected, the source being the São Paulo Stock Exchange's daily report, and $R_{p,t}$ was measured as the daily change in fund share value. As a measure of $R_{m,t}$, we used the daily change in the closing value of the São Paulo Stock Exchange Index, or IBOVESPA. The index is computed as a weighted average of stocks responsible for at least 85 percent of the exchange's volume of trading. It is not a market-value-weighted average but a trading-volume-weighted average. Both rates of return were computed as excess returns, that is, with the subtraction of the rate of return on the secondary market for treasury bonds (the so-called overnight market). A series of such rates is provided to us by Uniao de Bancos Brasileiros S.A. (UNIBANCO).

Sixteen mutual funds ("stock funds") were included in the sample. The results for each fund are presented in the next section of this chapter. Even though they are explicitly defined as "stock funds," government regulation permits that a portion of their resources be invested in treasury securities and other fixed-income assets. In the period covered by our study, those rules underwent some changes. In 1984 mutual funds were required to put at least 40 percent of the amounts not invested in equities in treasury securities, while in 1985 stock funds could invest up to 30 percent of their resources in fixed-income securities.

The aggregate value of the shares of the 16 funds included in this sample was 4.125 billion cruzeiros as of December 20, 1985 (approximately U.S. $395 million at the then-prevailing official exchange rate) and represented 24.48 percent of the net worth of all mutual stock funds in operation in Brazil at the time. Their share of total market capitalization of listed shares, which, for the São Paulo Stock

Exchange, was estimated at U.S. $42.77 billion by the end of 1985, was below 1 percent.

In 1984 and 1985 the market index (IBOVESPA) rose 442.0 percent and 268.4 percent in nominal terms, respectively. Corresponding inflation rates were 223.8 percent and 235.1 percent.

RESULTS

Tables 7.1 and 7.2 present the results obtained for each of the 16 funds for 1984 and 1985, respectively. These results are then used in rank-order correlation tests, whose conclusions are reported. Table 7.3 reports the results for estimating equation (7.3), with special attention to the dummy-variable coefficients as indicators of changes in stock-fund characteristics from 1984 and 1985.

The results reported in tables 7.1 and 7.2 are markedly different from those of other studies of Brazilian mutual-fund performance, particularly in the case of measures of "security selection." For 1984 the estimated a_p coefficients are significantly different from zero and positive for 15 of the 16 funds in the sample and for 1985 this occurs in 13 of the 16 funds. As to "market-timing ability," no surprising results are obtained, with only one fund (CRESCINCO) apparently displaying it in 1984.

All 16 stock funds in this sample were ranked in decreasing order according to their performance both in terms of "security selection" (magnitude of the estimate of the a_p coefficient) and "market timing" (magnitude of the estimate of the c_p coefficient) for each of the two years. Spearman's rho and Kendall's tau rank-order correlation coefficients were then used in an attempt to answer the third of the questions posed in the second section: Was there any consistency of performance from one year to another?

For the measure of "security-selection ability," the correlation coefficients obtained were 0.0824 (Spearman's rho) and 0.1333 (Kendall's tau). Thus we also failed to reject the null hypothesis for this measure.

The results reported in table 7.3 show that significant changes took place in the beta coefficients of only 3 of the 16 funds from 1984 to 1985—2 had lower and 1 had higher level of risk in 1985. No significant changes in performance were found.

Even though the aggregate net worth of stock funds is a small portion of total market capitalization of listed shares, the fact is that the turnover of these shares is very low in Brazil. Furthermore, mutual funds are important players in Brazilian stock exchanges when one considers that less than half of the trading volume is accounted for by transactions of individual investors. Given financial institutions' privileged access to the managements of listed firms, it is possible that their portfolio management divisions are among the first to obtain relevant information that is reflected in superior security selection. This could explain the results obtained in tables 7.1 and 7.2. At any rate, the preceding results which differ from those of previous studies of mutual-fund performance in Brazil and elsewhere, may be seen as giving indirect evidence in support of recommendations for stricter regulation of access to information potentially available from the managers of listed

Table 7.1
Estimation Results for Equation (2), 1984

Fund name	a	b	c		
ALPHA UNIBANCO	0.004377*	0.69797	0.852112	R^2= 0.521178	
	0.001276)	(0.044551)	(0.962002)	n = 231	
BBI BRADESCO	0.004104*	0.381840	.072741	R^2 = 0.363995	
	(0.000997)	(0.034713)	(0.734181)	n = 215	
BESC	0.002129*	0.464424	1.016109	R^2 = 0.632601	
	(0.001031)	(0.037908)	(0.621583)	n = 92	
BOZANO SIMONSEN	0.004921*	0.572330	.058646	R^2 = 0.494915	
	(0.001264)	(0.046285)	(0.961906)	n = 162	
CREFISUL	0.005079*	0.539460	.482418	R^2 = 0.545226	
	(0.000900)	(0.032010)	(0.691771)	n = 240	
CRESCINCO	0.004462*	0.533800	2.027677	R2 = 0.480220	
	(0.001067)	(0.038475)	(0.815738)	n = 222	
DENASA-MINERACAO	0.004354*	0.513040	.070996	R2 = 0.389445	
	(0.001194)	(0.042396)	(0.908703)	n = 23	
GARABNTIA	0.006241*	0.804074	0.950266	R2 = 0.701113	
	(0.002767)	(0.083224)	(2.236397)	n = 43	
GERAL DO COMERCI	0.001110	.616351	0.486928	R2 = 0.463757	
	(0.001253)	(0.044004)	(0.947684)	n = 232	
LONDON MULTIPLIC	0.005200*	0.331130	.424284	R2 = 0.513482	
	(0.000601)	(0.021161)	(0.456741)	n = 235	
MERCANTIL	0.003621*	0.629761	0.862940	R2 = 0.620366	
	(0.000983)	(0.034330)	(0.728958)	n = 210	
MERKINVEST	0.004816*	0.519134	0.216277	R2 = 0.494815	
	(0.000971)	(0.035532)	(0.756286)	n = 221	
PRIME	0.004419*	0.805870	.747733	R2 = 0.641811	
	(0.001136)	(0.040316)	(0.859238)	n = 226	
REAL	0.004074*	0.417366	0.344708	R2 = 0.339735	
	(0.001210)	(0.043657)	(1.126702)	n = 195	
SAFRA	0.003283*	0.639837	1.494452	R2 = 0.546844	
	(0.001079)	(0.038376)	(0.829348)	n = 240	
UNIBANCO	0.004710*	0.458339	0.328356	R2 = 0.433913	
	(0.000993)	(0.034940)	(0.750348)	n = 229	

* Significantly different from zero at the 1% significance level.

** Significantly different from zero at the 5% significance level.

Table 7.2
Estimation Results for Equation (2), 1985

Fund name	a	b	c	R²	n
ALPHA UNIBANCO	0.003819*	0.580720	0.426650	0.581056	
	(0.001251)	(0.033792)	(0.707057)		224
BBI BRADESCO	0.005386*	0.450850	0.092829	0.467042	
	(0.001222)	(0.033122)	(0.708946)		217
BESC	-0.00315	0.654244	2.445550	0.061485	
	(0.008089)	(0.206791)	(4.808795)		159
BOZANO SIMONSEN	0.005090*	0.469621	1.150679	0.340574	
	(0.001675)	(0.046561)	(1.039104)		202
CREFISUL	0.004716	0.631253	0.073755	0.302748	
	(0.002414)	(0.064509)	(1.369008)		230
CRESCINCO	0.004835*	0.595960	0.0064466	0.550860	
	(0.001357)	(0.036350)	(0.767927)		228
DENASA-MINERACAO	0.006953*	0.434080	0.404706	0.451498	
	(0.001302)	(0.034124)	(0.710667)		201
GARANTIA	0.005319*	0.729770	0.356363	0.619757	
	(0.001706)	(0.045019)	(0.983894)		167
GERAL DO COMERCI	0.001969	0.614197	0.530475	0.529835	
	(0.001553)	(0.046197)	(1.046551)		177
LONDON MULTIPLIC	0.005546*	0.357791	0.569627	0.518343	
	(0.000889)	(0.023886)	(0.500648)		223
MERCANTIL	0.006250*	0.621960	0.646121	0.410140	
	(0.001893)	(0.052026)	(1.072039)		209
MERKINVEST	0.005087*	0.405730	0.088983	0.363306	
	(0.001418)	(0.037546)	(0.784038)		212
PRIME	0.005161*	0.709930	0.543686	0.568328	
	(0.001538)	(0.041516)	(0.873725)		228
REAL	0.006166*	0.484340	0.065747	0.419162	
	(0.001511)	(0.040352)	(0.897205)		205
SAFRA	0.005286*	0.540720	0.352776	0.445398	
	(0.001501)	(0.040237)	(0.854942)		232
UNIBANCO	0.004914*	0.586822	0.288901	0.544118	
	(0.001361)	(0.036463)	(0.770319)		228

* Significantly different from zero at the 1% significance level.

** Significantly different from zero at the 5% significance level.

Table 7.3
Estimation Results for Equation (3): Changes from 1984 to 1985

Fund name	a	b	c	R^2	n
UNIBANCO	-0.000559	0.11	-0.425462	0.550892	
	(0.001792)	(0.055526)	(1.184161)		455
BBI BRADESCO	0.001289	0.069008	0.020088	0.428925	
	(0.001573)	(0.048764)	(1.036331)		432
BESC	-0.005280	0.189820	1.429442	0.072357	
	(0.009917)	(0.321997)	(5.943997)		251
BOZANO SIMONSEN	0.000160	0.102716	0.092033	0.394923	
	(0.002151)	(0.070364)	(1.500378)		364
CREFISUL	-0.000360	0.091786	0.556173	0.352657	
	(0.002489)	(0.077470)	(1.662328)		470
CRESCINCO	0.000378	0.062162	0.092143	0.525249	
	(0.001721)	(0.054298)	(1.149677)		450
DENASA-MINERACAO	0.002600	0.078960	0.333709	0.419121	
	(0.001774)	(0.054316)	(1.150727)		434
GARANTIA	-0.000920	0.074300	0.306629	0.634074	
	(0.003687)	(0.108311)	(2.830045)		210
GERAL DO COMERCI	0.000850	0.002181	0.043547	0.495828	
	(0.001986)	(0.063661)	(1.407815)		409
LONDON MULTIPLIC	0.000340	0.026659	0.993911	0.517448	
	(0.001056)	(0.032775)	(0.699243)		458
MERCANTIL	0.002620	0.007797	0.509061	0.476378	
	(0.002108)	(0.065914)	(1.383107)		419
MERKINVEST	0.000270	0.113400	0.305260	0.418714	
	(0.001691)	(0.053377)	(1.127953)		433
PRIME	0.000740	0.095939	0.204047	0.598890	
	(0.001902)	(0.059589)	(1.263825)		454
REAL	0.000200	0.055970	0.410455	0.392465	
	(0.001941)	(0.061590)	(1.515145)		400
SAFRA	0.002000	0.099115	0.847229	0.489029	
	(0.001829)	(0.057015)	(1.224019)		472
UNIBANCO	0.000200	0.128480	0.039455	0.508608	
	(0.001673)	(0.051920)	(1.107920)		457

* Significantly different from zero at the 1% significance level.

** Significantly different from zero at the 5% significance level.

firms, and even for enforcing greater independence between the management of portfolios in the mutual-fund industry and the operations of other types of financial intermediaries in Brazil.

REFERENCES

Brito, N. R. O. de, and Neves, A. R. M. (1984). "O Desempenho Recente de Fundos de Investimento." *Revista Brasileira de Mercado de Capitais* 10, no. 31 (July–September).

Contador, C. (1975). *Os Investidores Institucionais no Brasil*. Rio de Janeiro: Instituto Brasileiro de Mercado de Capitais.

Jensen, M. C. (1968). "The Performance of Mutual Funds in the Period 1945–64." *Journal of Finance* 23, no. 2 (May): 389–416.

Sharpe, W. F. (1966). "Mutual Fund Performance." *Journal of Business* 39 no. 1 (January): 119–138.

———. (1981). *Investments*. 2nd ed. Englewood Cliffs, N.J.: Prentice-Hall.

Sharpe, W. F., and H. B. Sosin. (1975). "Closed-end Investment Companies in the United States: Risk and Return." In *Proceedings, 1974 Meeting of the European Finance Association*, ed. Bernard Jacquillat. Amsterdam: North-Holland.

Treynor, J. (1965). "How to Rate the Management of Investment Funds." *Harvard Business Review* 43 (January): 63–75.

Vital, S. M. (1973). "Fundos de Investimento—Medida de Seu Desempenho." *Revista Brasileira de Economia* 27, no. 3 (September).

p 125: ## Discussant: Martin Laurence

This chapter sheds some light on Brazilian mutual funds' investment performance and institutional characteristics. Since little is known about this particular emerging capital market, the chapter adds to our knowledge.

The authors' review of three prior studies of Brazilian mutual-fund performance, each of which covered different earlier time periods, puts into perspective the state of Brazilian research on the topic. While two of the three previous investigations had substantially larger samples of funds and all covered longer time periods, the authors assert that some suffered from weak methodologies and inadequate numbers of return observations over long holding periods. Despite findings of inferior performance in all three foregoing studies, the authors seem skeptical. They contend that mutual funds' managements have "inside information" and should be able to outperform the market.

OBJECTIVES AND FINDINGS

Using daily return observations, the authors set the objective for themselves of looking for (1) evidence of superior asset (stock and fixed-income) selection and (2) evidence of superior timing (market) ability. They state that they found (1) superior asset selection during the period studied (1984–85), but (2) no evidence of superior timing ability.

The evidence they provide is based on regression coefficients only:

1. Mostly statistically significant alphas
2. Low betas ranging from 0.33 to 0.81
3. Timing coefficients, mostly nonsignificant
4. R-squares ranging from 0.34 to 0.70, with approximately half less than 0.5 and half greater than 0.5
5. Changes in these coefficients mostly nonsignificant from 1984 to 1985

METHODOLOGY

Alphas

Are alphas just the "garbage-can" effect of omitted variables or nonmarket risk? We really do not know whether alpha is a good measure of superior ability to select stocks or is simply a kind of "residual" or nonmarket risk and return measure.

Betas and R-Squares

The relatively low betas combined with low R-squares also tend to suggest large amounts of nonmarket risk. Furthermore, no information about the funds' objectives is given. For investors with other investments, these low beta portfolios may fulfill a need. But what about investors that have all their funds in one of these portfolios (funds)? If the measured betas are correct, they have not been provided with a well-diversified portfolio.

Characteristic Line and Market Index

The authors used the characteristic line to obtain the alphas and betas. Their proxy for the market (market index) was the São Paulo Stock Market Index. It seems inappropriate to use an all-equity index to develop characteristic lines for these portfolios that the chapter tells us consist of both fixed-income securities and equities. What is required is an index that incorporates all assets. Indeed, we may then find that the "true" performance of these portfolios (funds) was inferior. A proper market index should cause the characteristic line for each portfolio (fund) to rotate around the origin and have a slope either greater than, less than, or equal to the market index for all-equity portfolios when an all-equity index is used; likewise, both the index and the funds should have alphas approximately equal to zero.

The low betas combined with the low R-squares may reflect only the fact that the fixed-income securities are providing returns at times when the equity market is not. In other words, these are all conservative portfolios (relative to pure equities); aggressive portfolios would have provided high returns when the equity market's returns exceeded the interest rate. If 1984–85 was a time period when equity returns in general were lower than interest rates, the significant positive alphas may merely reflect that. The authors do not tell us whether that was the case in Brazil in 1984–85.

Possible Improvements

One possible improvement would be to design a market index of "passive" portfolio with characteristics similar to those of the individual funds, that is, fixed-income securities and equities in approximately the same proportions and having the same beta. Then this index (or perhaps several indices) could be used to generate alphas that are measures of average differential returns, that is, of superior performance.

A second improvement would be to use single-value measures instead of regression coefficients, for example:

Jensen's alpha: $R_p - R_f = J_p + B_p(R_I - R_f)$

Sharpe's total risk: $(R_p - R_f)/SD_p$

Treynor's market risk: $(R_p - R_f)/\beta_p$

These measures will provide evidence not only about nonmarket risk and return (Jensen's alpha), but also return adjusted for total risk for the nondiversified investor (Sharpe) and market risk-adjusted return for the diversified investor.

This chapter would also gain by reporting

1. percentage of fixed-income securities versus equities in each portfolio;
2. how returns (especially on fixed-income securities) were calculated;
3. any inflation-indexing effects that might possibly affect the reported returns, indexes, and other data;
4. total portfolio returns and standard deviations;
5. market returns (i.e., what did the equity market return (daily) during the study period and subperiods?);
6. risk-free rates of return, that is, T-bill rates during the study period.

Note that alpha is a positive function of the risk-free rate and a negative function of beta. This means that if the T-bill rate in Brazil was high (real rate) and the actual betas were low, high alphas would be expected.

Finally, superior methodologies exist to separate security-selection performance from fund-management market-timing activities. One methodology essentially isolates excess returns derived during "bear" markets from excess returns derived during "bull" markets. (See, for example, R. S. Henriksson and R. C. Merton, "On Market Timing and Investment Performance: Statistical Procedures for Evaluating Forecasting Skills," *Journal of Business*, October 1981.)

This chapter gives us a glimpse into mutual-fund performance in Brazil. With some methodological and data improvements it could reveal much more information and further contribute to our understanding of one more emerging capital market. Furthermore, policymakers, investors, and investment professionals in Brazil would certainly find it useful.

8

Market-Efficiency (Weak-Form) Tests of the Malaysian Stock Exchange

OTHMAN YONG

The stock-price behavior of the United States and Japan has been known to conform to the weak form of the efficient market hypothesis (EMH). The weak form of the EMH implies that the past history of prices cannot provide information that can be used to predict their movements in the future. According to the weak form of the EMH, stock prices are assumed to reflect all information that may be contained in the past history of the stock itself. Since the information itself is random, the stock-price movements should therefore be random.

Interest in the weak form of the EMH of small stock markets outside the United States has rapidly increased since Fama published his work in 1965 on the 30 stocks comprising the Dow Jones Industrial Average. Solnik (1973) did a study on European stocks; Conrad and Juttner (1973), on the behavior of stocks in Germany; Jennergren and Korsvold (1975), on Norwegian and Swedish stocks; Ang and Pohlman (1978), on Far Eastern stocks; and D'Ambrosio (1980), on Singaporean stocks. the findings were mixed, but most studies concluded that non-U.S. markets do deviate from the weak form of the EMH.

Nassir Lanjong (1983), Laurence (1986), and Barnes (1986) concluded that despite being a small and thinly traded market, the Malaysian stock market, surprisingly, is quite efficient in the weak sense of the EMH. Neoh Soon Kean (1985) suggested that the market is quite efficient in the weak form but not in the semistrong form. These studies, however, are not extensive enough and are not sufficiently representative of the market. Laurence (1986) used daily data of the 16 most active industrial stocks traded from June 1, 1973, to December 31, 1978, and Barnes (1986) used monthly data of the 30 most active stocks traded for the six years ended June 30, 1980, whereas many Malaysian stocks are not actively traded. Nassir Lanjong (1983) used monthly data of 104 stocks traded from January 1974 to June 1980, and Neoh Soon Kean (1985) used monthly data of 78 stocks for the period 1968 to 1983.

This chapter will explore the behavior of Malaysian stocks and the conformity of the Malaysian stock market to the weak form of the EMH. It will also examine in more detail the nature of the price changes using statistical measures such as mean, standard deviation, skewness, and kurtosis. The various tests to be performed will answer some questions relating to the statistical aspects of the random-walk model. The test results will also enable us to examine certain characteristics of the stock market in Malaysia and to provide some possible explanations. The summarized findings of the study on all 170 stocks traded from January 1977 to May 1985 inclusive will be presented, followed by a more detailed report on 30 stocks selected randomly from a pool of stocks comprising the Kuala Lumpur Stock Exchange Industrial Index and the *New Straits Times* Industrial Index. Possible explanations and implications of the findings will be discussed, and suggestions will be made to remedy the inefficiency that exists.

THE KUALA LUMPUR STOCK EXCHANGE

The securities industry in Malaysia began in the late nineteenth century as an extension of the British corporate presence in the rubber and tin industries. However, the first formal organization was established with the formation of the Singapore Stockbrokers' Association on June 23, 1930. This association was registered under the name of Malaya Stockbrokers' Association in 1938 and enjoyed moderately successful operations until the outbreak of World War II.

When the war ended in 1945, the association reestablished business. From 1946 to 1959 activity increased, but there was still no public trading of shares. The association was reregistered under the name of Malayan Stockbrokers' Association in July 1959 and changed its name to Malayan Stock Exchange on March 21, 1960. Also on this date the Malayan Stock Exchange was constituted. Public trading of shares started on May 9, 1960, when four stockbrokers gathered together in the clearinghouse of the Central Bank to mark prices. Clerical assistance and telephone facilities were provided by the Central Bank.

In November 1960 the Malayan Stock Exchange introduced the Trading Post System, under which trading became centralized. Additionally, the trading rooms in Kuala Lumpur and Singapore became more closely linked through the direct telephone or open-cry system. This link eliminated arbitraging, integrating the two trading rooms into a single market with the same stocks and shares listed at a single set of prices on both boards. By 1962 there were 20 stockbrokerage firms in both countries—10 in Singapore, 5 in Kuala Lumpur, 3 in Penang, and 2 in Ipoh. In November of the same year, the 33-year rule barring new brokers from membership was lifted. Membership was also extended to other states in Malaysia.

In an attempt to instill public confidence in the development of the market, a board was established in the exchange in 1963 to consider applications for new listings and to determine listing requirements. Toward the end of 1963, through an informal arrangement among the Central Bank, the Malayan Stock Exchange, and the Registrar of Companies, companies that intended to make public offers were requested to consult with the Central Bank prior to publicizing the terms of the issues.

On June 6, 1964, the Stock Exchange of Malaysia was formed. The operations of the exchange were strengthened in the same year with the adoption of new rules and bylaws, the creation of a fidelity fund, and the implementation of stricter listing requirements. In August 1965 the stock exchange became known as the Stock Exchange of Malaysia and Singapore.

To provide for a more comprehensive legal framework in supervising the operations of companies in the country, the Companies Act, 1965, came into force. the provisions of the act obliged companies to disclose more information to protect the investing public and promote the growth of a well-informed and discriminating body of investors. Given the new institutional and legal framework, the informal arrangements set up in 1963 among the Central Bank, the exchange, and the Registrar of Companies in guiding the development of the stock market were formalized in 1968 with the establishment of the Capital Issues Committee (CIC).

The most significant development in the stock market in 1973 was the announcement on May 8 of the preparations for the splitting of the Stock Exchange of Malaysia and Singapore and the establishment of a separate Malaysian stock exchange. This decision was taken because of the overriding need to develop a strong and healthy national capital market that could be closely identified with the country's overall objectives and development priorities. The split was also opportune in view of the termination of the currency-interchangeability arrangements between Malaysia and Singapore in May 1973, the rapid growth of a large and fairly diversified number of Malaysian incorporated companies whose shares were listed on the stock exchange, and the expansion and strengthening of financial institutions in Malaysia, including a growing body of stockbrokers. Another significant development was the enactment in June of the Securities Industry Act, 1973. This act provided for regulation of the securities industry aimed at protecting the interest of investors. It provided the government with powers to curb excessive speculation, insider trading, share rigging, and other forms of market manipulation. Also included were provisions for the licensing of dealers.

The Kuala Lumpur Stock Exchange Berhad was established on July 2, 1973, operating under provisional rules, bylaws, listing requirements, and a corporate disclosure policy. February 1974 saw the establishment of the Foreign Investment Committee (FIC).

As mentioned before, the Securities Industry Act (SIA) was formulated in June 1973 and given royal assent. Thus the Kuala Lumpur Stock Exchange Berhad was incorporated under the SIA, 1973, and the Companies Act, 1965. When the SIA was finally brought into force on December 27, 1976, a new company called the Kuala Lumpur Stock Exchange (KLSE), limited by guarantee, without a share capital, officially took over from the Kuala Lumpur Stock Exchange Berhad on the same day.

The KLSE experienced a boom period from September 1980 to July 1981. Since then, the KLSE has made advances in terms of computerization. The Data Processing Department was set up in May 1982 to establish a computerized clearinghouse for the industry. An IBM 43/41 was installed to start this process of computerization. The first "Daily Business Done Report" was published on February 7, 1983, and since then information dissemination has been an important area for further improvement. By November 1983 computerized clearing was initiated with 20 selected counters. Currently, SCANS (the Securities Clearing Automated Network Sendirian Berhad) takes care of the entire clearing and settlement system.

To provide for a more orderly conduct of the securities business in the country, the Securities Industry Act was revamped and amended in March 1983. This new act came into force in July 1983, replacing the SIA 1973. The new act incorporated up-to-date legislation providing for more effective supervision and control of the securities industry, mainly for the protection of investors, by regulating the operations of the dealers prohibiting artificial trading and market rigging, and empowering the minister of finance to amend the rules of the stock exchange. The status of the CIC was legally formalized in this new act.

During the next three years, the corporate securities market was dominated by bearish sentiment. Public pressure for the authorities to take steps to revive the KLSE was met by a review of the market that led to a number of changes. On the regulatory front, a major move was made to corporatize the stockbrokerage industry, the objective of which was to improve its financial strength, inject expertise and professionalism, and generate greater international interest in the KLSE. Initially, Malaysian corporate ownership was limited to only a 60 percent stake, but the allowed stake was increased to 100 percent in 1987. Foreign corporate ownership was limited to not more than 30 percent, but this limit was increased to 49 percent in July 1988.

To further promote efficiency in the market, the CIC made its set of guidelines more transparent to the public with its formal announcement of the guidelines in April 1986. The guidelines stated in clear terms the CIC criteria and standards for compliance by the public companies. Since then, the CIC has further clarified and strengthened the guidelines. The Malaysian Code on Takeovers and Mergers, 1987, came into force on April 1, 1987. It provides that the Panel on Takeovers and Mergers (which was established in May 1986) ensure that all takeovers are conducted in an orderly manner and that it protect the interest of minority shareholders.

To ensure proper development of the stock market, the Central Bank introduced a "Code of Ethics: Guidelines on Share Trading" for compliance by commercial and merchant banks. The guidelines are directed particularly to the merchant banks, which, as corporate advisers or underwriters for share issues, are privy to inside financial information of the companies concerned. These guidelines are designed to prevent any occurrence of grey-market and insider trading. Beginning from March 1989, the financial institutions are required to submit to the Central Bank quarterly reports on all breaches observed during the period and action taken against them. To complement these measures by the government, the KLSE itself has effected various changes and improvements. Among these was the implementation of the first phase of a computerized share scrips (stock certificates) clearing system in November 1983. The entire clearing system was fully computerized by March 1984. This was followed by the installation of the real-time share-price reporting system (MASA) for brokers in 1987. The Research Institute of Investment Analysts Malaysia (RIIAM) was formed in May 1985 to help the industry raise its level of security analysis and research. In 1986 the exchange's new composite index (KLSE CI) was launched.

The Advance Warning and Surveillance Unit (AWAS) was formed to alert the KLSE of stockbroking houses and public-listed companies facing problems, and in July 1987 the exchange introduced its new "Listing Manual" with an entirely new section on corporate disclosure policies and penalties. The listing of property trust was permitted effective April 15, 1989. On November 11, 1988, the KLSE also launched its second board to enable smaller companies that are viable and have strong growth potential to tap additional capital from the market through a listing on the KLSE.

Prior to the introduction of SCORE (System on Computerized Order Routing and Execution) in May 1989, the actual trading was carried out on the trading floor by authorized trading-room clerks. They were employees of each of the 50 member firms and member companies but were trained by the KLSE before they were authorized to trade. The trading clerks received orders to buy and sell through the direct telephone system provided, which linked them to their respective brokerage firms. Orders to buy and sell were called in to the board and were recorded by the KLSE posting clerks on the boards for all to see. Only the highest bid (buyer's price) and the lowest offer (seller's price) were recorded on the trading board. Each transaction was recorded on trading-room slips that were sorted out at the end of the day, and one copy was forwarded to SCANS. Once the transacted slips were passed to SCANS, they were entered into the data-entry terminals. From there they were transferred to the IBM 43/41 processor. The computer operated on a 24-hour basis and produced a reel by early the next day that carried all the necessary data regarding debiting and crediting of each broker's account with the clearing bank. The transacted "scrips" (stock certificates) were physically delivered or collected by a team of couriers who travelled all over Malaysia each day.

On May 15, 1989, the exchange took a leap into the technological age with the introduction of its new semiautomated trading system, SCORE. The conversion of trading from the open cry to an electronic system has tremendously improved the speed of transactions and also the volume.

Beginning on January 1, 1990, all Malaysian-incorporated companies were no longer allowed to be traded on the Singapore Stock Exchange. At the same time, no Singapore-incorporated companies were allowed to be traded on the Kuala Lumpur Stock Exchange. This split was viewed as an effort from the Malaysian side to become a totally independent stock exchange, separate from its neighbor.

In terms of size (based on market capitalization), as shown in table 8.1, the Malaysian stock market is ranked higher than the more established Singapore stock market and other emerging stock markets of Bangkok, Manila, and Jakarta in the

Table 8.1
Comparative Size (in Terms of Market
Capitalization) of Selected Stock Markets
in the World

Stock Market	Market Capitalization (Billions of U.S. Dollars)
Tokyo	$3,225
New York	3,208
London	867
Frankfurt	396
Paris	339
Taipei	159
Sydney	130
Seoul	124
Kuala Lumpur	49
Singapore	39
Bangkok	28
Manila	8
Jakarta	5

Source: ASIAWEEK Magazine, August 17, 1990, p.14.

Southeast Asian region. The Malaysian stock market, with its market capitalization of U.S. $49 billion, is only about 1.5 percent of the size of the New York stock market (market capitalization of U.S. $3,208 billion), about 5.6 percent of the size of the London stock market (market capitalization of U.S. $867 billion), and about 37.7 percent of the size of the Sydney stock market (market capitalization of U.S. $130 billion).

THE DATA

The data used in this study were the weekly closing prices of all 170 stocks traded on the KLSE from January 1977 to May 1985 inclusive. The 30 stocks chosen for detailed reporting were selected randomly from a pool of stocks listed in the KLSE Industrial Index and the *New Straits Times* Industrial Index. It should be noted that there are 30 stocks listed in each of these indices. These indices are widely referred to in Malaysia and are considered to be quite representative of the market. Closing prices were Friday's prices, and in case Friday was a holiday, the previously available trading price during the week was used. This study was conducted beginning in January 1977 in conjunction with the beginning of the current administrator of the Malaysian stock exchange, a company by the name of Kuala Lumpur Stock Exchange, taking over the management of the stock exchange from its predecessor, Kuala Lumpur Stock Exchange Berhad.

Heinkel and Kraus (1988) mentioned three possible alternatives in dealing with days (or weeks) with no transaction (or trading). One possibility is to ignore the days with no trading and use only return data for trading days. A second approach is to assign zero return for days with no trading. The third approach is to construct a linear model that can be used to estimate the "true" return for the day with no return, based on the assumption that prices change when there is information, regardless of whether or not there is trading. In this study, the second approach was followed for several reasons. First, it is not appropriate to ignore the weeks with no trading, since nontrading is a characteristic of a thinly traded market. Furthermore, by ignoring the nontrading weeks, the statistical analysis, as in the runs test, might conclude that the market is efficient (in the weak sese) even though in reality it might not be. Second, if a linear model is employed to fill in the missing observations, the values used are not the actual ones, but rather the estimates. Finally, assigning zero return to the week with no trading will at least reflect the actual return during that particular week. It should be noted here that the reason weekly closing prices were chosen over daily prices was to ensure that the percentage of nontrading observations included in this study would be reduced considerably. Furthermore, a week was dropped only if a stock was suspended from trading (for whatever reason), because, unlike the case of no transaction, which reflects an inactive market for the stock, suspension is an administrative matter in which no trading is allowed.

The stock prices were corrected for capital adjustments (splits, stock dividends, and rights). No adjustment was made regarding dividends, even though in the United States it is believed that on the ex-dividend date the price of a stock will fall by approximately the amount of the dividend. In Malaysia dividends accruing to an investor are taxable, but not capital gains realized from price appreciation. One would therefore not expect the price to fall exactly by the amount of the dividend declared. this omission, however, is not likely to produce any distortion in the results, as mentioned by Fama (1965). The corrected prices were then transformed into percentage price changes, as opposed to prior studies, which used log changes as a proxy for percentage changes. Osborne (1959) pointed out that the log changes only approximate percentage changes of less than plus or minus 15 percent, whereas some stocks used in this study exhibited changes greater than plus or minus 15 percent. The percentage change in stock price was used instead of the actual price of a stock because the percentage change in the stock price reflects the return to an investor. That is, an investor is more concerned about the return given by a stock than its actual price.

THE HYPOTHESES

Three main null hypotheses were tested:

1. The population correlation coefficients of successive price changes at all lags 1 through *k* are zero.
2. Percentage changes in stock prices are random.
3. Percentage price changes follow a normal distribution.

The first hypothesis was aimed at testing the independent nature of the successive percentage changes in the stock prices. The second hypothesis was aimed at testing the randomness (absence of trends) of percentage changes in stock prices. The third hypothesis was aimed at testing the distributional nature of the percentage changes in stock pries. In addition, the null hypothesis that states that the efficiency of the market is independent of continuity in trading was also tested, since discontinuity in trading (by suspension of trading) was a common occurrence in the Malaysian stock market during the period of the study. This tested Solnik's contention (1973) that discontinuity in trading does contribute to the inefficiency of a stock market.

STATISTICAL TESTS

Q-Statistic Test

An overall test for a flat serial correlation function is carried out using the Q-statistic (see Cornell and Dietrich 1978). Let the serial correlation at lag *j* be

$$r_j = \frac{cov(Z_t, Z_{t+j})}{var(Z_t)}, \tag{8.1}$$

where Z_t and Z_{t+j} are percentage changes at time *t* and time *t + j*, respectively. The standard error of the serial correlation (see Pankratz 1983, pp. 68–70) is given by

$$\left[1 + 2\sum_{j=1}^{k-1} r_j^2 \right]^{1/2} n^{-1/2}, \tag{8.2}$$

where r_j is the serial correlation at lag *j* and *n* is the number of observations. Most prior studies used an approximation formula $S(r_k) = [1/(N-k)]^{1/2}$.

Under the null hypothesis that all serial correlations are zero,

$$Q = N\sum_{j=1}^{k} r_j^2, \text{ where } N = \text{number of observations}, \tag{8.3}$$

is distributed as chi-square with k degrees of freedom. The null hypothesis is rejected if Q is greater than chi-square with k degrees of freedom at the corresponding 5 percent level of significance and 1 percent level of significance.

Runs Test

A run is defined as a sequence of percentage price changes of the same sign. For example, "+++ – – – – 000++" would constitute four runs, where "+" represents an increase in the percentage change of a stock price, "0" represents no price change, and "–" represents a decrease.

The expected number of runs, $E(R)$, was calculated as follows:

$$E(R) = \frac{\left[N(N+1) - \sum_{i=1}^{3} n_i^2 \right]}{N},$$ (8.4)

where n_i = number of percentage price changes for each sign and

N = total number of percentage price changes.

The standard error of runs, $S(r)$, was computed as follows:

$$S(r) = \left\{ \frac{\sum_{i=1}^{3} n_i^2 \left[\sum_{i=1}^{3} n_i^2 + N(N+1) \right] - 2N \sum_{i=1}^{3} n_i^3 - N^3}{N^2(N-1)} \right\}^{1/2},$$ (8.5)

where N and n_i are defined as in equation (8.4). Most prior studies also used this approach regarding runs tests. This approach to runs tests was introduced by Wallis and Roberts (1956, pp. 569–572).

The null hypothesis that states that the percentage changes are random was tested using the formula

$$Z\text{–(observed)} = [R - E(R) \pm 1/2]/S(r),$$ (8.6)

where R = actual number of runs,

$E(R)$ = expected number of runs,

$S(r)$ = sample standard error for number of runs, and

1/2 is the correction factor for continuity adjustment, in which the sign of the continuity adjustment is plus if $R \le E(R)$ and minus otherwise.

The null hypothesis that states that the percentage changes in stock prices are random is accepted if Z-(observed) is within plus or minus 1.96 at the 5 percent level of significance, or within plus or minus 2.576 at the 1 percent level of significance.

Test for Normal Distribution

When the Kolmogorov-Smirnov one-sample goodness-of-fit test is applied, the focus is on two cumulative distribution functions: a hypothesized cumulative distribution $(F_0(x))$ and the observed cumulative distribution $(F(x))$. Suppose that a random sample $S(x)$ is drawn from an unknown distribution function $F(x)$. If $F(x) = F_0(x)$, a close agreement between $F_0(x)$ and $S(x)$ can be expected. The objective of the Kolmogorov-Smirnov one-sample goodness-of-fit test is to determine whether the lack of agreement between $F_0(x)$ and $S(x)$ is sufficient to cast doubt on the null hypothesis that $F(x) = F_0(x)$.

Let x be the percentage change in stock prices. Then $S(x)$ equals the proportion of sample observations less than or equal to x. The test statistic

$$D = \sup_{\text{all } x} [S(x) - F_0(x)], \tag{8.7}$$

which is read "D equals the supremum, over all x, of the absolute value of the difference $S(x) - F_0(x)$." If the two functions are represented graphically, D is the greatest vertical distance between $S(x)$ and $F(x)$.

The null hypothesis, which states that the cumulative probability distribution of the percentage changes in stock price is normal, is rejected if $D > 1.36/N^{1/2}$ at the 5 percent level of significance, or if $D > 1.63/N^{1/2}$ at the 1 percent level of significance (see Daniel 1978, pp. 267–276). This null hypothesis can also be tested (as proposed by the SPSS-X procedures) using the formula

$$Z-(\text{observed}) = D(1/n)^{-1/2}. \tag{8.8}$$

The null hypothesis is accepted if Z-(observed) is within plus or minus 1.96 at the 5 percent level of significance, or within plus or minus 2.576 at the 1 percent level of significance.

Spearman Rank Correlation Test

The Spearman rank correlation coefficient was used to test the relationship between continuity in trading and the efficiency of the market. From the Q-statistic test, the stock with the highest Q-value was ranked lowest in efficiency. From the runs test, the stock with the highest absolute value of Z-(observed) was ranked lowest in efficiency. The number of trading weeks without suspension was assumed to correspond to continuity in trading. The stock with the lowest number of trading weeks was ranked lowest for continuity in trading.

The Spearman rank correlation coefficient (see Miller 1981) was calculated as follows:

$$r_s = 1 - \frac{6 \Sigma d_i^2}{n(n^2 - 1)}, \tag{8.9}$$

where d_i is the difference between efficiency ranking and continuity ranking, and n is the number of stocks in each sector of the Malaysian Stock Exchange. The null hypothesis, which states that the efficiency is independent of the continuity in trading, was tested using the formula

$$t\text{-(observed)} = \frac{r_s}{[(1 - r_s^2)/(n - 2)]^{\frac{1}{2}}}. \tag{8.10}$$

The null hypothesis is accepted if t-(observed) is within plus or minus t-table value with n - 2 degrees of freedom at the corresponding 5 percent and 1 percent levels of significance. For n greater than 30 the t-distribution is approximated by the Z-distribution, and thus the null hypothesis is accepted if the t-value is within plus or minus 1.96 at the 5 percent significance level and within plus or minus 2.576 at the 1 percent significance level.

STATISTICAL MEASURES OF THE DISTRIBUTION

Let r_i be the percentage price change for a stock at time period i, P_i be the probability of r_i, and $E(r)$ be the expected mean for r_i. Then we can discuss these variables in terms of four different statistical moments. The first moment, $M_1 = \Sigma p_i[r_i - E(r)]$, is always equivalent to zero. The expected mean, $E(r)$, is equivalent to $\Sigma p_i r_i$. The second moment, $M_2 = \Sigma p_i[r_i - E(r)]^2$, which is another name for variance, measures the distribution's dispersion or wideness. Its square root is the standard deviation, which measures the variability of price changes.

The third moment, $M_3 = \Sigma p_i[r_i - E(r)]^3$, measures the lopsidedness of the distribution. It is normalized by dividing it by the standard deviation cubed. This puts the third moments of different distributions in terms of a relative measure of lopsidedness called "skewness," $sk(r) = M_3/\sigma^3$.

The fourth moment, $M_4 = \Sigma p_i[r_i - E(r)]^4$, measures the peakedness of a probability distribution. The measure of kurtosis is normalized using the formula M_4/σ^4. In the SPSS-X procedure, the formula of kurtosis is modified to $[M_4/\sigma^4] - 3$. Under this procedure, a distribution is normal if the kurtosis is zero; leptokurtic, if kurtosis is greater than zero; and platykurtic, if kurtosis is less than zero. A leptokurtic distribution is more peaked than a normal distribution. It also tends to have more observation spread in the extreme tails than does a normal distribution. A platykurtic distribution has observations cluster less around a central point than a normal distribution; that is, it is flatter than a normal distribution.

A well-known statistical package, SPSS-X, was used to provide some statistical measures that describe the distributions of the weekly price changes. These measures are mean, median, mode, standard deviation, skewness, kurtosis, maximum value, and minimum value.

Table 8.2
Number and Percentage of Stocks for Each Stock Classification
Used in the Study

Stock Classification	Number of Stocks	Percentage of Stocks
Industrial	90	52.9
Finance	11	6.5
Hotel	10	5.9
Property	10	5.9
Plantation	32	18.8
Tin	17	10.0
Total	170	100.0

FINDINGS

The number and percentage of stocks used in this study for each stock classification are shown in table 8.2. These stocks met the requirement that they were traded on a weekly basis from January 1977 to May 1985 inclusive.

Q-Statistics and Serial Correlations

A serial correlation test was conducted to determine the dependency between the percentage price change at time t and the percentage price change at time $t + k$ for $k = 1, 2, 3, \ldots, 8$. Lags 1 through 8 were chosen in accordance with Cornell and Dietrich (1978), whereas Fama (1965) used lags 1 through 10. Percentage price changes are independent of each other if the serial correlation coefficient is zero. The number and percentage of stocks within each stock classification that have serial correlation coefficients significantly nonzero at the 5 percent and 1 percent levels for lags 1 through 8 are shown in table 8.3.

An overall test for a flat serial correlation function was conducted using the Q-statistic. All serial correlation coefficients for lags 1 through 8 are not significantly zero if the Q-statistic is greater than 15.507 at the 5 percent level with 8 degrees of freedom, or if the Q-statistic is greater than 20.09 at the 1 percent level with 8 degrees of freedom. The number and percentage of stocks within each stock classification with overall serial correlation coefficients significantly nonzero at the 5 percent and 1 percent levels are shown in table 8.4. About 10 percent of the stocks have an overall serial correlation coefficient significantly nonzero at the 1 percent level.

Table 8.5 shows the serial correlation coefficients of the selected 30 KLSE industrial stocks. Twelve of the 30 stocks exhibited significant correlation (the

Table 8.3

Number and Percentage of Stocks within Each Stock Classification with Serial Correlation Coefficients Significantly Nonzero for Lags 1 through 8 at the 5 Percent and 1 Percent Levels

Stock Classification	Lag 1		Lag 2		Lag 3		Lag 4		Lag 5		Lag 6		Lag 7		Lag 8	
	#	%	#	%	#	%	#	%	#	%	#	%	#	%	#	%
Industrial	27	30	11	12	6	7	5	6	3	3	4	4	3	3	4	4
	15	17	4	4	2	2	2	2	2	2	1	1	1	1	3	3
Finance	3	27	1	9	2	18	1	9	0	0	0	0	0	0	0	0
	2	18	1	9	0	0	1	9	0	0	0	0	0	0	0	0
Hotel	3	30	2	20	1	10	2	20	2	20	1	10	1	10	1	10
	1	10	1	10	1	10	1	10	2	20	0	0	1	10	1	10
Property	4	40	1	10	2	20	0	0	0	0	0	0	1	10	1	10
	1	10	1	10	0	0	0	0	0	0	0	0	0	0	1	10
Plantation	6	19	3	9	1	3	4	12	4	12	4	12	1	3	3	9
	3	9	0	0	0	0	1	3	1	3	1	3	0	0	0	0
Tin	4	24	2	12	1	6	3	18	2	12	1	6	1	6	1	6
	0	0	0	0	1	6	0	0	0	0	1	6	0	0	1	6

Notes: The number and percentage of serial correlation coefficients significantly nonzero at the 5 and 1 percent levels are given in the first and second lines, respectively, of each stock classification. These results are based on a two-tailed test. Percentages are rounded to the nearest whole number. It should be noted that a serial correlation coefficient significantly nonzero at the 1 percent level also implies that it is significantly nonzero at the 5 percent level, but not vice versa. This explains why the percentage of serial correlation coefficients significantly nonzero at the 5 percent level is always greater than at the 1 percent level.

Table 8.4
Number and Percentage of Stocks within Each Stock Classification
with Overall Serial Correlation Coefficients Significantly Nonzero
at the 5 Percent and 1 Percent Levels

Stock Classification	Nonzero at 5 Percent Level of Significance		Nonzero at 1 Percent Level of Significance	
	Number	Percent	Number	Percent
Industrial	21	23	8	9
Finance	2	17	1	9
Hotel	4	40	2	20
Property	2	20	0	0
Plantation	5	16	4	12
Tin	3	18	2	12

Note: Percentages are rounded to the nearest whole number.

correlation coefficient was at least twice its computed standard error) between past and future prices at lag 1. Sanyo stock had the largest correlation coefficient, –0.257, which can be translated to an R^2 (coefficient of determination) of 0.066. An R^2 of 0.066 means that 6.6 percent of the future price of this stock can be attributed to or explained by its past price (in this case its price last week). That is, only 6.6 percent of the variation in this week's price can be explained by last week's price. Twenty of the stocks exhibited negative correlation at lag 1. In most cases, correlations became smaller as the lag increased. That is, the further the time period lagged behind, the less influence it had in determining the future price. Table 8.5 also shows the overall serial correlations for lags 1 through 8. Nine (or 30 percent) of the 30 stocks had an overall serial correlation coefficient significantly nonzero at the 5 percent level. Three (or 10 percent) of the 30 stocks showed a deviation from the weak-form EMH at the 1 percent level of significance.

Table 8.6 shows the summary statistics of the weekly serial correlation coefficients distribution for Malaysia and for Australia and four Asian countries (see Ang and Pohlman 1978), eight European countries (see Solnik 1973), and the United States (see Fama 1965). It should be stressed here that a meaningful comparison cannot be made because of the differences in the time periods of these studies. However, there are a few observations that are worth mentioning. The average serial correlation of Malaysian stocks is higher than that of the American stocks and is quite comparable to those of the European stocks, but is lower than those of the Asian stocks with the exception of Hong Kong stocks. Forty percent of the Malaysian stocks exhibited departure from the weak-form EMH (the correlation coefficient was at least twice the standard error). With the exception of Australia,

Malaysia had the highest percentage of stocks that deviated from the weak-form EMH. Malaysian stocks are quite comparable to those of other countries in terms of the percentage of positive correlations. In fact, the Malaysian percentage is only slightly higher than that of the American stocks.

Runs Test

A runs test was conducted to test the randomness of the percentage price changes. The percentage changes in stock prices are random if the Z-(observed) is within plus or minus 1.96 at the 5 percent level of significance, or if Z-(observed) is within plus or minus 2.576 at the 1 percent level of significance. The number and percentage of stocks within each stock classification with percentage price changes significantly nonrandom are shown in table 8.7. Overall, over 50 percent of the stocks had percentage price changes significantly nonrandom at the 1 percent level.

Table 8.8 shows the results of the runs tests for the 30 selected industrial stocks. Fourteen of the 30 stocks showed a significant difference between the total actual numbers of runs and the expected numbers. This means that 47 percent of the Malaysian stocks showed a deviation from the weak form of the EMH. In fact, the average Z-(observed) of –2.27 indicates an overall slight departure from the weak form of the EMH. In all stocks, with the exception of Federal Cables and Wires, the actual runs were less than the expected runs. The results of the runs test on the U.S. stocks for the four-day time interval (Fama 1965) indicated that none of the stocks exhibited deviation from the weak-form EMH. In addition, total actual runs were less than the total expected runs in 16 of the 30 stocks.

Test for Normal Distribution and the Statistical Measures of the Distribution

All the Malaysian stocks chosen for this study showed a significant departure from the normal distribution (two-tailed observed value of significance, P-value = 0.000). No reporting of the D-values and the Z-values is made since the very low P-values indicate that it is quite meaningless to do so. This finding is consistent with the findings on the Asian and Australian stocks (Ang and Pohlman 1978), American stocks (Fama 1965), German stocks (Conrad and Juttner 1973), United Kingdom stocks (Dryden 1969), and Norwegian and Swedish stocks (Jennergren and Korsvold 1975).

Table 8.9 shows the distributional nature of the weekly price changes for the 30 Malaysian stocks selected for detailed reporting. The means of the weekly price changes vary from 0.058 percent for Malayawata to 0.670 percent for Esso, with an average of 0.340 percent. The medians, with the exception of Esso (median equals 1 percent), are all 0. Three of the stocks have a mode of 1 percent, 7 stocks have a mode of –1 percent, and the rest have a mode of 0 percent. It should be noted here that for a distribution to be normal, the values for mean, median, and mode should be the same. This means that none of the stocks exhibits a normal distribution.

Table 8.5

Weekly Serial Correlation Coefficients for Lags 1 through 8 and Q-Statistic for 30 Selected KLSE Industrial Stocks

Stock	Lag 1	Lag 2	Lag 3	Lag 4	Lag 5	Lag 6	Lag 7	Lag 8	Q-Stat
Alcom	.046	.045	.047	.014	-.034	.031	-.048	.053	6.01
Boustead	.100*	.035	.004	.087	.017	-.010	-.035	.101	13.38
Chem. Co.	-.016	-.050	-.137	.057	-.041	-.020	-.047	.072	14.93
Cold Storage	.015	-.018	-.065	.053	.056	.022	.005	.073	7.23
C & Carriage	-.191**	-.004	.030	.011	.068	.002	.018	.043	19.32[a]
Esso	-.010	-.098	-.018	-.047	-.064	-.019	-.030	.072	9.89
Fed. Cab. & W	-.152**	.067	.088	-.031	.083	-.059	-.037	.066	22.90[b]
F & N	.005	-.131**	.004	.073	-.073	-.047	.082	-.038	16.71[a]
Gen. Lumber	-.037	-.029	.108	.002	.036	-.009	-.060	.142**	17.05[a]
Genting	.017	.082	.077	.024	.060	-.040	.041	.037	9.34
Haw Par	-.099	-.009	.016	.050	-.031	.039	-.029	.039	7.61
Inchape	-.050	.000	.026	.025	-.012	.016	.062	-.009	3.50
Jack Chia	-.169**	.003	.001	-.012	.014	-.067	.044	.054	16.60[a]
M'yan Cement	-.217**	-.021	.015	-.023	.006	-.006	-.016	.018	21.14[a]
M'yan Tob'co	-.033	.033	.008	.046	-.026	-.006	-.003	.000	2.19
Malayawata	-.121*	-.101*	-.001	.022	-.032	-.010	.056	-.012	12.87
Matsushita	-.110*	.043	-.010	.049	.000	-.022	-.014	.026	7.78
New S. Times	.120*	.029	.027	-.093*	-.076	-.082	.053	.023	17.68[a]
Pan M. Cem't	-.130**	.010	-.004	-.018	.037	.007	-.039	-.032	9.16
Paper Prod't	.026	-.063	.050	.087	.037	.018	.019	.044	8.08
P'lis Plant.	-.020	-.027	.061	.071	.059	-.022	.000	.035	6.59
Roth. Mal.	.020	.010	-.012	-.021	.060	-.068	.027	.049	5.36
Sanyo	-.257**	.064	-.021	-.010	-.051	-.072	.027	-.086	9.28

Shell	-.095*	.014	-.013	-.032	-.028	.036	.006	.017	5.60
Sime Darby	-.032	-.159*	.054	.063	.031	.005	-.023	.047	16.06[a]
Str. S'ship	.024	-.034	.040	.003	-.017	.040	-.026	-.018	2.69
Str. Trading	.145*	.036	.072	-.008	.033	-.008	-.012	.053	13.81
Tan Chong	-.076	.027	.117*	.018	.062	.031	.058	.042	13.09
UMW	-.013	.116*	.028	.019	.072	-.033	-.010	-.010	9.26
Yeo H. Seng	-.061	.059	.033	.056	.074	-.053	.171**	.022	21.60

*Significant at 5 percent level.
**Significant at 1 percent level.
 Both * and ** mean that correlation $\geq$ 2 standard error.
[a]Significant at 5 percent level (chi-square value with 8 degrees of freedom is 15.507).
[b]Significant at 1 percent level (chi-square value with 8 degrees of freedom is 20.09).

153

Table 8.6

**Summary Statistics of the Serial Correlation Coefficients Distribution
for Eight European Countries, Four Asian Countries, Australia,
the United States, and Malaysia**

Country	Serial Corr. Average	Corr. ≥ 2 Std. Error Count	Corr. ≥ 2 Std. Error Percent	Positive Corr. Count	Positive Corr. Percent
France	−.049	17/65	26	21/65	32
Italy	.001	5/30	17	14/30	47
United Kingdom	−.055	7/40	18	8/40	20
Germany	.056	8/35	23	27/35	77
Netherlands	.002	3/24	13	14/24	58
Belgium	−.088	5/17	29	1/17	6
Switzerland	−.022	1/17	6	6/17	35
Sweden	.024	1/6	17	4/6	67
Hong Kong	.030	2/9	22	5/9	56
Japan	−.065	1/13	8	3/13	23
The Phillipines	−.055	1/9	11	2/9	22
Singapore	−.077	2/13	15	3/13	23
Australia	−.165	5/10	50	1/10	10
United States	−.038	5/30	17	9/30	30
Malaysia	−.046	12/30	40	10/30	33

Source: Adapted from studies by Ang and Pohlman (1978) on the four Asian countries and Australia,
Solnik (1973) on the eight European countries, and Fama (1965) on U.S. stocks.

Note: All percentages are rounded to the nearest whole number.

Table 8.7

**Number and Percentage of Stocks within Each Stock Classification
with Percentage Price Changes Significantly Nonrandom at the
5 Percent and 1 Percent Levels**

Stock Classification	Nonrandom at 5 Percent Level of Significance Number	Nonrandom at 5 Percent Level of Significance Percent	Nonrandom at 1 Percent Level of Significance Number	Nonrandom at 1 Percent Level of Significance Percent
Industrial	52	58	44	49
Finance	5	45	4	36
Hotel	9	90	8	80
Property	6	60	6	60
Plantation	25	78	23	72
Tin	14	82	14	82

Table 8.8
Results of Runs Tests for Thirty Selected Malaysian Stocks

Stock	Actual Run	Expected Run	Std. Error	Z (observed)
1. Alcom	236	237.47	9.64	−3.83**
2. Boustead	225	250.34	9.83	−2.53*
3. Chem. Co. 258	258	269.27	9.70	−1.11
4. Cold Storage	231	288.56	9.78	−5.83**
5. C & Carriage	232	251.13	9.79	−1.90
6. Esso	247	255.15	9.46	−.81
7. Fed. Cab. & W	260	250.29	9.87	.93
8. F & N	237	264.71	9.74	−2.79**
9. Genl Lumber	231	251.25	9.83	−2.01*
10. Genting	231	245.46	9.65	−1.45
11. Haw Par	238	245.89	9.87	−.75
12. Inchape	232	245.54	9.81	−1.33
13. Jack Chia	253	264.23	9.64	−1.11
14. M'yan Cement	234	280.33	9.68	−4.74**
15. M'yan Tob'co	262	275.65	9.61	−1.37
16. Malayawata	244	248.04	9.77	−.36
17. Matsushita	240	288.39	9.77	−4.90**
18. New S. Times	251	286.17	9.70	−3.57**
19. Pan M. Cem't	239	256.61	9.69	−1.77
20. Paper Prod't	225	246.02	9.82	−2.09*
21. P'lis Plant.	245	254.66	9.82	−.93
22. Roth. Mal.	241	267.58	9.64	−2.71**
23. Sanyo	247	287.88	9.74	−4.14**
24. Shell	244	266.33	9.73	−2.24*
25. Sime Darby	247	261.44	9.72	−1.43
26. Str. S'ship	226	285.65	9.73	−6.08**
27. Str. Trading	229	258.90	9.72	−3.23**
28. Tan Chong	228	245.14	9.71	−1.71
29. UMW	230	245.99	9.82	−1.58
30. Yeo H. Seng	246	253.11	9.83	−.67
Average				−2.27

*Significant at 5 percent level.
**Significant at 1 percent level.

Table 8.9

Distributional Nature of the Weekly Percentage Price Changes

Stock	Mean	Median	Mode	Standard Deviation	Skewness	Kurtosis	Range	
							Min	Max
1. Alcom	.170	0	0	5.313	1.150	6.190	-19	28
2. Boustead	.168	0	-1	5.379	-1.066	9.018	-36	20
3. Chem. Co.	.089	0	0	3.277	.640	5.805	-12	19
4. Cold Storage	.090	0	0	4.273	.011	4.660	.011	4.660
5. C & Carriage	.423	0	0	6.078	.932	16.896	-33	46
6. Esso	.670	1	1	3.122	.127	.930	-9	8
7. Fed. Cab. & W	.423	0	0	6.470	.374	3.727	-25	37
8. F & N	.134	0	0	3.687	-.979	6.173	-17	10
9. Genl Lumber	.447	0	0	6.9842	.515	4.071	-30	32
10. Genting	.646	0	0	4.900	.562	3.655	-17	25
11. Haw Par	.313	0	1	5.693	.541	6.132	-26	33
12. Inchape	.140	0	-1	4.677	.643	6.730	-22	25
13. Jack Chia	.433	0	0	5.189	1.013	9.406	-24	32
14. M'yan Cement	.403	0	0	3.836	.554	6.895	-24	20
15. M'yan Tob'co	.380	0	0	3.464	.914	10.437	-18	24
16. Malayawata	.058	0	-1	5.489	.900	16.814	-38	44
17. Matsushita	.494	0	0	4.431	.789	19.954	-27	33
18. New S. Times	.549	0	0	3.160	.617	5.561	-16	15
19. Pan M. Cem't	.585	0	0	5.879	.724	5.797	-28	31

20. Paper Prod't	.326	0	−1	5.806	.790	5.453	−28	32
21. P'lis Plant.	.356	0	0	5.120	.056	3.757	−24	24
22. Roth. Mal.	.425	0	0	4.462	−.238	8.634	−28	26
23. Sanyo	.237	0	0	4.517	1.867	16.227	−26	30
24. Shell	.420	0	0	5.031	1.725	18.226	−31	41
25. Sime Darby	.145	0	0	4.733	.372	11.843	−26	33
26. Str. S'ship	.082	0	0	4.524	1.096	6.673	−21	25
27. Str. Trading	.401	0	−1	4.364	.187	3.685	−19	19
28. Tan Chong	.652	0	1	5.101	.408	6.249	−25	29
29. UMW	.253	0	−1	5.452	.797	2.962	−18	26
30. Yeo H. Seng	.293	0	−1	4.683	−.901	12.861	−38	22
Average	.340	*	*	4.832	.504	8.181	−24	27

*Not meaningful. For a normal distribution, mean = median = mode. The annualized average mean is 17.68 percent. The annualized average standard deviation is 34.84 percent.

The values of the standard deviation vary from 3.122 percent for Esso to 6.842 percent for General Lumber, with an average of 4.832 percent. All but 4 stocks have positive skewness. The average skewness is 0.504. A normal distribution has a zero skewness; that is, these stocks deviate from a normal distribution.

All stocks have kurtosis (based on the calculation using SPSS-X) greater than zero. A normal distribution has a kurtosis (based on the SPSS-X procedure) of zero. A kurtosis greater than zero means that the stocks are leptokurtic. A leptokurtic distribution is characterized by relatively long and fat tails, and many observations are near the mean, resulting in a high peakedness.

On the average, the price changes range from –24 percent to +27 percent. The largest minimum value is –38 percent for Malayawata and Yeo Hiap Seng, and the largest maximum value is 46 percent for Cycle and Carriage.

The annualized means have an average of 17.68 percent. The annualized standard deviations have an average of 34.84 percent. Ibbotson and Sinquefield (1979) reported that the annual average return for U.S. stocks for the period 1926–78 was 11.2 percent, with a standard deviation of 22.2 percent. If we were to use this information as a basis for comparison (even thought it is not that accurate due to differences in the time period and the choice of time scale involved), we can say that on the average, the Malaysian stocks have a higher return than the U.S. stocks, but with a higher risk (the standard deviation is larger). It should be noted here that the price changes for Malaysian stocks do not really reflect the actual returns. We had to add dividend yield to the percentage change in order to get the actual return. If we add dividend yield, the average return for Malaysian stocks will be even higher than the average return for the U.S. stocks.

The comparison of riskiness will be more meaningful if we use the coefficient of variation, which is the standard deviation divided by the mean. The coefficient of variation measures the degree of change in the standard deviation as a result of a unit change in the mean. From the information in the previous paragraph, we can say that the Malaysian stocks have a coefficient of variation of approximately 1.97 and the U.S. stocks have a coefficient of variation of approximately 1.98. This means that the price changes of the Malaysian stocks are, on the average, as volatile as the price changes of the U.S. stocks.

Spearman Rank Correlation Test

The Spearman rank correlation test was conducted to determine whether the efficiency of a stock market is independent of continuity in stock trading. From the overall serial correlation test, the stock with the highest Q-statistic was ranked lowest in efficiency, and the rest of the stocks were ranked accordingly. From the runs test, the stock with the highest absolute value of Z-(observed) was ranked lowest in efficiency, and the rest of the stocks were ranked accordingly. The stock with the lowest number of trading weeks was ranked lowest inc continuity in trading, and the rest of the stocks were ranked accordingly. These rankings were divided into two subgroups: (1) rankings based on a pool of 170 stocks (i.e., all

Table 8.10
Results of the Spearman Rank Correlation Test Using Q-Statistic Rank as the Measure of Efficiency

Stock Classification	Number of Stocks	Spearman Rank Correlation	t-(observed)	P-Prob.
Industrial	90	−.2390	−2.014*	.023
Finance	11	−.0149	−.044	.965
Hotel	10	.4788	1.876	.162
Property	10	.2727	.904	.446
Plantation	32	.1076	.624	.558
Tin	17	−.1789	−.638	.492
All stocks combined	170	−.0925	−1.147	.230

*Efficiency is dependent on continuity in trading at the 5 percent level of significance.

Table 8.11
Results of the Spearman Rank Correlation Test Using Runs-Test Rank as the Measure of Efficiency

Stock Classification	Number of Stocks	Spearman Rank Correlation	t-(observed)	P-Prob.
Industrial	90	.1361	1.374	.201
Finance	11	.0795	.249	.803
Hotel	10	−.3697	−.893	.293
Property	10	−.5758	−1.297	.082
Plantation	32	−.1611	−.819	.378
Tin	17	−.0760	−.284	.772
All stocks combined	170	−.0504	−.637	.514

stocks combined as one group); and (2) rankings based on the individual stock classifications.

Efficiency is independent of continuity in trading if t-(observed) is within plus or minus t-table with n – 2 degrees of freedom at the corresponding 5 percent and 1 percent levels of significance. If the number of observations *n* is greater than 30, the t-distribution is approximated by the Z-distribution, and thus efficiency is independent of the continuity in trading if t-(observed) is within plus or minus 1.96 at the 5 percent level of significance and within plus or minus 2.576 at the 1 percent level of significance.

The results of the Spearman rank correlation test using the Q-statistic rank as a measure of efficiency are shown in table 8.10. The results of the Spearman rank correlation test using runs-test rank as a measure of efficiency are shown in table 8.11.

Based on the Spearman rank correlation test with the Q-statistic used as the measure of efficiency, only industrial stocks exhibit dependence between efficiency and continuity in trading at the 5 percent level of significance. All stocks exhibit independence between efficiency and continuity in trading at the 1 percent level of significance.

Based on the Spearman rank correlation test with the runs-test rank used as the measure of efficiency, all stock classifications exhibit independence between efficiency and continuity in trading at the 5 percent level of significance. Even when all stocks are combined, efficiency is still independent of continuity in trading at the 5 percent level of significance.

CONCLUSIONS AND IMPLICATIONS

Under the weak form of the EMH, stock prices are assumed to reflect all information that may be contained in the past history of the stock itself. Since the information itself is random in nature, the stock-price movements should therefore be random. This means that the past price movements are not predictive of the future price movements. In other words, past and future price movements are random and no related to each other.

Under the Q-statistic test, on the average, about 10 percent of the total stock exhibited a deviation from the weak form of the EMH at the 1 percent significance level. This finding indicated that a small percentage of stocks did exhibit dependence between past and future price changes. Whether or not this dependence can be exploited profitably is left to future research, using filter rules, for example. However, small R^2 values indicate that the model that can be constructed using the relationship between past and future prices will not be that meaningful from an investor's point of view.

The runs test was conducted to test the randomness of the percentage price changes. On the average, over 50 percent of the total stocks of each stock classification exhibited a departure from the weak form of the EMH at the 1 percent significance level. This finding is not consistent with the findings of the two previously published studies by Barnes (1986) and Laurence (1986). As indicated by Barnes, market thinness makes it difficult for traders to react to new information and therefore for prices to reflect it. This means that a thin market does not fully reflect the actual information, which is random in nature, and therefore the price changes are not random. The percentage of nonrandomness among these stocks is higher than that found in the European and the Far Eastern stocks. One possible explanation for this would be that the sample sizes of these two studies are small, and the data are selective; a bigger and more representative sample might support the finding of the present study. One would expect that a small and thinly traded capital market like the KLSE will exhibit a departure from the weak form of the EMH, as indicated by the finding of the runs test. The low trading volumes in most stocks and the possible price manipulations by the investors who own the majority of the stocks might help explain the finding of the runs test.

The finding on the serial correlation test suggests that an investor is capable of outperforming the market if he or she applies some statistical technique on the past prices of those stocks that exhibited a high serial correlation. The presence of nonrandomness in many of the stocks implies that the stock-price changes follow some trend. If this trend can be detected, an investor will be able to outperform the market and thus make an above-normal return.

The general results of the Spearman rank correlation test imply that the inefficiency of the Malaysian stock market is not dependent on discontinuity in trading (by suspension of trading). All stocks are equally responsible for the efficiency or inefficiency of the Malaysian stock market. In the case of the industrial sector, there is a slight dependence between discontinuity in trading and the inefficiency of the market if the Q-statistic ranking is used.

This chapter has also reported the nature of the distribution for Malaysian stock prices. The statistical measures to describe these distributions were presented. The coefficient of variation was used to compare the relative volatility of returns between U.S. stocks and the selected Malaysian stocks. Overall, Malaysian stocks have positive mean, exhibit leptokurtosis, and have positive skewness. In a nutshell, the price changes of the Malaysian stocks do not exhibit a normal distribution, which is consistent with the finding of studies performed on other markets. In addition, the coefficient of variation indicates that the Malaysian stocks are as volatile as the U.S. stocks in terms of the annualized returns.

The results of the runs test indicate that the price changes of some stocks are not random over time. This could imply that these stocks are inactively traded and/or that their prices are being manipulated. The low volumes of trading indicate that these stocks were in fact inactively traded. Market participants were small in many of these stocks, which resulted in inactive trading. The participation of many investors in the trading of a given stock will result in an active market for that stock.

Thinness of the market and discontinuity in trading are the basic characteristics of the Malaysian stock exchange. There is no market-making mechanism in Malaysia like specialists to provide continuity and depth in trading. Lack of sophisticated chartists and analysts may also contribute to the deviation from the random-walk model. It is widely believed that most investors act upon rumors rather than credible information. The distribution of the price changes in the

Malaysian stock market appears to conform to a stable Pareto model with alpha less than 2, whereas a normal distribution is a type of Pareto model with alpha equal to 2. This means that the path of the price level is usually discontinuous and tends to jump up and down by very large amounts during very short periods. A market such as this is inherently more risky due to the large numbers of abrupt changes. For an analyst, the usual measures of dispersion may not be good indicators of variability in this market due to the extremely erratic behavior of the price changes. Nonnormality implies that future tests employing price changes should be carried out using nonparametric tests that make no assumption regarding the distribution of the population of the sample under study.

SUGGESTIONS FOR IMPROVING THE EFFICIENCY OF THE MALAYSIAN STOCK EXCHANGE

In this section some measures that can be adopted to improve the efficiency of the market for Malaysian stocks are suggested.

Specialists

Specialists are a very important segment of a stock exchange in the United States. Specialists make up about one-fourth of the total members who own seats on the floor of the New York Stock Exchange (NYSE). Each stock traded has a specialist assigned to it, and most specialists are responsible for more than one stock. The specialist has two basic duties with regard to the stocks he or she supervises. First, he or she must handle any special orders that commission brokers or floor brokers might give him or her. the second major function (which is our utmost concern here) of specialists is to maintain continuous, liquid and orderly markets in their assigned stocks. This second function is difficult in those stocks with small or inactive trading. For example, suppose you placed an order to buy one lot of a given stock at the market price. If there is no seller for the stock at that time, your commission broker can buy the shares from the specialist who acts as a dealer, that is, buying for and selling from his or her own inventory. To ensure the ability to maintain continuous markets, the NYSE requires a specialist to have U.S. $500,000 or enough capital to own 50 lots of his assigned stock, whichever is greater.

Big and Sound Stockbrokerage Firms

One way to achieve sound stockbrokerage firms is through corporatization of the firms. It was believed that foreign institutional and individual investors were trading in Malaysian securities through Singapore, where better facilities are provided by the big brokerage firms in Singapore. If these foreign investors are to be encouraged to invest directly in the Malaysian market, then they have to be convinced that the Malaysian brokerage firms are able to cater to their needs. Furthermore, a big brokerage firm can bring in benefits such as a huge client base, expert management, quality research, and effective portfolio management. The Malaysian investors need solid advice from these brokerage firms. In addition, with big brokerage firms, it is possible to offer graduated commissions for big deals that come from these big investors (this has become a hot issue among Malaysian stockbrokers since Singapore proposed graduated commissions recently).

Public Education

The administrator of the stock exchange should educate the public about the stock exchange and encourage people to participate. The Research Institute of Investment Analysts Malaysia (RIIAM) should play its role effectively not only in doing research on the securities market, but also in educating the investing and general public on the securities industry and, in doing so, promoting the market to them. The participation of many existing and new investors in the trading of stocks will result in active markets for the stocks involved. Investors should be taught the fundamentals of analyzing and valuing stocks. This is important because many small investors in Malaysia buy or sell stocks based on rumors rather than on the "true" values of the stocks. In addition, the government can also introduce the investment course to pupils at the secondary level so that the new generation will have a correct view and perspective regarding the stock market. The stock exchange should be viewed as a place in which capital can be raised for the good of the company concerned, the investors, and the development of a developing country like Malaysia. A widespread belief among the average people from the street, who regard a stock exchange as a gambling place, should be eradicated. Buying a stock is like owning a piece of the company; it is not similar to gambling.

Stricter and More Effective Enforcement of Laws

The regulatory agency of the KLSE should pay closer attention to the problem of stock-price manipulations, market rigging, and false trading by those concerned (for example, substantial shareholders and the "top" persons of a given company). Since stocks with inactive trading are a likely target for price manipulation, these stocks should be watched more closely, and any sign of manipulation should be quickly investigated. Those people who are involved in manipulating the stock prices should be prosecuted and punished accordingly and not be let free. In addition, the disclosure of information and the prosecution of those involved in insider trading should be strictly and fully enforced. The law is there; what is needed is the strict enforcement of the law itself.

Liquid Shares

Companies should be required to maintain a certain proportion of "liquid shares." For example, the Tokyo Stock Exchange requires that a listed company must not have more than 80 percent of nonliquid shares. (Nonliquid shares are shares owned by the 10 largest shareholders.) A company that exceeds this limit is given three years to change the situation; if it does not, it faces delisting. In addition, nontrading companies (less than 10 percent of their shares traded in one year) should be delisted.

Listing of Big Companies

Big companies (those with paid-up capital of more than $100 million) should be required to be listed on the stock exchange. The entry of these big and strong companies will restore the confidence of investors in the market. On the other hand, companies that are in trouble for five years continuously should be delisted.

CONCLUDING REMARKS

Since 1986 the KLSE has introduced measures (Salleh Majid 1986) to improve the operational efficiency of the market in the hope of restoring investors' confidence in the market. These measures are briefly discussed here:

1. Under a program of corporatization, existing stockbrokerage firms take in corporate partners by giving them equity shares.
2. An interbroker fidelity fund has been created for brokers to fall back on the event of any unfavorable occurrence.
3. Each existing and new brokerage firm will have to pay a sum of money for a seat on the exchange, and the money contributed by each brokerage firm will form a fund that will serve as a "fall-back" security for brokers who need to use it.
4. Under real-time price dissemination, the system gives real-time prices quoted at any given moment on the trading floor at the stock exchange to brokers and subscribers.
5. "Listing Manual" amendments cover all the grey areas and present a clear set of rules for listed companies (and those companies seeking listing) to comply with.
6. The Research Analysts Early Warning System studies and investigates listed companies' performance and prospects in order to detect early signs of trouble that could lead to a drastic event such as the Pan-El crisis.
7. The Research Institute of Investment Analysts Malaysia (RIIAM) focuses on the educational and information-dissemination program to familiarize investors and the general public with the securities industry.
8. A new KLSE composite index serves as an accurate indicator, that is, representative of the market and responsive yet not too sensitive.

In 1987 the KLSE moved to bigger premises at Kompleks Bukit Naga, and the real-time price-dissemination system (MASA) was introduced. During the official launch of the new premises and the MASA system on August 14, Prime Minister Datuk Seri Mahathir Mohamad announced that the government had decided to grant brokerage licenses to the three top local banks—Malayan Banking, Bank Bumiputra, and the United Malayan Banking Corporation (UMBC). Maybank Securities and BBMB Securities started their operations on December 28, 1987, while UMBC Securities started trading on January 4, 1988.

On the corporatization front, W. I. Carr (Malaysia) and Public Consolidated Holdings became the second and third corporate members of the KLSE (Arab-Malaysian Securities was admitted first to the KLSE in 1986). W. I. Carr, a wholly owned subsidiary of the London-based stockbrokers W. I. Carr, took up a 30 percent stake in Seagroatt and Campbell. Public Consolidated, a wholly owned subsidiary of Public Bank, acquired 99.9 percent of the equity of G. P. Securities (subsequently renamed PB Securities). CIMB Securities was formed when Commerce International Merchant Bank acquired Ariffin and Low Securities.

The KLSE set up the Advanced Warning and Surveillance (AWAS) unit aimed at alerting the exchange of any stockbrokerage house or publicly listed company getting into difficulties so that appropriate action can be taken to prevent any possible crisis. The Securities Industry (Amendment) Act, 1987, which was passed by Parliament in 1986, became fully effective on October 1. The act incorporated the concept of corporatization and stated in definite terms the power of the registrar of companies. The act also removed anomalies in the principal act as well as facilitating its enforcement.

REFERENCES

Akgiray, V. (1989). "Conditional Heteroscedasticity in Time Series of Stock Returns: Evidence and Forecasts." *Journal of Business* 62, no. 1: 55–80.

Alexander, S. (1964a). "Price Movements in Speculative Markets: Trends or Random Walks." In *The Random Character of Stock Market Prices*, ed. P. H. Cootner, 199–218. Cambridge, Mass.: M.I.T. Press.

———. (1964b). "Price Movements in Speculative Markets: Trends or Random Walks No. 2." *Industrial Management Review* 5 (Spring): 25–46.

Ang, J. S., and R. A. Pohlman. (1978). "A Note on the Price Behavior of Far Eastern Stocks." *Journal of International Business Studies* (Spring/Summer): 103–107.

Bachelier, L. (1964). "Theory of Speculation." In *The Random Character of Stock Market Prices*, ed. P. H. Cootner, 17–78. Cambridge, Mass.: M.I.T. Press.

Barker, C. A. (1956). "Effective Stock Splits." *Harvard Business Review* 34: 101–106.

———. (1958). "Evaluation of Stock Dividends." *Harvard Business Review* 36 (July–August): 99–114.

———. (1959). "Price Changes of Stock-Dividend Shares at Ex-Dividend Dates." *Journal of Finance* 14: 373–378.

Barnes, P. (1986). "Thin Trading and Stock Market Efficiency: The Case of he Kuala Lumpur Stock Exchange." *Journal of Business Finance and Accounting* (Winter): 609–617.

Berkman, N. (1978). "A Primer on Random Walks in the Stock Market." *New England Economic Review* (September–October): 32–49.

Bowerman, B. L., and R. T. O'Connell. (1979). *Time Series and Forecasting: An Applied Approach*. North Scituate, Mass.: Duxbury Press.

Conrad, K., and D. J. Juttner. (1973). "Recent Behavior of Stock Market Prices in Germany and the Random Walk Hypothesis." *Kyklos* 26: 576–599.

Cornell, W. B., and J. K. Dietrich. (1978). "The Efficiency of the Market for Foreign

Exchange under Floating Exchange Rates." *Review of Economics and Statistics* (February): 111–120.

D'Ambrosio, C. A. (1980). "Random Walk and the Stock Exchange of Singapore." *Financial Review* 15 (Spring): 1–12.

Daniel, W. (1978). *Applied Nonparametric Statistics*. Boston: Houghton Mifflin.

Dryden, M. (1969). "Share Price Movements: A Markovian Approach." *Journal of Finance* 24 (March): 49–60.

Fama, E. F. (1965). "The Behavior of Stock Market Prices." *Journal of Business* 38 (January): 34–105.

Heinkel, R., and A. Kraus. (1988). "Measuring Event Impacts in Thinly Traded Stocks." *Journal of Financial and Quantitative Analysis* (March): 71–88.

Hong, H. (1978). "Predictability of Price Trends on Stock Exchanges: A Study of Some Far Eastern Countries." *Review of Economics and Statistics* 60 (November): 619–621.

Hsu, D. (1984). "The Behavior of Stock Returns: Is It Stationary or Evolutionary?" *Journal of Financial and Quantitative Analysis* 19, no. 1 (March): 11–28.

Ibbotson, R. G., and R. A. Sinquefield. (1979). *Stocks, Bonds, Bills, and Inflation: Historical Returns, 1926–1978*. Charlottesville, Va.: Financial Analysts Research Foundation, p. 12, exhibit 3.

Jennergren, L. P., and P. E. Korsvold. (1975). "The Non-random Character of Norwegian and Swedish Stock Market Prices." In *International Capital Markets*, ed. E. J. Elton and M. J. Gruber, 37–67. Amsterdam: North-Holland.

Kendall, M. G. (1964). "The Analysis of Economic Time Series—Part 1: Prices." In *The Random Character of Stock Market Prices*, ed. P. H. Cootner, 85–99. Cambridge, Mass.: M.I.T. Press.

Laurence, M. (1986). "Weak Form Efficiency in the Kuala Lumpur and Singapore Stock Exchanges." *Journal of Business Finance* 10: 431–445.

Miller, R. (1981). *Introductory Statistics for Business and Economics*. New York: St. Martin's Press.

Moore, A. G. (1964). "Some Characteristics of Changes in Common Stock Prices." In *The Random Character of Stock Market Prices*, ed. P. H. Cootner, 139–161. Cambridge, Mass.: M.I.T. Press.

Nassir Lanjong. (1983). "Efficiency of the Malaysian Stock Market and Risk-Return Relationship." Ph.D. thesis, Leuven.

Neoh Soon Kean. (1985). "An Examination of the Efficiency of the Malaysian Stockmarket." Ph.D. thesis, Edinburgh.

Osborne, M. F. (1964a). "Brownian Motion in the Stock Market." First published in *Operations Research* 7 (March–April 1959): 145–173; reprinted in *The Random Character of Stock Market Prices*, ed. P. H. Cootner, 100–128. Cambridge, Mass.: M.I.T. Press.

———. (1964b). "Periodic Structure in the Brownian Motion of Stock Prices." First published in *Operations Research* 10 (May–June 1962): 345–379; reprinted in *The Random Character of Stock Market Prices*, ed. P. H. Cootner, 262–296. Cambridge, Mass.: M.I.T. Press.

Pankratz, A. (1983). *Forecasting with Univariate Box-Jenkins Models: Concepts and Cases*. New York: John Wiley and Sons.

Roberts, H. V. (1964). "Stock Market 'Pattern' and Financial Analysis: Methodological Suggestions." In *The Random Character of Stock Market Prices*, ed. P. H. Cootner, 7–16. Cambridge, Mass.: M.I.T. Press.

Salleh Majid. (1986). "The Role, Challenge, and Future of the KLSE." Working Paper, National Seminar on KLSE, National University of Malaysia.

Solnik, V. H. (1973). "Note on the Validity of the Random Walk for European Stock Prices." *Journal of Finance* (December): 1151–1159.

Theil, H., and C. Leendeers. (1965). "Tomorrow on the Amsterdam Stock Exchange." *Journal of Business* 38 (July): 277–284.

Wallis, W., and H. Roberts. (1956). *Statistics: A New Approach.* Glencoe, Ill.: Free Press.

Watson, J. (1980). "The Stationarity of Inter-Country Correlation Coefficients: A Note." *Journal of Business Finance and Accounting* 7, no. 2: 195–205.

Working, H. (1958). "A Theory of Anticipating Prices." *American Economic Review* 48 (May): 188–199.

G14 016 168-69

p 137. **Discussant: G. Wenchi Kao**

While the efficient market hypothesis and/or random walk have been examined extensively in the finance literature, most of the empirical findings have been obtained using return data from the U.S. stock market. With the increasing globalization of the investment community, a study of an emerging stock market would be timely and educational for both academicians and practitioners. This chapter contributes to the finance literature by providing more detailed analysis of weak-form efficiency of the Kuala Lumpur Stock Exchange (KLSE) in Malaysia. In this study, the author conducted independence and randomness tests using weekly return data of 170 stocks and a subsample of 30 randomly selected industrial stocks. Weak-form inefficiency was detected in the KLSE. The distribution property of the return series was also examined. Results showed that returns on the KLSE stocks are not normally distributed. The following comments are prepared to address several issues regarding the empirical methodologies and findings of the study.

To determine if stocks on the KLSE are weak-form efficient, the author employed serial correlation tests (null hypothesis 1) and runs tests (null hypothesis 2). Although the serial correlation test is a popular method for studies of weak-form market efficiency, a proper use of the method requires that the return series be normally distributed. However, findings from most empirical studies of return series in the United States indicate that the series are not normally distributed. Similar findings have been obtained from most studies on markets outside the United States as well. In fact, the author examined the distribution property of stocks traded on the KLSE (null hypothesis 3) in a subsequent section of this chapter. He, too, found that return series of the KLSE stocks are not normally distributed. Consequently, one might question the validity of using the serial correlation test to examine the efficient market hypothesis. On the other hand, the runs test is not subject to the same limitation. This is because it is a nonparametric test. It does not require any assumption about the distribution of the return series. In addition to the two test methods used in this study, several alternative test methodologies such as the variance ratio test have recently been introduced to the literature in the area of the efficient market hypothesis. Some of the alternative methods are robust to return distribution. The author might want to consider using some of them instead of the serial correlation test.

One of the problems researchers of less developed markets encounter is that trading in these markets can be very thin. Although the author used weekly data, it is not clear if all stocks examined in this study had at least one trade every week during the entire time period. The point is that test results could be distorted if some stocks did not normally have trade every week. The author is encouraged to examine the data more closely. Proper adjustment should be made if a large percentage of the KLSE stocks do not trade at least once a week. Finally, since some readers may not be very familiar with the KLSE, tables containing descriptive statistics such as trading volumes, turnover, and market capitalization at the KLSE would be helpful.

My next comment concerns the comparison between findings on the Malaysian stock market and findings on several countries the author compiled from various studies. Cross-country comparisons are very helpful as long as these markets are evaluated on a comparable basis. Specifically, the same test methodology should be employed across countries, and data examined should be comparable (e.g., the daily return from the same time period for each country should be used). Unfortunately, this is not the case.

As indicated in the last section of the chapter, trading in shares of Malaysian firms has a unique feature. Since the split of the KLSE and the Stock Exchange of Singapore (SES) in 1973, publicly traded firms from Malaysia and Singapore are permitted to list their shares on both the KLSE and the SES. Investors from both nations are allowed to trade on both markets as well. Of the two markets, the SES is larger and more liquid. As a result, trading activity on Malaysian stocks cross-listed on both markets is normally heavier on the SES than on the KLSE. Given the close political, economic, and social ties of the two countries, and the dominance of the SES, a study of the price behavior of Malaysian stocks would not be complete without examining trading on both the KLSE and SES. Issues such as relative efficiency of the KLSE and the SES, possibilities of arbitrage between the two, impacts of nonsynchronous trading on the two markets, and regulatory differences should be examined.

In summary, this chapter investigates weak-form efficiency of the Malaysian stocks traded on the KLSE. The author is encouraged to explore alternative testing methodologies, address the issue of infrequent trading, and compare the findings across markets if comparable data can be obtained. Proper account of the effect of cross-listings on the SES should be made as well.

Part III

Asset Management

9

Financial Management and Goal Programming in Imperfect Capital Markets

EDGAR ORTIZ and GRACIELA BUENO

Financial management theory and tools have developed radically during the last three decades. The principles of finance have been mainly derived from studying the interrelationships between capital markets and the corporation and its environment.[1] Thus valuation and capital market indicators have become key variables for financial decision making for both private and public enterprises. Although full application of modern financial thought is far from being complete, corporations in most advanced countries have benefitted from these changes. Higher education, business training, and the presence of solid economies and nearly perfect markets, particularly securities markets, have contributed to a rather rapid and smooth transfering of financial know-how.

In the developing countries this is not the case. In addition to their own scientific developments and practices, a great deal of technological transfer has taken place from the most advanced to the less developed nations, in financial management as well as in other fields. Nevertheless, modern financial principles have been adopted in a limited way in corporate decisions. Often, financial managers in these nations choose outdated tools to solve their problems. They maintain that tools developed in the advanced nations are not relevant for their case due to market imperfections. Particularly, capital markets are thin and inefficient. There is a need to develop local administrative know-how based on serious research of local financial conditions. However, modern financial thought and theories can provide relevant principles and models to solve the problems related to financial decision making in the developing nations. Market imperfections should not constitute a barrier to rigorous decision making. Rather, financial principles derived under assumptions of perfect markets and perfect information should lead to a better understanding of the financial problems facing corporations in the developing countries. Although valuation might be imperfect, the goal remains maximizing the owners' wealth.

Moreover, in the case of state enterprises, this goal refers to the taxpayers and the nation at large. Similarly, market imperfections and economic instability can complicate the use of certain tools necessary for sound decision making. However, modern financial theory has developed an infinite array of sophisticated tools that can respond to such circumstances. A case in point is mathematical goal programming. In the developing countries, decisions are taken seeking optimization, traditionally profit maximization. However, market imperfections and limited information might lead to contradictory results. Particularly, the relationship between liquidity, leverage, asset expansion, and profits and sales growth might be weak. Similarly, market indicators might be limited in scope and insufficient to discipline managers to sound decision making. In turn, all these problems can lead to a weak financial structure and stagnation. Thus multioperational goals should be incorporated in business finance for sound decision making. Under these circumstances, goal programming is an adequate tool for decision making. It provides a framework for incorporating multiple goals and reconciling them in a satisfactory way. This chapter makes an application of goal programming, incorporating also integer programming, to the case of a large Mexican public enterprise, Pemex, the state's oil corporation. Previous to this application, taking the case of the Mexican Stock Market (MSM) as a benchmark, the next section of this chapter sums up some of the limitations faced by financial managers in the developing countries in carrying on their operations in the context of weak capital markets and identifies the problems affecting Pemex. The following section presents the goal-programming model and the results of five different applications. The chapter ends with a brief section of conclusions.

MODERN FINANCIAL THEORY AND ASSET MANAGEMENT IN THE DEVELOPING NATIONS

The building blocks of modern financial theory are efficient market theory, portfolio theory, capital asset pricing theory, option pricing theory, and arbitrage pricing theory. In the developing countries, although business education has taken important strides during the last two decades, these principles have not been fully incorporated in financial policy making. The main reasons are the limited size and the imperfection found in the domestic capital markets. In the case of the Mexican Stock Market, symptoms of market imperfections worth noting are the reduced number of corporations registered in the stock market as well as the high turnover in the corporations registered in it; the limited number of issues traded daily, and sporadic trading in the case of many stocks and bonds; the limited size of investment funds, for most operations concentrate in the money markets, mainly trading government-issued securities; the small number of investors because participation in the securities markets is limited to higher-income groups; and insufficient release of information by both corporations and the stock market itself. Descriptive studies by Basch,[2] Ortiz,[3] Otto,[4] and Rodriguez[5] have identified market thinness and concentration. Empirical studies on market efficiency using modern portfolio theory confirm these findings. A study on technical analysis, using monthly data and serial correlation tests for the 1967–80 period, suggested that there is a strong dependence (a correlation coefficient of .9) in successive price changes of securities active in the Mexican stock exchange.[6] Similarly, a runs test showed that the number of actual runs was markedly lower than the expected number of runs.[7] The average difference was –17 percent versus 13.3 percent in the seminal study by Fama on the U.S. stock market.[8] Finally, comparing the efficiency of the U.S. and Mexican markets in relation to earnings announcements, using monthly data for the 1975–80 period, a study by Haugen, Ortiz, and Arjona found a significant lag of at least six months in the Mexican market.[9] Using standard average performance index (API) and cumulative performance index (CAPI) analysis, according to one earnings model there was a difference in returns of 12 percent between favorable and unfavorable groups of corporations; the differential return for the corresponding U.S. groupings was only 3 percent. Thus investors in Mexico could profit by discriminating stocks on the basis of their expected profitability. Long and short positions could also be exploited to attain high profits.

In sum, taking the inefficiencies of the MSM as a reference, it can be affirmed that failures in the capital markets in the less developed countries contribute little to discipline investors and the firm to rational and efficient decision making. That is, market indicators become a limited source of information for corporate decision making. As a result, three important problems can be detected in financial management in Mexico: prevalence of traditional definitions of the goal of the firm, weak treatment of risk, and ill-treatment of multiple operative goals. This means that financial policy is formulated with a weak perception of the goal of the firm, since valuation is imprecise and market participation is limited to few corporations. Thus optimization of profits is often identified with the goal of the firm. Moreover, outdated accounting concepts are used, disregarding profit "normalization" and a cash-flow approach. Similarly, in the absence of market-equilibrium indicators, qualitative perceptions are used for risk management. Hence the degree-of-risk premiums associated with different investments are not properly weighted. As a result, although financial managers are risk-averse, their decisions are often over-optimistic. Growth and profits are emphasized without properly measuring risk. Finally, as a corollary of the previous two points, few financial indicators are used to plan and control financial performance. Moreover, short-run profits are given priority, and possible negative long-run effects in some areas are ignored. Particularly, the relationships between sales growth, profits growth, asset growth and turnover, leverage, and liquidity have not been fully understood. Often Mexico's leading corporations engage themselves in the acquisition of highly expensive fixed assets or else of other corporations. However, they overestimate the size of the market, their capacity to assimilate new capital, or synergy potentials. Thus resources are not properly used, which is reflected in low activity ratios. Similarly, expansion is mainly supported by borrowing. However, even high sales and profits growth becomes insufficient to cover operating and financial costs and sustain an

Table 9.1
Key Financial Ratios for Pemex, 1975–1985

	1975	1976	1977	1978	1979	1980	1981	1982	1983	1984	1985	
I. Liquidity												
1. Current	1.67	.74	.83	.52	.51	.51	.47	.38	2.70	3.41	2.54	times
2. Acid test	1.09	.42	.48	.27	.29	.26	.30	.26	1.95	2.38	1.79	times
II. Debt												
3. Total debt	49.49	64.74	36.47	46.20	54.84	49.63	54.03	74.48	57.16	42.71	48.46	%
4. Times interest earned	12.66	5.97	7.57	7.49	5.65	12.14	8.39	10.41	7.05	10.32	19.49	times
III. Activity												
5. Inventory turnover	5.35	5.16	6.64	6.90	8.80	11.13	9.80	11.24	12.53	10.54	9.47	times
6. Average collection period	60.66	57.54	68.58	44.20	29.73	39.02	65.58	81.54	68.14	65.98	62.47	days
7. Accounts receivable turnover	5.93	6.26	5.25	8.14	12.11	9.23	5.49	4.41	5.28	5.46	5.76	times
8. Fixed assets turnover	.86	.60	.32	.33	.44	.51	.45	.38	.55	.53	.46	times
9. Total assets turnover	.58	.42	.27	.29	.39	.45	.39	.33	.45	.44	.38	times
IV. Profitability												
10. Net margin	.67	.65	.44	.38	.20	.12	.09	.05	.04	.04	.03	%
11. Return on total assets	.39	.27	.12	.11	.08	.05	.04	.02	.02	.02	.01	%
12. Return on net worth	.76	.78	.19	.21	.17	.11	.08	.07	.05	.03	.02	%

Source: Derived from financial information reported by Pemex in the National Accounts, various issues. 1975–85.

adequate financial structure. Leverage increases, liquidity falls, and returns decay. In sum, the lack of strong and efficient capital markets promotes poor identification and management of corporate strategic and operative goals.

Poor identification of operating goals is not an uncommon problem in Mexico. Indeed, both public and private corporations share it. Two dramatic cases exemplify this. These are the cases of ALFA, a large domestic private corporation, and Pemex, Mexico's state oil corporation. ALFA engaged itself in a very aggressive program of corporate growth and acquisitions. Between 1977 and 1980 the number of corporations in the holding group increased from 37 to 157. To finance this rapid growth, ALFA resorted to internal resources, increased borrowing, and issuing additional stock. However, growth plans came to an abrupt end in 1981, when heavy losses and sales of corporate interests were reported. The growth rates of sales and profits were simply inconsistent with asset expansion, dividend payout policies, increased leverage, and liquidity. Taking profits as a benchmark, on the average, net earnings should have been 5.9 times higher than those actually obtained.[10]

The case of Pemex refers to its inability to maintain a sound financial position in spite of high export revenues.[11] Pemex is the largest and most important Mexican public corporation. In 1981 its assets neared $45.8 billion; total gross earnings amounted to $12.7 billion. Pemex also participates in the MSM, issuing three-year bonds, Petrobonos. Additionally, this corporation, not the federal government, was Mexico's main borrower in the Euromarkets from 1974 to 1982.[12]

Explorations to increase oil reserves and exploitation began in the early 1970s and were successful. Development plans initially aimed at covering increases in domestic demand. However, as a result of the 1973–74 world oil crisis, oil development plans were enlarged. Oil prices and international demand were unusually high, so substantial exports were planned. However, this required massive investments in fixed assets for oil exploration and exploitation, building up oleoducts, improving port facilities, and so on. Internal savings were insufficient. Hence Pemex and the Mexican state engaged in heavy borrowing. Large loans, mainly from private sources, were taken out from 1975 to 1981. A total of $19.235 billion was borrowed. This amounted to 44.7 percent of total public debt contracted during that period. Moreover, during 1980 and 1981 Pemex increased its foreign debt by $13.353 billion. Furthermore, in those years oil exports increased rapidly, becoming three-fourths of total national exports; in addition, domestic demand was booming.

Ex post results show that this situation was unsustainable. First, risk management was disregarded. Asset expansion continued in spite of high probabilities of a fall in international oil prices and of increased interest rates. Second, even before these problems appeared, financial overheating of the corporation was obvious. Table 9.1 shows some key financial ratios for the 1975–85 period. In the 1980–81 period, liquidity fell drastically, precisely during those years of heavy borrowing and previous to the full fledging of the Mexican debt crisis. Indeed, the acid-test ratios were .26 and .30, respectively. Nevertheless, debt increased sharply. From an all-time low of 36.47 percent attained in 1977, the ratio of total debt to total assets increased to 54.03 percent in 1981 and 74.48 percent in 1982. Similarly, total assets turnover was .45 and .39 times in 1980 and 1981, respectively. Finally, the net margin fell to less than 1 percent for the entire 1975–81 period, although it must be recognized that reserves for capitalization are treated as a cost in the earnings statement. However, the difference is not very significant. If these reserves are not treated as a cost, the net margin in 1981 was 2.07 percent.

A simple financial-ratio analysis, one of the most elemental tools of financial management, should have been enough to warn decision makers that attained sales and profits growth rates were incompatible with higher leverage, efficient asset turnover, and adequate solvency. In addition, the market was sending strong signals about possible oil-price falls and sharp interest-rate increases in the international capital markets. In sum, Pemex performance showed some incompatibility between its rate of profits growth, high leverage, and liquidity. To reconcile them, goal programming could have been used.

GOAL PROGRAMMING AS AN ALTERNATIVE TOOL FOR FINANCIAL MANAGEMENT IN THE DEVELOPING COUNTRIES

For the cases where multiple goals exist, mathematical goal programming becomes a viable alternative. Modern finance has made ample use of it.[13] Linear programming deals with optimizing a goal (maximize profits, minimize costs, and so on). Its standard formulation includes an objective function that is to be optimized subject to some constraints. The objective function contains a number of variables that must converge toward one specific goal. Multiple goals are included, but are subsumed as constraints. Goal programming takes into account more than one goal in arriving at a solution. It incorporates explicitly in the objective function all goals identified by management. It yields a satisfying solution in which the best compromise of all goals is made. The objective is to lead a set of functions to certain predetermined value-denominated goals. Moreover, each of these goals can be assigned different weights, depending on the priorities of the corporation, in relation to the rest of the goals. With all the goals incorporated in the objective function, only true constraints remain as such. Any linear programming problem can be reformulated as a goal-programming problem. The transformation is simple. Restrictions can become goals. This original value might be preserved, or management might set a new target level, for example, in the case of profits. Once the goals have been defined, two new dummy variables, y^+ and y^-, are included in each equation representing them. These dummy variables measure the discrepancy between the goals set by management and the realizable results according to the goal-programming model. Hence the objective of the goal-programming problem is to minimize the difference between these variables so that the predefined goals are achieved. Once the problem has been formulated, the solution can be pursued by the simplex method. Analytically, a goal-programming problem can be stated as follows:

Minimize:

$$f = y_1^+ + M_1 y_1^- + y_2^+ + M_2 y_2^- + \cdots + y_k^+ + M_k y_k^-$$

Objective
function

subject to:

$$a_{11}x_1 + a_{12}x_2 + \cdots + a_{1n}x_n \leq b_1 ,$$

$$a_{21}x_1 + a_{22}x_2 + \cdots + a_{2n}x_n \leq b_2 ,$$

.

.   .   Constraints

.

$$a_{m1}x_1 + a_{m2}x_2 + \cdots + a_{mn}x_n \leq b_n ,$$

$$a_{m+11}x_1 + a_{m+12}x_2 + \cdots + a_{m+1n}x_n - y_1^+ + y_1^- = c_1 ,$$

$$a_{m+21}x_1 + a_{m+22}x_2 + \cdots + a_{m+sn}x_n - y_2^+ + y_2^- = c_2 ,$$

Goals

.   .

.   .

.   .

$$a_{m+k1}x_1 + a_{m+k2}x_2 + \cdots + a_{m+kn}x_n - y_k^+ + y_k^- = c_k ,$$

$$x_j \geq 0 \text{ for } j = (1, \ldots, n),$$

$$y_j^+, y_j^- \geq 0 \text{ for } j = (1, \ldots, k).$$

An application to the case of Pemex shows the advantages of this technique. The main issue facing this corporation can be summed up as whether or not the contribution margin over variation costs can produce some satisfactory level of profits consistent with the debt obligations and liquidity needs of the corporation. Thus the key variables to be considered in the formulation of the linear programming model are contribution margin, working capital needs, sales levels, total fixed costs, and debt obligations. Since Pemex production is divided into five zones, information for all these areas is necessary. Table 9.2 shows the values of these variables. For the 1980 and 1981 years and for each zone the table includes average international prices, average production costs, the contribution margin, sales levels, and the relative share of reserves. Also shown are beginning net working capital,

Table 9.2
Pemex Goal-Programming Decision Variables

1980

Zone	Variable	Average Price[a]	Av. Prod. Costs[a]	Contribution[a]	Sales[b]	Percent Reserves
North	x_1	33.24	11.84	21.40	12,430,114	5.48
Center	x_2	33.24	8.18	25.06	27,957,828	4.41
South	x_3	33.24	8.73	24.51	10,506,569	2.23
Southwest	x_4	31.27	3.85	27.42	108,251,275	25.30
Ocean	x_5	31.27	3.21	28.06	112,968,214	62.58
					272,114,000	

Beginning Net Working Capital[c]	−2,051,730,100
Working Capital Needs, 2:1	14,454,309,000
Working Capital Needs, 1:1	7,227,154,500
Working Capital Needs, minim.	2,586,684,000
Estimated Fixed Costs	725,000,000

Earnings	10,697,861,000
Debt Payments	656,095,000

1981

Zone	Variable	Average Price[a]	Av. Prod. Costs[a]	Contribution[a]	Sales[b]	Percent Reserves
North	x_1	36.08	13.76	22.38	12,617,778	5.48
Center	x_2	36.08	9.32	26.76	30,410,818	4.41
South	x_3	36.08	10.40	25.68	31,100,854	2.23

Southwest	x4	32.87	16.85	16.02	209,869,160	25.30
Ocean	x5	32.87	2.34	30.53	208,883,339	62.58
					482,882,949	

Beginning Net Working Capital[c]	-3,224,785,400		Earnings	11,735,860,000
Working Capital Needs, 2:1	26,869,548,000		Debt Payments	1,500,367,007
Working Capital Needs, 1:1	13,434,774,000			
Working Capital Needs, minim.	6,653,180,400			
Estimated Fixed Costs	960,000,000			

Sources: Prices: *Petroleum Intelligence Weekly*, various issues. Production costs: Department of Finance, Pemex; see Francisco Colmenares, "Problemas de Rentabilidad y Productividad en la Industria Petrolera" (Master's thesis, UNAM, 1985). Sales: estimated from sales and production figures in Instituto Nacional de Estadística, Geografía, e Informática, *La Industria Petrolera en México* (México: SPP, 1985). Reserves: Pemex, *Memoria de Labores, 1970–84.*

[a]Dollars/barrel.
[b]Barrels.
[c]Dollars, for all financial data.

working capital needs based on a 1:1 current ratio, estimated fixed costs, and earnings and debt payments for each year. The formulation of the problem uses information drawn from Pemex financial statements, except for working capital needs. In other words, goal programming in this case is set to answer whether or not the liquidity of the corporation could have been strengthened from .51 and .47 to a 1:1 current ratio, taking as a goal realized earnings from oil operations and at the same time covering fixed costs and debt-servicing needs. Thus for 1980 the goal for working capital is the sum of the predefined level of net working capital plus beginning net working capital plus fixed costs. This is shown in the right side of the working capital goal equation ($10,003,884,600). Similarly, the profits goal is the sum of expected earnings (realized earnings from ex post results) plus fixed costs plus debt-servicing obligations. The goal for 1980, $12,078,956,000, is shown in the right side of the profits goal equation. It must be stressed that earnings have been adjusted to include only oil sales and costs. Revenues and costs from refinery and petrochemicals are excluded, mainly due to the lack of data.

The model, fully stated for the 1980 period, is as follows:

$$\text{Min } f = y_1^+ + y_1^- + y_2^+ + y_2^- \text{ subject to}$$

$$x_1 \le 12{,}430{,}114, x_1 \text{ integer,}$$

$$x_2 \le 27{,}957{,}828, x_2 \text{ integer,} \qquad \text{Sales-level constraints}$$

$$x_3 \le 10{,}506{,}569, x_3 \text{ integer,}$$

$$x_4 \le 108{,}251{,}275, x_4 \text{ integer,}$$

$$x_5 \le 112{,}968{,}214, x_5 \text{ integer,}$$

$$\sum_1^5 x_i = 272{,}114{,}000;$$

$$21.40x_1 + 25.06x_2 + 24.51x_3 + 27.42x_4 + 28.06x_5 + y_1^+ + y_1^- = \$10{,}003{,}884{,}600$$
$$\text{(working capital goal);}$$

$$21.40x_1 + 25.06x_2 + 24.51x_3 + 27.42x_4 + 28.06x_5 + y_2^+ + y_2^- = \$12{,}078{,}956{,}000$$
$$\text{(profits goal);}$$

$$x_1, x_2, x_3, x_4, x_5, y_1^+, y_1^-, y_2^+, y_2^- \ge 0.$$

No restrictions on capacity are included in this model since ex post data on realized sales are used as constraints. However, in an ex ante situation and in the real world these restrictions can be easily added to the model. Also, a 2:1 liquidity ratio is more recommendable. To illustrate the financial weakness of Pemex during the 1980–81 period, working capital needs under that assumption are also shown in table 9.2. They were not included in the goal-programming problem because their difference from the real situation, which is the point of departure of the model presented here, is too big. Finally, sales restrictions are defined as integers.

In addition of model 1, presented here, four other models were run. Model 2 assumes that both total sales and zone sales can be up to 5 percent larger than actual sales. Model 3 assumes that the levels of sales could vary 5 percent above or below realized sales. Model 4, besides making these assumptions on the levels of sales, lowers working capital needs based on reported current ratios for each year. The respective amounts, denominated minimum working capital needs, are shown in Table 9.2. Finally, model 5 assumes that the sales of each zone are based on their reserves, but total sales are equal to realized sales. That is, it assumes that to overcome labor immobility, oil exploitation and sales are based on reserve levels.

All these assumptions are shown in tables 9.3 and 9.4, which summarize the results.[14] The variations (y^+, y^-) from the goals are shown in the answers for working capital (WK) and profits (Π). Concerning 1980, in all cases working capital needs (based on a 1:1 ratio) become positive versus the negative working capital reported in the balance sheets (beginning working capital in table 9.2). However, profits fell short of the desired goals. The first model aimed at mirroring what actually happened except for the higher working capital goal than those reported in the 1980 and 1981 balance sheets (.51 and .47 current ratio, respectively). Thus the results imply that actual profits derived from oil sales should have been enough to maintain a 1:1 liquidity level. That is, refinery and petrochemical operations pressed profits and liquidity down. This is confirmed by the results of model 4. Assuming lower capital needs, losses would be present, but working capital would be much higher than the desired goal (y^+ equals an excess of $5,270,922,000). The remaining models show similar results. However, it is worth noting that introducing some flexibility in production and sales levels (models 2 and 3) yields better results which allow sales levels to vary ±5 percent from realized sales for each zone. The results improve those from model 1 meaning that greater flexibility in oil exploitation could lead to better results. Similarly, varying production and sales levels to shares in reserves levels yields even better results. These important possibilities should be explored by Pemex's financial managers to achieve a better allocation of resources.

In 1981 working capital needs were higher, reflecting overall growth and the growth in current liabilities of the corporation. Thus results show that both the profit and working capital goals were unattainable. Indeed, goal-programming results foretell the poor performance depicted in the financial ratios reported in table 9.1. The best solution is that given by model 4, which reduces the working capital needs and allows sales for each zone to vary 5 percent above or below realized sales. Then there is an excess in working capital in relation to the predefined goal. The best solution to working capital needs based on a 1:1 current ratio is model 5, which sets production and sales levels to the shares of oil reserves of each zone. This

Table 9.3
Goal-Programming Solutions, 1980

Working Capital Goal = $10,003,884,600
Profits Goal = $12,078,956,000

Model 1:

Assume: $X_i \leq$ actual sales
$\Sigma X_i \leq$ total actual sales

WK = +618,678,800
Π = −1,456,392,000
X_i = actual sales

Model 2:

Assume: $X_i \leq$ actual sales × 1.05
$\Sigma X_i \leq$ total actual sales × 1.05

WK = +1,157,401,000
Π = −917,669,000
X_i = actual sales + 5%

Model 3:

Assume: actual sales × .95 $\leq X_i \leq$ actual sales × 1.05
$\Sigma X_i \leq$ total actual sales

WK = +632,569,200
Π = −1,442,502,000
X_1 = 11,799,800
X_2 = 26,540,060
X_3 = 28,957,500
X_4 = 206,119,400
X_5 = 118,697,200

Model 4:

Assume: actual sales × .95 $\leq X_i \leq$ actual sales × 1.05
$\Sigma X_i \leq$ total actual sales
Working Capital Goal = $5,363,414,500

WK = +5,270,922,000
Π = −1,442,620,000
X_i = as in model 3

Model 5:

Assume: $X_i \leq$ reserve shares (actual total sales)
$\Sigma X_i \leq$ total actual sales

WK = +726,837,800
Π = −1,348,960,000
X_i = reserve shares (total actual sales)

Table 9.4
Goal-Programming Solutions, 1981

Working Capital Goal = $10,619,559,400
Profits Goal = $14,196,227,000

Model 1:

Assume: $X_i \leq$ actual sales
$\Sigma X_i \leq$ total actual sales

WK = −5,986,154,000
Π = −2,562,821,000
X_i = actual sales

Model 2:

Assume: $X_i \leq$ actual sales × 1.05
$\Sigma X_i \leq$ total actual sales × 1.05

WK = −5,393,298,000
Π = −1,970,098,000
X_i = actual sales + 5%

Model 3:

Assume: actual sales × .95 $\leq X_i \leq$ actual sales × 1.05
$\Sigma X_i \leq$ total actual sales

WK = −5,825,636,000
Π = −2,402,423,000
X_1 = 11,974,760
X_2 = 31,960,600
X_3 = 30,424,310
X_4 = 198,993,920
X_5 = 219,528,400

Model 4:

Assume: actual sales × .95 $\leq X_i \leq$ actual sales × 1.05
$\Sigma X_i \leq$ actual sales
Working Capital Goal = $10,837,965,800

WK = +995,997,800
Π = −2,402,303,000

Model 5:

Assume: $X_i \leq$ reserve shares (total actual sales)
$\Sigma X_i \leq$ actual sales

WK = −4,738,261,000
Π = −1,315,198,000
X_i = reserve shares (total actual sales)

changes radically production and sales quotas for each region from the shares originally realized. This means that Pemex should seek greater flexibility in its allocation of resources; it should move to exploit its most profitable wells; and to promote certain labor and production stability, it could assign quotas for each zone based on oil reserves available in each one.

In sum, sales growth from oil (mainly exports), although high, was insufficient to maintain increased levels of leverage and adequate levels of profits and liquidity. Assets and liabilities expansion should have been curtailed to avoid further deterioration of the financial structure of the corporation. Two important observations, however, are in order. First, the feverish expansion of Pemex during the 1977–81 period was a reflection of unrealistic high national development plan goals— 8 percent per year, according to the Global National Development Plan, 1980–82. These goals were achieved, but the economy was overheated, which led to the crisis still in process. Heavy foreign borrowing, fiscal and monetary indiscipline, and deficits in the balance of payments characterized the Mexican economy in that period. In that context, the crisis can also be seen as the result of the lack of correct goals in the cases of both the government and many public and private enterprises. Quick profits were sought without regard for risks and the long-run effects of high leverage and of an overheated investment and asset expansion.

Second, financial-ratio analysis and goal programming clearly show that Pemex was not a strong candidate for credits. International credit managers should have been more cautious in their allocation of credits. Since most public corporations from the developing countries are characterized by a weak financial structure, what probably led to aggressive lending policies from the international financial intermediaries was overoptimism and excessive emphasis on "country risk analysis" in lieu of traditional product analysis.[15] Finally, summing up the results, it can be affirmed that goal programming is a powerful technique that can be used to improve financial decision making in the case of Mexico and other developing countries.

CONCLUSION

Capital markets are thin and imperfect in the developing nations. The theoretical building blocks and tools of modern finance are unknown to many practitioners or else have limited value as guiding lights for financial decision making. As a result, problems commonly found in financial decision making are the prevalence of traditional goals of the firm, weak treatment of risk, and ill-treatment of multiple operative goals. The belief that modern financial principles are not relevant to the case of the less developed nations has also led to an extensive use of outdated financial tools by financial managers. However, modern finance can provide valuable concepts and tools to solve the problems facing corporations in these nations. The key lies in (1) identifying properly the problems affecting a corporation and identifying their interrelationships and priorities, and (2) selecting the appropriate model or tool.

Similarly, market imperfections should not become a barrier to sound decision making. Overemphasis on optimization and the lack of fair market indicators has often led in the developing countries to contradictory results. Poor financial performance is mainly reflected in unbalanced results concerning liquidity, leverage, assets expansion, and sales and profits growth. Overoptimism tends to predominate to the extent that corporations engage themselves in rapid asset expansion, but they often reveal a weak financial structure, and growth becomes unsustainable. To solve these types of problems, corporations should fix multiple operative goals. Mathematical goal programming could be used to reconcile these goals. An application of this technique to the case of Pemex, Mexico's largest state enterprise, shows that this technique can be a valuable aid in financial decision making in the developing countries. This also implies that other mathematical techniques can be applied in financial decision making in the developing countries: multiperiod goal programming, dynamic programming, stochastic optimization, Monte Carlo simulation, and so on. These techniques should be used not only for reconciling profit planning with other operative goals of the firm, but also for working capital management and capital budgeting decisions.

Finally, market thinness and imperfections should not limit the use of efficient market theory, portfolio theory, the capital asset pricing model, the arbitrage pricing model, the option pricing model, and agency theory in the case of the developing countries. Rigorous research should be encouraged in these areas so that valuation, the measurement and management of risk, securitization and financing of the firm, and the management of portfolios fully benefit from modern finance in the developing countries.

NOTES

1. Excellent surveys on the development of finance are Michael C. Jensen and Clifford Smith, Jr., "The Theory of Corporate Finance: A Historical Overview," in *The Modern Theory of Corporate Finance*, ed. Michael C. Jensen and Clifford Smith, Jr. (New York: McGraw-Hill 1984), pp. 2–16; Gerald A. Pogue and Kishore Lall, "Corporate Finance: An Overview," in *Modern Developments in Financial Management*, ed. Stewart C. Mayers (New York: Praeger, 1976), pp. 26–45; Mark E. Rubenstein, "A Mean-Variance Synthesis of Corporate Financial Theory," in *Modern Developments in Financial Management*, pp. 46–60; and J. Fred Weston, "New Themes in Finance," in *Frontiers in Financial Management*, ed. W. J. Serraino, S. S. Singhoi, and R. M. Soldofsky (Cincinnati: South Western Publishing Co., 1981), pp. 27–34.

2. Antonio Basch, *El Mercado de Capitales en Mexico* (Mexico, D.F.: CEMLA, 1968).

3. Edgar Ortiz, "Inflacion y la Estructura Financiera de las Empresas Inscritas en la Bolsa Mexicana de Valores," *Contaduria/Administracion*, no. 102/103 (Mexico) (October–December 1979); "Caminata al Azar en Mexico," *Contaduria/Administracion* (Mexico) (February–April 1980): 65–109.

4. Ingolf H. E. Otto, "Prospects of the Mexican Stock Exchange," in *Current Economic and Financial Issues in the North American and Caribbean Countries*, ed. Edgar Ortiz (Mexico, D.F.: NAEFA, 1984), pp. 254–267.

5. Roberto Rodriguez, "Algunos Aspectos de la Bolsa Mexicana de Valores" (Mexico, Secretaria de Hacienda y Credito Publico, 1979, Mimeo).

6. Edgar Ortiz, "The Behavior of Stock Prices in Mexico" (Research paper, Uni-

versidad Nacional Autonoma de Mexico (UNAM), presented at the Annual Congress of the European Finance Association, Graz, Austria, September 1980).

7. Ortiz, "Caminata al Azar en Mexico."

8. Eugene F. Fama, "The Behavior of Stock Prices," *Journal of Business* 38 (January 1965): 34–105.

9. Robert A. Haugen, Edgar Ortiz, and Enrique Arjona, "Market Efficiency: Mexico vs. the U.S.," *Journal of Portfolio Management* 12, no. 1 (Fall 1985): 28–33.

10. Edgar Ortiz and Alejandra Cabello, "Sales Growth and Debt Management among Mexican Corporations, 1975 1982" (DAP/CIDE [Centro de Investigacion y Docencia Economica], 1983, Mimeo).

11. Information concerning Pemex development and financial trends has been drawn from Pemex, *Memoria de Labores*, various issues, 1970–84; Francisco Colmenares, "Problemas de Rentabilidad y Productividad en la Industria Petrolera" (Master's thesis, UNAM, 1985).

12. See Alfonso Malagon Vera, *La Administracion de la Deuda Publica Externa* (Mexico, D.F.: INAP, 1987).

13. Goal-programming applications are fully developed in Cheng F. Lee, *Financial Analysis and Planning: Theory and Application* (Reading, Mass.: Addison-Wesley, 1985); James C. T. Mao, *Quantitative Analysis of Financial Decisions* (New York: Macmillan, 1969); George C. Philippatos, *Financial Management: Theory and Techniques* (San Francisco: Holden-Day, 1973); and F. M. Wilkes, *Capital Budgeting Techniques* (Chichester, England: John Wiley and Sons, 1978).

14. The software package used was developed by Graciela Bueno and Enrique Arjona, Colegio de Posgraduados, Chapingo. The model combines goal programming and integer programming. It is derived from the works by A. Charnes, W. W. Cooper, Yuri Ijiri, and R. E. Gomory. A summary of their concepts and applications in finance are included in the works by Lee, Mao, Philippatos, and Wilkes cited in note 13.

15. However, it must be acknowledged that leading banks used sophisticated models to determine levels of country risk. See Shelagh A. Heffernan, *Sovereign Risk Analysis* (London: Unwin Hyman, 1986); Ronald L. Solberg, *Sovereign Rescheduling: Risk and Portfolio Management* (London: Unwin Hyman, 1988).

10

Capital Budgeting in Countries with Less Developed Capital Markets: Financial and Ethical Issues

MARJORIE T. STANLEY

Capital budgeting models as they appear in today's finance literature have been developed within the context of the well-developed and efficiently organized financial markets of the industrialized world. These capital budgeting models claim to be financially normative, but this claim rests on certain assumptions with regard to the perfection, efficiency, and completeness of markets. The models may claim too much even in the context of highly developed financial markets (see, e.g., Findlay and Williams 1980; Hiley, 1987, especially p. 348). In countries with less developed capital markets, the conditions assumed by the models are unlikely to exist. This situation has implications for resource allocation and economic welfare. It has implications for local firms and for multinational corporations with operations or proposed operations in such countries. Existing capital budgeting models and procedures may not be appropriate for businesses operating in countries with less developed capital markets. Some models may need to be modified in order to be appropriate; other models may need to be avoided.

This chapter proposes to examine two separate but related sets of problems relevant to capital budgeting in countries with less developed capital markets: (1) technical problems and financial issues associated with the capital budgeting techniques themselves; and (2) ethical issues related to the ethical limitations of current (ethically utilitarian) financial models, particularly with given disparities in market development. The objective of the analyses of these sets of problems is to develop recommendations with regard to the appropriateness of capital budgeting models, processes, and techniques for firms operating in countries with less developed capital markets, and to develop recommendations with regard to the use and interpretation of the models by business managers.

The first part of the chapter will review the theoretical foundations and assumptions of selected capital budgeting models, the market conditions necessary for their effective operation, and the data required for their implementation and will specify the resultant criteria that must be met if the models are to be operationally relevant and useful. The capital budgeting models will then be evaluated as to whether and to what extent these criteria can be met with the context of less developed capital markets. This analysis will be separately applied to local firms and multinational corporations. This first subsection of the chapter will include suggestions for modifications of the models and processes and will conclude with recommendations with regard to which capital budgeting techniques are most appropriate in the case of less developed capital markets. A related subsection of the chapter will consider cash-flow analysis and some selected factors of importance to cash-flow analysis in less developed capital markets.

The second part of the chapter will analyze capital budgeting in less developed capital markets from the point of view of ethical issues, criteria, and models. A goal of this portion of the chapter is to emphasize the relevance of ethical analysis for business financial managers and other business decision makers operating in less developed capital market environments in which the "invisible hand" of market forces may be particularly unable to adequately perform the ethical tasks frequently assigned to it. The conclusions reached in this section will serve to end the chapter.

TECHNICAL PROBLEMS AND FINANCIAL ISSUES

Evaluation of Capital Budgeting Models

The modern capital budgeting models regarded as financially normative are models that stress the time value of money (the pure rate of interest), the opportunity cost of capital, and return/risk relationships. All of these factors are regarded as market determined. For example, the market pricing of risk and discovery of the investor-required rate of return entails investor portfolio decisions effectively carried out in open financial markets offering a range of alternative financial instruments, speedily available public information, low transaction costs, and other characteristics of highly developed markets. Thus it is necessary to acknowledge the importance of the existence of the requisite markets in which capital budgeting inputs are to be determined in order to evaluate whether or not the use of the models will lead to results that are indeed financially normative. The applicability of the models to capital-allocation decisions in countries with less developed capital markets is subject to question from the point of view of the national economy and from the point of view of the firm and its owners. In economies in which markets are not developed so as to enable investors to reduce risk via diversification, the pricing of risk may differ from that postulated in Capital Asset Pricing Model (CAPM) based models, and resource-allocation decisions may differ accordingly. It also seems probable that the modern models cannot always be relied upon to give financially normative results for the firm. This point may be illustrated by an examination of selected capital budgeting procedures: net present value, internal rate of return, adjusted present value, terminal rate of return, variability of returns, and arbitrage evaluation.

Net Present Value

Net present value (NPV) is the basic "textbook" discounted-cash-flow capital budgeting technique. I begin with it because it is the basic textbook model and will serve to highlight some of the problems with which we are here concerned. The present value of a proposed investment is the present value of the expected after-tax cash flows from the investment, that is, the expected after-tax cash flows discounted back to the present at an appropriate discount rate (the cost of capital); net present value is the present value thus calculated minus the initial cash outlay for the investment. A project with a positive net present value should be undertaken; in the case of two or more mutually exclusive projects, the one with the higher net present value should be undertaken.

Two assumptions of this method are important for consideration here. The method asserts or assumes that the overall economic worth of the project is the key to acceptance or rejection. The method also assumes that the appropriate cost of capital is known. The cost of capital is a market-determined rate, the rate of return required by investors. (Use of the unadjusted overall corporate cost of capital for project evaluation assumes that the proposed project does not change the corporation's risk classification.) Shapiro noted that a desirable property of NPV is that it evaluates investments as the firm's shareholders would if they had the opportunity and is consistent with stockholder wealth maximization (1986b, p. 431), the assumed financially normative goal of U.S. financial managers.

The applicability of the net present value method to less developed capital markets may be considered under two separate headings, the multinational corporation (MNC) and the local firm. Analysts of MNC capital budgeting have long raised the questions of whether parent cash flows or project cash flows are the appropriate cash flows to use in the analysis of foreign investment projects, whether overall corporate cost of capital or local subsidiary cost of capital is the appropriate discount rate to use, and what adjustment for risk should be made. In short, should the project be analyzed from a parent or project viewpoint (Eiteman and Stonehill 1986, pp. 332–336; Shapiro 1986, p. 51)?

Theoretical arguments strongly favor the use of the parent viewpoint (Eiteman and Stonehill 1986, p. 331; Madura 1986, p. 414): Dividends to stockholders, interest to corporate debt holders, and the allocation of reinvested funds to alternative international investment opportunities all depend upon cash flows to the parent. It is notable that these arguments are strongly influenced by capital market considerations: There are market-mediated alternatives available, and there are stockholders and bondholders whose required rates of return on investment shape the investment decision. On the other hand, while capital budgeting theory requires that financial cash flows and operating cash flows not be mixed (Eiteman and Stonehill 1986, p. 332), the cash flows to the parent from the project do just that: For example, operating flows may be blocked from repatriation to the parent and be temporarily placed in local financial instruments, or cash flows may be importantly influenced by local government financing subsidies. Governmental financing incentives, which most multinational corporations report to have an important effect upon cost or availability of capital in host countries (Stanley and Block 1983, pp. 66, 70), may be particularly relevant in host countries with less developed capital markets.

Theoretically, the multinational corporation should not make an investment in a local project unless the MNC's risk-adjusted return would be greater than the return that a local firm might make on the project (Eiteman and Stonehill 1986, p. 332). Although this "rule" has implications for local resource allocation, the theoretical argument hinges on the existence of an opportunity for the MNC's stockholders to buy shares in the local firm as an alternative to shares in the MNC. In the absence of developed capital markets in the host country, this opportunity does not exist in practice; indeed, the comparison of the MNC's risk-adjusted return with that of a local firm is likely to be purely hypothetical.

In short, the theorized normative results and the relevance of the modern net present value theory to actual capital budgeting practice are, step by step, highly dependent upon the existence of developed capital markets and conditions and relationships assumed to prevail in them. Given the dependence of the theory upon a high degree of capital market development, the net present value approach to capital budgeting appears to require some modification when it is applied by local firms operating in less developed capital markets. These firms may be family firms, originally financed by a family and friends and subsequently financed internally. Psychic income and the importance of family control of the enterprise may have an important impact upon the "required rate of return." In the absence of public stockholders, this return is not subject to market determination and measurement. Neither is there a market-determined adjustment for risk. On the other hand, the local owners of a closely held firm know their own required rate of return. Thus the local closely held firm could use a net present value approach, employing a subjective hurdle rate as the discount rate. This would be at least a satisficing form of owner behavior. If local owners were to apply such an approach to alternative projects, the results would presumably be wealth-maximizing for the local firms, given the owners' utility functions. The effect upon economic allocation of resources for the local economy as a whole is less clear, depending in part upon such factors as the range of alternative projects considered by the local firm and the presence or absence of local competitors. More detailed analysis of this issue is beyond the scope of this chapter.

Internal Rate of Return

A second discounted-cash-flow approach to capital budgeting is the internal rate of return (IRR) method. In this approach the focus shifts from a monetary unit of measurement, the net present value, to a percentage measure, the discount rate that causes the present value of the cash flows, including the initial outlay, to sum to zero. This discount rate is discovered by a trial-and-error procedure. Once discovered, it might be compared with a market-determined cost of capital that is, a market-determined return required by a multinational corporation's security holders. The decision rule would require acceptance of any project whose internal rate of return exceeded this cost of capital.

The internal rate of return method is applicable in situations involving negotiated (as opposed to open-market) borrowing, such as might be utilized by a local firm operating in a less developed capital market. The method can also be easily applied to projects for which project-specific financing is available and relevant to the required rate of return. In contrast, project-specific financing can create a problem for the net present value approach employing the weighted average cost of capital, because the cost of capital can vary with project scale, other things being equal. Thus the internal rate of return method has some advantages over the net present value method in the case of less developed capital markets.

In well-developed capital markets the internal rate of return method will not ignore information available in the form of a market-determined cost of capital. However, such a market-determined cost of capital is not necessary to the internal consistency of the internal rate of return model when it is applied in less developed capital markets, where the internal rate of return can be compared with the hurdle rate required by the owner of financial capital. The model can thus perform a resource-allocation function in the case of less developed capital markets, with the local economy as the relevant referent.

In the case of mutually exclusive investment projects, the net present value and internal rate of return approaches will not necessarily rank the projects in the same order. In this situation in well-developed capital markets, the net present value method will be reliable. The internal rate of return method will be reliable only for internal rates of return greater than the internal rate of return on the differential cash flows between two mutually exclusive projects (Bierman 1986, pp. 9–12). Another practical problem in the use of internal rate of return methodology is the fact that it assumes that cash flows are reinvested so as to earn the project internal rate of return. The less developed capital market and the economy associated with it may not afford such opportunities. Thus the internal rate of return approach is not without deficiencies.

Limitations to the net present value and internal rate of return approaches, particularly in the international case, have led to suggestions for their modification that may have relevance for local and/or multinational firms operating in less developed capital markets. One of these modifications is the adjusted present value approach (see, e.g., Lessard 1985, pp. 570–584); a second is the use of the terminal rate of return (see, e.g., Rodriguez and Carter 1984, pp. 444–447, 452).

Adjusted Present Value

The adjusted present value (APV) approach is an attempt to provide an improvement on the net present value method for the valuation of projects wholly owned by a multinational parent or by investors having access to the same relatively complete capital markets (Lessard 1985, pp. 572; Shapiro 1985, pp. 550–551). It discounts financial cash flows, such as tax shields on market-rate debt financing, and flows attributable to local concessionary-rate debt, at the before-tax "normal" cost of debt. The appropriate "base" for the determination of the systematic risk reflected in the all-equity cost of capital is the capital market relevant to the particular firm, that is, the home market (or, perhaps, as markets become more integrated, the international capital market) of the parent multinational firm.

The adjusted present value approach applies the value additivity principle (Haley and Schall 1979, pp. 230–237), which, in turn, focuses on the value of the component cash flows available for distribution to security holders. Lessard argued that the potential for investor arbitrage that is necessary if this principle is to hold in the case of incomplete markets (e.g., investment by the MNC in a host country with less developed capital markets) involves only investor arbitrage among corporate after-tax income streams available for distribution by the parent (1985, pp. 572–573); thus lack of investor access to local substitutes for the project income streams does not make the adjusted present value approach inapplicable to the multinational's capital budgeting decision in the less developed capital market.

Booth (1982) has disputed the advantage of simplicity that Lessard claimed for the APV model in the multinational case and has pointed to a disadvantage in the fact that the APV model needs to know the amount of debt financing, which is itself a complicating factor. This objection, of course, is blunted by the fact that concessionary project financing, varying with the size of the project, was one of the factors with which the APV method was designed to deal.

The cash flows to the multinational parent, of course, are of undisputed importance when the APV method is employed. Political-risk analysis, particularly with regard to foreign exchange restrictions affecting cash flows to the parent, assumes accordingly greater importance.

It is also important to note that a local firm and a multinational firm using the adjusted present value approach might put quite a different valuation on the same project. This difference in valuation could result from a different required rate of return on equity associated with a different market base for the determination of systematic risk and/or with a lack of opportunities for diversification in a local less developed capital market. The difference in valuation could also result from a difference in the financial cash flows from the project, especially those associated with concessionary debt (available to the local firm?), and/or from a difference in the discount rate applied to the cash flows. The difference in MNC versus local-firm valuation of a project can have important implications for local resource allocation. Presumably, concessionary financing offered to a multinational corporation is indeed designed to impact local resource allocation.

Terminal Rate of Return

The terminal rate of return (TRR) approach to capital budgeting (Rodriguez and Carter 1984, pp. 444–447, 452) is an alternative offered to meet practical problems caused by the internal rate of return assumption that all reinvestment is at the internal rate of return. This assumption may not hold for either a local firm or a MNC operating in a less developed capital market. The terminal rate of return approach employs a reinvestment rate for project cash flows as specified by the capital budgeter and allows for different reinvestment rates of return for different segments of the time encompassed by the investment. It thus allows for flexibility in the analysis. The rate of return specified might be the firm's cost of capital, a rate obtainable from investment in available short-term securities, or other alternatives locally available, including those available to a multinational firm in the event of currency blockage. An investment horizon is specified, and the specified reinvestment rate is used to compound cash flows forward to this point in time. The terminal rate of return is the rate that equates to zero the horizon value and the initial investment outflow.

Using this approach, a local firm and a multinational might arrive at different internal rates of return for the same project, with consequent implications for resource allocation and for the role of the local versus the multinational firm in economic development. Nevertheless, local alternative investment opportunities are explicitly considered in the capital budgeting of both the local and the multinational firm. The approach is applicable to less developed capital markets and to developing capital markets. For example, it makes possible the use of one assumed reinvestment rate for currently existing market conditions and differing reinvestment rates that could allow for expected future capital market developments. It may thus increase the financial manager's level of comfort with the capital budgeting process as applied to projects in not-yet-developed but rapidly developing capital markets.

Variability of Returns

A variability of returns capital budgeting model was evaluated by Sundem in a study of the cost/benefit performance of six capital budgeting models in simulated environments (1975, especially pp. 984–985, 989–991). The variability of returns approach "postulates that the variance of returns from a single project is an appropriate measure of the risk of that project" (Sundem 1975, p. 984). The decision rule calls for the acceptance of a project if the mean of the net present value minus the product of the variance of the net present value times a measure of the decision maker's aversion to variability of returns is greater than zero. The essentials of this approach were suggested more than two decades ago (Hertz 1964); it thus predates more recent theory that emphasizes the use of market-determined prices of risk.

A notable feature of this model is its use of a subjective risk-aversion measure. While market-determined measures of risk may have theoretical support, there is nevertheless dispute about what measure of risk the market is pricing (see, e.g., Findlay and Williams 1980, especially p. 13). Numerous empirical studies of capital budgeting practices in relatively recent time periods affirm the use of subjective measures of risk adjustment by sizeable percentages of survey respondents (Schall, Sundem, and Geijsbeek 1978, especially p. 286; Stanley and Block 1983; Gitman and Forrester 1977, especially p. 70). Although the variability of the returns model employed in Sundem's simulation study was biased against projects with significant individualistic components to the variance of their returns, components that would be diversifiable at a market or firm level in other models, Sundem concluded that the model may be a cost/benefit-efficient model (1975, pp. 984–985). Thus it may be particularly relevant for the local firm operating in an economy with less developed capital markets that provides little opportunity for diversification at the market level and limited opportunity for diversification at the firm level. Nevertheless, the fact that investments are "lumpy" for the local investor

(Bierman and Smidt 1980, p. 218), combined with the lack of an objective risk criterion, may negatively impact the optimal allocation of local resources.

Arbitrage Valuation

Another alternative approach to capital budgeting employs arbitrage valuation (Gehr 1981). A portfolio of assets providing the same cash flows as those from a proposed investment is valued, thereby valuing the project. The benefits claimed for this approach are that it avoids the use of the capital asset pricing model and its "troublesome assumptions" (Gehr 1981, pp. 14, 18). For example, there is no need to know the value of a market portfolio, and the approach is applicable in international instances in which the risk-free rate and the market price of risk vary. Thus the approach answers to avoid some problems that the net present value method presents for capital budgeting in less developed capital markets. However, it may present substantial difficulties of its own.

The problem is to find a portfolio of assets that will provide the same cash flows as the proposed investment and to value it, thereby valuing the project. For the local firm in the less developed capital market, finding and valuing such a portfolio in the local environment would involve substantial information and search costs, assuming that the necessary portfolio of marketed, publicly traded assets could indeed be found. Alternatively, the use of this method by the local firm might depend upon the firm's access to nonlocal capital markets. The method assumes that cash flows are fungible—a cash flow is a cash flow is a cash flow. The local owner of a closely held firm might not view the firm's expected cash flows in this light. The method appears to have serious deficiencies when it is evaluated as a practical guide to resource allocation in countries with less developed capital markets.

For the multinational firm considering a project in a less developed capital market, finding a portfolio of assets that will provide the same cash flow to the parent as that expected from the project is facilitated by the fact that the multinational does have access to international capital markets. However, it is not evident that this arbitrage valuation approach is superior to the adjusted present value approach for the multinational firm.

Conclusions about Selected Alternative Models

It is apparent from this analysis of selected alternative capital budgeting techniques that project evaluation by the multinational firm is increased in complexity when the proposed project is in a less developed capital market. Furthermore, some of the capital budgeting models are either irrelevant or practically inapplicable to project evaluation by the local firm in a less developed capital market because the criteria that must be met if the models are to be operationally relevant and useful cannot be met within the context of less developed capital markets. The best techniques for the local firm would appear to be a net present value approach, the internal rate of return approach or the terminal rate of return variation on it, or a variability of returns model.

The net present value method employing a subjectively determined discount rate represents a return to basics insofar as the model is concerned. It takes the time value of money into account, but the pricing of risk is that of the individual local entrepreneur, not that of the CAPM model.

The internal rate of return and terminal rate of return approaches also take into account the time value of money and are in this sense financially sophisticated, but they do not demand market-determined required rate-of-return inputs that are not obtainable in less developed capital markets. The methods allow an evaluation of independent projects against the firm's hurdle rate, and the IRR method provides a limited means of ranking mutually exclusive projects. However, given the lack of opportunities for risk-reducing diversification, and the use of a subjectively determined discount or hurdle rate, the NPV, IRR, and TRR approaches as employed by the local firm may lead to resource-allocation decisions that differ from those that might result in a market environment in which opportunities for risk-reducing diversification were available.

The advantages and disadvantages of the variability of returns model for the local firm both hinge upon its lack of dependence upon data on market-determined cost of capital. This model is pragmatically useful for the local firm, but does entail previously noted shortcomings with regard to optimal resource allocation.

For the multinational firm, the adjusted present value and terminal rate of return models provide financially sophisticated capital budgeting approaches that are adaptable to the environment of less developed capital markets and do not require a marked departure from capital budgeting procedures employed by the multinational in other environments. It is clear that current capital budgeting theory provides the multinational firm with more sophisticated tools for project evaluation in the environment of less developed capital markets than those provided for the local firm in the same environment.

In a later section, this chapter will turn to an analysis of some ethical implications of this disparity. Before doing so, however, it is important to consider a problem common to all of the capital budgeting models and to their application in both developed and less developed capital markets. The problem is that of determining a project's cash flows.

Cash-Flow Analysis

Expected cash flows are core data in capital budgeting procedures, and errors originating in cash-flow data can negate the results of the most sophisticated capital budgeting models. This, of course, is widely recognized: Uncertainty over cash flows is a source of uncertainty in capital budgeting, and bias in cash-flow estimates has been associated with bias in capital budgeting. Textbooks on international finance urge that cash flows rather than the discount rate employed in net present value models be adjusted in the multinational corporation's capital budgeting for foreign projects (Eiteman and Stonehill, chap. 10). Sensitivity analysis is prescribed for cash flows (Eiteman and Stonehill, chap. 10). These observations and recommendations serve to highlight the fact that at each step of the capital budgeting analysis, the determination of expected cash flows is dependent upon assumptions made with regard to sales, prices, factor inputs, factor costs, taxes, inflation, exchange rates, and other economic variables. For the multinational firm, in particular, it is also dependent upon assumptions with regard to political risk and the prospects for managing it, including attendant costs and benefits. In many instances, political risk is closely related to the economic variables.

Problems associated with the determination of cash flows can assume new dimensions in the less developed capital market. Where capital markets are less developed, other markets may be less developed also. In such cases, there are fewer market data available to guide projections with regard to sales volume and prices and input costs. Market imperfections provide profitable investment opportunities; they also provide conditions in which human agency and use and abuse of individual and corporate power can affect distributive shares.

Cash Flows and Multinational Labor Costs

A critical factor here is labor. The multinational firm considering an investment project in a less developed capital market environment may find that it would have a monopsonistic or oligopsonistic position in the labor market. Wages would then have an administered-price as opposed to a competitive-price quality. The project cash flows of the project could then depend importantly upon the corporation's wage- and labor-relations policies.

Critics of multinational operations often single out for criticism the MNC's allegedly exploitative treatment of local labor in host countries, or, alternatively, the sociocultural distortion caused by the MNC's payment of above-average wages (see, e.g., LaPalombara and Blank 1979, pp. 180–181; Gunnemann 1975, p. 61). A corporation's labor-relations and financial decision making may not be integrated; labor-relations policymaking may be decentralized and financial decision making may be centralized. Nevertheless, to the extent that the corporation does have some monopsony power in the local labor market, it would do well to consider how cash-flow projections might vary with different assumed conditions for labor, that is, what posture toward its work force the corporation would be assuming in order to realize certain alternative cash-flow scenarios. Making these assumptions explicit would heighten the corporation's awareness of its socioeconomic and political role in the host country; it might serve to eliminate investment projects whose positive net present values were dependent upon labor-practice assumptions that would not meet a corporation's "social responsibility" criteria.

If the output of a multinational's proposed investment would be intended for international markets, product prices prevailing in these markets would constrain the multinational's pricing policy, its derived demand for labor, and its wage policy. It may be particularly difficult for the capital budgeter to quantify the potential impact on future cash flows as world market factors impact internal markets in rapidly changing market environments. Thus sensitivity analysis of future cash flows may be of particular importance to capital budgeting in less developed markets.

Cash-Flow Analysis and Political Risk

A multinational corporation's wage- and labor-relations policies may impact the corporation's political-risk situation, which has its own impact on cash-flow projections. Wages and working conditions superior to those that might be required by competitive local market conditions might even be regarded, from a practical as opposed to an altruistic point of view, as a cost of managing political risk.

It is also relevant to ask what other cash-flow adjustments should be made for the multinational's costs of managing political risk. One study, for example, has shown that multinationals whose executives initiated more contacts with host governments experienced statistically significantly less host-government intervention than those who did not initiate such contacts (Poynter 1982, pp. 19–20). Assuming that a multinational corporation was considering an initial investment project in a host country, the capital budgeting cash-flow analysis might well include a cost/benefit analysis of such "contacts" under given behavioral-model assumptions. Such considerations may be of particular importance in less developed markets, where resource allocation and market access may be importantly affected not by impersonal market pressures but by governmental executive, legislative, and administrative decisions. Capital budgeting that concentrates solely on market forces in such an environment may lead the corporate decision maker astray.

Cash-Flow Analysis and the Local Firm

The local firm's capital budgeting analysis is also made more complex in a rapidly changing market environment, where product and factor markets may change in rather unpredictable and perhaps unanticipated ways, creating conditions with which the local investor is not familiar. A great deal of uncertainty may be associated with the would-be local investor's cash-flow analysis. Under such circumstances, it may be tempting (and seemingly cost-effective) to resort to less sophisticated capital budgeting techniques; for example, what is the likely payback period? But cash-flow projections are needed in any case; to the extent that the assumptions underlying these projections are made explicit and their results quantified, the quality of capital budgeting will be improved. Incorporated in an internal rate of return or variability of returns capital budgeting approach, such cash-flow analysis should provide the local decision maker with a better guide to project analysis than would be provided by a crude payback model.

ETHICAL ISSUES RELATED TO CAPITAL BUDGETING IN LESS DEVELOPED CAPITAL MARKETS

The specific question of ethical issues involved in capital budgeting in less developed capital markets arises in part because of the reliance of existing models upon market-determined data as the basis for financially normative results. The financially normative results, in turn, are expected to produce ethically normative results in the sense that the allocation of financial resources in accordance with the model will lead to an allocation of real resources that meets posited ethical criteria. Financial resource allocation guided by stockholder wealth maximization is a descendant of ethically utilitarian models that posit the "greatest good to the greatest number" arising from resource allocation guided by expected future returns, with resources going to those uses in which the highest returns are expected. The more modern theory adds to the return dimension a risk dimension, for example, the market-determined risk premiums of the capital asset pricing model. Furthermore, from an ethical point of view, capital budgeting's use of data inputs from product, labor, and other factor markets in arriving at expected cash flows encompasses distributive as well as allocational issues. It is apparent that ethically normative results cannot be expected to follow from the application of capital budgeting techniques that cannot be relied upon to produce financially normative results when applied in environments that depart markedly from those assumed by the models.

The question of ethical issues related to capital budgeting can also be addressed at a more basic level, the question of values and of the ordering of values. This issue arises out of the nature of capital budgeting models, which are concerned with the allocation of resources to the best uses as measured by a quantification of returns expected from the production of certain goods and services. The assumption that scarce resources will be best allocated when they go to those uses that will produce the best returns as measured by NPV, IRR, APV, and related capital budgeting approaches is an assumption that depends upon a valuing of material goods and services as synonymous with "good" or with "welfare."

This ethical issue is relevant to any capital budgeting. The assumption of the capital budgeting models may seem to be more realistic and relevant in poorer countries than in wealthier countries that have reached high material standards of living; given conditions of extreme poverty, material welfare will rank high in a hierarchy of needs. In any case, from an ethical point of view it should be noted that values such as freedom, human dignity, and spiritual growth and well-being are not encompassed by the models, which are explicitly concerned with economic good and welfare as reflected in financial measures. Even economic "good" is narrowly defined, in the sense that the emphasis is upon value in consumption, not upon the value of jobs or the satisfaction derived from engaging in creative productive work. Nevertheless, now that we have noted this basic ethical limitation of capital budgeting models, ethical issues will be viewed mainly from within the economic constraints of the models in the remainder of this chapter.

Some Ethical Approaches

Pareto Efficiency

An advantage claimed for market systems from an ethical point of view is that they are generally Pareto efficient; that is, generally, the welfare of all or virtually all will be increased in the long run (McKenzie 1987, pp. 168–169). In a narrower sense, Pareto efficiency requires that increased welfare for some should not be at the expense of reduced welfare for others at the same time (McKenzie 1987, p. 169).

The extent to which international financial markets are integrated versus segmented is an important issue in international finance literature. As international financial markets become increasingly developed and integrated, the "all" with whom Pareto efficiency is concerned will increasingly extend beyond domestically circumscribed boundaries and markets. In the meantime, we are unlikely to be satisfied that increased welfare for some is not coming at the expense of reduced welfare for others at the same time.

A related ethical deficiency of our capital budgeting models in today's global economy is the fact that they do not provide a way to distinguish among kinds or qualities of material want-satisfaction, for example, luxuries versus necessities. In economic terms, a util of want satisfaction is a util of want satisfaction, even if we have had to expend resources to create the want in one case and not in the other. This is a serious ethical dilemma for market economies, especially those encompassing a broad range of wealth and poverty, a condition certainly characteristic of the global economy and often characteristic of countries with emerging market economies and less developed capital markets. Furthermore, the ethical outcomes of the capital budgeting models depend upon an implicit assumption that those who have a demand for want-satisfaction have the wherewithal to bid to satisfy those wants. If, through sheer poverty, their demand (e.g., for food) is not effective, the Pareto-optimal result claimed for market systems will not be achieved in practice.

The finance literature is replete with articles that focus on problems associated with allocation decisions. My purpose here is not to provide an inventory of this work, but simply to establish the fact that limitations of the models have long been acknowledged in the finance literature. For example, Arzac noted that "except for those special cases in which CPO [constrained Pareto optimal] investment plans are unanimously supported by stockholders . . . the theory of the firm in incomplete markets lacks a suitable maximization criterion" (1983, p. 175). Arzac proposed an internal allocation mechanism to deal with allocation in a stock-market economy lacking a complete set of contingent claims markets. Sundem noted that "the optimality of the NPV model under certainty and perfect capital markets is easily proved; however, the theoretically appealing qualities of the model dissipate if uncertainty is introduced" (1975, p. 986). Sundem evaluated six capital budgeting models from the point of view of the cost/benefit efficiency of the models in simulated environments; the net present value model achieved a very low level of performance in uncertain environments (1975, pp. 990–991). Litzenberger and Joy (1975) considered the implications of decentralized decision making on stockholder wealth maximization. They noted that "in an imperfect market, where the firm is able to influence the probability distribution of aggregate output, a social welfare function does not exist" (p. 993n). Yet, tantalizingly, in another view Findlay and Williams noted that "in equilibrium, it is necessary to assume an imperfection in one or more of the factor or output markets . . . to contemplate the existence of positive net present value projects" (1980, p. 10).

The major point for our purposes here is that operational ethical deficiencies in the models have been recognized with regard to their application even in highly developed financial markets, and various suggestions have been made with regard to possible refinements in the models or changes in their usage that might produce more normative results. This may reduce our level of expectations with regard to the ability of extant capital budgeting models to produce ethically normative results in economies with less developed capital markets.

The dynamic nature of markets is such that change may be costly for some individuals and communities in the short run, even though they benefit in the longer run. In a country with less developed capital markets that is moving toward more developed capital markets, the short-run costs of change may seem to dominate any long-run market benefits, especially if substantial social as well as economic change is involved. In a country with less developed capital markets that finds itself in the position of host to multinational corporations, resource allocation will be affected by international market pressures and by industrial organization that internalizes some international interdependencies (see Calvet 1981, especially p. 48; Hennart 1982, especially chap. 6). Multinational corporations may be more efficient than markets in organizing these interdependencies, but analysis of the welfare implications must move beyond the question of the Pareto efficiency of market systems (Hennart 1982, p. 17; Calvet 1981, p. 48).

Distributive Justice and Spheres of Justice

An analysis employing the concept of distributive justice and spheres of justice may be helpful. The spheres of justice approach set forth by Walzer (1983) evaluates welfare and distributive justice within a particular "sphere" on the basis of conventions and understandings within that sphere. It is thus a relativistic theory of justice: "Justice is relative to social meanings" (Walzer 1983, p. 312). In countries with less developed capital markets, local entrepreneurs are likely to share local meanings, conventions, and understandings; multinational corporations, however, operate in a broader sphere and in different spheres. Walzer argued that justice is lacking if special dominance in one sphere is extended, by conversion, to other spheres without regard to the distinctions between the spheres and the distinctive meanings of relevant social goods.

The relevance of this conceptual approach to capital budgeting in countries with less developed capital markets lies, first of all, in the very application of models and techniques valued as normative in the well-developed capital market sphere to the less developed capital market sphere. The spheres of justice concept warns us that what is just in one economic/financial environment may not be just in a differing economic/financial environment. It also alerts us to the fact that when people disagree about the meaning of social goods, or when understandings are controversial, some means must be found to express the differences and work them out. Walzer argued that the society must provide institutional means by which differences can be expressed and adjudicated (1983, p. 313). Even a well-developed capital market may need some "help" in mediating these differences.

Furthermore, a country with less developed capital markets that is nevertheless open to multinational corporate investment is likely to be experiencing socioeconomic change and changing social meanings. The spheres of justice approach argues that as these meanings change, the content of justice changes. In this view, then, justice is both relative and dynamic. From a capital budgeting point of view, the spheres of justice approach might seem to suggest that there is a reason for subjecting expected future cash flows to sensitivity analysis emphasizing differing future ethical "states."

Justice as Fairness

An academically influential approach to justice, justice as fairness, has been developed by John Rawls (1971) who stressed a hypothetical "original position" that would lead to two principles of justice. The original position is defined as one in which no one knows his or her "place in society," "class position or social status," or "fortune in the distribution of natural assets and abilities" (Rawls 1971, pp. 11–13). The two resultant principles of justice that would be chosen by people, given the original position, are that there should be equality in the assignment of basic rights and duties, and that social and economic inequalities should exist only if they result in compensating benefits for everyone, particularly the least advantages (Rawls, 1971, pp. 14–15).

Of course, social and economic inequalities do exist. One company's capital budgeting decisions and investment decisions may possibly serve to either increase or reduce them. Awareness of this possibility might lead a company to evaluate the effect of its activities upon social and economic inequalities (though not necessarily as part of the capital budgeting process). Given existing inequalities, most businesses contemplating an investment and subjecting it to capital budgeting analysis would probably maintain that an acceptable project in a market economy would contribute to overall economic welfare, including that of the least advantaged, by providing employment and producing want-satisfying economic goods and services.

In countries with less developed but developing capital and other markets, the relevance of the Rawlsian approach to the ethics of capital budgeting might be considered in terms of the fairness of the wage costs, working conditions, and other factor and product prices factored into cash-flow estimates utilized in the capital budgeting process. However, it is difficult to abstract oneself into the hypothetical original position, and outside of this position fairness may be perceived differently by different parties, for example, the presumably advantaged financial manager and the possibly least advantaged potential employee. It is possible that the employer might be willing to offer as fair something more than what the worker would be willing to accept as fair. An attempt to apply Rawlsian justice as fairness to the capital budgeting process is likely to result in ambiguity. One critic of the Rawlsian theory of justice argued that his theory will not be convincing or rational to people in social settings differing from those in which the theory was produced thereby seriously limiting its usefulness (McCoy 1985, p. 115).

Commutative Justice

Another concept of justice is that of commutative justice. Commutative justice is concerned with justice in exchange. Thus it is particularly relevant to market societies. Exchange occurs, however, even in the absence of organized markets. Commutative justice is therefore a useful concept regardless of the level of market development, and the concept of commutative justice may be applied to the capital budgeting decision in less developed capital markets. Commutative justice requires that harm not be done in exchange, and it thus requires equivalence in exchange. the market-clearing price in a competitive market economy is generally considered to represent equivalence in exchange, that is, to be a "just" price. However, it is important for commutative justice that the market participants have "shared meanings" and "mutual knowledgeability" about what they are exchanging (Gunnemann 1986, see especially pp. 102–104).

Shared meanings are likely to be present in exchanges between individual members of a local economy and local society; mutual knowledgeability may be more of a problem, given differences in education, relative social status, and so forth. For the capital budgeter analyzing an investment proposal, especially an investment proposal involving an economic activity new to the local economy, it seems that the local entrepreneur has an "advantage" over a multinational firm in terms of making cash-flow estimates using cost and return data that are likely to meet the requirements of commutative justice.

Exchanges between local economic units and multinational corporations are much more likely to lack shared meanings and mutual knowledgeability about what is being exchanged. This does not mean that the multinational is being intentionally unjust. It does reveal a potential source of social unrest and political risk for both the host government and the multinational corporation if local parties to an exchange become more knowledgeable ex post and feel or believe that they have made a "bad deal." It would probably be good long-run policy for both the government and the multinational to accept a teaching role designed to increase shared meanings and mutual knowledgeability about the exchanges that are to take place. In the nature of the case, the country with less developed capital markets lacks the financial and economic infrastructure that would contribute to mutual competence in exchange between local parties and the multinational, and the multinational's capital budgeters may not have the background and experience that would make them able to share local meanings.

There is a distance between the local producing market and the final consuming market when the latter is an international one. This distance is, in effect, bridged by the multinational, and the ability to bridge the distance is a source of the profit potential existing in the project for the multinational. But the very circumstances that create the opportunity for a positive net present value also create the potential for commutatively unjust exchanges. I believe that it is important for multinational corporations to be aware of this factor and to take it into consideration as they adapt their capital budgeting procedures to economies with less developed capital markets and evaluate the results of these procedures. Economic theory tells us that opportunities to earn above-normal profits in competitive markets are at best rare. This point has been the basis of a recommendation for the use of Bayesian decision rules in capital budgeting (Miller 1987). For the "socially responsible" or ethically aware corporation, it might also be the basis for a search for possibly unjust exchanges embedded in the projected cash flows of potential investment projects with high positive net present values.

Conclusion

It is possible that ethical awareness on the part of decision makers may operate so as to compensate, at least in part, for the welfare deficiencies attributable to imperfect, incomplete, or absent markets. It is certain that capital budgeting in less developed capital markets provides an important role for human agency in resource-allocation decisions and in decisions affecting distributive shares. Some observers (favoring the impersonal role of markets and fearing the power of corporations) would find in this fact an important reason for countries to promote capital market development.

One positive step that might be taken to strengthen capital budgeting in less developed capital markets from an ethical point of view would be to subject expected cash flows to adjustment and to sensitivity analysis that would reflect differing ethical "states of the world." This would be particularly useful to the extent that these ethical states are subject to the influence, determination, or control of the capital budgeting entity and its managers. If the corporation, particularly the multinational, has a corporate statement of goals, objectives, principles, or philosophy concerned with corporate responsibility (e.g., McCoy 1985, app. M), the responsible financial manager should ensure that there is congruence between the inputs into the capital budgeting process and the corporate responsibility statement. Such procedures would provide a form of ethical audit within the constraints of the existing capital budgeting process. They would highlight the particularly important role of human agency in the less developed capital market environment and heighten awareness that responsibility for ethical decision making cannot always be laid off on impersonal market forces.

REFERENCES

Arzac, Enrique R. (1983). "A Mechanism for the Allocation of Corporate Investment." *Journal of Financial and Quantitative Analysis* 18, no. 2 (June): 175–188.

Bierman, Harold, Jr. (11986). *Implementation of Capital Budgeting Techniques*. Tampa: Financial Management Association.

Bierman, Harold, Jr., and Seymour Smidt. (1980). *The Capital Budgeting Decision*. 5th ed. New York: Macmillan Publishing Co.; London: Collier Macmillan Publishers.

Booth, Laurence D. (1982). "Capital Budgeting Frameworks for the Multinational Corporation." *Journal of International Business Studies*, Fall, 113–123.

Calvet, A. L. (1981). "A Synthesis of Foreign Direct Investment Theories and Theories of the Multinational Firm." *Journal of International Business Studies*, Spring/Summer, 43–59.

Drake, P. J. (1977). "Securities Markets in Less-developed Countries." *Journal of Development Studies* 13, no. 2 (January): 73–91.

Eiteman, David K., and Arthur I. Stonehill. (1986). *Multinational Business Finance*. 4th ed. Reading, Mass., and Menlo Park, Calif.: Addison-Wesley Publishing Co.

Findlay, M. C., and E. E. Williams. (1980). "A Positivist Evaluation of the New Finance." *Financial Management* 9, no. 2 (Summer): 7–17.

Gehr, Adam K., Jr. (1981). "Risk-adjusted Capital Budgeting Using Arbitrage." *Financial Management* 10, no. 5 (Winter): 14–19.

Gitman, Lawrence J., and John R. Forrester, Jr. (1977). "A Survey of Capital Budgeting Techniques Used by Major U.S. Firms." *Financial Management* 6, no. 4 (Fall): 66–71.

Gunnemann, Jon P., ed. (1975). *The Nation-State and Transnational Corporations in Conflict.* New York: Praeger Publishers.

———. "Capitalism and Commutative Justice." *Annual, Society of Christian Ethics, 1985,* ed. Alan B. Anderson, 101–122. Washington, D.C.: Georgetown University Press.

Haley, C. W., and L. D. Schall. (1979). *The Theory of Financial Decisions.* New York: McGraw-Hill Book Co.

Hennart, Jean-François. (1982). *A Theory of Multinational Enterprise.* Ann Arbor: University of Michigan Press.

Hertz, David D. (1964). "Risk Analysis in Capital Investment." *Harvard Business Review,* January–February, 95–106.

Hiley, David R. (1987). "Power and Values in Corporate Life." *Journal of Business Ethics* 6: 343–353.

LaPalombara, Joseph, and Stephen Blank. (1979). *Multinational Corporations and Developing Countries.* New York: Conference Board.

Lessard, Donald R. (1985). "Evaluating International Projects: An Adjusted Present Value Approach." In *International Financial Management,* ed. Donald R. Lessard, 2nd ed., 570–584. New York: John Wiley and Sons.

Litzenberger, Robert H., and O. Maurice Joy. (1975). "Decentralized Capital Budgeting Decisions and Shareholder Wealth Maximization." *Journal of Finance* 30, no. 4 (September): 993–1002.

McCoy, Charles S. (1985). *Management of Values.* Marshfield, Mass.: Pitman Publishing Co.

McKenzie, Richard B. (1987). *The Fairness of Markets.* Lexington, Mass.: Lexington Books of D. C. Heath and Co.

Madura, Jeff. (1986). *International Financial Management.* St. Paul: West Publishing Co.

Miller, Edward M. (1987). "The Competitive Market Assumption and Capital Budgeting Criteria." *Financial Management* 16, no. 4 (Winter): 22–28.

Poynter, Thomas A. (1982). "Government Intervention in Less Developed Countries: The Experience of Multinational Companies." *Journal of International Business Studies,* Spring/Summer, 9–25.

Rawls, John. (1971). *A Theory of Justice.* Cambridge, Mass.: Belknap Press of Harvard University Press.

Rodriguez, Rita M., and E. Eugene Carter. (1984). *International Financial Management.* 3rd ed. Englewood Cliffs, N.J.: Prentice-Hall.

Schall, Lawrence D., Gary L. Sundem, and William R. Geijsbeek, Jr. "Survey and Analysis of Capital Budgeting Methods." *Journal of Finance* 33, no. 1 (March): 281–287.

Shapiro, Alan C. (1985). "International Capital Budgeting." In *International Financial Management,* ed. Donald R. Lessard, 2nd ed., 548–569. New York: John Wiley and Sons.

———. (1986a). *International Corporate Finance.* Tampa: Financial Management Association.

————. (1986b). *Multinational Financial Management*. 2nd ed. Boston: Allyn and Bacon.

Stanley, Marjorie, and Stanley Block. (1983). "An Empirical Study of Management and Financial Variables Influencing Capital Budgeting Decisions for Multinational Corporations in the 1980s." *Management International Review* 23 (March): 61–72.

————. (1984). A Survey of Multinational Capital Budgeting." *Financial Review*, March, 36–54.

Sundem, Gary L. (1975). "Evaluating Capital Budgeting Models in Simulated Environments." *Journal of Finance* 30, no. 4 (September): 977–992.

Walzer, Michael. (1983). *Spheres of Justice*. New York: Basic Books.

Part IV

Credit and Financing Policy

11

Uruguay

Macro Shocks and Industrial Portfolio Responses: An Econometric Model for LDCs

JAMES TYBOUT and TAEHO BARK

INTRODUCTION

Macroeconomic conditions change frequently and dramatically in the semi-industrialized countries. In this turbulent environment, policymakers hope that the industrial sector not only remains financially sound, but manages to grow rapidly. This study identifies the macro conditions under which industrial growth and financial stability are most likely, and those conditions that are most prone to create disaster.[1]

We model interest rates, exchange rates, and aggregate demand conditions as affecting industrial growth and financial risk through two channels. First, because these variables affect firms' income, they affect firms' net worth expansion. Second, because the link between macro variables and income depends on the proportions in which firms hold fixed capital, inventories, financial assets, and debts (hereafter the "portfolio mix"), changes in macro variables also induce portfolio adjustments. This chapter develops an empirical model that allows us to calibrate the strength and timing of each effect.

The model has several antecedents in the literature (Taggart 1977; Yardeni 1978; Jalilvand and Harris 1984). However, it breaks new ground by (1) treating corporate net income and savings as endogenous functions of macroeconomic and firm-specific variables; (2) treating fixed capital accumulation as endogenous; (3) distinguishing between domestic and foreign-currency-denominated balance sheet items; and (4) relaxing assumptions regarding functional forms and error structures. The model is also unique in that it is estimated with micro data from a developing country.

When fit to Uruguayan data, the model yields several basic findings. First, corporate income is very sensitive to output demand and the cost of dollar credit. Second, fluctuations in corporate income have a clear direct effect on the rate of net worth expansion. Third, firms absorb most short-run fluctuations in net worth via adjustments in assets, not debts. Finally, the interest elasticity of corporate demand for peso debt is very small. Inter alia, these findings imply that rapid changes in the exchange rate have large effects on corporate-sector leverage and liquidity.

The remainder of the chapter has two major sections: one to develop the model, and one to report an application to Uruguayan data. There is also a brief summary section.

A GENERAL MODEL OF CORPORATE INCOME AND PORTFOLIO ADJUSTMENT

The Basic Model

Our model can be summarized as follows. Each firm's net income is a function of macroeconomic variables (like output demand and interest rates) and firm-specific factors (like physical asset stocks, currency exposure, and overall indebtedness). Once earned, some portion of this income is retained by each firm, depending upon dividend policy and past earnings performance. Retained earnings increment net worth and are distributed among specific assets and liabilities according to, once again, macroeconomic and firm-specific variables. These increments to assets and liabilities set the stage for the next period's adjustment behavior.

Suppressing firm subscripts, the complete model is presented in table 11.1. For future reference we first call the reader's attention to the portfolio vector, $\mathbf{a}'_t = [a_{1t}, a_{2t}, \dots, a_{kt}]$, which is the focus of our analysis. This vector is defined to include a financial asset subvector $\tilde{\mathbf{a}}'_t = [a_{1t}, a_{2t}, \dots, a_{k-2,t}]$, inventories $(a_{k-1,t})$, and fixed capital (a_{kt}). Debts enter the financial asset subvector negatively, so summing the portfolio vector over all items yields net worth (equation (5)).

We now review the model's structure, beginning with the determination of income and net worth. By accounting identity we write real net income for a

Table 11.1
The Model

Stochastic Equations

$$\ln(G_t) = \theta_0 + \theta_1 \ln(a_{k-1,t-1}) + \theta_2 \ln(a_{k,t-1}) + \theta_3 \ln(Q_t) + \theta_4 \ln(w_t) + e_t^g \tag{2}$$
$$\Delta W_t = \phi_1 Y_t + \phi_2 Y_{t-1} + \phi_3 \Delta W_{t-1} + e_t^w \tag{3}$$
$$\mathbf{a}_t = \mathbf{MB} \mathbf{x}_t W_t + [\mathbf{I} - \mathbf{M}] \mathbf{a}_{t-1} + \mathbf{M}\delta + \mathbf{e}_t^a \tag{9}$$

Identities

$$Y_t = G_t + \tilde{\mathbf{a}}'_{t-1} \tilde{\mathbf{x}}_t \tag{1}$$
$$W_t = \Sigma a_{it} \tag{5}$$
$$W_t = W_{t-1} + \Delta W_t \tag{4}$$

*Precise variable definitions are provided in table 11.2.

representative firm in period t as equation (1). Here Y_t is real net income, G_t is operating earnings, and $\tilde{a}'_{t-1}\tilde{x}_t$ is the vector product of financial assets $(\tilde{a}_{t-1})$ held by the firm with the real yields $(\tilde{x}_t)$ these assets generate. Financial assets and real yields may be of either sign, so the second right-hand-side term of equation (1) may be positive or negative.

Real financial yields will be viewed as determined by macro conditions, and hence exogenous to the firm. So, since $\tilde{a}_{t-1}$ is predetermined, some assumptions regarding the determinants of operating earnings will complete the linkage between macro conditions and current net income. Suppose output (q_t) is Cobb-Douglas in labor (L_t) and beginning-of-period nonfinancial assets; that is, fixed capital and inventories:

$$q_t = L_t^\eta \left(\prod_{j=k-1}^{k} a_{j,t-1}^{\gamma_j} \right).$$

Also let the market for manufactured products be represented as in Dixit and Stiglitz (1977), so that under Bertrand competition the representative firm believes that it can sell output level q_t for price

$$p_t = (Q_t/q_t)^\sigma.$$

(Here σ^{-1} is the perceived elasticity of demand and Q_t is an index of total real expenditure on manufactured goods.) Then the representative firm will attempt to maximize short-run profits at wage rate w_t by choosing output such that operating earnings, $G_t = p_t q_t - w_t L_t$, are

$$G_t = \left(\xi^{\xi/(1-\xi)} - \xi^{1/(1-\xi)} \right) \left(Q_t^{\sigma/(1-\xi)} \right)$$

$$\times \left(\prod_{j=k-1}^{k} a_{j,t-1}^{\gamma_j(1-\sigma)/(1-\xi)} \right) \left(w_t^{-\xi/(1-\xi)} \right),$$

where $\xi = \eta(1 - \sigma)$. From this it follows that operating earnings are loglinear in the beginning-of-period quasi-fixed factors, the cost of labor, and total demand for manufactured products (equation (2)).[2] Note the correspondence between θ and structural parameters introduced above.

Equation (3) translates into net worth changes, that is, earnings retention.[3] This equation is simply a restatement of the dividend model that worked best for Fama and Babiak (1968). It is based on the assumptions that desired dividends are a weighted average of current and lagged income, and since shareholders want to smooth their earnings streams, adjustment that this desired level is partial in any period.

The linkage between macro conditions and firms' net worth is completed by the identity stated in equation (4).

It remains to motivate equation (9), which indicates how the representative firm allocates its net worth across specific portfolio items, setting the stage for next period. Suppose that, if conditions prevailing at time t were to continue indefinitely, the representative firm would like to hold some portfolio a_t^* in steady state. Moreover, let the elements of this desired portfolio each be linear in net worth:

$$a_{jt}^* = \alpha_{jt} W_t + \delta_j. \tag{6}$$

Here each δ_j is a (firm-specific) intercept term, and each α_{jt} is some linear function of a vector of variables x_t which are considered by firms when choosing their optimal portfolio:

$$\alpha_{jt} = \beta_j' x_t. \tag{7}$$

(The vector of financial yields, $\tilde{x}$, is a subvector of x.) Clearly, for the preferred portfolio to be feasible it must be that $\Sigma_{j=1}^k \alpha_{jt} = 1$ and $\Sigma_{j=1}^k \delta_j = 0$ for all t.

Finally, assume that discrepancies between a and a^* are eliminated via a partial adjustment process:

$$a_t - a_{t-1} = M[a_t^* - a_{t-1}] + e_t^a, \tag{8}$$

Here M is a matrix of partial adjustment coefficient, I is a conformable identity matrix, and a disturbance vector e^a has been added to establish exact equality.[4]

Combining equations (6), (7), and (8), the portfolio adjustment model may be expressed in terms of observable variables (equation (9)) where[5]

$$B' = [\beta_1, \beta_2, \ldots, \beta_k], \quad \delta' = [\delta_1, \delta_2, \ldots, \delta_k].$$

This system of k equations can be estimated along with equations (2) and (3), then used in conjunction with identities 1 and 4 to analyze the short-run and longer-term effects of changes in the economic environment on corporate income and portfolio choices. The variables G_t, W_t, Y_t, x_t, a_t, the disturbance terms e_t, and the intercept parameters δ will all take i subscripts to index firms.

Econometric Issues

Several problems arise in estimating the system of equations (2), (3), and (9). First, because panel data will be used, serial correlation will be likely: The idiosyncrasies of certain firms will give them disturbances with expected values that are systematically positive or negative. Hence we view the error term in each equation as composed of a "fixed" firm effect, υ, and an orthogonal random component ε that is serially and cross-sectionally uncorrelated. For the mth equation we write this $e_{it}^m = \upsilon_t^m + \varepsilon_{it}^m$. Note that because this fixed effect is equivalent to a firm-specific intercept term, its use implies that estimates of the vector δ_t cannot be obtained.

Second, because the data to be used include a wide range of firm sizes, a correction for heteroskedasticity is necessary. We first perform ordinary least squares with the deviation-form data and construct firm-specific mean squared residuals (equation by equation). The square roots of these statistics are then used to weight observations for associated firms (e.g., Fomby, Hill, and Johnson 1984).[6]

Finally, equation (5) implies that all columns of the parameter matrices **MB** and **[I − M]** in equation (9) must sum to zero except for the first column of **MB**, which must sum to unity. These constraints can be imposed on the asset demand system (9) by employing a constrained Zellner-efficient estimator (e.g., Theil 1971, chap. 6) after converting the data to mean deviation form and correcting for heteroskedasticity.

Interpreting Parameters

When interpreting our findings, it will be pedagogically helpful to distinguish between "substitution effects" and "wealth effects." The former pertain to changes in portfolio composition induced by changes in exogenous variables, holding net worth constant. The latter pertain to the effect of exogenous variables on net worth and the scale of asset holdings (via equations (1), (2), and (3)), holding constant the long-run desired portfolio composition.[7] This decomposition will be used to establish such things as whether increases in interest rates have their primary impact on firms via induced shifts in desired portfolio composition, or via reductions in income and net worth growth. Mathematically, the total impact effect of a change in some exogenous variable x_{kt} can be decomposed into the sum of these substitution and net worth effects by differentiating equation (9):

$$\partial a_t / \partial x_{kt} = \mathbf{MB}_{.,k} W_t + \mathbf{MB} x_t (\partial W_t / \partial x_{kt}). \tag{10}$$

Estimates of equation (9) provide the matrix **MB**; estimates of equations (2) and (3) provide the partial derivatives $\partial W_t / \partial x_{kt}$. (The subscript $.,k$ refers to the kth column of the subscripted matrix.)

Our model can also be used to contrast the impact effects of an exogenous shock with transitional and long-run effects. However, because our estimates reveal all these to be qualitatively similar, we focus on impact effects.

AN APPLICATION TO URUGUAY: 1973–1982

We now consider an application to Uruguay. But before discussing our variable definitions and findings, it is useful to review the major changes in the Uruguayan economy that took place during our 1973–81 sample period.[8]

The Uruguayan Economy

In 1973, the Uruguayan economy was on the bring of disaster. Inflation was accelerating toward 100 percent, the public-sector deficit was growing, and despite numerous controls on international capital flows, the Central Bank was rapidly losing reserves. These problems were widely perceived as the cumulative result of two decades of import substitution and a heavy reliance on state intervention.

When the military seized control in 1973, a dramatic shift toward laissez-faire policies began. Interest controls were quickly phased out, restrictions on holdings of dollar deposits were eliminated, the tax system was reformed, and numerous measures to restore trade flows were taken. In addition to a large real devaluation, these latter included the removal of controls on capital good imports, a gradual reduction in the level of tariffs, and various subsidies to exporters.

The economy responded miraculously. Real GDP growth, which had averaged less than 1 percent per annum during the import-substitution period, jumped to over 5 percent, and manufacturing investment responded in kind. However, despite these welcome developments, inflation remained stubbornly around 60 percent per annum. Hence by 1978 policymakers had begun to focus their attention more on price stabilization and less on liberalization per se. In particular, it was decided that the traditional measures of monetary restraints were inadequate in an open economy, and that the inertia of inflationary expectations was the problem. A new, unconventional policy designed to break expectations through exchange-rate management was enacted in 1979. This policy, nicknamed the "*tablita*" (little tableau), was a preannounced schedule of devaluations, each smaller than the last and all significantly less than the difference between world and domestic inflation rates.

The initial impact of the *tablita* was to induce large capital inflows that brought real interest rates back to negative levels not seen since the years of regulatory ceilings (–20 percent). But this boom period ended abruptly two years later when it became clear that the stabilization program was unsustainable. Capital inflows ceased, and peso interest rates soared to record heights. Simultaneously, external demand for Uruguayan goods rapidly dropped with maxi-devaluations in Argentina. Our sample period ends in the year of these developments, on the eve of Uruguay's own maxi-devaluations and financial crisis.

The Data

To link the changing Uruguayan macro environment with industrial-sector growth and financial structure, we fit our model to panel data on Uruguayan firms (augmented by several macro time series). The raw data for this exercise describe 74 manufacturing firms on an annual basis from 1972 through 1981. They were collected with surveys in 1975, 1980, and 1981, then corrected for inflation bias using a variant of the "general purchasing power" system of adjustment.[9] The sample, which represented roughly 65 percent of the total manufacturing labor force during the period of analysis, was stratified on the basis of employees (see Pascale 1982 for details). In cases where balance sheet or income statement identities did not hold exactly, the discrepancy was corrected with the assistance of the accountants who had prepared the statements. Firms whose inflation-adjusted books showed negative net worth were omitted from the sample, as were meat-packing firms, which operated subject to many special government regulations. This left 60 firms for our analysis.

Variable Definitions

Variable definitions for our applications to Uruguay are presented in table 11.2. Several aspects of these definitions merit brief discussion.

1. The Net Income Determinants: To begin, the net income variable (Y) which appears in equations (1) and (3) is real value added net of taxes, wages, and net financial outlays.[10] Hence the appropriate definition of operating earnings (G) in equations (1) and (2) is real value added net of taxes and wages. Other accounting identities imply that real financial income ($\widetilde{a}'\widetilde{x}$) amounts to real earnings on interest-bearing assets (a_2 and a_3) less the inflation loss on cash balances (a_1), less real interest payments on debt (a_4 and a_5). Note finally, that when estimating equation (3), we add a trend term to pick up productivity growth.

2. The Asset Demand Equations: Our asset categories represent something of a departure from convention. First, because Uruguayan securities markets are basically limited to government paper, corporate bond and stock issues can be ignored. Second, because Uruguay's dual-currency system has led to important changes in the dollar exposure of firms, and because many feel that this dollar exposure was a critical element of the financial crisis, we break down financial

Table 11.2
Variable Definitions

	Net Assets		Strictly Exogenous Variables
a_1	Cash and securities	x_1	intercept term
		x_2	inflation rate
a_2	Net peso trade credit	x_3	peso interest rate
		x_4	LIBOR rate
a_3	Net dollar trade credit	x_5	nominal peso devaluation rate
		x_6	real sales growth (firm specific)
a_4	Peso debt (sign reversed)		
		x_7	lagged real sales growth (firm-specific)
a_5	Dollar debt (sign reversed)		
		x_8	log [mean net worth during sample period] (firm-specific)
a_6	Inventories		
		w	real industrial wage rate
a_7	Fixed Capital	Q_t	real output demand (sample-wide)[a]

Vector Definitions

$\mathbf{a}'_t \equiv [a_{1t}, a_{2t}, a_{3t}, a_{4t}, a_{5t}, a_{6t}, a_{7t}]$
$\mathbf{x}'_t \equiv [x_{1t}, x_{2t}, x_{3t}, x_{4t}, x_{5t}, x_{6t}, x_{7t}, x_{8t}]$
$\widetilde{\mathbf{a}}'_t \equiv [a_{1t}, a_{2t}, a_{3t}, a_{4t}, a_{5t}]$
$\widetilde{\mathbf{x}}'_t \equiv [-x_{2t}, (x_{3t} - x_{2t}), (x_{4t} + x_{5t} - x_{2t}), (x_{3t} - x_{2t}), (x_{4t} + x_{5t} - x_{2t})]$

[a] Our output demand index is defined as sales of the entire sample divided by a manufacturing price deflator. Given that our sample is representative of manufacturing, this variable is roughly a Laspeyres quantity index.

items by currency denomination wherever possible. Finally, unlike other studies, we include fixed capital among the set of assets whose size can be adjusted endogenously. In our view, this is an important improvement.

There are several novelties in our vector of exogenous variables as well. First, because we distinguish peso- and dollar-denominated assets, we include the rate of nominal devaluation in $\mathbf{x}$.[11] Second, we include current and lagged real sales growth among our set of exogenous portfolio determinants. These are intended as proxies for the expected returns from "real" operations.[12] Finally, because of scale economies in certain items (e.g., cash balances), large firms may have different marginal allocations of wealth than small firms, given interest rates, and other factors. To account for this possibility, we define $\mathbf{x}$ to include a firm-size index— the logarithm of average net worth over the sample period. Thus, given the presence of a firm-specific intercept in equation (6), both the slope and the intercept of the linear relation between wealth and asset demands can shift from firm to firm.

Findings

Estimates of equations (2) and (3) are reported in table 11.3, and estimates of the system (9′)) are reported in table 11.4. Below we present interpretations.

1. Income and Net Worth Effects: from equation (10), the total impact of a change in an exogenous variable on firms' portfolios can be broken into a net worth effect and a substitution effect. In this section we interpret our findings regarding the former. For this exercise it is convenient to further break down the net worth effect of a change in the kth exogenous variable into the marginal impact of the variable on income, times the marginal impact of income on net worth:

$$\mathbf{MBx}_t(\partial W_t/\partial x_{kt}) = (\partial Y_t/\partial x_{kt})\mathbf{MBx}_t/\partial Y_t).$$

We now examine each right-hand-side component of this expression.

(a) Determinants of Net Income: Equations (1) and (2) link exogenous and predetermined variables to net income. Estimated parameters for the latter appear in the supper portion of table 11.2. All coefficients have expected signs, and most are of plausible magnitude. Coefficients for fixed capital and wages are exceptions, being unexpectedly small, but these are not estimated with much accuracy. (For the wage coefficient, this may be partly due to the fact that the only available series is of poor quality.) We therefore tentatively conclude that the effects of wages and fixed capital stocks on operating earnings appear to be small in the short run, and we turn our attention to other variables.

Output Demand: Operating earnings do appear sensitive to fluctuations in the demand for manufactured goods (table 11.3, $\hat{\theta}_3$). A 10 percent drop in expenditures on manufactured goods reduces operating earnings by almost 12 percent. Or, using the fact that operating earnings are about 0.22 of net worth, the effect is to reduce net income by an amount equal to 0.026 of net worth. One can thus imagine that the sudden reduction in Argentine demand for Uruguayan products that took place in 1981 had a major effect on industrial-sector profitability.

Table 11.3

Estimates of θ and φ from Equations (2) and (3)[a]

Equation 2: (Dependent Variable is Operating Earnings)[b]

Coefficient	
$\hat{\theta}_1$ (lagged inventories)	0.15[c]
	(7.40)
$\hat{\theta}_2$ (lagged fixed capital)	0.01
	(0.73)
$\hat{\theta}_3$ (manuf. output demand)	1.15[c]
	(11.51)
$\hat{\theta}_4$ (manuf. wage rate)	−0.18
	(−1.33)
$\hat{\theta}_5$ (trend, total revenue)	−0.01
	(−1.05)
$\hat{\theta}_6$ (trend, operating costs)	−0.02[c]
	(−2.55)

Equation (3): (Dependent Variable is Change in Net Worth)

Coefficient	
$\hat{\phi}_1$ (current net income)	0.64[c]
	(12.57)
$\hat{\phi}_2$ (lagged net income)	−0.11
	(−1.88)
$\hat{\phi}_3$ (lagged change in net worth)	−0.05
	(−0.98)

[a]Equations are estimated using data in firm-specific deviation form, hence intercepts are not estimated. Reported results are after heteroskedasticity correction.
[b]All variables in equation (2) are measured in logarithms. Operating earnings were not directly regressed on the explanatory variables. Rather, coefficients from the operating earnings equation were obtained by fitting a total revenue and an operating cost function simultaneously, imposing the appropriate cross-equation constraints. This afforded some gain in efficiency.
[c]1% significance.

Borrowing Costs: By equation (1), increases in real borrowing cost reduce net income to the extent that firms have net financial liabilities in the associated currencies. Conversely, increases in the inflation rate reduce net income to the extent that firms have net monetary assets. To give an idea of the magnitudes involved, it is useful to consider some examples based on the consolidated balance sheet for the entire sample. Specifically, in 1980, the ratio of net peso liabilities to net worth was about 0.15, so a 10 percentage point increase in real peso interest rates (e.g., from 0 percent to 10 percent) would have cut net income by an amount equivalent to about 0.015 of net worth. By similar calculations, a 10 percentage point increase in the cost of dollar credit would have cut net income by about 0.035 of net worth, and an increase in the inflation rate by 10 percentage points would have resulted in capital losses on monetary assets of about 0.015 of net worth. The average ratio of net income to net worth was about 0.07 in 1980, so fluctuations on this order of magnitude clearly are significant. It is noteworthy that by 1980 firms were the most sensitive to fluctuations in the cost of dollar credit and hence were

Table 11.4
Estimates of MB and (I − M) from Equation (9)

Explanatory Variables	a_1 Cash and Securities	a_2 Peso Trade Credit	a_3 Dollar Trade Credit	a_4 Peso Loans	a_5 Dollar Loans	a_6 Inventories	a_7 Fixed Capital
x_1 constant	0.51[b] (5.07)	−0.00 (−0.02)	−0.11 (−1.53)	0.05 (0.70)	−0.11 (−0.88)	0.49[b] (2.36)	0.17 (1.27)
x_2 inflation	−0.06[b] (−3.69)	−0.03 (−1.14)	0.00 (0.31)	−0.00 (−0.07)	−0.02 (−1.16)	0.09[b] (2.72)	0.03 (1.36)
x_3 peso interest rate	−0.00 (−0.25)	0.03 (1.11)	−0.03[a] (−2.23)	0.00 (0.37)	−0.03 (−1.42)	0.24[b] (7.07)	−0.21[b] (−8.80)
x_4 LIBOR rate	0.05 (0.73)	0.05 (0.48)	0.07 (1.18)	−0.03 (−0.78)	0.12 (1.57)	−0.01 (−0.09)	−0.25[b] (−2.88)
x_5 devaluation rate	−0.02 (−1.21)	−0.06[b] (−2.36)	−0.03[b] (−2.58)	−0.01 (−1.40)	0.06[b] (3.49)	0.14[b] (4.96)	−0.08[b] (−4.21)
x_6 sales growth	0.06[b] (6.34)	−0.05[b] (−2.97)	−0.00 (−0.19)	−0.00 (−0.01)	−0.02[b] (−2.51)	0.03 (1.60)	−0.02 (−1.45)
x_7 lagged sales growth	0.04[b] (3.92)	−0.03[a] (−1.94)	−0.00 (−0.25)	0.01 (0.88)	0.00 (0.38)	0.05[b] (2.60)	−0.06[b] (−5.31)
x_8 log of firm size	−0.04[b] (−4.55)	0.01 (0.82)	0.01 (1.88)	−0.00 (−0.66)	0.01 (1.20)	−0.02 (−0.81)	0.02 (1.58)
$a_1(-1)$ lagged cash and securities	0.45[b] (12.71)	−0.16[b] (−3.30)	−0.02 (−0.84)	−0.02 (−1.00)	−0.05 (−1.45)	−0.16 (−3.07)	−0.05 (−1.51)
$a_2(-1)$ lagged peso trade credit	−0.01 (0.47)	0.40[b] (9.90)	−0.02 (−1.21)	−0.02 (−0.99)	−0.08[b] (−3.21)	−0.19[b] (−4.42)	−0.09[b] (−4.01)
$a_3(-1)$ lagged dollar trade credit	0.02 (0.80)	−0.13[b] (−2.35)	0.23[a] (5.16)	0.02 (0.86)	0.10 (1.81)	−0.16[b] (−2.39)	−0.09[b] (−2.49)
$a_4(-1)$ lagged peso loans	0.02 (1.11)	−0.13[b] (−2.85)	0.04[b] (2.20)	0.41[b] (10.15)	0.03 (0.89)	−0.24[b] (−4.60)	−0.14[b] (−4.85)
$a_5(-1)$ lagged dollar loans	0.02 (1.41)	−0.10[b] (−2.58)	−0.01 (0.59)	−0.03 (−1.41)	0.51[b] (13.29)	−0.28[b] (−6.10)	−0.11[b] (−4.51)
$a_6(-1)$ lagged inventories	0.04[b] (4.29)	−0.02 (−0.68)	0.01 (0.62)	−0.01 (−0.53)	−0.06[b] (−2.84)	0.11[b] (3.45)	−0.07[b] (−4.57)
$a_7(-1)$ lagged fixed capital	−0.01 (−0.97)	−0.15[b] (−6.21)	−0.01 (−1.19)	0.00 (0.17)	−0.06[b] (−2.69)	−0.38[b] (−12.12)	0.61[b] (25.67)

Note: The transpose of **MB** appears as the first 8 rows; the transpose of **(I − M)** appears as the last 7 rows.
Estimated as a constrained Zellner-efficient system after expressing data in firm-specific deviation form and correcting for heteroskedasticity.
[a] Significant at the 5% level.
[b] Significant at the 1% level.

vulnerable to large devaluations. The large Uruguayan devaluations that took place in 1982 must have greatly worsened earnings problems due to slack product markets and turned net income negative for a large fraction of the manufacturing sector.

(*b*) *Translating Income Effects into Wealth Effects:* Once income is earned, firms must decide how much to retain, and how much to pay out to shareholders. We have represented this decision with equation (3), for which estimates are reported in the bottom half of table 11.3. Very simply, it appears that roughly 64 percent of each peso of current net income is retained. Other terms in the equation have signs that confirm our basic model: Desired dividends are a weighted average of current and lagged income, and only partial adjustment toward desired payout levels takes place each period. However, there appears to be a heavy bias toward current rather than lagged income in determining desired payments, and the fraction of adjustment that takes place in the current period is not significantly less than 1.

Combining equation (2) estimates with equation (3), we now have a complete representation of the chain of causation from interest rates, devaluation rates, and real output demand to net worth effects. For example using the relationship $\partial W_t/\partial x_{kt} = (\partial W_t/\partial Y_t)(\partial Y_t/\partial x_{kt}) = .64(\partial Y_{kt}/\partial x_{kt})$, we can calculate the short-run wealth effect of a 10 percentage point increase in peso interest rates as $\partial W_t/\partial x_{2t} = .64(.10)(a_{4t-1} + a_{2t-1})$, which for a typical portfolio composition amounts to roughly a $0.01W_t$ reduction in net worth growth (recall that a_{4t} is negative). Alternatively, a 10 percent real devaluation would reduce net worth growth by more than $0.02W_t$, reflecting the fact that firms relied more heavily on dollar debt. Finally, a 10 percent fall in manufacturing output demand reduces net worth growth by slightly less than $0.02W_t$.

(*c*) *Wealth Effects and Portfolio Composition:* What influence do these short-run wealth effects have on portfolio composition? Referring back to equation (10), one sees that wealth effects are translated into portfolio changes by the vector **MBx**$_t$. This vector reflects the influence of long-run desired portfolio composition (via **Bx**$_t$) and adjustment costs (via **M**). To gauge the net effect of these influences, we use estimated elements of **MB** and actual **x** to construct this vector year by year. For example, in 1980, a typical year, a one-unit change in net worth would have led to a 0.07 increase in cash, a 0.10 increase in net peso trade credit, virtually no change in net dollar trade credit, a 0.48 increase in inventories, a 0.42 increase in fixed capital, a 0.02 increase in peso borrowing, and a 0.06 increase in dollar debt. (Figures for other years are available upon request.)

In some sense this distribution of the shock is just what one would expect—earnings increases become liquid assets and induce fixed capital expansion. But it is surprising that virtually no adjustment to peso borrowing takes place. The implication is that standard indices of corporate financial risk—liquidity measures and leverage—are quite sensitive to fluctuations in income. A firm that suffers negative earnings reduces its liquid asset stock, and because there is no reduction in peso borrowing the overall debt/equity ratio clearly rises.

2. Induced Substitution: We now turn our attention to substitution effects. Referring back to equation (10), one sees that the kth column of the matrix **MB**, multiplied by W, represents the short-run changes in portfolio holdings induced by a unit change in the kth exogenous variable. Or equivalently, the kth column of **MB** is simply the substitution-induced change in the asset vector expressed as a ratio to net worth. This fact is used below to interpret the **MB** and **I − M** matrices reported in table 11.4.

Inflation Rates: consider first the short-run substitution effects of a change in the rate of inflation. Holding net worth constant, an increase in this variable changes the predicted portfolio mix according to the coefficients reported in the second row of table 11.4. For example, a 100 percentage point change in the inflation rate results in a 0.06 reduction of cash and securities, a 0.03 unit reduction in peso trade credit, and a 0.09 increase in inventories (each expressed as a ratio to net worth). Overall, then, substitution takes place away from peso-denominated assets toward inflation hedges—especially inventories. Notice, however, that peso borrowing is completely insensitive to the inflation rate.

Peso Interest Rates: The substitution effects of peso interest rates also seem to conform largely to our priors. From the third row of table 11.4 one sees that increases in peso rates tend to strongly discourage fixed capital holding and encourage inventory accumulation.[13] Also, dollar borrowing increases while net dollar trade credit falls, so the combined effect is clearly to increase currency exposure. Interesting, there is once again no effect on peso borrowing. Recalling from earlier that the net worth effect of peso rates on peso borrowing is also very small, one may conclude that peso credit demand is very inelastic. This result suggests that considerable increases in interest rates may accompany minor increases in credit demand, and in particular, it may help explain the extremely high and volatile interest rates that emerged in all Southern Cone countries following interest-rate decontrol. Surprisingly, previous analyses of Southern Cone interest rates have tended to overlook this explanation.

LIBOR and Devaluation Rates: The return on dollar-denominated balance sheet items is the sum of the dollar interest rate (LIBOR) and the rate of peso devaluation. To test whether this sum can be treated as one explanatory variable, we imposed within-equation equality of their respective coefficients and obtained an $F(7,2850)$ statistic of 2.23, which has a marginal significance level of about 97 percent. Thus, in view of the large number of degrees of freedom, it appears that the differences between the effects of the two variables are small, and we will not discuss each separately.

The main effect of rising dollar costs is to discourage fixed capital holding and encourage the holding of inventories and trade credit. So when Uruguay slowed the devaluation rate in the latter 1970s, capital accumulation was induced by both net worth expansion (due to higher net earnings) and by shifts in portfolio composition.[14] No doubt part of the explanation for the latter lies in the high import content of manufacturing-sector capital.

Recalling that the net worth effects of a devaluation were also found to be strong, it is worth asking how they combined with the substitution effects identified above.

Referring back to the section on Wealth Effects and Portfolio Composition, one may confirm that net worth effects compound the negative substitution effect of a devaluation on cash and trade credit. So devaluation strips firms of their most liquid assets because strong net worth and substitution effects compound one another.

Sales Growth: Rapid sales growth appears to induce short-run substitution toward cash, securities, and inventories. This shift is financed by reductions in fixed capital (per unit net worth) and by increased dollar borrowing. Except for the latter effect, therefore, firms that improve their sales performance tend to become more liquid, at least initially. Some of the substitution effects induced by sales growth might seem, at first glance, counterintuitive. But one must keep in mind that the total portfolio response to a change in sales includes net worth effects as well. Hence, for example, the positive impact of sales on income and net worth identified in earlier discussions easily outweighs the tendency to shift the portfolio away from fixed capital, and the familiar accelerator relationship obtains. Similarly, sales growth tends to increase net peso trade credit, once net worth effects are accounted for.

Firm Size and Portfolio Composition: It was noted earlier that scale economies and other factors may cause large firms to desire different portfolios than small firms operating in the same economic environment. We observe in passing that table 11.4 confirms that such effects are indeed significant, but only for cash and securities.

SUMMARY AND CONCLUSIONS

Generally, Uruguayan data fit our model of corporate financial behavior well. The portfolio composition equations suggest significant substitution effects in expected directions when real yields or expected revenue growth rates change. Also, there appears to be a straightforward linkage between net income and net worth expansion. Finally, the adverse effects of contractions in output demand or financial cost increases on firms' profitability are severe in the short run. Hence, for example, major changes in the exchange regime can mean boom or bust for the industrial sector.

Examining the short-run effects of net worth expansion on balance sheet composition, we find that liquid asset stocks correlate positively with net worth growth, and peso debt does not correlate at all. So the results imply that when maxi-devaluations or other shocks reduce corporate income, operating expenses are met by drawing down net liquid assets. Of course, once these stocks are exhausted, slack markets for inventories and fixed capital could mean that firms have no way to meet their operating expenses. This problem could have been the proximate cause of the Uruguayan financial crisis that emerged in 1982 after the aggregate demand collapse.

Although net worth effects appear to be more important than substitution effects when explaining balance sheet changes, a number of the latter are noteworthy. Reductions in inflation reduce inventories and increase peso asset holdings. Increases in peso interest rates strongly discourage fixed capital formation, while inducing a shift into inventories and increasing net dollar exposure. But the effect of this variable on demand for peso-denominated items is insignificant. (The rate of devaluation appears to play a much larger role in predicting peso-dollar substitution.) One implication is that a financial liberalization program that amounts basically to interest-rate decontrol is unlikely to induce much expansion in the stock of peso-denominated financial wealth. Indeed, Uruguay's expansion was apparently traceable to other factors. Equally interesting, the extremely small interest elasticity of demand for peso credit suggests a possible source of financial market instability when interest rates are decontrolled.

NOTES

Funding for this research was provided by the World Bank. The authors wish to thank Douglas Brown, Yoon Je Cho, John Cuddington, Dale Henderson, Jaime de Melo, Daniel Westbrook, and two anonymous referees for comments on an earlier draft. They are also grateful to Jackson Magargee for typing, and to Gabriel Casillo, Ty Mitchell, and Shoihi Katayama for assistance with data preparation.

The World Bank does not accept responsibility for the views expressed herein, which are those of the author(s) and should not be attributed to the World Bank or to its affiliated organizations. The findings, interpretations, and conclusions are the results of research supported by the Bank; they do not necessarily represent official policy of the Bank.

1. Tybout (1986) presents descriptive interpretations of the relationships between macro variables and industrial financial statements in the Southern Cone countries. However, unlike the present chapter, that study does not attempt behavioral modelling.

2. An earlier version of this chapter assumed that gross earnings depended on total financial costs, the wage rate, and output demand. However, this specification was difficult to reconcile with product market equilibrium and it fit poorly, so the above alternative has been adopted. The reported figures should thus be viewed as resulting from a specification search.

3. We ignore new stock issues as a source of net worth expansion because they are of negligible empirical significance in the country to which the model will fit.

4. Variants on equation (8) may be found in Taggart (1977), Yardeni (1978), and Jalilvand and Harris (1984). Unlike Taggart, we place no zero constraints on elements of M. Also, unlike Jalilvand and Harris, we do not require that the off-diagonal elements of M within a column be equal. Cross-equation consistency constraints implied by the identity 5 (Brainard and Tobin 1968) are nonetheless imposed by our estimation technique, as will be seen below.

5. Equation (9) resembles the dynamic factor demand system derived by Prucha and Nadiri (1986) if we assume that exogenous variables in the system follow a first-order autoregressive process. Details of the analogy are available on request.

6. Jalilvand and Harris (1984), in the only other panel-data study of industrial portfolio adjustments we are aware of, employ the same mean square error correction we use.

7. Such effects have been generally ignored in earlier empirical portfolio balance models.

8. For more details, see Hanson and de Melo (1985) and de Melo and Tybout (1986).

9. General patterns that emerge from the data are described in de Melo, Pascale, and Tybout (1985). Details of the inflation adjustment procedure are provided in the World Bank Staff Working Paper version of this same study, and in Tybout (1988).

10. Uruguay had a value-added tax rather than a profit tax during the sample period. Wages should be interpreted to include administrative and marketing expenses.

11. An earlier version of the model incorporated the real exchange rate as a proxy for expected devaluation rates. Since the results suggested that firms were able to accurately anticipate devaluation rates for the current year, we have simply included the nominal devaluation rate directly in this version. Accurate prediction was no doubt aided by the fact that devaluation rates were preannounced by the Central Bank during much of the sample period.

12. An alternative model was estimated in which operating earnings per unit assets played this role—it yielded very similar results. The version of the model with sales growth is reported here because expected sales proxies seem to be standard in the literature (Taggart 1977; Yardeni 1978).

13. This strongly suggests that previous portfolio models that treat physical capital as exogenous are misspecified.

14. De Melo and Tybout (1986) found a negative association between the real exchange rate and the level of investment during the post-1973 period using Uruguayan macro data. Since low real exchange rates are associated with low rates of devaluation, this finding seems to conform to the micro results reported here.

REFERENCES

Brainard, William, and James Tobin. (1968). "Pitfalls in Financial Model Building." *American Economic Review*, May, 99–122.

Dixit, Avinash, and Joseph Stiglitz. (1977). "Monopolistic Competition and Optimal Product Diversity." *American Economic Review*, 279–308.

Fama, E., and H. Babiak. (1968). "Dividend Policy: An Empirical Analysis." *Journal of the American Statistical Association*, 1132–1161.

Fomby, Thomas, R. Carter Hill, and Stanley Johnson. (1984). *Advanced Econometric Methods*. Heidelberg: Springer-Verlag.

Hanson, James, and Jaime de Melo. (1985). "External Shocks, Financial Reforms, and Stabilization Attempts in Uruguay During 1974–83." *World Development*, August, 917–939.

Jalilvand, Abolhassan, and Robert Harris. (1984). "Corporate Behavior in Adjusting to Capital Structure and Dividend Targets: An Econometric Study." *Journal of Finance*, March, 127–145.

Melo, Jaime de, Ricardo Pascale, and James Tybout. (1985). "Uruguay, 1973–81: The Interplay of Real and Financial Shocks." *World Development*, August, 995–1015.

Melo, Jaime de, and James Tybout. (1986). "The Effects of Financial Liberalization on Savings and Investment in Uruguay." *Economic Development and Cultural Change*, April, 561–588.

Pascale, Ricardo. (1982). *El Comportamiento Financiero de la Industria Manufacturera Uruguaya*. Montevideo: Banco Central de Uruguay.

Prucha, Ingmar, and Ishaq Nadiri. (1986). "A Comparison of Alternative Methods for the Estimation of Dynamic Factor Demand Models under Non-Static Expectations." *Journal of Econometrics* 33: 187–211.

Taggart, Robert. (1977). "A Model of Corporate Financing Decisions." *Journal of Finance*, December, 1467–1484.

Theil, Henri. (1971). *Principles of Econometrics*. New York: John Wiley and Sons.

Tybout, James. (1986). "A Firm-Level Chronicle of Financial Crisis in the Southern Cone." *Journal of Development Economics*, December, 371–400.

———. (1988). "The Algebra of Inflation Accounting." *International Economic Journal*, Summer, 83–100.

Yardeni, Edward. (1978). "A Portfolio-Balance Model of Corporate Working Capital." *Journal of Finance*, May, 535–552.

N|A

öt6

unuguay

p211: # Discussant: Ashok Vora

I think that this is an interesting chapter: interesting because hard-to-find data from a Southern Cone country are used; interesting also because it reveals more about our profession than it does about Uruguay. The authors do much fancy econometric footwork and find things that can be found very easily in other ways. Whatever happened to Occam's razor? Does one need all these many regressions to conclude that "the sudden reduction in Argentine demand for Uruguayan products that took place in 1981 had a major effect on industrial-sector profitability," or "increases in the inflation rate reduce net income to the extent that firms have net monetary assets"? The authors conclude that "generally, Uruguayan data fit our model of corporate financial behavior well." So we played our game and we won. But does this research help any of the 60 firms used for the analysis? I doubt it very much. How about Uruguay? I don't think I can know.

Now, about the detailed results. What is a plausible explanation for "lagged inventories" to have a highly significant coefficient in explaining "operating earnings" in table 11.3? Why use, for Uruguay, the dividend model that worked best for Fama and Babiak? Fama and Babiak had tested numerous specifications on American corporate data. Why assume that a model that fits American data well is the best specification for Uruguay?

Finally, table 11.4. The authors give us estimates of 105 coefficients. The problem is that the authors do not give a cogent discussion of how we should "digest" these estimates, what the relationships are among them, how some of them make good sense, and how some of them make no sense at all. In short, I think that this is an interesting chapter, but the authors should have worked to make it more useful for others.

12

Optimal Corporate Debt Financing and Real Investment Decisions under Controlled Banking Systems

MANSOOR DAILAMI

The debate over the determinants of optimum corporate capital structure and its interaction with corporate real investment decisions has been in the forefront of the literature on the theory of finance at least for the past two decades. The discussion, however, has centered almost exclusively on the experience of a few industrialized countries where capital markets are assumed to be perfect and the existence of well-developed securities markets for pricing of various debt and equity claims on corporate assets is taken for granted. Within this context one important goal of research has been to modify the implications of the original Modigliani-Miller (1958) leverage irrelevance theorem by taking explicit account of the influences of taxes and bankruptcy cost (Baxter 1967; Scott 1976), the agency cost (Jensen and Meckling 1976), and the asymmetry of information (Ross 1977; Leland and Pyle 1977) on the determination of corporate financial leverage. These studies have generally treated the corporate real investment decisions as exogenous and have focused on the financing aspects of corporate investment behavior. In contrast, there is the important strand of research on the neoclassical theory of private investment behavior, which either in its original context (Jorgenson 1963; Jorgenson and Hall 1971) or in its modified cost-of-adjustment context (Lucas 1967; Hayashi 1982) assumes a perfect capital market and no uncertainty.[1] In this case it follows that the firm's real investment policy is independent of how it is financed.

Such a separation of research activity on the theory of investment and finance has often been a source of dissatisfaction and criticism (Vickers 1970; Ciccolo and Fromm 1979, 1980; Hite 1977) where both logic and evidence are invoked to support the argument that the firm's real and financial investment decisions are in reality linked and are made simultaneously. Thus it is argued that the cost of capital to a firm is not determined completely exogenously but depends on its means of financing, and the timing of a firm's investment expenditures is conditional upon the availability of funds. This integrative view of the firm's real and financial investment decisions has in fact been empirically established both for the case of developed countries (Artus, Muet, Palinkas, and Pauly 1985) and more strongly for developing countries (Sundararajan and Thakur 1980; Blejer and Khan 1984). In these studies it is generally found that both the dynamics and the level of aggregate private investment tend to respond positively to the availability of bank credit or to the quantity of cash flows.

The aim in this chapter is to develop an integrated approach toward the problem of optimal corporate real investment and finance in the context of a financial model of a developing economy characterized by credit rationing, a controlled banking sector, and an organized equity market.[2] In this model there are two financial instruments, equity and debt; equity is traded publicly in the stock market and is priced competitively, while debt is placed only with the financial institutions, including both domestic and foreign banks and nonbank financial institutions. No organized corporate bond market exists, and the interest rate on bank loans is administratively set and is treated as a policy variable. It is further assumed that the banking sector imposes an upper bound on the amount of debt finance available.[3] This upper bound is postulated to depend on the borrower's financial circumstances and its creditworthiness. Given the condition that interest rates are administratively set, such an upper bound may be viewed as a reflection of rational behavior on the part of banking sector dictated by loan safety considerations.[4] In a world characterized by uncertainty and business risk, the loan safety factor will depend on the borrower's financial leverage and on the risk-return characteristics of its investment schedule. In the absence of uncertainty, then, it is the borrower's leverage, that is, the extent to which the firm is financed by borrowing, that bears upon the willingness of the bankers to extend new loans.

The chapter is organized as follows. In the first section we develop an optimal model of corporate real and financial investment decisions within the cost-of-adjustment-theoretic framework. In this sense the model can be viewed as an extension of the cost-of-adjustment approach to the neoclassical theory of private investment, extended to incorporate the influence of debt financing in the form of bank loans. Thus the firm's optimal rate of real investment is derived as a function of Tobin's marginal q, that is, the ratio between the market's valuation of an incremental unit of capital to its cost of replacement and the financial parameters characterizing the supply of bank credit. Changes in these financial parameters are then shown to affect corporate real investment both directly through their impacts on the cost and availability of debt finance, and indirectly through their impacts on the valuation ratio. The simultaneous impact of these financial policy changes on corporate real investment are then evaluated by focusing on the steady-state solution of the model.

The second section contains an application of the model to the nonfinancial corporate sector (NFCS) of the Korean economy, using annual data from 1963 to 1983. Using both capital market and balance sheet data, a measure of the valuation ratio is provided and its relevance and limitations for explaining corporate real investment behavior in the Korean economy are discussed. This provides a new perspective on the relation between capital market development and corporate real investment, an issue that has so far been explored only in the context of industrialized countries with well-developed securities markets.[5] Finally, a brief summary concludes the chapter.

THEORETICAL FRAMEWORK

The Basic Model

To focus on the basic essentials of the relationship between corporate financial and real investment decisions, we abstract from the complexities of personal taxation of dividends and capital gains and only consider a proportional tax on corporate income with deductible interest expenses. We also assume that there exist no uncertainty and no bankruptcy costs. We assume, however, that the supply of bank credit is limited. This limitation, furthermore, is formulated to apply to the flow of debt as a function of the corporation's rate of investment and its leverage. Formally this is expressed in linear form as

$$b(t) = hP(t)I(t) + \beta_1 P(t)K(t) - \beta_2 B(t), \tag{12.1}$$

where $b(t)$ is the maximum level of bank credit extended at time t, $B(t)$ is the stock of corporate debt outstanding, $K(t)$ is the stock of real capital, $I(t)$ is gross corporate real investment, $P(t)$ is the price of capital goods, and h, β_1, and β_2 are nonnegative parameters of the underlying supply function of bank credit.

By virtue of the assumptions that interest payments are tax deductible and the cost of equity is higher than the cost of financing, the firm has always the incentive to resort to the maximum level of borrowing possible. Thus in this model the firm's flow demand for bank credit coincides with the maximum supply of bank credit available. This, then, implies that equation (12.1) can also be interpreted as expressing the equilibrium condition between the flow demand for and the supply of bank credit.

By virtue of the assumptions that interest payments are tax deductible and the cost of equity is higher than the cost of financing, the firm has always the incentive to resort to the maximum level of borrowing possible. Thus in this model the firm's flow demand for bank credit coincides with the maximum supply of bank credit available. This, then, implies that equation (12.1) an also be interpreted as expressing the equilibrium condition between the flow demand for and the supply of bank credit.

The equity market is in equilibrium when share owners are satisfied to hold the existing stock of equity. For this condition to hold, it is necessary that the return to equity, consisting of dividends and capital gains or losses, be equal to the investor's required rate of return. Thus this condition takes the form

$$\rho = \frac{\dot{E}(t) + d(t)}{E(t)}, \tag{12.2}$$

where $E(t)$ is the stock of equity outstanding at time t, $d(t)$ is the corporate dividend payment, ρ is the investor's required rate of return, and the dot denotes time derivative: $\dot{E}(t) = dE(t)/dt$. Furthermore, equation (12.2) implies

$$\dot{E}(t) = \rho E(t) - d(t). \tag{12.2a}$$

Solving equation (12.2a) for $E(t)$ yields an expression for the market value of equity:

$$E(t) = \int_{t}^{\infty} \exp(-\rho s) d(s) ds, \tag{12.3}$$

which is the present value of the future stream of dividend payments.

The objective of the firm is to maximize the market value of its equity as given by equation (12.3), subject to a set of constraints. The first constraint is that dividends cannot be negative, that is,

$$d(t) \geq 0. \tag{12.4}$$

The second constraint refers to the equality between the use and sources of funds. Given the assumption that there is no issue of new equity, the sources of funds consist basically of two items: (1) after-tax operating profits net of interest payments and (2) net borrowing. On the use side, there are also two main items: (1) payments of dividends and (2) expenditures on new capital goods, including costs of installation and adjustment. Under these conditions dividends can be derived as operating profit plus new borrowing minus investment expenditures. Therefore

$$d(t) = (1 - \tau)[\pi(K(t)) - rB(t)] + b(t) - aB(t) - P(t)I(t)[1 + c(I(t), K(t))], \tag{12.5}$$

where π is before-tax profit, taken to be an increasing and concave function of K, that is, $\dfrac{\partial \pi}{\partial K} > 0, \dfrac{\partial^2 \pi}{\partial^2 K} \leq 0$; r is the interest rate; a is the amortization rate on debt; I is gross corporate real investment; τ is the corporate profit tax rate; and c is the adjustment-cost function per unit of investment.

The cash-flow constraint (12.5) is straightforward, although two features require comment. First, it should be noted that interest payments are treated as tax deductible. This conforms to the prevailing tax regulation in many countries including Korea, where tax allowances are made for corporate interest payments. This in effect lowers the cost of borrowing and thus induces firms to substitute debt for equity financing. The limit to this process of substitution is determined either by some legal and institutional restraints on the debt finance available, or through consideration of bankruptcy costs associated with increasing corporate leverage.[6] Second, we have included a unit cost-of-adjustment item $c(I,K)$ in equation (12.5) to capture the additional installation expenses associated with the process of investment. The rationale is based on the models of Lucas (1967), Gould (1968), and Treadway (1969), in which the cost of adjustment was introduced in the neoclassical theory of investment to obtain an explicit solution for the firm's optimal rate of investment. Furthermore, following Hayashi (1982) and Summers (1981), this cost function is assumed to depend positively on I/K and specifically to take the form

$$c(I,K) = \frac{\alpha}{2}\left(\frac{I}{K}\right),$$
(12.6)

where $\alpha \geq 0$ is a constant parameter.

Two other constraints are the evolution of the firm's stocks of capital and debt as given by

$$\dot{K}(t) = I(t) - \delta K(t) \text{ and}$$
(12.7)

$$\dot{B}(t) = b(t) - aB(t),$$
(12.8)

where δ is the rate of depreciation of physical capital. Equation (12.7) describes the familiar perpetual method of capital accumulation, wherein real capital increases at the rate of gross investment less depreciation due to obsolescence and wear and tear. The rate of depreciation is further taken as a constant fraction of existing capital stock. In equation (12.8) the net flow of loans from the banking sector is defined as the difference between new loans contracted and the amortization payment on the existing loans, where the rate of amortization is assumed to remain unchanged over time.

The maximization problem facing the firm, stated formally, is to choose $b(t)$, $I(t)$, and $d(t)$ to maximize the present value of its market equity, $E(t)$, subject to the constrains (12.1), (12.4), (12.5), (12.7), and (12.8) and given initial conditions $B(0)$ and $K(0)$. This problem can be solved by means of standard control techniques. Thus we treat $b(t)$, $I(t)$, and $d(t)$ as control variables and $B(t)$ and $K(t)$ as state variables and formulate the current-value Hamiltonian H as

$$H = d + \lambda(I - \delta K) + \mu(b - aB),$$
(12.9)

where λ and μ are the associated shadow prices of capital and debt, respectively.

Taking into account the constraints (12.1), (12.4), and (12.5) we define the Lagrangian L as

$$L = H + \theta\left\{(1-\tau)[\pi(K) - rB] - aB + b - PI\left[1 + \frac{\alpha}{2}\left(\frac{I}{K}\right)\right] - d\right\}$$

$$+ \psi_1(hPI + \beta_1 PK - \beta_2 B - b) + \psi_2(d - \xi^2),$$
(12.10)

where θ, ψ_1, and ψ_2 are the Lagrangian multipliers associated with constraints (12.5), (12.1), and (12.4), respectively, and ξ is a slack variable, introduced to convert the inequality constraint (12.4) into equality. The necessary conditions for an optimal solution are the following:

$$\dot{\lambda} = (\rho + \delta)\lambda - \theta\left[(1 - \tau)\frac{\partial\pi}{\partial K} + \left(\frac{\alpha}{2}\right)P\left(\frac{I}{K}\right)^2\right] - \psi_1\beta_1 P, \qquad (12.10a)$$

$$\dot{\mu} = (\rho + a)\mu + \theta[(a + (1 - \tau)r] + \beta_2\psi_1, \qquad (12.10b)$$

$$\frac{\partial L}{\partial b} = \theta + \mu - \psi_1 = 0, \qquad (12.10c)$$

$$\frac{\partial L}{\partial I} = -\theta p\left(1 + \alpha\frac{I}{K}\right) + \lambda + \psi_1 hp = 0, \qquad (12.10d)$$

$$\frac{\partial L}{\partial d} = 1 - \theta + \psi_2 = 0, \qquad (12.10e)$$

$$\psi_1 > 0, \text{ and} \qquad (12.10f)$$

$$\psi_2\xi = 0, \qquad (12.10g)$$

and the transversality conditions are

$$\lim_{t\to\infty} \exp(-\rho t)\lambda(t)K(t) = 0 \text{ and} \qquad (12.10h)$$

$$\lim_{t\to\infty} \exp(-\rho t)\mu(t)B(t) = 0. \qquad (12.10i)$$

A priori, there are two possible optimal paths or regimes corresponding to whether the firm maintains a positive stream of dividend payments or not. These two paths correspond to whether $\psi_2 = 0$ or $\psi_2 > 0$. We will assume here that the firm maintains a positive stream of dividend payments and resorts to the maximum level of borrowing possible. Under these circumstances we have $\psi_2 = 0$, which from equation (12.10e) implies that $\theta = 1$. To derive formally the firm's optimal investment rule and its financing, we use this value of q to solve equation (12.10b) and (12.10c) for m and ψ_1 and substitute the results into equations (12.10a) and (12.10d) to obtain

$$P\left[1 + \left(\frac{\alpha}{2}\right)\left(\frac{I}{K}\right)\right] - \left[h\frac{\rho - (1 - \tau)r}{\rho + a + \beta_2}\right] = \lambda \text{ and} \qquad (12.11a)$$

$$\dot{\lambda} = (\rho + \delta)\lambda - \left[(1 - \tau)\frac{\partial \pi}{\partial K} + \left(\frac{\alpha}{2}\right)\left(\frac{I}{K}\right)^2 + \beta_1 \frac{\rho - (1 - \tau)r}{\rho + a + \beta_2} \right]. \tag{12.11b}$$

Equation (12.11a) describes the equilibrium condition for the firm's optimum level of real investment. It states that an optimizing firm will continue to invest until the marginal cost of an additional unit of investment is equal to the marginal value of that investment. The marginal cost of investment, as shown in equation (12.11a), is composed of two factors: (1) the marginal cost of acquisition and installation associated with investment and (2) a term that reflects the impact of the firm's substitution of debt for equity. The latter term depends on the cost of debt relative to equity financing and on the institutional restraint on the availability of debt finance. Clearly, to the extent that debt financing is cheaper than equity financing, that is, that $(1 - \tau)r < \rho$, firms are in a position to decrease the marginal cost of their investment through substitution of debt for equity. The limit to this substitution is set, in our model, by the credit ceiling imposed by the banking sector.

In equation (12.11b) the evolution of λ, the marginal value of investment, is described to depend on three main factors: (1) the marginal profitability of capital, $\frac{\partial \pi}{\partial K}$, (2) the extent to which an increase in K reduces the installation cost, $\left(\frac{\alpha}{2}\right)\left(\frac{I}{K}\right)^2$, and (3) the extent to which an increase in K shifts outward the supply of bank credit, $\beta_1 \frac{\rho - (1 - \tau)r}{\rho + a + \beta_2}$. Note that the first two terms depend on the firm's underlying production function and its output market characteristics, while the last term depends on its financial policy and the underlying financial market characteristics. Thus in this model the marginal value of a unit of investment depends not only on the underlying market and technological factors that govern the profitability of that investment but also on its mode of financing. This interaction between finance and investment is, in fact, an important distinctive feature of our model. To highlight this aspect of the model, let us solve equation (12.11a) for the firm's optimal rate of real investment I and obtain

$$I = \frac{1}{\alpha}\left[q - 1 + h\frac{\rho - (1 - \tau)r}{\rho + a + \beta_2} \right]K, \tag{12.12}$$

where $q = \lambda/p$ is the familiar Tobin's marginal q, defined as the ratio of the market value of an additional unit of capital to its replacement cost.

Equation (12.12) offers some important insights into the relationship between the firm's real investment decisions and its financial policy. Thus it is readily seen that $\frac{\partial I}{\partial h} > 0$, $\frac{\partial I}{\partial r} < 0$, and $\frac{\partial I}{\partial \beta} < 0$. But since q depends also on these financial parameters, the results just indicated can only provide a partial view of the relationship between investment and finance. To derive a more general view, we rewrite equation (12.11b) in terms of q and note that the resultant equation, in conjunction with equation (12.12), describes a system of two first-order differential equations in K and q, namely,

$$\dot{K} = \frac{1}{\alpha} \left[q - 1 + h \frac{\rho - (1-\tau)r}{\rho + a + \beta} - \alpha\delta \right] K \quad \text{and} \tag{12.13a}$$

$$\dot{q} = (\rho + \delta - \hat{p})q - \left[(1-\tau)\frac{\pi_K}{p} + \left(\frac{\alpha}{2}\right)\left(\frac{I}{K}\right)^2 + \beta_1 \frac{\rho - (1-\tau)r}{\rho + a + \beta_2} \right], \tag{12.13b}$$

where $\hat{p} = \dfrac{\dot{p}}{p}$ denotes the rate of inflation in capital goods prices, and $\pi_K = \dfrac{\partial\pi}{\partial K}$.

The system of equations (12.13a and (12.13b) describes the joint determination of the optimal time path of K and q and provides the basis for our analysis of the short- and long-term implications of various exogenous changes in the underlying financial market conditions.

Steady-State Equilibrium

The system attains its steady-state equilibrium when $\dot{K} = \dot{q} = 0$. the phase diagram corresponding to this system is shown in figure 12.1. In the figure, the $\dot{K} = 0$ line is based on equation (12.13a) and depicts the locus for which the rate of change of the capital stock is zero. The downward-sloping curve $\dot{q} = 0$ is based on equation (12.13b) and describes the locus for which the marginal value of investment is zero. By virtue of the assumption that the profit function is concave, the steady-state equilibrium of the system, denoted by (K*,q*), is unique and lies on the saddle-point path of the system as indicated by the dark curve in the figure.

Consider now the consequences of an increase in h brought about, for instance, as a result of an expansionary credit policy. An increase in h lowers the $\dot{K} = 0$ locus and leaves the $\dot{q} = 0$ locus unaffected. The new intersection will involve a higher level of capital stock and a lower q, as shown in figure 12.2. Thus an increase in the marginal debt/capital ratio has favorable impacts on the firm's optimal capital stock and on its rate of investment, but has adverse effect on its marginal valuation:

$$\frac{\partial K}{\partial h} > 0, \quad \frac{\partial I}{\partial h} > 0, \quad \frac{\partial q}{\partial h} < 0.$$

Next consider a decrease in the rate of interest (figure 12.3). From equations (12.13a) and (12.13b) it can be inferred that a decrease in the rate of interest shifts both loci; the $\dot{K} = 0$ locus shifts upward because the lower interest rate tends to induce the substitution of debt for equity and thus lowers the marginal cost of investment. The $\dot{q} = 0$ schedule shifts to the right because of the positive impact of

Figure 12.1
Phase Diagram of the System of Equations (12.13a) and (12.13b)

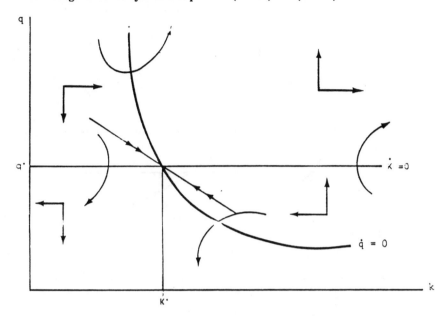

Figure 12.2
Response to an Increase in the Supply of Bank Credit

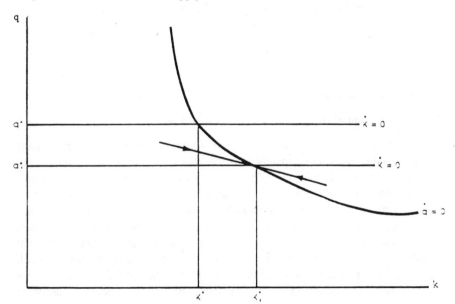

Figure 12.3
Response to a Decrease in the Rate of Interest

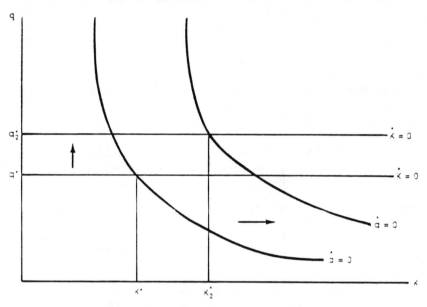

higher availability of debt financing on the firm's marginal values of capital. Formally, the responses in the firm's optimum level of capital stock, its rate of investment, and the valuation ratio are as follows:

$$\frac{\partial q}{\partial r} > 0, \ \frac{\partial I}{\partial r} < 0, \ \frac{\partial K}{\partial r} < 0.$$

EMPIRICAL RESULTS

Specification of the Corporate Investment Function

In this section we use evidence from the corporate sector of the Korean economy to gain some quantitative insight into the relationship between corporate real investment behavior and financial policy as elaborated in the previous section. It was shown in the previous section that changes in financial policy operating via changes in the rate of interest and/or changes in the supply of bank credit could have important effects on the firm's optimal rate of investment. The main objective in this section is to establish the quantitative dimension of these relationships. The starting point is the modification of equations (12.1) and (12.13a) into some suitable empirical forms that can be estimated. We extend equation (12.1) to account for any short-term variation in bank credit that may stem from cyclical fluctuations in the overall level of economic activity. Thus the basic equations to be estimated, expressed in discrete time, are

$$\frac{I_b}{K_t} = \frac{1}{\alpha}\left[q_t - 1 + h\frac{\rho_t - (1 - \tau_t)r_t}{\rho_t + a + \beta_2}\right] + \varepsilon_{1t} \text{ and} \tag{12.14a}$$

$$b_t = \beta_0 + hp_t I_t + \beta_1 p_t K_t - \beta_2 B_{t-1} + \beta_3 y_t + \varepsilon_{2t}, \tag{12.14b}$$

where y_t in equation (12.14b) is the deviation of real GDP from its long-term trend, included as a measure of the business cycle, and ε_{1t} and ε_{2t} are disturbance terms assumed to be normally distributed with definite variance-covariance matrix and zero means.

Before we turn to the estimation of equations (12.14a) and (12.14b), one obstacle remains. As emphasized originally by Tobin and Brainard (1977) and subsequently by Hayashi (1982) and Summers (1981), q in equation (12.14a) is not directly observable, and so this equation is not empirically operational. What is, in principle, observable and under certain conditions can serve as an appropriate proxy for q is the "average q" to be denoted by Q and defined as the ratio of the market value of existing capital to its replacement cost. The market value of existing capital can be inferred from the market's valuation of various security claims over total corporate assets. This includes the market value of equity as well as the market value of debt if debt is publicly issued. If, on the other hand, no organized corporate bond market exists, and if debt is mostly financed by bank loans or loans from other financial institutions, then there is no meaningful empirical counterpart to the market value of debt. In this case one possible approach would be to measure debt at its book value by referring directly to the liability side of the corporate balance sheet. This measure of corporate debt has the advantage of being free from estimation error, but it suffers from one major drawback: It reduces the informational content of the q ratio as a determinant of corporate investment. The loss in the informational content of q and thus in its predictive power is proportional to the ratio of debt to equity in the firm's capital structure.

With these considerations in mind, we proceed to measure the average q in the nonfinancial private corporate sector of the Korean economy as the ratio of market value of equity plus book value of debt to the replacement cost of capital. With the exception of data on the book value of corporate debt, which are directly available from the flow-of-funds tables published by the Bank of Korea, other variables had to be estimated. In the process we relied on both national income accounts and balance sheet data to generate the necessary information. Data coverage, sources, and variable definitions are discussed in the Appendix to this chapter. In brief, here, our estimates of both market value of equity and replacement cost of capital follow conventional approaches.[7] The market value of equity was estimated by capitalizing corporate dividend payments, using annual average yield on equity as the discount rate; and the replacement cost of capital was calculated by a perpetual

Table 12.1
Market Value of Equity, Book Value of Debt, and Replacement Cost of Capital, Korean Nonfinancial Private Corporate Sector, 1963–1983 (Billions of Won)

Year	Market Value of Equity	Debt	Capital Stock
1963	17.30	37.11	43.17
1964	23.33	48.63	75.26
1965	27.28	72.90	110.69
1966	50.67	139.14	199.11
1967	67.41	252.37	299.69
1968	105.47	488.52	493.76
1969	183.41	768.79	699.07
1970	184.41	1,029.38	1,006.89
1971	180.48	1,301.67	1,222.51
1972	262.17	1,558.32	1,449.81
1973	806.22	2,051.61	2,038.67
1974	1,164.77	2,937.14	3,196.41
1975	1,557.05	4,833.34	4,441.23
1976	2,418.48	6,093.79	5,574.14
1977	2,726.74	7,726.19	7,138.39
1978	2,839.92	10,022.89	9,719.55
1979	1,984.55	13,898.99	14,751.13
1980	2,891.89	18,556.19	22,022.11
1981	3,687.00	23,807.59	26,762.91
1982	3,944.14	27,399.99	30,725.79
1983	5,960.67	31,758.09	34,440.35

Sources: See the Appendix to this chapter.

inventory method, using an average depreciation rate of 8 percent per annum. These estimates are reported in table 12.1.

Table 12.2 provides estimates of Tobin's q average as well as the ratio of the book value of debt to the total book value of debt plus the market value of equity in the nonfinancial private corporate sector of the Korean economy for the 1963–83 period. The latter ratio represents a measure of corporate financial leverage and, as expected, is relatively very high. For the decade of the 1970s, for instance, corporate leverage in Korea averaged 0.787 which, in a rough comparison, is close to a level of 0.722 observed for Japan[8] and is significantly higher than a level of 0.315 observed for the United States[9] over the same period. This high level of the debt/capital ratio observed in Korea is indicative of the dominant role of debt financing in the corporate capital structure and has significant potential implications for the implementation and management of financial policy.[10] A high debt/capital ratio renders the corporate sector very vulnerable to the effects of contractionary changes in credit and monetary policy and thus may limit the ability of policymakers to pursue stabilization policies.

Two features of the estimates of the average q shown in the second column of table 12.2 are worth noting. First, the estimates appear quite reasonable despite the fact that the denominator and the numerator of q were estimated independently of each other. The estimates for the period 1963–83 are generally greater than one, which reflects the market's optimistic expectation of the pattern of corporate profitability during that period. Second, the broad movements in q seem to have been closely paralleled by the pattern of corporate real investment expenditures. These movements have followed a cyclical pattern, characterized by a phase of upward movement from 1976 until 1980 and a phase of downward movement since 1981.

Estimation Method and Results

Turning to the estimation of the system of equations (12.14a) and (12.14b), we substitute Q_t for q_t in equation (12.14a) and after slight modification obtain

$$\frac{I_t}{K_t} = \frac{1}{\alpha}(Q_t - 1) + \frac{h}{\alpha}X_t(\beta_2), \tag{12.15}$$

where $X_t(\beta_2) = \dfrac{\rho_t - (1 - \tau_t)r_t}{\rho_t + \bar{a} + \beta_2}$, and $\bar{a}$ is a given value of the rate of amortization taken to be 10 percent per year. Note that for a given value of β_2, X_t is empirically observable and thus can be used as part of the data set.

To obtain consistent and efficient estimates of the parameters α, h, β_0, β_1, and β_3, we performed an iterative grid search over β_2 and chose the value that maximized the log likelihood function corresponding to the system of equations (12.14b) and (12.14c). The grid search was conducted over the interval

Table 12.2
Tobin's Average q Ratio and the Ratio of Debt to Total Capital: Korean Nonfinancial Private Corporate Sector, 1963–1983

Year	Debt/Capital Ratio[1]	Average q[2]
1963	0.68202	1.26043
1964	0.67577	0.95609
1965	0.72764	0.90510
1966	0.73304	0.95336
1967	0.78920	1.06706
1968	0.82243	1.20301
1969	0.80738	1.36209
1970	0.84807	1.20548
1971	0.87823	1.21239
1972	0.85599	1.25568
1973	0.71789	1.40181
1974	0.71604	1.28329
1975	0.75634	1.43888
1976	0.71588	1.52710
1977	0.73914	1.46433
1978	0.77921	1.32340
1979	0.87506	1.07677
1980	0.86517	0.97482
1981	0.86590	1.02734
1982	0.87417	1.02012
1983	0.84197	1.09519

Sources: See the Appendix to this chapter.

[1]Ratio of book value of debt to total market value of equity plus book value of debt.
[2]Ratio of book value of debt plus market value of equity to replacement cost of capital.

$\{\hat{\beta}_2 \pm k\hat{\sigma} \mid k = 0,1,2,3,4\}$, where $\hat{\beta}_2$ and $\hat{\sigma}$ are, respectively, the OLS estimates of β_2 and its standard error obtained from the regression of equation (12.14b) using annual data for the years 1963–83. The regression results of this equation are

$$b_t = 176.2 + 0.76p_tI_t + 0.2p_tK_t$$
$$\quad\ (71.07)\ \ (0.114)\quad (0.044)$$

$$\quad - 0.337B_{t-1} + 383.12y_t, \qquad \bar{R}^2 = 0.98 \tag{12.16}$$
$$\quad\ (0.049)\qquad (171.76)$$

(standard errors are in parentheses).

The final results of the maximum-likelihood estimates of equations (12.14b) and (12.15) are reported in table 12.3. The table also shows the corresponding asymptomatic standard error of the estimates. These estimates correspond to the value of $\beta_2 = 0.287$, which led to the maximum value of the log likelihood function. Our estimation results seem quite satisfactory, as all have the right sign and all, with the exception of the coefficient of cyclical fluctuation of real output, are significantly different from zero at the 5 percent level. The estimated value for h is 0.88, which is consistent with the high leverage characteristic of the Korean corporate sector. The implied value for the coefficient of cost of adjustment is $\alpha/2 = 1.19$, which suggests an unusually high cost of adjustment per unit of investment.

We are now in a position to provide a quantitative measure of the extent to which government policy over the past two decades has yielded positive investment incentives to the private corporate sector. Let us then formally introduce the concept of "investment incentive space," to be denoted by S and defined as

$$S = \{Q_t \geq q_t^* \mid t = 1963, \ldots, 1983\},$$

Table 12.3
Maximum-Likelihood Estimates of the Parameters
of Equations (12.14b) and (12.15)

Parameters	Estimates	Standard Error
β_0	143.25	63.98
h	0.88	0.092
β_1	0.212	0.012
β_3	116.	146.3
α	2.38	0.408

Figure 12.4
Tobin's Average Q and Investment Incentive Space in the
Korean Nonfinancial Corporate Sector, 1963–1983

Year	Debt-Capital Ratio 1	Average Q 2
1963	0.68202	1.26043
1964	0.67577	0.95609
1965	0.72764	0.90510
1966	0.73304	0.95336
1967	0.78920	1.06706
1968	0.82243	1.20301
1969	0.80738	1.36209
1970	0.84807	1.20548
1971	0.87823	1.21239
1972	0.85599	1.25568
1973	0.71789	1.40181
1974	0.71604	1.28329
1975	0.75634	1.43888
1976	0.71588	1.52710
1977	0.73914	1.46433
1978	0.77921	1.32340
1979	0.87506	1.07677
1980	0.86517	0.97482
1981	0.86590	1.02734
1982	0.87417	1.02012
1983	0.84197	1.09519

Note: (1) = Ratio of book value of debt to total market value of equity plus book value of debt.

(2) = Ratio of book value of debt plus market value of equity to Replacement Cost of Capital.

Sources: See Table A1 in appendix A.

where q_t^* is the steady-state value of q_t given by

$$q_t^* = 1 - \hat{h}\frac{\rho_t - (1-\tau_t)r_t}{\hat{\beta}_2 + \bar{a} + \rho_t}. \tag{12.17}$$

Thus, when $Q_t > q_t^*$, firms have an incentive to expand real investment, and the larger the distance between Q_t and q_t^*, the greater the incentive for investment.

Figure 12.4 shows the plots for Q_t and q_t^* for the Korean nonfinancial corporate sector over the 1963–83 period. The shaded area between Q_t and q_t^*, as shown in the figure, represents a measure of incentive accorded to the corporate private sector during this period. As can be seen, these incentives were greatest from the mid-1960s to the late 1970s, which, interestingly, was a period of vigorous expansion of corporate investment.

CONCLUDING REMARKS

In many developing countries corporations rely heavily on bank borrowing to finance their long-term investment expenditures. This has reflected partly the effects of past governmental policy to encourage debt financing through a variety of measures, including low interest rates, generous tax allowances for interest payments, and a tacit commitment against bankruptcy and business failures. Thus the resultant comparative advantage in favor of debt financing has generally led to high corporate leverages, with potential adverse implications for the conduct of credit and monetary policy. To gain an understanding of how corporate investment may respond to various policy-induced changes in the corporate financial environment, this chapter has developed a dynamic optimization model of the firm's investment and financial behavior. The model was estimated for the nonfinancial corporate sector of the Korean economy, using annual data from 1963 to 1983. On the basis of the estimates obtained, we constructed a quantitative measure of the extent to which governmental policy encouraged corporate investment through lax interest-rate and tax policies. It was shown that the private corporate sector in Korea benefitted from substantial investment incentives from the mid-1960s to the late 1970s.

Appendix: Data Sources and Definition

The primary source for most of the data used in this study is the *Economic Statistics Yearbook* (ESYB), Bank of Korea, various issues. Two sets of flow-of-funds tables, the "Integrated Accounts of National Income and Financial Transactions" and "Financial Assets and Liabilities," contained in this publication, were utilized to generate the necessary balance sheet data for the total nonfinancial private corporate sector for the years 1963–83. These data were supplemented, when necessary, by drawing on two other sources: International Monetary Fund (IMF), *International Financial Statistics* (IFS), and *Major Statistics of Korean Economy* (MSKE), Economic Planning Board, various issues.

The definitions of variables are as follows:

1. $PI =$ fixed capital formation (in current prices) (ESYB).
2. $P =$ price deflator for fixed capital formation constructed as a weighted arithmetic average of wholesale price indices of construction materials and capital goods (MSKE).
3. $I =$ real fixed capital formation, (1) deflated by (2).
4. $b =$ gross borrowing, consisting of special and commercial bank loans, insurance and trust loans, and net foreign loans (ESYB).

5. $B =$ total corporate debt, consisting of total bank debt, foreign debt, and debt owed to insurance and trust companies (ESYB).

6. $d =$ dividends, from national income accounts (ESYB).

7. $\rho =$ annual average yield on stocks traded on the Korea Stock Exchange (ESYB).

8. $r =$ interest rate on commercial bank loans for machines, industry, and promotion (MSKE).

9. $\tau =$ corporate income-tax rate constructed from data obtained from ESYB.

10. $K =$ capital stock, constructed by means of the perpetual inventory method, $K_t = I_t + (1 - \delta)K_{t-1}$, where the average depreciation δ is estimated to be 8 percent per annum using the straight-line depreciation rule based on the average lifetime of 35 years for structures and 15 years for machinery and equipment.

11. $y =$ cyclical fluctuation of real aggregate output constructed as the deviation of real GDP from its long-term trend.

NOTES

I would like to thank Indermit Gill, Mohsin Khan, Ashok Lahiri, and Sweder Van Wijnbergen for helpful comments and suggestions, and Boubker Abisourour for research assistance.

The World Bank does not accept responsibility for the views expressed herein, which are those of the author and should not be attributed to the World Bank or to its affiliated organizations. The findings, interpretations, and conclusions are the results of research supported by the bank; they do not necessarily represent official policy of the bank. The designations employed, the presentation of material, and any maps used in this document are solely for the convenience of the reader and do not imply the expression of any opinion whatsoever on the part of the World Bank of its affiliates concerning the legal status of any country, territory, city, area, or of its authorities, or concerning the delimitation of its boundaries, or national affiliation.

1. For an extension of the neoclassical theory of investment to include uncertainty, see Lucas and Prescott (1971).

2. These characteristic features are typical of the financial market structure of most new industrialized developing countries, including, for example, Argentina, Brazil, Chile, Korea, Mexico, and the Philippines, as well as some developed countries such as Japan. In all these countries there exists a relatively well functioning equity market that serves to generate essential information regarding investors' attitudes and their expectations of future profitability and provides a limited amount of equity financing. Admittedly, the equity market's role in terms of providing corporate finance is still comparatively limited, but it seems to be growing in almost all these countries. Between 1981 and 1985 the market value of equity shares traded in the stock markets of Brazil (São Paulo), Korea, and Mexico, for instance, grew at an average annual rate of 365.2, 23.5, and 73.5 percent in local currencies, respectively, and at a rate of 45, 16.1, and 5.25 percent in terms of U.S. dollars. By the end of 1985 the aggregate market capitalization of the equity shares in these three countries' stock markets amounted to $89.4 billion, which is about one-fourth of the size of London's equity market. See Fédération Internationale des Bourses de Valeurs for recent information

and van Agtmael (1984), Wai and Patrick (1973), Sakong (1977) and Ness (1974) for a survey and analysis of stock-market developments in developing countries.

3. Here and through this chapter, the banking sector refers to both commercial and special banks, nonbank financial institutions, and foreign banks. The important point here is that both the cost and the supply of credit from this sector are directly or indirectly controlled by the monetary authorities.

4. Even in circumstances where interest rates are free from administrative control, banks may ration credit as a rational response toward imperfect information and business risk. See, for instance, Hodgman (1960), Freimer and Gordon (1965), and Jaffee and Russell (1976) for an analysis of credit rationing along these lines.

5. For example, von Fustenberg (1974) and Summers (1981) for empirical applications of the q theory of investment to the U.S. data and Poterba and Summers (1985) for an application to the British data.

6. See Miller (1977) for a consideration of taxes, Scott (1976) for a consideration of bankruptcy costs, and Auerbach (1985) for an empirical investigation of corporate leverage in the United States.

7. See, for instance, Taggart (1985) and Holland and Myers (1979).

8. This figure is based on Wakasugi et al. (1984).

9. This figure is based on Taggart (1985).

10. See Sundararajan (1985) for a theoretical analysis of the macroeconomic effects of high corporate leverage in developing countries.

REFERENCES

Arthus, P., P. A. Muet, P. Palinkas, and P. Pauly. (1985). "Tax Incentives, Monetary Policy, and Investment in France and Germany." In *Stabilization Policy in France and the Federal Republic of Germany*, ed. G. de Menil and U. Westphal, 105–180. Amsterdam: North-Holland.

Auerbach, A. J. (1985). "Real Determinants of Corporate Leverage." In *Corporate Capital Structures in the United States*, ed. B. M. Friedman, 301–322. Chicago and London: University of Chicago Press.

Baxter, N. (1967). "Leverage, Risk of Ruin, and the Cost of Capital." *Journal of Finance* 22: 395–404.

Blejer, M. I., and M. S. Khan. (1984). "Government Policy and Private Investment in Developing Countries." *IMF Staff Papers* 31: 374–403.

Ciccolo, J., and G. Fromm (1979). "'Q' and the Theory of Investment." *Journal of Finance* 34: 535–547.

———. (1980). "'Q,' Corporate Investment, and Balance Sheet Behavior." *Journal of Money, Credit, and Banking* 12: 294–307.

Fédération Internationale des Bourses de Valeurs. *Activities and Statistics*. Various issues. Paris, France.

Freimer, M., and M. J. Gordon. (1965). "Why Bankers Ration Credit." *Quarterly Journal of Economics*, no. 79: 397–416.

Hayashi, F. (1982). "Tobin's Marginal q and Average q: A Neoclassical Interpretation." *Econometrica*, January, 213–224.

Hite, G. L. (1977). "Leverage, Output Effects, and the M-M Theorems." *Journal of Financial Economics* 13: 177–202.

Hodgman, D. R. (1960). "Credit Risk and Credit Rationing." *Quarterly Journal of Economics* 74: 258–278.

Holland, D. M., and S. C. Myers. (1979). "Trends in Corporate Profitability and Capital Costs." In *The Nation's Capital Needs: Three Studies*, ed. R. Lindsay. New York: Committee for Economic Development.

Jaffee, D. M., and T. Russell. (1976). "Imperfect Information, Uncertainty, and Credit Rationing." *Quarterly Journal of Economics* 90: 651–666.

Jensen, M., and W. Meckling. (1976). "Theory of the Firm: Managerial Behavior, Agency Costs, and Ownership Structure." *Journal of Financial Economics* 3: 305–360.

Jorgensen, D. W., and R. E. Hall. (1971). "Application of the Theory of Optimum Capital Accumulation." In *Tax Incentives and Capital Spending*, ed. G. Fromm, 9–60. Washington, D.C.: Brookings Institution.

Leland, M. E., and D. H. Pyle. (1977). "Informational Asymmetries, Financial Structure, and Financial Intermediation." *Journal of Finance* 32: 371–387.

Lucas, R. E. (1967). "Adjustment Costs and the Theory of Supply." *Journal of Political Economy* 75: 321–334.

Lucas, R. E., and E. Prescott. (1971). "Investment under Uncertainty." *Econometrica* 39: 659–681.

Miller, M. (1977). "Debt and Taxes." *Journal of Finance* 32: 261–275.

Modigliani, M., and M. Miller. (1958). "The Cost of Capital, Corporation Finance, and the Theory of Investment." *American Economic Review* 48: 261–297.

Ness, W. L., Jr. (1974). "Financial Markets Innovation as a Development Strategy: Initial Results from the Brazilian Experience." *Economic Development and Cultural Change* 22: 436–453.

Poterba, J. M., and L. H. Summers. (1985). "The Economic Effects of Dividend Taxation." In *Recent Advances in Corporate Finance*, ed. E. I. Altman and M. G. Subrahmanyam. Homewood, Ill.: Richard D. Irwin.

Ross, S. A. (1977). "The Determination of Financial structure: The Incentive-Signalling Approach." *Bell Journal of Economics* 8: 23–40.

Sakong, I. (1977). "An Overview of Corporate Finance and the Long-Term Securities Market." In *Planning Models and Macroeconomic Policy Issues*, ed. Chuk Kyo Kim, 228–262. Seoul: Korea Development Institute.

Scott, J. H. (1976). "A Theory of Optimal Capital Structure." *Bell Journal of Economics* 7: 33–54.

Summers, L. H. (1981). "Taxation and Corporate Investment: A *q* Theory Approach." *Brookings Papers on Economic Activity*, no. 1: 67–122.

Sundararajan, V. (1985). "Debt-Equity Ratios of Firms and Interest Rate Policy." *IMF Staff Papers*, no. 3 (September): 430–473.

Sundararajan, V., and S. Thakur. (1980). "Public Investment, Crowding Out, and Growth: A Dynamic Model Applied to India and Korea." *IMF Staff Papers*, December, 814–855.

Taggart, R. A., Jr. (1985). "Secular Pattern in the Financing of U.S. Corporations." In *Corporate Capital Structures in the United States*, ed. B. M. Friedman, 13–75. Chicago and London: University of Chicago Press.

Tobin, J., and W. C. Brainard. (1977). "Asset Markets and the Cost of Capital." In *Economic Progress, Private Value, and Public Policy: Essays in Honor of William Fellner*, ed. R. Nelson and B. Balassa, 235–262. Amsterdam: North-Holland.

van Agtmael, A. W. (1984). *Emerging Securities Markets*. London: Euromoney Publications.

Vickers, D. (1970). "The Cost of Capital and the Structure of the Firm." *Journal of Finance*, no. 1 (March): 35–46.

von Fustenberg, G. (1974). "Corporate Investment: Does Market Valuation Matter in the Aggregate?" *Brookings Papers on Economic Activity*, no. 2: 347–397.

Wai, U. T., and H. T. Patrick. (1973). "Stock and Bond Issues and Capital Markets in Less Developed Countries." *IMF Staff Papers* 20 (July): 264–272.

Wakasugi, T., K. Nishina, F. Kon-ya, and M. Tsuchiya. (1984). "Measuring the Profitability of the Nonfinancial Sector in Japan." In *Measuring Profitability and Capital Costs*, ed. D. M. Holland, 345–386. Lexington, Mass.: Lexington Books.

p229 : # Discussant: Cheng Few Lee

The intent of this chapter is useful in applying corporate finance theory in macro-economic research. In my opinion, an integration of macroeconomic research with corporate finance theory can establish some linkage models for corporations' financial analysis, planning, and forecasting.

Recently, several papers have developed implications of corporate capital structure on macro policy decisions. For example, the paper by Kose John and Lemma Senbet (1988) entitled "Limited Liability, Corporate Leverage, and Public Policy" provided one rationale for the tax deductibility of debt from the public perspective. In addition, the authors showed why there exists optimal capital structure in the macroeconomic structure.

This chapter is a good start for doing research to integrate corporate finance theory and macroeconomic theory; however, further research can expand in the following directions:

1. A stochastic instead of a deterministic approach can be used.
2. Industry data instead of aggregate national data can be used to study how different industries will behave differently.
3. The stability of the phase diagram as indicated in the chapter can be more explicitly investigated in accordance with different growth conditions.

Overall, I enjoyed reading this chapter. I hope that the author can do more research in this area in the near future.

REFERENCE

John, K., and L. Senbet (1988). "Limited Liability, Corporate Leverage and Public Policy." New York University Working Papers.

13

Financial Reform, Inflation, and Investment Behavior in Developing Countries: Evidence from Peru

UWE CORSEPIUS

Raising real interest rates is a central element of financial reforms in developing countries. This chapter presents a theoretical model in which higher levels of inflation risk reduce private real capital formation. Using Peruvian data the negative relationship between inflation volatility and private investment is confirmed. Since inflation variability increases with the level of inflation, financial reforms should include measures to reduce inflation, if private real capital formation is to be stimulated effectively.

In the 1980s foreign capital inflows into many developing countries declined dramatically, so that these countries had to finance investment mostly by domestic resources. The financial sector can play an important role in helping to increase domestic resource mobilization and the efficiency of resource use (World Bank 1989). However, extensive government regulation hampers efficient intermediation in many developing countries. Therefore, the importance of financial reforms is frequently stressed in the theoretical and empirical literature.[1] Raising real interest rates is usually a central element of the reform proposals. Basically, real interest rates may be raised by lowering inflation rates or increasing nominal interest rates. Most analyses advocating financial reforms do not distinguish between these possibilities. Typically, lifting interest-rate controls is favored, because governments are thought to be unable to control inflation (e.g., Moore and Chowdury 1981).

This chapter challenges the view that the different means to raise real interest rates are symmetrical in their impact on the success of financial reforms. It can be demonstrated that savings mobilization can be improved by lowering inflation or by full indexation of the financial sector (Corsepius 1989). However, the principal aim of financial liberalization is to increase the volume and the allocative efficiency of investment. Thus in the following it is shown that only the dampening of high inflation rates can assure that financial liberalization leads to more fixed investment. In the next section a model is presented that accounts for the effects of inflation on private investment behavior. Subsequently, the model is tested with Peruvian data.

THE MODEL

Empirical evidence for several developing and industrial countries supports a positive correlation between the level of inflation and its variability.[2] Fluctuating inflation rates render it more difficult for firms to estimate the profitability of investment projects for several reasons. Volatile inflation rates hamper the projection of trends in demand, as price increases that indicate excess demand can hardly be distinguished from those that are part of the general inflation. Unexpected changes in inflation rates affect the reliability of cost estimates, because real financing costs change with the level of inflation. In addition, tax laws, bookkeeping, and depreciation rules are generally based on nominal values.[3] Furthermore, relative prices fluctuate with inflation (Fischer and Modigliani 1978), so that choosing the optimal production structure on the basis of price signals becomes more difficult.

As the validity of investment appraisals declines with higher rates of inflation, the probability of failures grows. This is not to say that the profitability of individual investments is generally negatively affected. However, the riskiness of investments increases, because the variance of investment returns is larger if inflation rates fluctuate widely. The effects of an increase in the investment risk are captured in the following model.

In developing countries decisions on consumption and investment are often taken simultaneously. This is most evident in the case of small household firms, where firms often do not form a legal entity and most employees are family members.[4] Nevertheless, even in bigger companies the influence of individual families is considerably larger than in public companies in industrialized countries.

In the model, household firms maximize their utility over two periods. With a given initial endowment they can consume their funds in the first period (C_t) or invest them in risky projects. The investments provide consumption possibilities in the second period (C_{t+1}). The utility of consumption in the second period is discounted by the rate of time preference. If σ is the investment risk, the utility function U of risk-averse household firms may be written as follows:

$$U = a(C_t, C_{t+1}, \sigma), \text{ with } U_{C_t} > 0, U_{C_{t+1}} > 0, U_\sigma < 0.$$

Assuming a utility function of the type of von Neumann and Morgenstern and no consumption in the first period, the relationship between utility and investment risk can be described by figure 13.1. Investment leads to expected future consumption possibilities $E(C_{t+1})$. If the investment risk equals σ_1, a value of $C_{t+1}(P_1)$ will be realized with probability P_1 only, while the probability for achieving $C_{t+1}(1 - P_1)$ is $1 - P_1$. The utility of the household firm equals $U(\sigma_1)$, with the certainty equivalent being C_{t+1}^S. C_{t+1}^S is smaller than the expected value of C_{t+1} because risk-averse household firms demand a risk premium if future consumption possibilities are uncertain. Raising the investment risk to σ_2 lowers the utility, while the expected return to the investment remains constant.

The certainty equivalent are used to derive the intertemporal allocation of the household firm's funds (figure 13.2). The household firm distributes its funds between consumption in the first period and investment according to the system of indifference cures (I_1, I_2). A higher indifference curve represents a higher level of utility. The line AB shows possible distributions for the investment risk σ_1. Accordingly, the household firm realizes the combination X_1. As the increase in the investment risk leads to smaller certainty equivalents, the risk can be represented by turning the line AB at point B to $A'B$. Consequently, risk-averse household firms lower their investment outlays in favor of current consumption (X_2). In the next section the hypothesized negative relationship between inflation-induced risk and investment expenditure will be tested with Peruvian data.

Figure 13.1
The Utility of Household Firms in the Presence of Inflation Risk

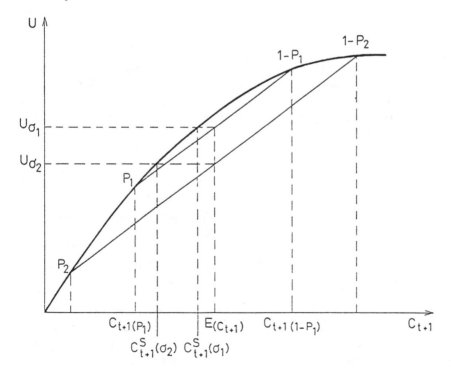

Figure 13.2
Consumption and Investment with Different Levels of Inflation Risk

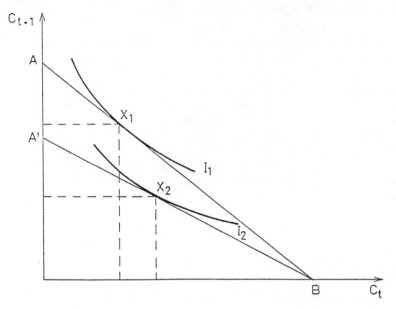

INFLATION AND INVESTMENT: THE PERUVIAN CASE

After a short introduction to Peru, the effects of inflation volatility on private investment are evaluated in two steps. First, we investigate whether in Peru the level of inflation is positively associated with its variability. Otherwise, policies to lower inflation will not be able to reduce uncertainty. Second, we estimate an investment model incorporating inflation effects for Peru.

Inflation in Peru

After the first oil-price shock, inflation accelerated in Peru, and due to inflexible interest-rate ceilings, real interest rates became negative in 1974 (table 13.1). In an attempt to stimulate financial savings, in late 1978 and again in January 1981 the authorities partly reformed the financial system. Interest-rate ceilings were adjusted significantly upward in order to account for the rising rates of inflation, and deposits denominated in U.S. dollars were introduced. Since the devaluation of the sol against the dollar roughly compensated for the higher rate of inflation in Peru relative to that of the United States, the dollar deposits were actually indexed deposits meant to stop currency substitution and capital flight. The inflation rate, however, could not be brought down. Therefore, increasing inflation rates soon eroded the positive effect of the shifts in interest-rate ceilings on real interest rates,

Table 13.1
Private Investment, Inflation, and Interest Rates
in Peru, 1973–1985 (Percentages)

Year	Private Investment/GDP	Rate of Inflation[a]	Inflation Variability[b]	Nominal Effective Interest Rate on Credits[c]
1973	7.4	9.5	3.7	15.3
1974	7.6	16.9	1.1	15.3
1975	9.6	23.4	2.5	15.3
1976	8.5	33.1	7.5	18.2
1977	7.4	38.5	5.5	23.4
1978	6.8	56.9	12.1	31.7
1979	7.5	68.2	5.0	52.5
1980	8.9	59.4	4.0	53.0
1981	10.3	75.5	4.4	71.1
1982	9.7	63.9	4.6	69.6
1983	6.8	108.7	17.1	76.2
1984	6.1	111.8	8.3	96.1
1985	5.6	160.1	23.4	114.8

Source: Banco Central de Reserva del Perú, *Memoria*, various issues, and unpublished material; author's calculations.

[a] Average annual change in the CPI.
[b] Standard deviation of monthly inflation rates, annualized.
[c] Includes commissions, discounting of credits, and quarterly compounding of interest.

thus favoring the growth of dollar deposits relative to financial savings in national currency. In 1984 about 65 percent of all quasi-money was held in U.S. dollars.

The Level of Inflation and Its Volatility

We will distinguish between the absolute and relative measures of inflation volatility. The latter are calculated by normalizing the variability by the mean level of inflation. This assumes, for example, that a deviation of 2 percentage points from an average inflation of 4 percent has the same consequences as a deviation of 50 percentage points from an average inflation rate of 100 percent. However, most authors agree that this assumption cannot be sustained, since economic decisions are influenced by absolute deviations.

However, absolute measures also suffer from shortcomings, as they generally measure only partially the uncertainty caused by fluctuating inflation rates. Therefore, three different measures are used to capture all effects. Similarly to Logue and Willet (1976) and Heitger (1985), the standard deviation of yearly inflation rates is applied to proxy inflation volatility. In particular, the standard deviation *PSTD* is calculated from monthly changes in the price level P relative to the price level of the same month of the preceding year:

$$PSTD_t = \sqrt{\frac{1}{12} \sum_{i=1}^{12} \left(\left(\left(\frac{P_{i,t}}{P_{i,t-1}} - 1 \right) \times 100 \right) - \Delta \overline{P}_t \right)^2},$$

$$\text{with } \Delta \overline{P}_t = \frac{1}{12} \sum_{i=1}^{12} \left(\left(\frac{P_{i,t}}{P_{i,t-1}} - 1 \right) \times 100 \right). \tag{13.1}$$

However, as Foster (1978, p. 347) noted, the standard deviation cannot distinguish between a situation with continuously increasing inflation rates and inflation rates that fluctuate around their mean. In both cases the standard deviation may be the same, but the continuously increasing inflation causes less uncertainty, as firms can adjust their expectations to the stable growth of inflation. In order to correct for this deficiency, Foster (1978) and Blejer (1979) measured uncertainty by the absolute mean of changes in past inflation rates.

A similar variable has been constructed using the absolute differences of monthly changes in the price level relative to the preceding year:

$$PDIFM_t = \frac{1}{12} \sum_{i=1}^{12} \left(\left(\left| \frac{P_{i,t}}{P_{i,t-1}} - \frac{P_{i-1,t}}{P_{i-1,t-1}} \right| - 1 \right) \times 100 \right). \tag{13.2}$$

Finally, uncertainty results from false projections of future inflation rates. This type of inflation-induced uncertainty is proxied by the absolute difference of expected inflation ($\Delta \overline{P}^e$) and actual inflation ($\Delta \overline{P}$):

$$PUN_t = \left| \Delta \overline{P}_t^e - \Delta \overline{P}_t \right|. \tag{13.3}$$

It is assumed that individuals form their expectations on the basis of past levels of actual inflation (adaptive expectations). Expected inflation is then substituted by actual inflation lagged one and two periods, where the weights decline geometrically and are constrained to one.

Each measure of uncertainty has been regressed on the level of inflation using the only data available, that is, changes of the consumer price index. All regressions were run over the period 1968 to 1985 with the ordinary least squares technique.

Table 13.2
The Relation between the Level of Inflation and Uncertainty
in Peru, 1968–1985

Measure of Uncertainty	Const.[a]	$\Delta\bar{P}^a$	$\bar{R}^2$	D.W.	Q^b	N^c
PSTD	0.55	0.115***	0.71	2.19	5.75	18
	(0.48)	(6.47)			(0.76)	
PDIFM	0.60*	0.043***	0.80	1.60	2.83	18
	(1.77)	(8.28)			(0.97)	
PUN	1.20	0.252***	0.72	2.16	4.01	18
	(0.50)	(6.70)			(0.91)	

Source; BCRP, *Memoria*, various issues;author's calculations.

[a]t-values in parentheses.
[b]Ljung-Box Q-statistic, level of significance in parentheses.
[c]Number of observations.
*Significant at the 10 percent level.
***Significant at the 1 percent level.

From table 13.2 it can be seen that in the case of Peru the uncertainty of inflation increases unambiguously with the level of inflation irrespective of the uncertainty measure used. In all regressions the coefficient for the level of inflation is positive and statistically significant at the 1 percent level.

The Effects of Inflation Volatility on Investment

Models of private investment behavior generally being used in theoretical and empirical applications do not allow for a separate influence of inflation.[5] An exception is the work of Maloney, Prinzinger, and Ulbrich (1982), who introduced the actual rate of inflation in a modified quarterly accelerator model of investment for the United States. They found a negative and statistically significant relationship between inflation and the real change of expenditures for new plants and equipment. They attributed their results to the interaction of inflation and a progressive tax structure that reduces the profitability of funds invested in real capital formation relative to other uses such as gold or investment in housing.

However, in highly inflationary developing countries tax considerations are less important for investment decisions. Tax rates are lower, while tax evasion is easier and more frequent. In addition, high rates of inflation reduce the real value of tax obligations if firms succeed in delaying tax payments. Instead, this chapter postulates that any negative impact of inflation on private fixed investment in developing countries is rather due to the uncertainty being caused by variable inflation rates.

Table 13.3
The Impact of Inflation Uncertainty on Private Fixed Investment in Peru, 1970–1985

	Const.[a]	Y[a]	K[a]	PSTD[a]	PDIFM[a]	PUN[a]	$\overline{R}^2$	D.W.	Q[b]	N[c]
1.	-21483.6***	0.11***	0.04*	-551.3***			0.92	2.05	6.66	15
	(-3.32)	(11.38)	(1.90)	(-6.28)					(0.47)	
2.	-25356.7***	0.12***	0.04*		-1660.6***		0.92	2.19	4.58	14
	(-3.40)	(10.65)	(1.84)		(-5.54)				(0.71)	
3.	-7185.3	0.10***	0.02			-211.8***	0.75	2.0	7.0	16
	(-1.12)	(6.20)	(0.45)			(-4.51)			(0.54)	

Sources: BCRP 1976; BCRP, *MemoriaL*, various issues; INE, *Cuentas Nacionales del Perú*, various issues; own calculations.

[a]t-values in parentheses.
[b]Ljung-Box Q-statistic, level of significance in parentheses.
[c]Number of observations.
*Significant at the 10 percent level.
***Significant at the 1 percent level.

The empirical analysis is based on a flexible accelerator model. Household firms decide on their investment outlays I_t by considering expected demand Q_t^e and the investment risk (R_t). An increase in expected demand induces household firms to enlarge their productive capacity, while higher risks are hypothesized to lower investment in favor of consumption. In addition, gross investment is determined by the capital stock lagged one period, K_{t-1}.[6]

$$I_t = a_0 + a_1 Q_t^e + a_2 R_t + a_3 K_{t-1} . \qquad (13.4)$$
$$ (+) \quad\ (-) \quad (+/-)$$

In empirical applications the expected level of output in period t is proxied by a sum of lagged values of actual output. In highly inflationary economies such as that of Peru, the planning horizon of household firms is relatively short. consequently, it is reasonable to consider actual output lagged one period only:[7]

$$Q_t^e = bQ_{t-1}, \quad \text{with } b > 0. \qquad (13.5)$$

Substituting (13.5) into (13.4) yields

$$I_t = c_0 + c_1 Q_{t-1} + c_2 R_t + c_3 K_{t-1} . \qquad (13.6)$$

In the following each measure of inflation volatility will be used consecutively to proxy R_t.

An initial estimation of (13.6) with annual observations over the period 1970 to 1985 and the ordinary least squares technique revealed autocorrelation of the residuals. The Durbin-Watson test statistics lay in the inconclusive range. However, the values of the Ljung-Box Q-statistic rejected the hypothesis that the first nine (eight in equation 13.2) autoorrelation coefficients are white noise. In order to determine the nature of the autocorrelation process, the autoregressive parameters were estimated. On the basis of these estimates, the filtered least squares technique was applied. The results are shown in table 13.3.

According to the adjusted coefficients of determination, the overall fit of the regressions is reasonably good. The problems of autocorrelation have been solved. As expected, the lagged output turned out to be the single most important variable in determining the current level of real private capital formation. The relatively poor performance of the lagged capital stock may at least partially be attributed to the lack of reliable capital stock estimates in Peru. The coefficients for all three variables measuring inflation-induced uncertainty are negative and statistically significant at the 1 percent level. The results, therefore, confirm the proposition that firms reduce fixed investments if the inflation variability is relatively high.

SUMMARY

Financial reforms in developing countries generally include measures to raise real interest rates. In order to be able to discriminate between alternative measures, an investment model has been formulated that incorporates the effects of inflation-induced uncertainty on the business forecasts of risk-averse investors. The empirical analysis with Peruvian data confirmed the theoretical proposition that firms reduce their real capital formation if the inflation variability rises. The empirical investigation also showed a close relationship between the level and the variability of inflation. It can thus be concluded that financial liberalization has to be accompanied by measures to reduce inflation if private real capital formation is to be stimulated effectively. Otherwise, an increased credit supply will not lead to more long-term investments but rather will be used to finance consumption and short-term speculative investments.

NOTES

1. For an overview of the theoretical and empirical literature, see Fischer (1982), Fry (1982), Gupta (1984), and World Bank (1989).

2. See Logue and Willet (1976); Blejer (1979); Fischer (1981); Bulkey (1984).

3. Halloran and Lanser (1983) showed that even inflation-adjusted accounting is not free from inflation biases due to the inherently uncertain nature of inflation forecasts.

4. In developing countries household firms are of considerable quantitative importance in agriculture and the manufacturing sector. Firms with fewer than five employees account for 80 percent or more of all firms in the manufacturing sector (Bruch 1983, p. 4).

5. For an overview and an empirical comparison of various investment models, see Kopcke (1985).

6. With respect to the dependent variable, gross investment is preferred to net investment, since the latter cannot be explained without considering depreciation losses. Firms generally plan net additions to the existing capital stock and the replacement of worn-out parts simultaneously (Heil 1985).

7. Further lags did not prove to be significant, nor did they improve the coefficient of determination, adjusted for the degrees of freedom.

DATA SOURCES

Banco Central de Reserva del Perú (BCRP). (1976). *Cuentas Nacionales del Perú: 1960–1974*. Lima.
———. *Memoria*. Various issues.
———. "Tasas de Interes en Moneda Nacional." Unpublished paper, Lima.
Instituto Nacional de Estadistica (INE). *Cuentas Nacionales del Perú*. Various issues.

REFERENCES

Blejer, Mario I. (1979). "The Demand for Money and the Variability of the Rate of Inflation: Some Empirical Results." *International Economic Review* 20, no. 2: 545–549.
Bruch, Mathias. (1983). *Kleinbetriebe und Industrialisierungspolitik in Entwicklungsländern*. Kieler Studien, no. 182. Tübingen: Mohr.
Bulkey, George. (1984). "Does Inflation Uncertainty Increase with the Level of Inflation?" *European Economic Review* 25: 213–221.

Corsepius, Uwe. (1989). *Kapitalmarktreform in Entwicklungsländern: Eine Analyse am Beispiel Perus.* Kieler Studien, no. 225. Tübingen: Mohr.

Fischer, Bernhard. (1982). *Liberalisierung der Finanzmärkte und wirtschaftliches Wachstum in Entwicklungsländern.* Kieler Studien, no. 172. Tübingen: Mohr.

Fischer, Stanley. (1981). "Towards an Understanding of the Costs of Inflation: II." In *The Costs and Consequences of Inflation,* ed. Karl Brunner and Allan H. Meltzer, 5–42. Carnegie-Rochester Conference Series on Public Policy, vol. 15. Amsterdam: North-Holland.

Fischer, Stanley, and Franco Modigliani. (1978). "Towards an Understanding of the Real Effects and Costs of Inflation." *Weltwirtschaftliches Archiv* 114, no. 4: 810–833.

Foster, Edward. (1978). "The Variability of Inflation." *Review of Economics and Statistics* 60 no. 3: 346–350.

Fry, Maxwell J. (1982). "Models of Financially Repressed Developing Economies." *World Development* 10, no. 9: 731–750.

Gupta, Kanhaya L. (1984). *Finance and Economic Growth in Developing Countries.* London: Routledge.

Halloran, John A., and Howard P. Lanser. (1983). "Inflation-induced Biases in the Evaluation and Selection of Capital Investments." *Financial Review* 18, no. 4: 314–325.

Heil, Johann. (1985). *Akzelerationstheorie.* Regensburg: Transfer Verlag.

Heitger, Bernhard. (1985). "Bestimmungsfaktoren internationaler Wachstumsdifferenzen." *Weltwirtschaft,* no. 1: 49–69.

Kopcke, Richard W. (1985). "The Determinants of Investment Spending." *New England Economic Review,* July/August, 19–35.

Logue, Dennis E., and Thomas D. Willet. (1976). "A Note on the Relation between the Rate and Variability of Inflation." *Economica* 43, no. 170: 151–158.

Maloney, Michael T., Joseph Prinzinger, and Holley Ulbrich. (1982). "Capital Formation in an Inflationary Environment." *Southern Economic Journal* 48, no. 3: 651–661.

Moore, Basil J., and A. H. M. Nuruddin Chowdhury. (1981). *Domestic Savings in Selected Developing Asian Countries.* Asian Development Bank Economic Staff Paper, no. 2. Manila: Asian Development Bank.

World Bank. (1989). *World Development Report 1989.* Washington, D.C.: World Bank.

Discussant: Esmeralda O. Lyn

This chapter is well written and is presented in a very clear and organized manner. The theoretical model is developed rigorously, with its theoretical underpinnings discussed comprehensively. The hypothesis that financial reform leads to higher deposit rates but not necessarily to higher interest rates for bank credit is proven mathematically under certain assumptions.

My most important criticism of the chapter is the tenuous link between the theoretical model and the empirical test. The hypothesis is tested in quite a circuitous manner. The author uses ordinary least squares to find whether there is a relationship between inflationary volatility and private capital formation using the Peruvian case. He finds that high inflationary volatility is a significant explanatory variable of the decline in Peru's private investments after its financial reform and concludes that financial reform can stimulate private real capital formation more effectively if deflationary measures are employed to increase real interest rates. The author cannot make a definitive conclusion such as the one he makes—he can only infer it given the empirical test he uses. To determine the validity of the test, it is crucial that the financial reform Peru instituted in the 1970s and the relationship of the formal and informal markets be discussed more extensively. Did the financial reform take the form of variable interest rates, or gradual increases in interest-rate ceilings (the latter reform is used by some countries to avoid economic and financial shocks or disruptions to their financial markets)? During the time financial reform was introduced, was the Peruvian informal market large in relation to the formal market, and what are its characteristics?

The author uses annual data to test his accelerator model of private investment spending. There are only 18 observations. Serial correlation is a serious problem in time-series analysis that the author mentions but does not rectify in his chapter. To reduce the problem, the change in private investments may be a better dependent variable than the level of private investments.

I am suggesting two alternatives that the author may explore. If the sample can be enlarged, the model may be tested by using two regimes—a prereform regime and a postreform regime—to determine if the model exhibits significant difference in behavior. Since the chapter alludes to the fact that in a stable economy, increasing real interest rates and adopting deflationary measures will produce identical results, then a better case to use is a country with a relatively stable economy, or at least one that is not subject to hyperinflation (and possibly, one with not too large an informal market). This will test more effectively the impact of financial reform on private capital formation.

The last suggestion I have is probably more cosmetic than substantive. To make this chapter more interesting and informative, there should be a more detailed discussion of financial reforms and informal markets in general, and those of the Peruvian economy in particular. Financial reform takes different forms. It may be interest-rate reforms or deflationary measures. It may be gradual or a one-shot deal. It may take the form of nationalization of banks, as in Pakistan, or privatization of banks, as in South Korea. Informal markets also have different characteristics. For example, Indonesia has a well-developed informal market in the form of rotating credit societies; Pakistan's informal market is fueled by funds generated from unofficial imports and exports and from corporate or individual undeclared income; and in the Philippines informal lending occurs among smaller businesses, families, and households.

Part V

Theory of the Firm

14

Enterprise Governance and Growth: Notes on the Theory of the Firm in Less Developed Capital Markets

STAVROS B. THOMADAKIS

The received neoclassical theory of the firm assumes that there are markets for inputs and outputs in which each item is priced and from which the profit-maximizing firm derives optimal input and output decisions, given its technology. Competitive financial theory supplements the neoclassical paradigm with several elements. The three most critical ones are the following: First, the firm maximizes the market value of its invested capital by appropriately choosing its investments. Second, the value of the firm is reflected in the aggregate value of its outstanding securities, which, however, can be made up of different classes or categories (for example, debt or equity securities). Third, each type of security earns a rate of return commensurate to risk assumed by its holders, and the firm's cost of capital is some weighted average of these required returns. These three elements together constitute the foundation for a theory of the firm.

Market valuation is a linchpin in the competitive financial theory of the firm. It is a mechanism of allocation of resources, since capital is presumably invested in the highest-valued uses before being allocated to lower-valued ones. It is also a barometer of performance, since any errors or negligence in management's decisions will presumably be reflected in a reduction of the firm's value. This, in turn, will both make it more expensive to raise new capital and expose the firm to the threat of takeover and installation of better management policies. Thus, on one hand, market-value processes enable the optimal allocation of new capital to be realized. On the other hand, they also set down a discipline for the best utilization of capital already invested. It is clear that this theory of optimal firm behavior is grounded much more on what goes on outside the firm than on what goes on inside it. It is the capital market environment of the firm that supports the process of valuation and that gives rise to the benchmarks of optimal investment choice and competitive performance.

    The "orthodox" competitive financial theory of the firm that yields the conclu-
sions briefly summarized in the previous paragraph has become a source of policy
inspiration in many quarters. It leads to the recommendation that arm's-length
markets for financial claims be boosted and that institutional reforms be directed
more specifically to the enhancement of equity markets (Cho 1986). It is presumed
that in the absence of such markets firms will be led to inefficient choices, whereas
within such markets inefficiencies will be eliminated. Unfortunately, this logic is
somewhat circuitous and flawed. The main reason for being suspicious of it is that
it only prescribes conditions outside the firm and disregards what goes on inside it.
    The issue of enterprise governance has been raised in several ways in the context
of developed arm's-length markets for financial claims. Two sources of problems
appear to lie at the core of the issue. The first is that access to information may be
unequal and costly for various capital market participants. The second is that
control of a firm is not synonymous with ownership of financial claims against the
firm. These two problems complicate substantially the question of enterprise
governance. It is worthwhile to offer a brief account of complications. Imperfect
information usually implies an asymmetry between how informed the "insiders"
and the "outsiders" of an enterprise are. Insiders can be owner-managers, a
controlling shareholder holding a majority of a firm's shares, or, finally, a financial
institution holding debt claims in private placement. Outsiders can be minority
shareholders, holders of publicly issued debt and other securities, or short-term
creditors. If insiders have differential information, their private valuations of the
firm will diverge from the market value arrived at by outsiders. This generates
pressure for conveying information from insiders to outsiders, and under certain
conditions the attempts to signal the information can inhibit the firm from taking
the most efficient decisions (Myers 1977; Myers and Majluf 1984). If in addition
insiders' interests are not identical to those of outsiders, the problem of monitoring
insiders' actions can also lead to severe impediments for most efficient decisions
(Jensen and Meckling 1976). The literature on signaling and agency problems is
replete with examples of divergence from efficiency. Conflicts of interest may arise
both between insiders and outsiders and between classes of claimants such as
shareholders and creditors.
    In the context of less developed capital markets, these issues are not exactly
reproducible. That is, one cannot take for granted the existence of a sufficiently
effective arm's-length market that furnishes the mechanism for "objective" firm
valuation. The dissemination of information may be extremely sparse or haphazard,
the quality of information and the reputation of the firm issuing it may be hard to
establish, and there may be very few outsiders who can fit the mold of diversified
portfolio investors. In a developed capital market the "base case" for the competitive theory of the firm is a world of fully informed, well-diversified investors who
participate in the firm's profits and share its control. In less developed capital
markets the "base case" must be defined differently: I would simply suggest that
it consists of an owner-entrepreneur who controls the firm exclusively. The
rationale for this choice of "base case" is obvious. Less developed capital markets
are much less conducive to the solicitation of external finance, and one is therefore

much more likely in such environments to encounter the prototype of owner-entrepreneur than in developed capital markets.

The owner-entrepreneur who exclusively controls a firm makes all the decisions and nominally bears all the consequences. There are no insider/outsider problems, no divergence of interest between managers and owners, and no potential conflicts between different classes of security holders. In a certain sense the world of the owner-managed firm is the most idyllic example of the neoclassical firm in which self-interest enforces efficient choices. The only anomaly to this paradigm as the ideal standard of competitive efficiency is the lack of diversification and the consequent distortion in the cost of capital as perceived by the owner-entrepreneur, since some risks that would be avoidable in a portfolio setting must now be borne and priced. I do not plan to focus on this point, however, as it seems not directly relevant to issues of governance.

This chapter will focus on two primary issues that make the paradigm of owner-entrepreneur more complex than its apparent neoclassical virtues would suggest. the first issue is that of limited liability. The second issue is that of growth opportunities. Both are related to issues of firm growth, as I will argue. I will portray the former as an issue related to "downside" risks and sudden pressures for winding down enterprise activity. I will correspondingly portray the latter as an issue related to "upside" risks and sudden pressures for expanding enterprise activity. In both cases the owner-entrepreneur encounters decision choices that are not always apparent in the traditional neoclassical setting. In the case of sudden pressure to wind down enterprise activity, the existence of limited liability enables him or her to pass on losses to providers of other factors of production. In the case of sudden pressures to scale up enterprise activity, the possible need to raise external capital poses a challenge to his or her control of the enterprise. Each of these cases requires treatment since they have different implications for the choices of the owner-entrepreneur, for his or her incentives to invest, and for his or her preferred way of formulating and organizing investment projects.

LIMITED LIABILITY AND ENTERPRISE DECISIONS

The enactment and use of limited liability historically antecedes the development of capital markets. Limited liability is also present as an institutional arrangement in many countries where capital markets are not well developed today. It is therefore plausible to discuss the choices and actions of owner-entrepreneurs in a legal context offering limited liability. There are two main economic consequences of limited liability. The first is that the extent of entrepreneurial loss is limited to the amount of capital committed to the enterprise. The second is that the protection of limited liability afforded to each enterprise separately enables an insulation of one enterprise from a possible disaster that befalls the other.

The limitation of loss to the amount of committed capital has significant consequences that must be carefully screened. Although the modern theory of finance has underscored the character of these consequences in some instances (e.g., in the discussion of the default option held by shareholders in the presence of risky debt (Black and Scholes 1973]), the theory of the firm has not recognized the full range of consequences. Limited liability is operative when the firm fails. We can suppose that of all possible states describing the firm's profit outcomes, there is a nonempty subset that includes failure. Failure implies that all the capital owned by the firm in a particular state does not suffice for it to discharge fully its obligations. These obligations can be of several kinds. Three major ones are obvious: obligations to debt holders, obligations to suppliers of noncapital factors of production, and obligations to third parties who are bearers of contingent claims arising from the firm's actions (e.g., disgruntled customers, industrial accident victims, and so on). Let us disregard debt claims for the sake of argument, on the assumption that the owner-entrepreneur employs only his own capital. Obligations to suppliers of noncapital factors of production usually assume a short-term character. Thus taxes owed, utility bills and wages owed, or suppliers' credits are normally short-term claims upon the firm. One could therefore surmise that the default option provided by means of these claims to the firm is of relatively small value. Hence the effects of limited liability protection are also negligible. I believe that this is the implicit presumption that most theorists make when they focus on limited liability only as a result of debt contracts. However, the presumption is not always correct since tax claims, wage claims, or suppliers' claims may in fact be based on implicit or explicit long-term contracts. A good example, not uncommon in less developed countries, occurs when the state offers tax subsidies to a new firm for a specific period of time, which could be five or ten years. There is an expectation that after the special period expires, tax liability will resume its normal levels and that tax receipts will be magnified since the firm will have in the meantime grown and solidified its operations. This claim against higher future tax receipts is annihilated if the firm fails. Similar examples can be obtained in the context of long-term employment practices or long-term relationships with suppliers. For a second example, if a supplier of the firm is willing to offer lower prices in exchange for a prospective long-term relationship that will furnish him with a secure market, the supplier has an implicit long-term claim on the firm. Again, this is annihilated if the firm fails. In each of these cases we can argue that the ongoing firm obtains the present value of near-term benefits in exchange for longer-term claims. Limited liability protects against these claims in the subset of states where the firm fails. Product warranties and general legal requirements that the firm indemnify third parties for any damages caused by its actions (as in the case of industrial accidents) also constitute claims against the firm that will be forgone in the event of failure. In short, the firm controlled by an owner-entrepreneur is enveloped by a nexus of contingent claims owned by a variety of private or social agents. Limited liability creates for the firm a bundle of default options against these claims.

The existence of limited liability for the owner-entrepreneur suggests two propositions. The first is well known in the case of debt: Given a level of contingent claims against the firm, incentives will arise for choice of riskier projects and investment policies. As in the case of debt holders, so also in the case of other claimants it is not possible to fix contractually the investment policies of the firm

(John and Senbet 1988). The firm has an incentive to engage in selections of riskier projects, thereby changing the distribution of risks to the disadvantage of other claimants and to the advantage of shareholders or to the owner-entrepreneur, who in our case is the only residual claimant of the firm.

The second proposition is that given a particular project or set of investment policies, the owner-entrepreneur may seek to shape factor employment in such a fashion as to maximize the value of default options held against private or social claimants, as long as these claimants are unable to price the default options that they write. Thus, for example, the owner-entrepreneur has an incentive to choose a more labor-intensive technique if he or she does not have to bear the cost of unemployment insurance. Or he or she may opt for low-cost and reduced-safety techniques if he or she is not required to purchase insurance for possible damages caused by his or her industrial practices. Since the default options of this type held by the owner-entrepreneur do not arise from explicit capital market transactions, there is no guarantee that they will be appropriately priced. In that case factor proportions will be affected.

It is clear from the argument summarized here that the consequences of limited liability are operative even in the absence of debt claims and even if the firm does not operate in an environment of fully developed arm's-length markets for financial instruments of various kinds. Focusing on the second economic consequence of limited liability, I will now argue that the logic of limited liability also affects the preferred pattern of growth of entrepreneurial capital. Let us consider, to start with, that growth opportunities appear in the form of new "projects." These do not have to be independent of existing firm activities. Risky projects are usually described by a random distribution of returns that they offer. Any risky project, if considered on a "stand-alone" basis, enjoys the protection of limited liability if realized returns fall below a critical level (which we may call y^*). The same project, however, when embodied within the structure of an existing firm that owns other projects as well, may lose some of its limited liability protection. Even if its realized returns fall below the critical level y^*, its losses can be absorbed by the rest of the firm. In other words, bad states for the particular project may be coinsured by other projects that enjoy contemporaneous good states. Thus, unless the new project's returns are either riskless or perfectly positively correlated to the returns of other projects held by the firm, the value of a project to the owner-entrepreneur will be greater on a stand-alone basis than within a firm with other projects. It makes sense, therefore, that an owner-entrepreneur who allocates his or her own capital to various projects will have an incentive to constitute these projects as limited liability entities, that is, as separate firms, rather than to incorporate them into existing firms. The benefits of limited liability lead to a rational choice that argues against firm growth and in favor of proliferation of separate firms. Naturally, the latter choice also represents growth of the entrepreneur's capital as a whole.

Taken to its ultimate consequences, the incentive for proliferation of firms underlies the formation of complex enterprise groups whose existence is well documented in many countries. Firms included in these groups may enjoy mutual dependencies in production, vertical relationships, or even a certain degree of commonality of management. Economic rationality and efficient decisions can also be a feature not of specific firms within a group but of the group as a whole. Interdependence between the firms created by the growth of entrepreneurial capital poses special problems when steps are contemplated for the solicitation of external equity by these firms. We shall return to this problem later.

The incentives to constitute projects as "stand-alone" limited liability entities are countered by two types of economic factors about which we can theorize. One is the possible existence of managerial economies when projects are bunched together, especially if the projects are interdependent economically. Synergies that arise between two projects can be more easily internalized within a single firm, whereas when separate legal entities control them, there is always a potential conflict over the distribution of synergies even if both firms belong to the same entrepreneurial group. A second type of disincentive is more germane to the issue of arm's-length financial markets. If a new project is to be funded not by the entrepreneur's own capital but (at least fractionally) by the issue of external securities, informational barriers can make it easier to fund the issue as part of an existing firm than as a new venture. The firm's existing assets, proven record, and reputation can facilitate the process of external finance, whether it be of the debt or the equity variety. The project considered on a "stand-alone" basis may pose too many informational imponderables and may require the disclosure of so much information that the disclosure may prove strategically disadvantageous. It must always be remembered that information made public about a project can be used both by a firm's claimants and by its competitors to their advantage. In conclusion, the force of limited-liability-based incentives for proliferation of separate firms will be stronger in environments of close control of capital by owner-entrepreneurs than in environments of developed arm's-length markets and diversified investors. Owner-entrepreneurs who allocate their own capital do not suffer from informational problems the way external capital providers may.

To the economic consequences of limited liability we must adduce a final point. Given the incentives of the owner-entrepreneur to engage in risk shifting against other claimants, there is an incentive on the part of the latter to monitor and attempt to control the choices of the firm. This effect has been recognized in the analysis of debt claims. It must also be recognized in the case of other claimants, for example, providers of nonfinancial factors of production, customers, or the state. Since the claims whose protection these parties seek are rarely explicit contracts and are not traded in arm's-length markets in any case, the attempts to safeguard their value all too often take the form of regulation. In this context regulation cannot be construed or criticized as interference with "private initiative." However, although the motives for regulation are justifiable within the economic argument we have developed about limited liability, the forms of regulation can easily go astray. This is clearly a tall subject, but the main principle that should be pointed out here is to use the logic of insurance pricing and the formation of reserve funds contributed to by the firm as protection against default contingencies. The issue of monitoring and of attempts to control the choices of the owner-entrepreneur can be enriched further if we admit explicit debt claims. The owners of such claims also have an interest in safeguarding their value and may undertake private actions that create external benefits for all other claimants. This observation would imply that private solutions can replace the need for public regulation (John and Senbet 1988). There are, however, two general caveats that must be noted in this instance. The first refers to the priority of claims. If the particular legal system (or custom) of a given country gives priority to debt claims over other third-party claims, including state claims, there will still occur a residual requirement for monitoring by third-party claimants; lower priority implies that third-party claimants own assets with different contingent outcomes than debt claimants do. The second caveat refers to the character of debt claims in less developed capital markets. Casual observation suggests that in such environments debt is mostly an arrangement between the owner-entrepreneur and a bank in the context of a repetitive and quasi-permanent relationship between the two. If the debt is collateralized against specific assets, as a matter of course, we fall back to the previous issue of the priority of claims. If, on the other hand, the holdings of debt are combined with equity holdings, as happens in many countries whose legal systems do not force a separation between "commercial" and "investment" banking (Langohr and Santomero 1985), then the nominal lenders partake in the owner-entrepreneur's incentives to shift risks and to unilaterally devalue third-party claims by his or her investment actions.

GROWTH OPPORTUNITIES AND
THE PROBLEM OF CONTROL

The owner-entrepreneur, who is the starting point for our thinking, combines ownership and control of his or her enterprise. As usual, ownership is meant as a claim on the profits of the enterprise. Control requires a somewhat more careful definition. Agency theorists have pointed out, in the context of separation of ownership and control, that managers who are partial owners of an enterprise value control because it enables them to appropriate "perquisites" at the expense of external equity holders (Jensen and Meckling 1976). The same effect can occur in the presence of other external claimants, such as those we discussed in the previous section. Therefore, even in the absence of external equity or debt, the owner-entrepreneur may engage in unilateral transfers, thus diverting value from other actual or potential claimants. The value attached to these diversions constitutes a part of the "rents from control" (Ragazzi 1981). This explanation of the desirability of control, however, is limited to a static setting. If we expand our horizon to more dynamic circumstances, the value of control extends to the ability to fashion strategy, make investment decisions, and choose the legal-organizational entities under which a particular project will be launched. Our discussion in the previous section explained some of the important aspects of these choices.

The appearance of growth opportunities poses a major challenge to the maintenance of control by the owner-entrepreneur. The timing and the size of new investment opportunities are frequently matters that cannot be regulated by his or her discretionary actions. Developments of new production techniques, the pressures of competition, and the opening up of the economy to foreign entry are examples of factors that can convert the emergence of new investment opportunities to a process with random and exogenous elements outside the owner-entrepreneur's control. If the timing and size of investment opportunities are exogenous, there is no guarantee that the entrepreneur's own capital will be sufficient for undertaking the requisite investment in the appropriate time. On the other hand, the solicitation of external finance—be it equity or debt—will bring new players into the arena of enterprise decisions and distributions. As a result, the owner-entrepreneur's demand function for external finance will include at least two arguments: (1) the exogenously determined schedule of benefits of the investment opportunity and (2) the forgone benefits from dilution of control via external financing. Actual investment will be regulated by the trade-offs between these two components.

From the perspective of the entrepreneur, the problem of dilution of control may be actually more severe in less developed capital markets. In more developed capital markets external finance can take the form of circulation of claims to a multitude of investors, each of whom holds only a small portion of the aggregate claim against the firm. It can be argued that in that context external investors will undermonitor the firm's choices because of free-riding problems. On the other hand, in less developed capital market environments the holdings of a firm's external claims are much more likely to be highly concentrated in the hands of another entrepreneur, a bank, or the state. Large claimants are more apt to exercise effectively the monitoring function. The incentive to maintain control of the enterprise can be explicitly embodied in a variety of entrepreneurial strategies that seek to attenuate the tension between investment-opportunity generation and own-capital availability. A broad category of strategic options is, of course, to attempt to limit competitive pressure through entry barriers enforced either at the level of state regulations or at the level of industry actions. (Limiting competitive pressures allows some flexibility, if not in terms of size, at least in terms of timing of investments. Although this type of political economy can take us far beyond the scope of this chapter, it should at least be pointed out that limits to competition can be sanctioned by the state in an attempt to reduce the risks of existing investments and to safeguard the value of existing claims against the firm.) Another strategic option, which is more directly related to our subject matter, is the preference for measures that maintain and expand the availability of internal funds. The maintenance of large liquid reserves is an obvious example. A somewhat less obvious one is the preference for investments that turn a quick profit and that therefore do not tie up funds for extended periods of time. The "quick-profit" motive, for which entrepreneurs in less developed countries are frequently criticized, can at least in part be explained by the high shadow price of internal fund availability and the implicit costs of loss of control that external finance can bring about.

If the timing, size, and competitive pressure associated with an investment opportunity make the solicitation of external finance inevitable, the strategic choice to incorporate the investment into an existing firm or to set it up as a separate legal entity is also relevant. If the provision of external capital is to be concentrated in the hands of a few large claimants who will effectively possess a portion of control, the creation of a separate legal entity for a particular investment offers two specific advantages from the viewpoint of the original entrepreneur. First, the external control by a new claimant does not automatically extend to his or her preexisting investments; rather, they remain insulated from external interference. Second, and perhaps more important, maintaining full control of one enterprise and only partial control of another creates opportunities for interfirm transfers if the two firms trade with one another. Imagine, for example, that an owner-entrepreneur has 100 percent equity in firm A and only 60 percent equity in firm B. He or she can exercise the management function in both firms, since he or she is the majority shareholder in each instance. If the two firms trade with each other, he or she clearly has an incentive to transfer a dollar of total profit from firm B to firm A. The transfer reduces the benefit from firm B by $0.60 but increases the benefit from firm A by $1, thereby giving him or her a net gain of $0.40. The transfer can of course be effected by overpricing firm A's goods or services sold to B, or by underpricing firm B's corresponding transactions.

The proliferation of enterprises and the formation of entrepreneurial groups is reinforced as a form of growth by other similar considerations. For example, the ability to shift profits among enterprises within the group may be valuable as a device of minimizing taxes if different firms are subject to different tax regimes. The formation of separate enterprises can also offer insulation from regulatory interventions geared to specific activities, or expanded opportunities for the exploitation of fiscal incentive schemes offered by governments to selected activities. In the same vein, it may be advantageous from the viewpoint of selective credit restrictions or incentives.

Within the logic of well-developed entrepreneurial groups of enterprises, the tension between the emergence of lucrative investment opportunities and the availability of types of finance that do not dilute the original control structure is at least partially relaxed by the possibility that one firm will finance the other. Even if we suppose that internal fund generation is a noisy process with random elements for each firm, the variation of activities among different firms within the group can ensure a smooth-enough process of internal fund generation for the group as a whole. This would imply that the various firms in the group would engage in cross-finance, and that eventually a very complex set of interfirm claims would arise. The observation of entangled equity holdings among firms belonging to an entrepreneurial group is quite a frequent phenomenon in countries with less developed capital markets. The entangled thread of equity holdings in these cases does not necessarily reveal the structure of control or the "chain of command" within the group. It simply reveals past outcomes of the random process of internal fund generation that may endow with ample disposable reserves one firm at one time and another firm at another time.

As we mentioned before, a basic strategic option available to the owner-entrepreneur for the defense of his or her control is the maintenance of a reserve fund. In the context of developed entrepreneurial groups the same strategic option can take a more advanced form. The ultimate mechanism for the resolution of the tension between lucrative investment opportunities and the availability of finance that does not dilute control is a mechanism that can solicit external but nondilutive finance. That mechanism is a bank. Consider the simple case in which the liquid (but permanent) reserve that is required for the maintenance of control is converted into bank equity. A bank can solicit external finance in the form of deposits. It can therefore multiply the availability of funds compared to the amount of its initial equity capital. Depositors' claims are not a threat to the control of enterprise financed by the bank. Presumably these are riskless claims, but even in the event of bank failure it is not customary anywhere to have the bank's depositors take it over. This is the fundamental difference of deposits from firm bonds. Furthermore, in a number of countries deposits may enjoy state-sponsored insurance, and this frees depositors from any pretension of control over the bank's portfolio. It appears very plausible, therefore, to argue that the establishment or acquisition of a bank with access to deposits constitutes for the entrepreneurial group a strategic tool for the solicitation of external finance laundered and purified from actual or potential threats to entrepreneurial control. In my opinion, bank deposits are the purest form of claim against a stream of returns, fully devoid of elements of control over the return-generating entity. The incentive for an entrepreneurial group to acquire control of (or at least a close repetitive relationship to) a bank does not differ much from the incentive of the industrial company that integrates into its upstream activities in order to ensure an orderly flow of raw materials to its plants.

Two parenthetical observations are required in this context. Both, in my view, are significant for the interpretation of international differences in financial systems. The first is that banks that are incorporated within the structure of an entrepreneurial group are not subject to the same rules of competition or the same measure of efficiency as other banks. The reason for this is again that what may be rational for a group as a whole may not be rational for some of its component entities. Banks that operate as external finance arms of an entrepreneurial group may allocate their placements on the basis of intragroup shadow prices rather than marketwide value indices. If finance professors exercise their wizardry to discover compliance to efficient decision rules, they should properly focus on the entrepreneurial group as a whole and not on any particular component of it. The second observation has to do with the character of debt incurred by firms from a bank within their entrepreneurial group. Whether this is debt only in name, but in fact an equity claim, or whether it is in fact debt, is a matter that requires specific analysis of intragroup relationships. It is certainly true, however, that debt ratios shown on balance sheets are not necessarily comparable between firms belonging to a group and firms not belonging to one. Direct comparison of stated debt ratios may be very misleading since the requisite claims may in fact be quite different in their terms, in their implications for potential control, and in the implicit promises for renewal or nonrenewal of the debt after the current claim expires.

Theorizing about growth and enterprise governance is really an open agenda. Most received theory focuses on "downside" crises as the source of governance issues. Our viewpoint in the previous comments has taken the owner-entrepreneur as a starting point and has presumed that he or she follows a certain logical unraveling of incentives without being disturbed by a spontaneous growth of arm's-length markets and financial transactions. Clearly, however, a logical argument can be varied, and the emergence of arm's-length markets can interfere with both the logic and the actual process by which things happen. Our important point that must be addressed is whether in fact the absence of well-developed arm's-length markets for finance operates as an objective impediment for enterprise (or entrepreneurial capital) growth. In the received neoclassical theory of full-information, competitive financial markets the solicitation of external finance appears like almost an effortless task. Imperfect information and agency problems endow the solicitation of external finance with a variety of complications. If the mechanisms and the logic of growth-induced strategies in less developed capital market environments are taken into account, it is really not clear whether growth impediments can be located in that area of the finance functions or at some other point of the economic mechanism. In terms of international experiences, of course, the evidence is inconclusive also. We have witnessed formidable growth of enterprises and whole economies both with and without a primary role played by arm's-length financial markets.

ON SUPPLY PROBLEMS IN CAPITAL MARKET DEVELOPMENT

Previous remarks on the owner-entrepreneur and his incentives in the context of less developed capital markets can be supplemented by a few reflections on the question of capital market development. In every particular instance the development of arm's-length financial markets must be based on a supply of securities. Owner-entrepreneurs are to act (and have acted historically) as the primary issuers of securities in developing capital markets. My foregoing arguments suggest at least three necessary conditions for owner-entrepreneurs to be willing to proceed to issues of securities. The first is sufficient pressure from investment opportunities in a competitive environment that does not allow their postponement. The second is a systematic insufficiency of internally generated funds that forces the solicitation of external finance. The third is a lack of sufficient control over a bank mechanism of external fund solicitation. The last condition is really a question of how far institutional arrangements have been consolidated between entrepreneurs and banks in particular countries. The more secure the bank mechanism of external fund acquisition, the less urgent will be the need to proceed to direct security issues.

The first two conditions are related to economic growth and competition. Competitive investing is bound to increase the pressure for timely investment activity, and this in turn may not match a firm's time pattern of internal fund generation. Economic growth per se is not a sufficient inducement for the issue of securities. Certain types of growth favor internal fund generation and blunt the pressure for external finance. For example, growth that occurs mainly in established sectors and through established activities will generate timely profits for expansion. On the other hand, if the growth stimuli involve new activities and a restructuring of the economy, sufficient internal profit generation is not guaranteed. The current phase of the world economy with increasing global competition and pervasive needs for industrial restructuring is a good example of the conditions for development of external finance markets and instruments. Indeed, such a tendency is observable on an international scale.

The development of arm's-length financial markets can be hampered, however, even if entrepreneurs are willing to supply securities and investors' incomes have grown sufficiently to create a demand for securities. The contracts offered to investors may be so burdened with informational asymmetries and moral-hazard problems that they end up heavily underpriced and scarcely marketable. For example, it is worth wondering whether a full-fledged equity market can function when all traded shares are minority shares and each owner-entrepreneur keeps for himself a nontraded majority block of shares. The external investors in the shares would bear the brunt of the full power of the majority owner to appropriate rents from the firm. The example that was mentioned previously by which an owner-entrepreneur could divert profits from a partially owned to a fully owned firm is an easy illustration of the problem. More generally, the preexistence of well-formed entrepreneurial groups of firms with tangled equity holdings and economic inter-relationships may create a veil of misinformation about each firm that small investors will find impenetrable.

In a more general vein, it seems to me that there can be no transition from a system dominated by owner-entrepreneurs to a system of a multitude of diversified investors without some resolution of monitoring problems and some safeguards for minority owners' rights. The formulation of rules of ex post disclosure is not a sufficient step, since it does not enable ex ante intervention. It is well known that it is practically impossible to fix in any contract the investment activity of the firm without running the danger of choking it altogether. Basically, what is needed to attract and maintain a multitude of diversified investors in an arm's-length market is a powerful-enough champion of their interests who can expend resources for timely monitoring activities and who can contest, if necessary, the discretionary power of the owner-entrepreneur. This role could perhaps be filled by a new brand of development bank, whose function would be streamlined to these requirements and whose activities would include the potential takeover of the firm under certain conditions. Such a development bank could either be publicly funded (at least in part) so as to offer the public good of monitoring, or it could be initially funded by a multitude of investors who would buy its shares but would have a right to exchange them at a later date for the constituent securities of the bank's portfolio. Furthermore, such a bank would hold not only shares but also arm's-length debt claims of specific term against firms, so as to wield the bargaining instrument of credit renewal against owner-entrepreneurs.

The problem of transition from an undeveloped to a fully operative arm's-length financial market is replete with unanswered questions. In the interest of a future research agenda, I should perhaps list a few: What should be the role of banks, and does the separation of "investment" from "commercial" banking have a positive impact on the transition? If public-sector-sponsored institutions (such as a version of the development bank) undertake a role in the transition, what should be the limits of their power and when should they be phased out, if at all? Should there be any limitations on private takeover activity that would on one hand spur interest in speculative security holdings, but on the other lead to concentrations of control in systems that already suffer from that problem? Is it sensible to give policy priority to the trading development of particular instruments (e.g., debt over equity)? The list of questions is quite long, and the answers are scarce and sometimes context-specific. As a research agenda for international financial economists, I think that they constitute a serious challenge in the years ahead.

REFERENCES

Barnea, A., R. Haugen, and L. Senbet. (1985). *Agency Problems and Financial Contracting*. Englewood Cliffs, N.J.: Prentice-Hall.

Black, F., and M. Scholes. (1973)."The Pricing of Options and Corporate Liabilities." *Journal of Political Economy* 81 (May/June): 637–654.

Cho, Y. J. (1986). "Inefficiencies from Financial Liberalization in the Absence of Well-functioning Equity Markets." *Journal of Money, Credit, and Banking* 18: 191–199.

Holmstrom, B. (1979). "Moral Hazard and Observability." *Bell Journal of Economics* 10 (Spring): 74–91.

Jacquemin, A., and E. deGhellinok. (1980). "Familial Control, Size, and Performance in the Largest French Firms." *European Economic Review* 13: 81–91.

Jensen, M., and W. Meckling. (1976). "Theory of the Firm: Managerial Behavior, Agency Costs, and Ownership Structure." *Journal of Financial Economics* 3: 305–360.

John, K., and L. Senbet. (1988). "Limited Liability, Corporate Leverage, and Public Policy." New York University Working Paper.

Langohr, H., and A. Santomero. (1985). "The Extent of Equity Investment by European Banks." *Journal of Money, Credit, and Banking* 17: 243–252.

Leland, H., and D. Pyle. (1977). "Informational Asymmetries, Financial Structure, and Financial Intermediation." *Journal of Finance* 32: 371–387.

Miller, M., and K. Rock. (1985). "Dividend Policy under Asymmetric Information." *Journal of Finance* 40: 1031–1051.

Myers, S. (1977). "Determinants of Corporate Borrowing." *Journal of Financial Economics* 5 (November): 147–175.

Myers, S., and N. Majluf. (1984). "Corporate Financing and Investment Decisions When Firms Have Information That Investors Do Not Have." *Journal of Financial Economics* 13: 187–221.

Ragazzi, G. (1981). "On the Relation between Ownership Dispersion and the Firm Market Value." *Journal of Banking and Finance* 5: 216–276.

Rybczynski, T. (1984). "Industrial Finance System in Europe, U.S., and Japan." *Journal of Economic Behavior and Organization* 5: 275–286.

Sarig, O. (1983). "On Mergers, Divestments, and Options: A Note." *Journal of Financial and Quantitative Analysis* 20 (September): 385–390.

Snowden, P. (1987). "Financial Market Liberalization in LDCs: The Incidence of Risk Allocation Effects of Interest Rate Increases." *Journal of Development Studies* 24: 83–93.

Stiglitz, J. (1985). "Credit Markets and the Control of Capital." *Journal of Money, Credit, and Banking* 17 (May): 133–152.

Stiglitz, J., and A. Weiss. (1981). "Credit Rationing in Markets with Imperfect Information." *American Economic Review* 71 (June): 393–410.

Discussant: Lemma W. Senbet

Professor Thomadakis suggests a set of interesting perspectives on the theory of the firm in less developed capital markets. He uses an owner-manager of the firm as a "base case" in contrast to the value-maximizing paradigm of the Fisherian separation principle and well-functioning capital markets. This case is picked because it appears observationally relevant in less developed economies. Thomadakis argues that efficient choices are forced by an owner-manager who faces no other outside financiers similar to the manner in which functioning markets force value maximization. Self-interest forces efficiency, so to speak. I think, though, that self-interest also motivates expansion of span of control.

Since there are no outside financiers, there are no agency conflicts among capital contributors of the type familiar in the agency literature. However, the existence of limited liability engenders agency conflicts with noncapital contributors, including the society at large, as those presented by John and Senbet (1988). Thus the owner-manager has an incentive (1) to set up the productive processes in a more risky fashion, (2) to parcel up firms into separate entities to overcome the "coinsurance effect," and (3) to engage in activities that protect and expand span of control. These incentives follow if the entrepreneur-manager is risk-neutral. Thomadakis then traces the evolution of the entrepreneurial firm economy into growth patterns, the emergence of banks, and the evolution of equity markets.

Admittedly, the chapter lacks structure and model. The arguments do not follow from first principles. I would have preferred a theoretical development with some structure that allows comparative statistics. I realize that it is difficult to come up with a coherent model for this ambitious agenda without making strong assumptions. However, it is useful to start from somewhere and then add arguments consistent with the framework.

The basic economic consequences of limited liability are recognized in prior literature (e.g., John and Senbet 1988). However, what I like about the current chapter is that it makes a specific prediction regarding the impact of the "coinsurance" effect on the nature of entrepreneurially controlled firms. Under coinsurance the value of an option on a portfolio is less than the sum of the values of component options. Thus the private value of a project is worth more on a stand-alone basis, and hence limited liability discourages firm growth. Thomadakis predicts that this leads to an incentive for proliferation of firms and to the formation of complex enterprise groups. I have found this particular prediction interesting, and this observation is new, at least in the context of less developed economies.

As I mentioned earlier, the economic consequences of limited liability have been analyzed earlier. In the John and Senbet paper (1988) it was shown that the private firm overinvests in risky projects relative to social optimality, because the equity holders of the firm escape negative externalities by virtue of limited liability. Examples that engender such potential "social agency problems" are abundant; they include chemical accidents, oil spills, product malfunctions, and even federal deposit insurance. John and Senbet showed that risky corporate debt has an effect of aligning social and private interests, along with the current tax system. Indeed, the existence of corporate taxation and tax subsidization of debt provide self-enforcing devices for the society as an alternative to government regulation. In the John and Senbet paper the very two things, namely bondholder-stockholder conflict and tax discrimination between debt and equity payments, that have troubled financial economists turn out to be useful from the social perspective.

Thomadakis argues that in the course of enterprise growth, the owner-manager's control can be threatened by the emergence of growth opportunities that cannot be postponed due to competitive pressure. Again, this reinforces his earlier observation that the entrepreneur would wish to engage in a complex setup of separate entities and heavy reliance on internally generated funds. External capital markets, of course, must be accessed when the alternatives, including entrepreneurial capital, are exhausted, resulting in further dilution of control. Thomadakis suggests that entrepreneurial banks develop to issue deposits and that depositors presumably do not threaten control. This is an interesting observation, although I am not fully persuaded. This strategy is similar to issuing loans by using the bank as a conduit. These loans can be riskless only if the government insures them. But then the insurer, the government, becomes the creditor and will engage in activities that threaten the entrepreneur's control. Alternatively, the entrepreneur could have issued nonvoting shares or preferred stock, but then there will be informational asymmetry and monitoring problems. On another issue, Thomadakis ignores the risk-sharing aspects of entrepreneurial problems, which presumably call for the necessity and evolution of financial markets, as well as a mechanism for discipline provided by takeover threats. However, this discussion is beginning to look like a story on the emergence of capital markets and their evolution over time. Indeed, Thomadakis's discussion of development banks in resolving asymmetric information begins to look like Leland and Pyle's (1977) rationalization of financial intermediaries. It may well be that the existing literature on agency and information asymmetry is more applicable to less developed capital markets than to the advanced economies. That is, the extant financial theory of imperfect information may just be a theory of finance in less developed capital markets.

Overall, I enjoyed reading this chapter. Thomadakis advances very interesting perspectives on issues relating to enterprise evolution in less developed capital markets.

REFERENCES

John, K., and L. Senbet. (1988). "Limited Liability, Corporate Leverage, and Public Policy." Wisconsin working paper.

Leland, H., and D. Pyle. (1977). "Informational Asymmetries, Financial Structure, and Financial Intermediation." *Journal of Finance* 32 (May): 371–387.

15

Financial Management in
Public Enterprises in India

V. N. HUKKU

The foundations of the public sector in India go back to the early years of planning. The Industrial Policy Resolution of April 30, 1956, which is still the basis of present policy, proposed that all basic and strategic industries and public utilities should be in the public sector, given the objective of a socialistic pattern of society and the need for planned and rapid development. Public enterprises (PEs) have achieved a great deal in terms of their contribution to quantitative targets of production, to the establishment of a modern industrial structure, to balanced regional development, and to the formation of technological skills. They have become principal instruments of planning in India, occupying commanding heights of the economy and controlling and directing in a large measure the whole course of its development. Over the last 30 years or more, the growth of the PEs has been phenomenal in terms of investment and production as well as the scope of activities. But in spite of this phenomenal growth, the overall performance of public enterprises has remained unsatisfactory, especially in terms of their contribution to the generation of resources and financial profitability. Consequently, the net contribution of PEs to the requirements of funds for their investment proposals is small, resulting in pressures on budgetary resources. The ability of the budget to finance further public investment has been seriously eroded because of low returns on past investment and the rising burden of defense and other nonplan expenditures.

The rationale of the operation of PEs and the expectations that their management should be run on commercial and business lines, that they should earn profits to contribute to the revenues of the state, that they should be judged for their total results, and that subject to these performance criteria they should have full freedom of operation were clearly set out in the Industrial Policy Resolution of 1956. In accordance with this rationale, most of the activities of the public sector have been organized in the form of corporations or companies set up either under the statute or under the Companies Act, while some activities continue to be organized within the framework of departmental undertakings or statutory boards; their numbers are few, and their operational methods are dictated by specific requirements of the government. This chapter pertains only to PEs set up as corporations or companies, which are supposed to function "along business lines."

PERFORMANCE APPRAISAL

Issues involved in appraising the performance of the public sector are so conflicting in nature that they often bewilder both politicians and economists all over the world where economies are in practice. This makes a proper assessment of the performance of the public sector difficult.[1] Public sentiments are often exploited by politicians who may push the government to the wall in defending the efficiency of the PEs run by it. The economic viability of any public-sector unit depends much on its profit-earning capacity. While the political lobby raises cries of exploitation when profit earning is involved, the Public Accounts Committee regards a unit as inefficient if it incurs losses.[2] The public-sector enterprises thus suffer under this cross-fire. This situation is not peculiar to India. In the United Kingdom also an urgent need was felt for setting up proper guidelines for appraising the performance of public-sector units. Some performance standards were prescribed in 1967 but had to be amended again after a trial of about a decade.[3]

Leaving aside the political aspect, it must be understood that the successful performance of any unit largely depends on effective financial management. Hence a well-designed financial management system is essential for the effectiveness of financial decisions. Financial decisions contribute to the achievement of financial and overall corporate goals in PEs. PEs in developing countries have often been criticized for lack of effective financial management. Lack of financial planning, defective investment decisions, and low or negative profits are the common areas of criticism.

It has often been observed that there is a lack of financial consciousness in PEs. Noneconomic considerations largely influence decision making, due to which performance evaluation in financial terms is rendered difficult.[4] Moreover, there is a lack of professionalized management. The managers in some cases have a background that leads to achieving target expenditure rather than ensuring financial discipline, which would motivate a better input-output relationship in financial management. There are certain other areas also in which deficiencies exist, such as standardization of procedures for maintenance of accounts, effective internal audits, cost recording, inventory control, and weak credit collection leading to blocking of large investment in inventories and receivables.[5] All these reflect the system of financial management, which is the real problem.

The expectation that PEs as commercial ventures should "augment the revenues of the State" and provide a return that can be used for further investment and growth has not been fulfilled.[6] Even for units that are making losses because of the nature of their products or because of their serving some specified social objectives, the efficiency of operation has often deteriorated. In actual practice, the freedom of operation of the management has quite often been curtailed or interfered with by formal or informal government intervention. While PEs were to be judged by their "total results," the monitoring and evaluation system of the government has not been adequate to the task. The strict enforcement of performance standards on PEs would entail having a closer look at the constraints of the operation. While some of these arise from the general nature of India's economic structure and some from incorrect investment decisions of the past, others stem from poor managerial practices within the enterprises and formal and informal interference by the government. The object of this chapter is to critically examine the system and practices prevalent in India for financial management in public-sector enterprises involving financial decision-making practices.

FINANCIAL MANAGEMENT

The finance function is of great significance in PEs, but several of them are not adequately equipped with the basic framework in which efficient financial management could be operative. There is an obvious lack of professionalization of management.[7] In most of the PEs there is a finance director, financial adviser, or financial controller. Like the government, the finance person rules supreme, unlike in private enterprises where every functional area manager is responsible for the financial implications of his or her proposal. These financial advisers belong to the bureaucratic order and are often nominated by the government. This has often led to a situation of dichotomy, though the basic idea was that the financial adviser should be nearer to the heart of management and out of the periphery of unnecessary details in which he is involved today. The financial adviser has a large number of functions, in the performance of which he enjoys the position of the principal adviser of the chief executive on all financial matters. In such a situation it is essential that the financial adviser have a wider and deeper understanding of the concept and essentials of financial management in addition to his knowledge of bookkeeping, accounting, and auditing. The government has accepted in principle the need for providing training to the financial adviser in the techniques of financial management. In actual practice, this often does not happen, and even if training is provided, the frequency of transfers nullifies its advantage.

INVESTMENT APPROVALS

Decisions regarding investment in PEs are guided by the overall national considerations of resource mobilization and allocation. Approval of the cabinet is also necessary in certain cases such as the creation of new corporations in the public sector, an increase in existing investment in a PE by more than 20 percent, and participation of the central government or a PE in the share capital of any existing corporation or company. In 1972 the government set up a Public Investment Board (PIB) to which all investment proposals are referred that involve an investment of 10 million rupees and above. It examines the broad contours of an investment proposal at the project-formulation stage and even decides whether the feasibility report should be prepared.

The present system of investment financing for PEs integrates their plans fully into the total public-sector plan. As a consequence, the investment activities of PEs are subject to government approval at several stages. The intimate links between PE investment plans and the budget has led to a complex system of governmental approval for individual proposals. In order to integrate its plans with the national plan, an enterprise has to interact with the government at several stages. Despite such rigorous scrutiny and government intervention, in practice the system does not really provide greater leverage in regulating the public sector's draft on resources. At the same time, it probably leads to a measure of financial irresponsibility in the PE.

The direction of reforms in the present system of investment financing has to be in line with the importance of PE investments in the national plan.[8] In this regard, a distinction has been made between (1) core-sector enterprises, (2) financially viable enterprises in the noncore sector, and (3) enterprises in the noncore sector that are incurring losses. The Public Accounts Committee was of the view that in the case of core-sector enterprises, the existing system of fully integrating their plans with the total public-sector plan must continue since in most cases the PE plans are coterminous with the national sectoral plans. Many of the core sectors are highly interlinked, and, therefore, this calls for coordination with other sectoral plans. The resource requirements of these sectors are also very large, and, therefore, the present system of scrutiny of all their investment proposals, whether they are financed through the national budget or through the funds raised by the enterprises themselves, has to continue. In the case of the financially viable noncore sector, there does not seem to be any need for such detailed scrutiny, and the public-sector investment plan should include only the flows through the budget. To the extent that these enterprises can finance their investment requirements by raising funds from the public through deposits or debentures or by borrowing from the financial institutions, they need not be subjected to any process of governmental clearance.

At present, proposals that fall beyond the delegated powers of a PE but are estimated to cost 10 crores or less (one crore equals 10 million rupees) are brought before the Expenditure Finance Committee (EFC) for approval. Investment proposals costing above 10 crores require the approval of the cabinet, and these are brought before the PIB. It is suggested that these limits be raised as follows:

1. EFT: Investment proposals costing above 5 crores but not above 25 crores

2. PIB: Investment proposals costing over 25 crores

Corresponding changes should be made in the delegated powers of the PEs. We would also suggest that the EFC and the PIB should be served by a single appraisal agency that should be the principal point of contact between a PE and the various agencies that scrutinize the investment proposals. We feel that the Project Appraisal Division of the Planning Commission should be this nodal agency, and for this purpose it should be suitably strengthened.

BUDGETING

In accordance with the recommendations of the Administrative Reforms Committee, the PEs are required to prepare comprehensive budgets. However, the budgets of all types of PEs are not presented to the Parliament. The government should discuss every year with the PE the general lines of its short-term (five years) and long-term capital budgets. It is also useful to apply the system of performance budgeting so as to establish more clearly the input-output relationship. This will direct attention to ends and not means as the significant element in financial planning.

Performance budgeting should be used as a control mechanism, but it suffers from behavioral problems.[9] Cost-control measures are important, and the Parliamentary Committee on Public Undertakings also recommended their application.[10] The committee also recommended that norms be established for determining standard costs, but consciousness about cost control is generally lacking.

FINANCIAL RESOURCE MANAGEMENT

The major sources of finance of PEs are not much different from those of private enterprises in character. The differences are those of participation, powers of acquisition, and procedures related to the raising of funds. These sources of finance can be classified as follows:

1. Equity and grants by government
2. Loans from government
3. Loans from public and financial institutions
4. Public participation in equity
5. Foreign investments
6. Public deposits
7. Working capital arrangements with banks
8. Internal financing

EQUITY FINANCING

Depending on the type of organization of a public enterprise, the initial funds provided by the government take the form of share capital (equity) or loans. The government has generally been earmarking funds for investment in these PEs. The burden on the national exchequer, therefore, has been counting. It is felt that government funds are either cost-free (as in the case of share capital) or low-cost funds because of the insignificant, rather formal rate of interest charged on loans, which are sometimes interest free as well. This sort of feeling renders financial management less effective. With these considerations, there has been a change in the outlook of the government. The PEs have been allowed to raise funds in the open market either through seeking deposits from the public by offering interest as approved by the government or by seeking public participation in equity or bonds.

The idea for public participation in the equity of PEs was supported by the Estimates Committee. The Krishna Menon Committee (1959) justified the option of limited private participation in investment in PEs.[11] However, the Sengupta Committee (1984) did not approve private participation in equity. The committee did make the following recommendations:

1. For financially viable enterprises in the noncore sector, the government would contribute only toward equity. Investment proposals for equity participation in such cases would be dependent on the enterprise meeting performance criteria and payments of dividends at the prescribed rates. the remaining requirements for project investment should be raised outside the budget through borrowing or nonconvertible debentures but without government guarantee.

2. Where noncore enterprises are used as agencies for other than commercial objectives, either the government should undertake additional equity contribution or the additional net cost of such activities should be reimbursed.

3. Since selling of shares may create problems of ownership without giving the public-sector enterprise any great advantage, the committee did not recommend selling of shares to the public by existing PEs.[12]

BORROWINGS FROM THE OPEN MARKET

Ordinarily, loans from public commercial banks and other financial institutions hardly constitute a significant proportion of the total financial structure of public enterprises in India. Therefore, PEs should be encouraged to raise funds from the open market to supplement their capital base. The Administrative Reforms Committee Study Team has examined the suggestion that "Government financing offers fail to create the necessary financial discipline in the PEs and that it will, therefore, be better if they are asked to resort to borrowing from market on their own credit even for capital expenditure." The study team felt that the amount of capital required by the public enterprises is very large and is to be raised in the open market without the support of the government guarantee.

Nothing is a better index of a company's good health than its market quotation, which, in essence, signifies the degree of confidence of the public in the company's future. Thus in the present-day context there is a very strong case for permitting the public enterprises to approach the capital market. Recently the government has allowed selected public enterprises to approach the capital market for public deposits and selling of bonds.

ISSUE OF BONDS

In view of the increasing demand of PEs for financial resources, the government of India announced guidelines on September 7, 1985, permitting PEs to issue bonds with the prior approval of the government. The objects for the issue, the period for redemption, the rate of interest, and the value of the bonds are all prescribed by the government, keeping in view the permitted debt/equity ratio. Although these bonds are not guaranteed by the government as in the case of other such bonds, they have been declared an authorized security and as such have been made as attractive as possible. These bonds are listed on all the major stock exchanges in the country and are freely transferable without the requirement to pay the transfer-stamp duty. The biggest advantage to the subscriber is that there is no deduction of tax at the source, and the benefit under section 80L of the Income Tax Act will be available, which would mean that up to a limit of 7,000 rupees, minus the interest, dividend income will stand exempted from the Income Tax Act, 1961.

In addition, there is a total exemption from the wealth tax on these bonds, which is currently not available in respect of debentures being issued by the private-sector companies. It is also interesting to note that the new guidelines specify that the interest for the entire seven-year period of these bonds will be payable in advance in the form of interest coupons along with the issue of bonds. This would mean that along with the transfer of these bonds, the owners can also trade in the interest coupons.

PUBLIC DEPOSITS

In the budget of 1980–81 the government made a provision for public deposits to be accepted by the public enterprises. The government companies have been allowed to accept up to 35 percent of the aggregate of their paid-up share capital and free reserves from the public. The rate of interest is 11.5 percent per annum for one year, 12.5 percent for two years, and 14 percent for three years.

This was a good decision taken by the government, as this scheme is quite useful for all the concerned parties—public enterprises, investors, and the government. It will help the general public to put their savings in these secured companies and also help the government's own liquidity funds. With the help of this scheme, the dependence of public enterprises on the state exchequer can be minimized to a considerable extent, and sufficient funds can be made available through the capital market for expansion and modernization programs.

WORKING CAPITAL FINANCING

Requirements for working capital generally differ from enterprise to enterprise depending upon the type and nature of the business, its size, its operating cycle, its costs of production, the marketability of its products, the availability of raw materials, stores, and spares, and banking policies pursued by the nationalized banks. To overcome the difficulties of working capital, these enterprises should try their best to reduce the costs of production and to increase production to the maximum. Similarly, the government should take adequate steps to resolve the problems of working capital faced by the public enterprises.

FINANCIAL PROBLEMS

While the public enterprises have made a great contribution to the nation's economy, their performance has not been satisfactory. The main financial problems of these enterprises can be summarized as follows:

1. Overcapitalization
2. Faulty pricing policy
3. Deficient planning and budgeting
4. Problems of raising financial resources
5. Inadequate profitability
6. Unfavorable debt/equity ratio
7. Heavy burden of social overheads
8. Extravagance of expenditure
9. Deficient working capital management
10. Inadequate attention to cost accounting
11. Overall lack of professional financial management

ACCOUNTABILITY AND FINANCIAL PERFORMANCE

It is essential to make the PEs more accountable for their performance. It is necessary, therefore, to develop a general set of performance criteria. The criteria for financial performance are the most important, in that PEs are expected to play an important role in the mobilization of resources, and they can do so only if they are financially viable. Three basic criteria can be the following:

1. Gross margin on assets (for all enterprises)
2. Net profit on net worth (for core-sector and profit-making enterprises)
3. Gross margin on sales (for service enterprises)

The standards against which financial performance has to be evaluated will have to vary for (1) core-sector enterprises, (2) financially viable enterprises in the noncore sector, and (3) loss-making units. Enterprises in the core sector are generally subject to price control, and their financial performance is affected by this fact. However, some normative rate of return is often implicit in price-fixation procedures and can provide a standard for comparison. In general, after allowing for distortions induced by lags in price adjustment, the rate of net profit, measured by the ratios listed above, should be at least a stipulated percentage that can be fixed for each enterprise at the beginning of the year. The gross margin on assets should be improving over time. In the noncore sector, manufacturing enterprises in the public sector generally operate in a competitive environment with a substantial private-sector presence. Some of them (e.g., cement, drugs) are subject to price control. In general, for these enterprises, the criteria for comparison should be the industry average both for gross margin on assets and the rate of net profit. This will of course only apply to profit-making units. Many service enterprises in the public sector operate as monopolies or have special privileges that allow them to function on a cost-plus basis. Moreover, the capital base in these service units is very different from what it is in manufacturing enterprises. In service enterprises it may be more useful to focus attention on the direction of change in the gross margin on sales, though the other measures of financial profitability should also be examined. Wherever service enterprises operate in a competitive environment, a comparison with private-sector units would also be useful. In the third category, loss-making units, it is clearly not possible to examine measures of profitability. However, the gross margin should be positive so that the loss-making unit is at least covering operating costs. In addition, it may be useful to monitor the direction of change in a few other measures like (1) the ratio of loan liabilities to assets, (2) the ratio of wages to value added per workers, and (3) cash loss per worker.

There are many PEs incurring cash losses continuously over a period of years, and in many of these cases the average value added per employee per month is even less than the average monthly emoluments per employee. Whatever steps are taken, such enterprises can seldom break even or make good. Such enterprises, particularly when they are not in the core sector, could hardly justify their existence by eating into government resources. It is, therefore, recommended that the Bureau of Public Enterprises (BPE) on its own initiative take up special studies of the operations of such enterprises, with the help of consultants if need be.

TRAINING FINANCIAL MANAGERS

In order to attain the desired national objectives, it is essential to provide for an efficient management of public-sector enterprises, whose contribution to the national economy is growing day by day. To ensure efficient and effective management, it is necessary to have an efficient staff at all levels of management. Efficiency of the staff is dependent partly on ingrained skill, knowledge, and experience and partly on specialized training related to specific functional areas of management.

An essential aspect of training is to instill among the managers a sense of belonging to the undertaking served by them. It has been observed that there is a feeling that "government's business is nobody's business" and that "government losses are nobody's losses." The financial manager needs to develop the feeling that his or her stake in his or her career coexists with efficiency in financial administration. Realization is a psychological phenomenon for which formal training is rather unthinkable unless we can devise a technique of thorough brainwashing, which does not appear to be feasible in the democratic setup of overall administration in the country. An attempt can, however, be made to pick up persons who have an aptitude for the nature of specific work. Hence a proper and effective training system has its own advantage.

There is no guarantee that a financial manager trained to meet the financial administrative requirement in an undertaking will continue to serve the same organization for all time to come. It would therefore be desirable that the training should be so designed that the basic principles and elements of financial management in PEs are well understood by the prospective and existing financial managers. This basic and grass-roots training can thereafter be applied with related modifications based on the specific nature of the undertaking.

NOTES

1. H. Bhattacharya, "Public Sector Units, A Framework for Appraisal." *Economic Times* (India), December 14, 1986, p. 5.

2. The Public Accounts Committee is a body of the Parliament of India entrusted with the task of reviewing the performance of public-sector units and the working of government departments and agencies.

3. *A Review of Economic and Financial Objectives* (London: HMSO, Cmnd. 3437, 1967).

4. Laxmi Narain, *Principles and Practice of Public Enterprise Management* (New Delhi: S. Chand, 1980), p. 343.

5. *Report of the Comptroller and Auditor General of India—Union Government (Commercial)* (New Delhi, 1977).

6. Government of India, *Report of the Committee to Review Policy for Public Enterprises* (1984), p. 2 (Sengupta Committee Report).

7. Narain, *Principles and Practice*, p. 243.

8. Government of India, *Report of the Committee to Review Policy for Public Enterprises* (Sengupta Committee Report), pp. 11–13.

9. Ishwar Dayal, *New Concepts in Management* (Bombay: Lalvani Pub. House, 1970).

10. Committee on Public Undertakings, *Report No. 67 Submitted to the 4th Lok Sabha*, p. 88.

11. *The Report of the Sub-Committee of Congress Party in Parliament*, November 1959, p. 34.

12. *Loc. cit.*

Part VI

International Capital
and Enterprise Incentives

16

Financial Contracting between Non-OPEC Developing Countries and Multinationals for Oil Extraction

DANIEL D. TZANG

The role oil and gas will play in meeting the world's energy requirements will remain significant in the foreseeable future. The recent oil-price decline has reduced concern about new exploration activities and new sources of oil supply in the world, but oil shortages may well occur by the end of the present decade when the economies of both developed and developing countries increase the oil demand to fuel their renewed economic growth. The developing countries as a whole are estimated to have 53 billion barrels of ultimately recoverable oil reserves, 24 billion barrels in established oil-producing countries and 29 billion barrels in the remaining developing countries.[1] There is considerable evidence that the prospects for discovering petroleum resources in developing countries are promising.[2] One important source of new oil supply in 1990s could be the non-OPEC developing countries (NODCs).

During the past decades the NODCs have been importing crude oil and crude-oil products at a rapidly rising rate. There are two identifiable dangers in this pattern of rising oil imports by NODCs. The first is that these imports will influence crude-oil availability in the world petroleum market and exert inflationary pressures on world petroleum prices, especially in times of global oil shortage. Second, huge oil-import bills have been placing severe strains on these countries' balances of payments and their economies in general. The rising oil imports by NODCs are bound to create further balance-of-payments strains on these nations and, by extension, on the world financial markets. Increasing indigenous supplies of petroleum resources can relieve the burden of imports and spur domestic economic activity.

Petroleum exploitation involves a substantial investment outlay, sophisticated technical and managerial skill, and marketing outlets. Most NODCs do not have sufficient expertise or technical capacity to exploit petroleum resources within their jurisdictions. The participation of multinational oil companies is often sought to provide these capabilities. Effective working relations between the two parties require a contractual arrangement that will not only secure the principal interests of both parties, but will also reduce the possibility of tensions or conflicts.

This chapter is organized in the following manner. The first and second sections discuss risks and alternative financial contracting in petroleum recovery. In the first part of the third section, the theory of incentive contracting in the principal-agent relation is applied to characterize efficient contract structures. Characteristics of the optimal arrangement derived from the analysis provide us with criteria to compare the desirability of alternative arrangements (the remaining parts of the third section). The implications for NODCs' choice of contract form are discussed in the fourth section. Finally, we draw conclusions in the fifth section.

RISKS IN PETROLEUM EXTRACTION

The development of petroleum resources involves four phases: exploration, development, production, and marketing. A crucial difference between petroleum production and other types of industrial ventures is the degree of risk involved. The risks associated with petroleum extraction include both technical (geological) and nontechnical (economic) factors. Geological risk arises because large exploration expenses have to be incurred, with a high probability that no resources will be discovered. In addition, uncertainty about the volume and quality of the deposit and the degree of oilfield accessibility is also involved in this stage. Economic risks are involved in petroleum extraction because future prices of petroleum products and costs of extraction are difficult to predict. Geological and cost risks arise mainly at the exploration and development stages. At the production and marketing stages oil-price (or revenue) risks become the dominant considerations.

In the case of international cooperation in petroleum extraction, the situation becomes more complicated. Petroleum exploitation involves a long-term commitment of capital and other resources. The environment for cooperation, considered favorable to both the host government and the oil company at the time the agreement was settled, might change radically before the completion of the project. Contracting risks refer to potential unilateral alterations in cooperation agreements by one party (usually the host government) that jeopardize the other party's position. Actions that give rise to such risks include expropriation, alteration of host-country tax codes, restrictions on expatriation of profit, and imposition of price controls on domestic sales of crude oil or refined products.

FINANCIAL CONTRACTING IN OIL LEASING

Throughout the history of international cooperation in petroleum extraction, various forms of cooperation between host governments and foreign oil companies have been designed. They can be categorized into two basic arrangements: concessions and contracts (production-sharing contracts, service contracts).[3] The joint venture has been widely misunderstood as being a separate type of agreement. It is not. It is merely a partnership arrangement wherein the host government receives an equity interest in concessions or production-sharing agreements.

Agreements for petroleum exploration and extraction are distinguished by the stipulated fiscal regimes, that is, the set of ex ante rules specifying the distribution of the project's cash flow between the parties involved. A concession basically gives all production to the concessionaire while imposing high tax and royalty rates. The production-sharing contract divides production between the host government and the contractor after allowing a portion for cost recovery. Relative to the concession arrangement, the production-sharing contract imposes lower income-tax and royalty rates. The service contracts give none of the production to the contractor but pay him for his risk and expertise in cash generated from his production.

The fiscal regimes entail various distributions of risks. With the service contract, the oil company bears geologic risks but none of the cost or revenue risks. Under a production-sharing contract, the foreign oil company receives a share of output (or its monetary equivalent) in return for its investments. The company bears all the geological and cost risks and a proportionate share of the revenue risk. In theory, both parties should share all types of risks under the joint-venture concession. In practice, geologic risks are borne by the oil company alone; only cost and price risks are shared jointly.

FISCAL REGIMES AND EFFICIENCY IN CONTRACTING

In this study different fiscal regimes are analyzed from the perspective of efficiency. The concept of Pareto efficiency in economics literature is used here. Contracts are said to be efficient when no changes are possible in their specific terms that would result in net gains for one party while leaving the other party indifferent. Moving toward contract efficiency is a positive-sum undertaking in which both parties can gain or one can gain while the other does not lose.

The efficiency in contracting between non-OPEC developing countries and multinational oil companies can be analyzed in terms of three specific dimensions:[4]

1. The way the fiscal terms allocate risks and returns between the two contracting parties.
2. The extent to which the fiscal terms provide the appropriate incentives for investment.
3. The extent to which the fiscal terms introduce contracting risks, that is, risks of non-performance by one or both parties.

Principal-Agent Model of Contracting

Oilfields are often classified into five size categories: small oilfields (less than 50 million barrels of petroleum resources), medium oilfields (50 to 100 million barrels), large oilfields (100 to 500 million barrels), giant oilfields (500 million to 5 billion barrels), and supergiant oilfields (more than 5 billion barrels). In the model developed here, these size categories are captured in six distinct states of nature, $Q = (Q_i \mid i = 0, 1, \ldots, 5)$. In the state i, Q_i barrels of recoverable oil resources exist.

$Q_0 = 0$ denotes that no resource exists for the state 0. Uncertainty occurs insofar as the lease must be settled before the state of nature is known.

Under cooperation, the oil company selected by the host government is assumed to make an investment X to search for the resource.[5] Since an oil company's investment in exploration has a significant impact on the success of the search for oil, we assume that the probability of discovering a tract containing Q_i barrels of oil is a function of the exploration investment X and denote it as $f(Q_i \mid X)$. If the search is successful and the discovery is of commercial value, further investments D, Y, and M are required for development, production, and marketing.

To facilitate the analysis, investment expenditures during the development, production, and marketing periods are assumed to be a function of revenues that will be generated by the recoverable resource Q_i:

$$q(D_i + Y_i + M_i) = s_i P Q_i \quad (0 < s_i < 1), \quad i = 1, \ldots, 5,$$

where D_i, Y_i, and M_i are capital goods required for lifting and processing the Q_i barrels of oil, P is the price of oil per barrel, q denotes the cost of the capital goods and includes the principal and interest charges, and s_i is a parameter to reflect the economic scale in operation. It is assumed that P and q are known, that is, there is no uncertainty with respect to the oil price and the cost of capital goods invested. The only risk involved in the project comes from the stochastic amount of reserve, Q_i.

The net worth of the tract in the state i, V_i, can be expressed as

$$V_i = PQ_i - qX - q(D_i + Y_i + M_i)$$

$$= P(1 - s_i)Q_i - qX, \text{ for all } i.[6] \tag{16.1}$$

A crucial question in cooperation is how the net rents should be allocated between the host government and the company to establish an efficient distribution of risks and rewards. The allocation is often governed by the fiscal regime (financial terms specified in the contract and tax provisions promulgated by the host government). For simplicity, the division of V can be represented by a payment schedule,

$$I = (I_i \mid i = 0, 1, \ldots, 5), \tag{16.2}$$

negotiated or specified in the agreement of cooperation and before realization of the state of nature. I in (16.2) represents the payments made by the company to the host government. The remainder,

$$R = (R_i = V_i - I_i \mid i = 0, 1, \ldots, 5),$$

is the return to the oil company.

The host government and the oil company are each assumed to act according to continuously differentiable objective functions $G(I)$ and $F(R)$ defined over the parties' respective shares. Both the host government and the foreign company are assumed to be risk averse, with $G'(I)$ and $F'(R) > 0$ and $G''(I)$ and $F''(R) < 0$; that is, the objective functions are strictly concave. Each party is assumed to maximize the expected value of its objective function from cooperation in petroleum extraction. Since V in (16.1) is a function of the random variable Q, we can suppress the state of nature Q and instead view the net worth of the tract V as a random variable with a conditional probability density function $f(V|X)$. Given a distribution of Q, $f(V|X)$ is simply the distribution induced on V via the equation (16.1). The probability $f(V_i|X)$ represents the two parties' subjective assessment of the tract's value given that the exploration investment X is made. It is assumed that both parties agree on the probability distribution of V.[7]

The expected value of the objective functions for the host government and the company can be expressed as

$$E(G) = \sum_{i=0}^{5} G(I_i)f(V_i|X) \quad \text{and}$$

$$E(F) = \sum_{i=0}^{5} F(R_i)f(V_i|X),$$

where E is the expectation operator with respect to the party's subjective probability distribution over states of nature. It is assumed that the host government guarantees the oil company a minimum expected value $F(0)$ comparable to that of other petroleum projects in the world. Under this assumption, an optimal payment schedule can be characterized by maximizing the host government's expected utility subject to the company's expected utility level, $F(0)$. In other words, a lease or payment schedule that solves the maximization problem

$$\text{Max } E[G(I)]$$
$$I$$

subject to   (16.3)

$$E[F(R)] \geq F(0)$$

is referred to as an optimal lease.

Sharing in Risks and Returns

The first-order conditions for the maximization problem (16.3) with respect to the payment schedule I can be derived, using the Lagrangian optimization method, as

$$G'(I_i)f(V_i|X) = L_1 F'(R_i)f(V_i|X), \text{ for all } i, \tag{16.4}$$

where primes denote derivatives with respect to corresponding variables I_i and R_i. L_1 is the Lagrangian multiplier attached to the constraint in (16.3). The concavity assumption of the utility functions $G(I)$ and $F(R)$ guarantees the sufficiency of conditions (16.4). An optimal cooperation arrangement, by definition, will be one that leads the oil company to invest exploration and production capital in a way that satisfies the conditions given in (16.4). The nature of the optimal payment schedule is examined in the following propositions.

PROPOSITION 1: *Outcome V should be allocated up to a point where the government's marginal rate of substitution between I_i and I_j is equal to the corresponding marginal substitution rate of the company between R_i and R_j.*

Proof: Since the host government and the oil company are assumed to have identical subjective assessments of a tract's value, we can cancel out $f(V_i|X)$ in (16.4) and reduce it to

$$G'(I_i)/F'(R_i) = L_1, \text{ for all } i. \tag{16.5}$$

Condition (16.5) must hold for each state. Let i and j denote two of the possible states of nature. Dividing (16.5) as defined for state i by the same condition for state j yields the following expression:

$$G'(I_i)/G'(I_j) = F'(R_i)/F'(R_j), \quad i, j = 0, 1, \ldots, 5. \tag{16.6}$$

Proposition 1 implies that the uncertain outcome V should be divided in accordance with the two parties' attitudes toward risk. An efficient allocation will come about if the payment schedule adequately reflects differences between the two parties in terms of their risk-bearing attitudes. The less risk-averse party should bear the greater risk in cooperation. Otherwise, a higher overall value can be achieved by reallocating the outcome between the parties.

Different contractual arrangements allocate risks and distribute rewards of oil-exploration and development investments in varying degree between the two contracting parties. It is interesting to examine the implications of the parties' attitudes toward risk on the choice of the contract form. To look into this issue, it is often convenient (1) to have an explicit measure of risk sharing in alternative agreements and (2) to assume specific forms for the parties' objective functions.

Let i and j denote two different states of nature, with state j representing a higher return state. Define the differences $\hat{I}$ and $\hat{V}$ and the ratio $\hat{I}/\hat{V}$ as $\hat{I} = I_j - I_i$, $\hat{V} = V_j - V_i$, and $\hat{I}/\hat{V} = (I_j - I_i)/(V_j - V_i)$. The ratio $\hat{I}/\hat{V}$ represents the portion of additional economic rent captured by the host government and can thus be viewed as a local measure of risk sharing. Two extreme cases in leasing policies can be described as follows: (1) cash-bonus bidding, in which

$\hat{I}/\hat{V} = 0,$ that is, $I_i = I_j$ for $V_i \neq V_j$, and

(2) service contract, in which

$\hat{I}/\hat{V} = 1,$ that is, $\hat{I} = \hat{V}.$

In the cash-bonus-bidding case, the payment made by the oil company to the host government consists of a fixed amount and is invariant to different values of V ($\hat{I}/\hat{V} = 0$). Under this system, the company will bear all risk while enjoying the whole outcome from petroleum extraction. At the other end of the spectrum is the service-contract case, in which the host government garners all incremental gains from the resource extraction and bears all risks ($\hat{I}/\hat{V} = 1$). The oil company is hired for a fixed fee to develop the resource. As the ratio $\hat{I}/\hat{V}$ varies from zero to one, the oil company transfers the risk bearing to the host government.[8]

Consider a situation in which both the host government and the company have constant relative risk-aversion objective functions of the following forms:

$G(I) = 1/(1 - m) \times (I)^{1-m},$ and

$$F(R) = 1/(1 - n) \times (R)^{1-n}, \tag{16.7}$$

where m and n are the coefficients of relative risk aversion for the host government and the company, respectively. If m (or n) is zero, the government (or firm) is risk-neutral, while values greater than zero indicate relative risk aversion.

PROPOSITION 2: *When both the government and company exhibit risk averseness, contracts with risk-sharing provision are more appropriate. The cash-bonus-bidding arrangement (service contract) is optimal if the firm (the host government) is risk-neutral.*

Proof: Marginal rates of substitution corresponding to equation (16.6) for objective functions such as (16.7) can be obtained as

$(I_i/I_j)^{-m} = (R_i/R_j)^{-n},$ or

$$(I_j/I_i)^m = (R_j/R_i)^n, \quad i, j = 0, 1, \ldots, 5. \tag{16.8}$$

If the oil company is risk-neutral ($n = 0$) while the host government is risk averse ($m > 0$), (16.8) reduces to

$(I_j/I_i)^m = 1,$

which implies that $I_i = I_j$. The cash-bonus-bidding arrangement is optimal if the company is risk-neutral and the government is risk-averse. In the opposite case ($m = 0$ and $n > 0$), (16.8) becomes

$$1 = (R_j/R_i)^n,$$

which implies that $R_j/R_i = 1$. Since Ri is equal to $V_i - I_i$ by definition, $R_i = R_j$, in turn, implies that $\hat{V} = \hat{I}$. The service contract is optimal if the host government is risk-neutral and the firm is risk-averse.

Proposition 2 states that the optimal contractual form depends upon the characteristics of the parties involved. If one of the parties is risk-neutral, then that party should bear all risk. The optimal payment arrangement will merely require a fixed (state-invariant) payment to the risk-neutral party. Contracts that share risks will perform more efficiently if both parties are risk-averse.

Incentives for Investments

The previous sections examine optimal payment schedules I where the oil company always takes the action X in accordance with the host government's interest. It was presumed that the host government can observe or monitor the company's action directly. Normally the company's performance under cooperation cannot be evaluated accurately by the host government due to lack of required expertise and knowledge. This is almost certainly the case for governments of non-OPEC developing countries. In this case the host government can only observe the outcome V or the payment I made by the firm. The action taken by the oil company can only be inferred from the observed V or I that results from it.

More generally, firms are informed of the payment schedule and choose their actions in light of it. A multinational company's extraction decision is determined on the basis of its global operations. The firm might be inclined to commit less of its scarce resources to a particular tract. The resulting action taken by the company on the tract under cooperation does not necessarily line up with the host government's interest. In this case the host government must seek a payment schedule to

$$\underset{I, X}{\text{Max }} E[G(I)]$$

subject to   (16.9)

$$E[F(R)] \geq F(\emptyset) \quad \text{and}$$

$$X \in \text{argmax } E[F(R)],$$

where the notation "argmax" denotes the set of arguments that maximizes the objective function that follows. The first constraint in (16.9) guarantees the oil company a minimum expected value from petroleum extraction. The second constraint reflects that the host government can observe the outcome V, but not the action X taken by the firm. The agent retains freedom to choose the action by solving its own objective function,

$$\underset{X}{\text{Max }} E[F(R)].$$

The first-order condition of the company's maximization problem with respect to X is

$$\sum_{i=0}^{5} F(R_i) f_X(V_i|X) = qF'(R_i).^9 \tag{16.10}$$

The investment made by the company that satisfies (16.10) is not necessarily viewed as optimal by the host government.

PROPOSITION 3: *Allocation in accordance with parties' risk attitudes might not provide appropriate incentives for the firm to take actions in line with the government's interest.*

Proof: Replacing the second constraint in (16.9) with the first-order condition (16.10), we get the maximization program

$$\underset{I}{\text{Max }} E[G(I)]$$

subject to $\tag{16.11}$

$$E[F(R)] \geq F(0) \quad \text{and}$$

$$\sum_{i=0}^{5} F(R_i) f_X(V_i|X) = qF'(R_i).$$

If we attach Lagrangian multipliers L_1 and L_2 to the two constraints in (16.11), optimization of the Lagrangian expression yields the following characterization of the payment schedule:

$$G'(I_i) f(V_i|X) = L_1 F'(R_i) f(V_i|X) + L_2 F'(R_i) f_X(V_i|X), \quad \text{for all } i.$$

Dividing both sides by $F'(R_i) f(V_i|X)$, we obtain

$$G'(I_i)/F'(R_i) = L_1 + L_2 f_X(V_i|X) / f(V_i|X), \tag{16.12}$$

for all i.

If we compare (16.12) with the optimal risk-sharing rule (16.5), the second term of the right-hand side in (16.12),

$$L_2 f_X(V_i|X) / f(V_i|X),$$

can be interpreted as a deviation from Pareto-optimal risk sharing.[10] For a given L_1, we have the following relationship between payment schedules indicated by (16.12) (denoted as I^+ *and* R^+) and those indicated by (16.5):

$$G'(I_i^+) / F'(R_i^+) = L_1 + L_2 f_X(V_i|X) / f(V_i|X)$$

$$\geq L_1 = G'(I_i)/F'(R_i), \quad \text{for all } i, \tag{16.13}$$

if $L_2 > 0$ and $f_X(V_i|X) \geq 0$. The relationship (16.13) implies that

$$G'(I_i^+) / F'(R_i^+) \geq G'(I_i) / F'(R_i), \quad \text{for all } i. \tag{16.14}$$

Under the assumption of concave objective functions $G(I)$ and $F(R)$, the marginal value of the party's share is low when the total value is high. The inequality (16.14) implies that R^+ is greater than or equal to R.

The ratio $f_X(V|X) / f(V|X)$ in (16.12) is the derivative of the maximum-likelihood function, log (f) when X is viewed as an unknown parameter. Because the probability density function $F(V|X)$ represents the subjective assessment of the tract's value given that the investment X is made, the ratio $f_X(V|X) / f(V|X)$ can be used as a signal about the action taken by the firm. Equation (16.12) indicates that incentives (as expressed by deviations from optimal risk sharing) should be provided in proportion to this measure. The incentive effect is stronger the larger that $f_X(V|X)$ is, and it is more costly with higher values of $f(V|X)$.

Two remedies to the problem can be suggested. One is to allow the host government to participate in the extraction operation. The other is to let the level of exploration taken by the oil company be specified explicitly in the contract (the "work program," as it is called). Through participation the host government can obtain information about the firm's performance and the state of nature. This additional information is of value because it allows a more accurate judgment and a better appreciation of the oil company's efforts. Under a work program, the second constraint in (16.11) is not effective (the multiplier L_2 will equal zero), and conditions (16.12) reduce to the optimal risk-sharing rule (16.5).

The Optimal Work Program

A related question is what level of exploration should be specified in the contract.

PROPOSITION 4: *Exploration should be carried to the point where the sum of parties' marginal benefits (in terms of expected incomes) from information gathering equals the marginal cost of exploration investment.*

Proof: The optimal level of exploration can be determined by solving the maximization problem with respect to the exploratory investment X:

$$\text{Max } E[G(I)]$$
$$X$$

subject to (16.15)

$$E\{F[P(1-s)Q - qX - I]\} \geq F(0),$$

where $[P(1-s)Q - qX - I] = (V - I) = R$ by definition. In the following analysis, the notations used are simplified as $G = G(I_i), F = F(R_i), f = f(V_i|X), G' = dG(I_i)/dI_i$, $F' = dF(R_i)/dI_i$, and $f_X = df/dX$. The conditions for optimal exploration can be expressed as

$$L_1 q \sum_{i=0}^{5} F'f = \sum_{i=0}^{5} Gf_X + L_1 \sum_{i=0}^{5} Ff_X, \tag{16.16}$$

where L_1 is the Lagrangian multiplier attached to the constraint in (16.15). Dividing (16.16) by $(\Sigma_{i=0}^{5} G'f)$, we obtain

$$\frac{L_1 q \sum_{i=0}^{5} F'f}{\sum_{i=0}^{5} G'f} = \frac{\sum_{i=0}^{5} Gf_X}{\sum_{i=0}^{5} G'f} + \frac{L_1 \sum_{i=0}^{5} Ff_X}{\sum_{i=0}^{5} G'f}. \tag{16.17}$$

Summing up the equations in (16.4) for states 0 through 5, we have

$$\sum_{i=0}^{5} G'f = L_1 \sum_{i=0}^{5} F'f.$$

Substituting $L_1 \Sigma_{i=0}^{5} F'f$ for $(\Sigma_{i=0}^{5} G'f)$ in (16.17), we obtain

$$q = \frac{\displaystyle\sum_{i=0}^{5} Gf_X}{\displaystyle\sum_{i=0}^{5} G'f} + \frac{\displaystyle\sum_{i=0}^{5} Ff_x}{\displaystyle\sum_{i=0}^{5} F'f}, \tag{16.18}$$

for all i.

The two terms in the right-hand side of (16.18) represent host government's and company's marginal rates of substitution between investment for gathering information X and its expected income. Equation (16.18) indicates that the output of production is a private good that must be allocated between the host government and the oil company for an optimal outcome, but the output of exploration activities is information that can be jointly consumed by both parties. Conditions (16.18), therefore, are much like the rule for the optimal supply of public goods in economics literature, which requires that the sum of the two parties' marginal rates of substitution between exploration investment X and the party's expected share in outcome from the petroleum extraction equal the cost of exploration capital q. Exploration should be carried to the point where the sum of the two parties' marginal benefits (in terms of expected incomes) from information gathering equals the marginal cost of exploration investment.[11]

IMPLICATIONS FOR NON-OPEC DEVELOPING COUNTRIES

In deciding which party should bear what proportion of risk, it is necessary to consider whether either of the two contracting parties has a comparative advantage in doing so. If so, the efficiency criteria require the party with the comparative advantage in bearing risks to take a higher proportion of risk. A party's comparative advantage in bearing risks depends on the extent to which it is exposed to risks and its ability to manage those risks.

There are two dimensions of risk diversification. One type of risk (systematic risk) is related to all petroleum-extraction projects. Systematic risks derive from national or world economic forces. For example, economic risks (the variability of oil prices and extraction costs) will affect all petroleum-exploitation projects to some degree. Another type of risk (project-specific risk) is associated with particular petroleum projects. Geological risks (the quantity and quality of petroleum resource in a specific site) is primarily a project-specific risk. Project-specific risks can be diversified away to some extent by taking on other exploration and development projects. However, project diversification cannot eliminate or reduce the economic risk that is inherent in all petroleum projects.

According to modern finance theory, the riskiness of an investment from the perspective of a specific investor depends on two things: the riskiness of the investment when it is viewed by itself, and the extent to which the risk can be diversified away in the investor's portfolio. The former will be the same for all investors, but the latter may vary significantly among investors. From the perspective of international oil companies, geological risks in a specific country are diversifiable. These risks should not lead to an upward adjustment in required expected returns. In addition, large oil companies usually have a comparative advantage in bearing cost and price risks because their long-term survival depends critically on efficient management of such risks.

On the other hand, NODCs' exposure to risks is different. Oil projects to which these countries can get access are relatively fewer. Furthermore, huge oil-import bills in the past decades have been placing severe strains on these countries' balances of payments and their economies in general. Successful development of petroleum resources can relieve the burden of imports and spur domestic economic activities. Consequently, NODCs will opt for contracts that transfer risks to foreign partners. This posture is incompatible with service contracts. In other words, service contracts might be inefficient in terms of risk shifting.

One of the major reasons for NODCs to involve foreign oil companies in offshore petroleum extraction is to obtain their technology and expertise, which are in scarce local supply. This implies that NODCs are not in a position to fully specify all actions by the foreign contractors, as service contracts require. Service contracts, in practice, are limited to those countries like the Persian Gulf nations of the Middle East, Argentina, Brazil, and Venezuela that have existing production and a certain level of indigenous expertise in petroleum development.[12]

Managerial deviations from the host government's desires, such as underexploring, or under- or overspending on development, are more likely for service contracts. Because the oil company has nothing to gain through a better exploration strategy or a cost-saving extraction program, it may not make full use of its expertise and technology to seek resources or control costs. Moreover, under the service agreement the oil company obtains the payments based on its services offered. The oil company might supply the host government with distorted information in order to get more oilfields developed. Resources might be wasted to develop marginal or even uncommercial oilfields.

Past experience in international cooperation indicates that a host government might default on promised payments to the oil company or unilaterally reduce them if the discovery is large or there is an escalation in oil prices. At first glance, the host government might appear to gain from the unilateral action. However, the oil company, recognizing the likelihood of such action, would reduce its investment or provide less advanced technology. Reduction of contracting risks is of mutual benefit because such risks typically reduce the overall attractiveness of the project. A contract that is subject to frequent disputes will not be efficient.

Contracts differ in the degree to which they introduce contracting risk. Joint-venture concessions and production-sharing contracts that split price or discovery windfalls between the two parties are more likely to be stable than the cash-bonus-bidding and service contracts that allow one party to capture such windfalls. In addition, under the tax laws of many home countries, such as the United States, an oil company must prove to the tax authority that it has an interest in the oil or gas project in order to deduct intangible drilling costs for oil and gas or to obtain the benefit of a depletion allowance. This leads U.S. companies to prefer agreements such as joint-venture concessions and production-sharing contracts, under which they own the resource, to service contracts, under which they do not.

CONCLUSION

Under sharing of risk and incentives for investment consideration, service contracts are not a suitable contract form from either party's consideration. Joint-venture concessions and production-sharing contracts, which share risks and allow the host government participation in petroleum operations, are more likely choices.

The efficiency criteria require the party with the comparative advantage in bearing risks to take a higher proportion of risk. Usually the sharing rate for exploration and production specified in the cooperation agreement is 51/49 in favor of the host government. The majority participation sought by the government is often a response to political considerations. Moreover, optimal conditions (16.5) and (16.18) indicate that the oil product is a private good that must be allocated between the parties, but the output of exploration is information that can be shared. The sharing rates in these two different stages in cooperation are not necessarily identical.

The major instrument used in joint-venture concessions to allocate economic rent is the income tax. Although the merit of an income tax is well known to economists, its disadvantages come from administrative difficulties. Use of profit sharing requires that adequate procedures for cost accounting have been developed in the host country. The taxable income must be carefully defined to coincide with the realized economic rent. If the defined profit base is not an accurate measure of economic rent, misincentives to the firm are likely to result.

Production-sharing contracts have economic as well as institutional advantages. They capture economic rent for the host government while allowing the foreign oil company a fair rate of return. Moreover, they are easier for NODCs to administer. A possible disadvantage of production sharing is that the oil company will experience the full range of price risk on its share of oil. If prices rise above expected levels, then the company may be accused of reaping windfall profits. If prices fall below expected levels, the company may withdraw from extraction or pressure the government to provide more favorable terms. In either case, the government is vulnerable to criticism of its contractual arrangements, and high contracting risks may result.

NOTES

1. Ghadar 1982.
2. Broadman 1983, p. 8.
3. The essence of a joint-venture concession is that the government and the company become partners in an operating company in which each owns a specific percentage of equity

share (usually 51/49 in favor of the host government). Although the operating company is jointly owned, all capital for exploration is furnished by the foreign partner.

A service contract is used by the host government to hire or buy technical, financial, and commercial services from foreign oil companies. All petroleum deposits and products belong to the host country. A service contract stipulates a fixed payment for services rendered. No extra returns accrue to the company even if the undertaking is successful.

Under a production-sharing contract, the oil company is responsible for carrying on all exploration and development activities. If there is no commercial discovery, the loss is borne by the contractor. In each year, a specific percentage (40 percent in most production-sharing contracts) of crude oil produced is allotted for such reimbursement. The remaining portion of the production is to be shared in a proportion specified in the agreement.

4. Blitzer, Lessard, and Paddock, 1984.

5. All exploratory wells are assumed to be drilled by the oil company at a single point in time. The more realistic dynamic case in which the oil company drills sequentially based on conditional probabilities is not considered.

6. A typical petroleum-production pattern includes (1) a production buildup period during which production is increasing each year as installed capacity is coming on stream; (2) a flat production period; and (3) a declining production period. Although these dynamic factors are not explicitly modelled in this study, V in (16.1) can be thought of as the present value of the stream of net cash flows involved in resource extraction.

7. This assumption seems warranted if government and oil company share information and the company's interpretation of the exploration.

8. Under the cash-bonus system, legislation fixes in advance all requirements that the company must fulfill. Competitive bidding on advance cash payments for the right to extract petroleum is used to encourage applicants to compete with one another, and the license is awarded to the highest bidder. The United States is the only country that uses this system regularly.

9. Since $f(V|X)$ is a probability density function and probabilities over all events must sum to one, the right-hand side of (16.10) can be simplified to $qF'(R)$.

10. Borch (1962, p. 427) pointed out that $G'(I_i)/F'(R_i)$ being constant is required for optimal risk sharing between the two contracting parties. The condition (16.12) could be optimal from the risk-sharing point of view if (1) the term $f_X(V_i|X)/f(V_i|X)$ in (16.12) is constant, or (2) the Lagrangian multiplier L_2 for the second constraint in (16.11) is equal to zero, that is, the constraint is not binding. Holmstrom (1979, pp. 78–80) proved that both conditions are violated if the host government and the oil company have different objectives.

11. Hyde and Markusen 1982.

12. Broadman 1983, p. 25.

REFERENCES

Arrow, Kenneth. (1970). *Essays in the Theory of Risk-Bearing*. Amsterdam: North-Holland.

Barrows, Gordon H. (1983). *Worldwide Concession Contracts and Petroleum Legislation*. PennWell Publishing Company.

Blitzer, Charles R., Donald R. Lessard, and James L. Paddock. (1984). "Risk-Bearing and the Choice of Contract for Oil Exploration and Development." *Energy Journal* 5, no. 1: 1–27.

Borch, K. (1962). "Equilibrium in a Reinsurance Market." *Econometrica* 30: 424–444.

Broadman, Harry G. (1983). *Determinants of Oil Exploration and Development in Non-OPEC Developing Countries.* Washington, D.C.: Resources for the Future.

Dam, Kenneth W. (1976). *Oil Resources: Who Gets What How?* Chicago: University of Chicago Press.

Ghadar, Fariborz. (1982). *Petroleum Investment in Developing Countries.* The Economist Intelligence Unit, London, Special Report no. 132.

Grossman, Sanford J., and Oliver D. Hart. (1983). "An Analysis of the Principal-Agent Problem." *Econometrica* 51, no. 1 (January): 7–45.

Harris, Milton, and Artur Raviv. (1979). "Optimal Incentive Contracts with Imperfect Information." *Journal of Economic Theory* 20: 231–259.

Holmstrom, Bengt. (1977). "On Incentives and Control in Organizations." Ph.D. diss., Graduate School of Business, Stanford University.

———. (1979). "Moral Hazard and Observability." *Bell Journal of Economics* 10: 74–91.

Hossain, Kamal. (1979). *Law and Policy in Petroleum Development: Changing Relations between Transnationals and Governments.* London: Francis Pinter.

Hyde, Robert, and James R. Markusen. (1982). "Exploration versus Extraction Costs as Determinants of Optimal Mineral-Rights Leases." *Economic Record*, September, 224–234.

Leland, E. Hayne. (1978). "Optimal Risk Sharing and the Leasing of Natural Resources, with Application to Oil and Gas Leasing on the OCS." *Quarterly Journal of Economics*, August, 413–437.

Ramsey, James B. (1980). *Bidding and Oil Leases.* Greenwich, Conn.: JAI Press.

Reece, D. (1979). "An Analysis of Alternative Bidding Systems for Leasing Offshore Oil." *Bell Journal of Economics* 10: 659–669.

Ross, S. (1973). "The Economic Theory of Agency: The Principal's Problem." *American Economic Review* 63: 134–139.

Shavell, Steven. (1979a). "Risk Sharing and Incentive in the Principal and Agent Relationship." *Bell Journal of Economics* 10: 55–73.

———. (1979b). "On Moral Hazard and Insurance." *Quarterly Journal of Economics*, November, 541–562.

Stiglitz, J. E. (1974). "Incentives and Risk Sharing in Sharecropping." *Review of Economic Studies*, 219–256.

p295 Discussant: Jeffrey Weiss

My comments will be limited to the sections from "Incentives for Investments" to the end of Professor Tzang's chapter. I will discuss (1) the appropriateness of using the first-order approach to solve his principal-agent problem and (2) his "solutions" to the inefficiency inherent in the short-run principal-agent relationship.

To understand my reservations concerning how he solved his principal-agent problem, it is necessary to take a close look at the general principal-agent model (as described in Rogerson 1985). An agent picks an action $a \in [\underline{a}, \bar{a}] = A$. The outcome $x_i \in X = \{x_1, \ldots, x_n\}$. Let $p_j(a)$ be the probability of outcome j occurring, given that action a is taken by the agent, and let $F_j(a) = \Sigma_{i=1}^{j} p_i(a)$ be the corresponding distribution function. The principal's utility function $u(y)$ depends on income and the agent's, $v(y) - a$, depends positively on income and negatively on his action (effort).

A contract $w = (w_1, \ldots, w_n)$ is an agreement between the principal and the agent that awards w_i to the agent when outcome x_i occurs. Finally, define

$$U(w,a) = \sum_{j=1}^{n} p_j(a)u(x_j - w_j)$$

and

$$V(w,a) = \left[\sum_{j=1}^{n} p_j(a)v(w_j) \right] - a$$

as the expected utility of the principal and the agent, respectively.

DEFINITION: *A contract w solves the short-run principal-agent problem if it solves the following problem:*

max $U(w, a)$
$\quad$ w,a

subject to

$V(w, a) \geq V*,$

$a \in \underset{\hat{a} \in A}{\text{argmax }} V(w, \hat{a}),$ $\qquad\qquad\qquad$ (16D.1)

where V* is the minimum utility level the agent must achieve.

Problem (16D.1) corresponds to (16.9) in Tzang's chapter. For later reference let $(\overline{w}, \overline{a})$ solve (16D.1) and let $\overline{U} = U(\overline{w}, \overline{a})$ and $\overline{V} = V(\overline{w}, \overline{a})$.

As far as tractability is concerned, (16D.1) is a very difficult problem to deal with because the second constraint is actually a continuum of constraints of the form

$$V(w, a) \geq V(w, \hat{a}) \quad \text{for all } \hat{a} \in A. \tag{16D.2}$$

To overcome this messy situation, many authors, including Tzang, have used the first-order approach, where this constraint is replaced with the requirement that the effort level be a stationary point for the agent, that is

$$\frac{\partial V}{\partial a}(w, a) = 0.$$

Let (16D.2) denote this modified principal-agent problem. The question then becomes whether the solutions to (16D.1) and (16D.2) are identical. Mirrlees (1975) was the first to show that in general they are not, since the stationary point chosen in (16D.2) may be a local, but not a global, maximum, or a local minimum or a saddle point.

Fortunately, there are conditions (Mirrlees 1979) under which the solution of (16D.2) is the solution of (16D.1). The first is the monotone likelihood ratio condition. The functions $\{p_j(a)\}_{j=1}^{n}$ satisfy this condition if $\hat{a} \leq \hat{\hat{a}}$ implies that $p_i(\hat{a})/p_i(\hat{\hat{a}})$ is nonincreasing in i. The second condition is that $F_j'' \geq 0$ for all j and $a \in A$.

My question for Tzang is whether or not these two conditions are satisfied in oil exploration. While I am not an expert in that field, I am not very sanguine, especially since the second condition is a difficult one to satisfy. It will not be satisfied, for example, if output in each state of nature is determined by a diminishing-returns-to-scale stochastic production function.

On the second issue, one of the "remedies" to the inefficiency problem has the host country participating with (monitoring) the company in oil exploration. Now it is quite possible that the benefits from this action are positive, but that does not mean, as Tzang seems to imply, that this action would increase the country's welfare over that level achieved at (16.9)'s solution. The reason is simply that the costs of participation may exceed these benefits.

Another proposed solution is a "work program," where the level of "effort" is specified in the contract. Such a contract is, essentially, an "all-or-nothing" offer, which means that it may be rejected by the firm. Even if it were accepted, the country must still monitor the agreement, which again means that this plan suffers from the defect of the participation plan.

There is another remedy that I will briefly describe. Since, as Tzang says, this is a long-term arrangement between the company and the country, the game between the players would be better modeled as a repeated principal-agent game. Here the players play a one-period game infinitely often, and at each of these one-period games, their actions can be based on the history of outcomes and rewards up to that point in time. In this setting, Radner (1985) has shown that the inefficiency in the solution of (16D.1) can, to a large degree, be overcome. Specifically, he showed that for every pair $(\hat{U}, \hat{V})$ that is efficient and Pareto-superior to $(\overline{U}, \overline{V})$, one can contract "review strategies" that will result in equilibrium outcomes for the players that are arbitrarily close to $(\hat{U}, \hat{V})$, just as long as the players do not discount the future "very" much. I refer interested readers to this fascinating paper for further details.

REFERENCES

Mirrlees, J. (1975). "The Theory of Moral Hazard and Unobservable Behavior: Part I." Nuffield College, Oxford. Mimeo.

————. (1979). "The Implications of Moral Hazard for Optimal Insurance." Seminar given at Conference held in honor of Karl Borch, Bergen, Norway. Mimeo.

Radner, Roy. (1985). "Repeated Principal-Agent Games with Discounting." *Econometrica* 53: 1173–1198.

Rogerson, William P. (1985). "The First-Order Approach to Principal-Agent Problems." *Econometrica* 53: 1357–1367.

17

Investment Incentives and Renegotiation in International Lending

GEORGE C. ANAYIOTOS

Debt finance creates incentives for underinvestment when a country does not precommit its investment decision. This is partly the result of inefficient risk sharing between the debtor and the creditor in international lending. Considering the fact that international debt contracts have not been written to delegate risks to the two parties efficiently, it is not a surprise that a debt crisis would arise when adverse developments affect either debtors or creditors. In addition to these problems of risk sharing, we consider incentive problems that are present in international lending. The distortion of investment incentives in a country where there is a need for repayment of external debt arises in a one-period model. It is a well-established result in agency theory that when some aspect of investment (level, riskiness, productivity) is a private decision of the country-agent and is not observed or monitored by the lender, the country has incentives to underinvest by passing up positive net present value projects. Even if the international loan contract is designed to provide incentives for high levels of investment, risk sharing between lenders and borrowers will typically be inefficient. It is difficult to avoid this trade-off between optimal risk sharing and incentives in international lending. To achieve efficient risk sharing along with high incentives for investment, we need more complex financial contracting and more complete international financial markets.

This chapter addresses the problem of underinvestment that arises when countries do not precommit their investment level at the time of signing a loan agreement. The issue that precommitments by countries are not generally credible is analyzed together with the fact that international debt contracts are not enforceable. In the presence of sovereign risk and because it is costly for lenders to impose various penalties on countries that default, there is a strong incentive for both parties to act cooperatively and renegotiate their initial agreement when default is likely.

It is precisely this possibility of renegotiation that generates an ex post payoff function for the borrower that leads to ex ante underinvestment incentives. The experience of reschedulings as a form of renegotiation between lenders and borrowers since the emergence of the debt crisis and the experience of declining levels of investment in debtor countries provide some evidence supporting the formulation and the results of this chapter.

In the environment described here, where country policies are heavily weighted toward ex post utility maximization, the solution of incentive problems that arise is a difficult task. An extension of this chapter could examine whether the fact that the country has to return to the market for external financing will improve its investment incentives. The one-period model shows how disincentives in investment arise when a country cannot precommit its investment decision and when international debt contracts are not enforceable. As is known, these disincentive effects will not be ruled out in finite repetitions of the same game with no intertemporal linkage. In the presence of sovereign risk, this inefficiency will only be ruled out when the possibility of renegotiation is allowed at the end of the first period. In a two-period model, for example, the need for a country to maintain some reputation because it is returning to the loan market and the external cost of default that is imposed could alleviate the problem of underinvestment incentives.

The chapter is organized in the following way: In the first section sovereign risk is modelled and the implicit nature of international loan contracts is discussed. Simple payoff schedules are derived based on bargaining considerations. In the second section the underinvestment problem is examined in a simple model. In the third section the supply of loans is examined and some credit-rationing results are derived. Conclusions and possible extensions are presented in the fourth section.

THE IMPLICIT DEBT CONTRACT IN THE PRESENCE OF SOVEREIGN RISK

In international lending there are no bankruptcy procedures to transfer the assets of a defaulting country to its international creditors. Instead, when a country is unable to service its foreign claims, it faces the possibility of incurring various penalties. These penalties may take the form of trade embargoes, permanent exclusion of the debtor from any future loans, or seizure of the debtor's assets that are abroad. For major primary commodity producers whose income is based on commodity exports, trade embargoes could have a dramatic effect on their income. For countries with extensive investment opportunities or widely fluctuating output streams, continuous access to international capital markets is of vital importance. Such costs of default might be high enough to discourage loan repudiation. In the literature Eaton and Gersovitz (1981a), Sachs (1982), and Sachs and Cohen (1982) consider these penalties as costing the debtor country a fraction of its national product. This fraction reflects all possible costs incurred by the debtor when lenders retaliate in the case of default. It is further assumed that retaliation and imposition of penalties is costly also for the lenders. Eaton (1986) has considered this possibility. In a situation like this where repudiation is costly to the debtor and imposition of penalties is costly to the lender, the incentive to renegotiate the initial agreement is strong for both parties. This renegotiation process is what we have observed since 1982, when the debt crisis erupted. Bulow and Rogoff (1986) and Ozler (1986) analyzed the process of bargaining between lenders and borrowers and discussed the debt reschedulings as a result of these renegotiations. In this analysis the possibility of renegotiation of the initial debt contract is taken into account by the debtor when it makes its investment decision. Before modelling of a debtor's investment decision, which is the subject of the next section, an explicit model of the bargaining process between the two parties is presented here.

Suppose that at the time when repayment comes due the debtor owes an amount D. The total output is Q_2, and if the debtor pays the creditor in full, then output will be reduced to $Q_2 - D$. If no repayment is made, the creditor can expropriate the debtor's assets abroad and can seize undelivered trade products still in ports. As a result, output will be curtailed. Before such actions take place, it is likely that the two parties will enter into negotiations. These negotiations take place between the debtor and a cartel of lenders that is formed after the country declares its inability to pay D. The bargaining between the two parties is modelled as in the bilateral monopoly situation with fixed threats. The asymmetric Nash solution is used here to determine the outcome of the bargaining game.

Let L_0 and B_0 represent the threat points of the creditor and debtor in the noncooperative outcome. These threat points are the payoffs to the parties when total default takes place. If we assume that when this happens the creditor can extract a zero net payoff from the debtor, and that the debtor will incur a reduction of its output of proportion equal to μ,[1] then $L_0 = 0$ and $B_0 = (1 - \mu)Q_2$, and

$$L_0 + B_0 < Q_2 . \tag{17.1}$$

Considering now the case in which the two parties act cooperatively and renegotiate the initial debt contract, we write the asymmetric Nash solution of the bargaining process that will take place:[2]

$$L = L_0 + \alpha(Q_2 - L_0 - B_0), \tag{17.2}$$

$$B = B_0 + \beta(Q_2 - L_0 - B_0). \tag{17.3}$$

L and B represent the payoffs of the creditor and debtor, respectively, α represents the bargaining power of the creditor, β represents the bargaining power of the debtor, and $\alpha + \beta = 1$. The level of α depends crucially on the determination of the debtor to keep to its decision not to pay D, while it knows that its output would be curtailed by μQ_2. On the other hand, the level of β depends on the credibility of the creditor's threat to impose various penalties on the debtor that will lead to a reduction of output.

If we substitute in equations (17.2) and (17.3) the values of L_0 and B_0, we get

$$L = \alpha\mu Q_2 \equiv aQ_2 \text{ and} \tag{17.4}$$

$$B = (1 - \alpha\mu)Q_2 \equiv (1-a)Q_2. \tag{17.5}$$

This result is presented in figure 17.1. B_0 represents the threat point where the debtor refuses to pay D, renegotiation of the initial debt contract does not take place, and the creditor carries out its threat to impose penalties on the debtor. The creditor's payoff is $L_0 = 0$, and the debtor's payoff is $B_0 = (1 - \mu)Q_2$. When the two parties act cooperatively, no outright default or imposition of penalties takes place. Instead, the initial debt contract is renegotiated and an efficiency gain from cooperation equal to μQ_2 is realized. The bargaining solution that allocates this gain lies on the line YZ. The symmetric Nash bargaining solution for $\alpha = \beta = 1/2$

Figure 17.1
The Asymetric Nash Bargaining Solution

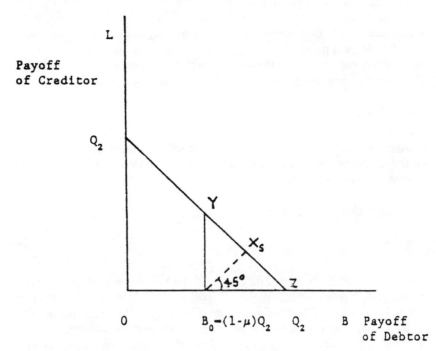

is given by the midpoint X_s. The asymmetric Nash bargaining solution will lie on X_sY if $\alpha > \beta$, or on X_sZ if $\alpha < \beta$.

In this context of renegotiation, we view the international loan contract as a debt contract with a call option that can be exercised by the debtor. D represents the face value of the loan plus the accrued interest. The debtor can choose to renegotiate the terms of the repayment, and it will do this whenever $D > aQ_2$. The creditor's payoff is given by

$$R_2 = \text{Min } (D, aQ_2). \tag{17.6}$$

Whether the debtor will choose to exercise the option of renegotiation and, instead of paying back D, lose aQ_2, depends crucially on the following factors: the amount of loan D_0 given to the debtor in the beginning of the period, the interest rate R charged for the loan [note that $D = D_0(1 + R)$], the productivity of investment, which will determine the level of Q_2, the credibility of the threat by the creditor to impose the cost of default, and the negotiating power of the parties. These factors are examined in detail in the remaining sections of the chapter.

THE DEBTOR'S INVESTMENT DECISION

Precommitments by countries are not generally credible. There is no international enforcement agency, and governments abrogate the agreements signed by their predecessors without losing legitimacy. On the contrary, governments that do not act in the ex post interest of their constituents are likely to be deposed. Thus country policy is heavily weighted toward ex post utility maximization. In this section the investment decision takes place after the loan is arranged. This is a more natural assumption in international lending because the debtor country will have an incentive to renege on a promised level of investment once it gets the money from the lender. To study the investment behavior of the debtor, we also consider the possibility of renegotiation. This possibility generates ex post payoff functions for the debtor that lead to underinvestment incentives. The setup from which the country takes its investment decision is the following:

The country receives a loan at the beginning of the first period without precommitting itself to undertake a specific level of investment. The decision about investment is taken after the country observes a state of the world s that determines the productivity of investment $i(s)$. This investment decision is taken by solving the following problem:

$$\underset{I}{\text{Max }} U(C_1, C_2) = C_1 + C_2/d \tag{17.7}$$

subject to

$$C_1 = Q_1 + D_0 - I, \tag{17.8}$$

$C_2 = Q_2 - R_2$, and   (17.9)

$Q_2 = Q_1 + i(s)I$,   (17.10)

with $I < I^M$, $i(s) \in [0,i^*]$, and $\partial i/\partial s > 0$. C_1 and C_2 are consumption levels at $t = 1$ and $t = 2$, respectively, and d is the discount factor. The investment level will determine the amount R_2 that will be repaid at $t = 2$. It will be either $R_2 = D$, if the contract is adhered to, or $R_2 = aQ_2$, if renegotiation takes place. Notice that R_2 depends on I. The country at time $t = 1$ determines simultaneously the investment level and the repayment mode.

We solve backwards. At $t = 2$, the optimal strategy depends on the size of D in relation to the size of aQ_2. Thus, using (17.6), the strategy is to renegotiate if $D > aQ_2$ and to pay D otherwise. At $t = 1$, I is set either to zero when $\partial U/\partial I < 0$ or to I^M otherwise. This is derived from the first-order conditions (FOC) of the maximization problem:

$\partial U/\partial I = -1 + i/d$ if $R_2 = D$,   (17.11a)

$\partial U/\partial I = -1 + (1 - a)i/d$ if $R_2 = aQ_2$.   (17.11b)

In the case where $R_2 = D$, the investment opportunity is undertaken in states where the return on investment is larger than the discount factor. (As in the case of a lump-sum tax, repayment considerations do not distort the investment decision.) In the case where $R_2 = aQ_2$, however, only a portion of $(1 - a)$ of the marginal return of investment is retained for consumption. Thus no investment takes place unless the marginal increase in future consumption $(1 - a)i$ exceeds the discount factor. This outcome of the investment decision hinges crucially on the assumption that the threat point in the renegotiation process is an increasing function of Q_2. To trace out the pattern of investment, we construct table 17.1, which presents the levels of investment as a function of D and the realized state of nature.

The level of investment undertaken by the debtor depends on both the level of D and the realized state of nature. As D rises, the set of states in which the debtor prefers to renegotiate the terms of debt service gets larger. As a result, investment occurs in a smaller set of states. This is what is illustrated by the solution of the simple model presented here. To construct table 17.1 we derive the choice of the debtor among the following four possible actions;

1. $I = I^M$, $R_2 = D$

2. $I = I^M$, $R_2 = aQ_2$

3. $I = 0$, $R_2 = D$

4. $I = 0$, $R_2 = aQ_1$

Table 17.1
Optimal Investment and the Level of Debt Repayments
under Different Values of D and $i(s)$

return on investmt	0	d	i_1	$d/(1-a)$	i_2	i^*
Level of D						
$D < D_1$	$I = 0$ $R_2 = D$			$I = I^M$ $R_2 = D$		
$D_1 < D < D_2$	$I = 0$ $R_2 = aQ_1$			$I = I^M$ $R_2 = D$		
$D > D_2$	$I = 0$ $R_2 = aQ_1$			$I = I^M$ $R_2 = aQ_2$	$I = I^M$ $R_2 = D$	

where

(12) $D_1 = aQ_1$

(13) $D_2 = aQ_1 + adI^M/(1-a)$

(14) $i_1 = d + [(D-aQ_1)/I^M]$ (spread over d)

(15) $i_2 = (D - aQ_1)/aI^M$

The calculations for comparisons of the levels of utility under different values of D and $i(s)$ are given in the appendix to this chapter.

As the level of the debt-repayment obligation rises, there are two threshold levels at which there is a quantitative change in the debtor's optimal strategy in terms of choosing I and R_2. When $D < aQ_1$, the repayment and investment decisions are uncorrelated. The debtor does not exercise its option to renegotiate the debt repayment in any state of nature. Thus D acts as a fixed cost, and the optimal level of investment is determined solely by the marginal return on investment. R_2 is always equal to D, and $I = 0$ for $i(s) < d$, $I = I^M$ for $i(s) > d$. For levels of D above this first threshold aQ_1, the borrower prefers to pay aQ_1 of its output in the low states in which it is not profitable to grow. However, when the investment opportunity is undertaken, debt renegotiation is not optimal. $D < aQ_2$ and $R_2 = D$.

Investment occurs only above $i_1 = d + [(D - aQ_1)/I^M]$, where the term $[(D - aQ_1)/I^M]$ shows the spread above d that is required for the value of $i(s)$ to make investment profitable. The set of states where investment occurs gets smaller because the marginal return on the project must now be higher than d in order to allow the debtor to decide to pay $R_2 = D$ instead of $R_2 = aQ_2$. Thus the required spread over d is $(D - aQ_1)/I^M$ per unit invested.

There is also a second threshold of the level of D at which D is large enough (above D_2) to make debt renegotiation profitable in a subset of states (the low ones) where investment occurs. The debtor will start investing when $i > d/(1 - a)$ and will repay $R_2 = aQ_2$ when $d/(1 - a) < i < i_2$. The debtor will invest and repay $R_2 = D$ when $i > i_2$. In general, no renegotiation will occur for realizations of states that are very good. In such states the debtor will pay $R_2 = D$.

We now derive the expected investment function and the expected repayment function. At the time when the loan is arranged, the expected levels of future investment and future repayment depend on D. The larger the D, the smaller the expected investment. Thus the debt renegotiation option is exercised more often, and the lender expects to get more often an amount that is smaller than D. Typically, we expect the present value of the lender's claim to be concave in D. We concentrate again on the simplest case, assuming that $i(s)$ is uniformly distributed on the interval $[0, i^*]$ with $i^* = (d/(1 - a)$. Using the results in table 17.1, we can compute the investment level that is expected to occur in $t = 1$ as a function of D:

$$E[I] = \text{pb}[i > d]I^M = \left(\frac{i^* - d}{i^*}\right)I^M = \left(1 - \frac{d}{i^*}\right)I^M \quad \text{if } D < D_1,$$

$$= \text{pb}[i > i_1]I^M = \left(\frac{i^* - i_1}{i^*}\right)I^M$$

$$= \left[\frac{i^* - \{d + [(D - aQ_1)/I^M]\}}{i^*}\right]I^M$$

$$= (1 - d/i^*)I^M - (D - aQ_1)/i^* \quad \text{otherwise.} \tag{17.12}$$

Clearly, $E[I]$ is nonincreasing in D on the whole range of D. Note that $E[I]$ is nondecreasing in a and in i^* but is decreasing in d.

We now compute the expected repayment function:

$$E[R_2] = D \qquad\qquad \text{if } D < D_1,$$

$$= \text{pb}[i < i_1]aQ_1 + \text{pb}[i > i_1]D$$

$$= (i_1/i^*)aQ_1 + [(i^* - i_1)/i^*]D$$

$$= aQ_1/i*[d + (D - aQ_1)/I^M] + D/i*[i* - d - (D - aQ_1)/I^M]$$

$$= -d/i*(D - aQ_1) - [(D - aQ_1)/i*I^M](D - aQ_1) + D$$

$$= D - [(D - aQ_1)/i*] [d + (D - aQ_1)/I^M] \quad \text{otherwise.} \tag{17.13}$$

The exact behavior of this expected repayment depends on the probability distribution of i. In our example, $E[R_2]$ is concave with an interior maximum for a D that is larger than D_1 but smaller than D_2. (When $i*$ gets larger, the maximum occurs at D_2 when $i* = d(1 + a)/(1 - a)$ and then gets above D_2.) Note that in the interesting case, $E[R_2]$ increases in $i*$ and in a, but decreases in d.

THE SUPPLY OF LOANS, CREDIT RATIONING, AND THE PROBABILITY OF RENEGOTIATION

We now investigate the level of capital that rational creditors would advance to the country. We assume that the loan market is competitive. Risk-neutral creditors are willing to buy a claim that promises to pay R_2 at $t = 2$ at the price of

$$D_0 = E[R_2]/(1 + R_f), \tag{17.14}$$

where R_f denotes the world's risk-free rate. Denoting by R the interest paid when the debt contract is not renegotiated we have

$$D = D_0(1 + R).$$

The relationship between D_0 and R represents the lenders' supply-of-funds function. This is presented in figure 17.2.

Since $E[R_2]$ is concave in D, increasing D_0 and R is initially profitable, and thus the supply function is initially increasing in R. However, at large-enough D, an increase in R or in D_0 reduces $E[R_2]$, and the supply schedule becomes completely inelastic. From equation (17.14), and for $D_0 < D_0^*$, we obtain

$$\partial D_0 / \partial R = \frac{\partial E[R_2]/\partial R_2}{1 + R_f}$$

$$= \frac{(\partial E[R_2]/\partial D)(\partial D/\partial R)}{1 + R_f}$$

$$= \left\{ D_0 / (1 + R_f) \right]/(\partial E[R_2]/\partial D) \right\}. \tag{17.16}$$

Figure 17.2
The Supply of Loans and Credit Rationing

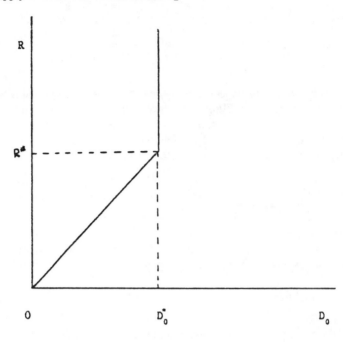

The credit ceiling is given by $D_0^* = D*/(1 + R_f)$. $D*$ is determined by setting the derivative $\partial E[R_2]/\partial D$ equal to zero. From equation (17.13) we obtain

$$\partial E[R_2]/\partial D = 1 - \{(1/i*)[d + (D* - aQ_1)/I^M] + (1/I^M)[(D* - aQ_1)/i*]\} = 0,$$

$$1 - d/i* - [(D* - aQ_1)/i*I^M] - [(D* - aQ_1)/i*I^M] = 0,$$

$$1 - d/i* - [2(D* - aQ_1)/i*I^M] = 0,$$

$$D* = aQ_1 + (i* - d)I^M/2.$$

Therefore

$$D_0^* = \frac{D*}{1 + R_f} = \frac{aQ_1 + (i* - d)I^M/2}{1 + R_f}. \tag{17.17}$$

Note that the credit ceiling is increasing in a and in $i*$ but decreasing in d and in R_f.

Suppose that R_f is uncertain when the loan is contracted at the beginning of the period. In practice, commercial bank loans to LDCs were made contingent on LIBOR.[3] Let us represent the interest rate R charged on the loan as a function of the unknown R_f of the form

$$R = rR_f, \quad \text{with } r > 1. \tag{17.18}$$

Under the assumption of risk neutrality for the lenders, the credit ceiling D_0^* is determined by an expression similar to (17.17) where R_f is replaced by $E[R_f]$. Assume that R_f is observed before the investment decision is made, and that a very high value is realized. Then $D = D_0^*(1 + rR_f)$ would be high and indeed would exceed D^*. In such a case, where $D > D^*$ due to the high value of the interest rate, it might be beneficial to the lenders to decrease the level of D by forgiving part of the principal D_0 owed by the debtor.[4] Why might this be in the interest of the lenders? Because reduction of the required amount of repayment D, if $D > D^*$, increases the expected output by enough to lead to an increase in both the borrower's payoff and the lender's expected payoff. This increase will come from higher incentives to invest when the required amount of repayment is reduced. From table 17.1 we can see that by reducing D investment will increase in all states where $i > i_1$. Thus Q_2 gets bigger. However, the lender's expected payoff increases in D for $D < D^*$. Only for $D > D^*$ will we observe an increase in $E[R_2]$ when reduction of D takes place. Figure 17.3 shows how the lender's expected payoff $E[R_2]$ is related to the level of the required repayment D.

Using equation (17.13) and the derivative $\partial E[R_2]/\partial D$, we find that $E[R_2]$ reaches a maximum value $E[R_2]_{max}$ at point A where $D = D^*$. Above D^*, $E[R_2]$ starts to decline. If $D = D_3$ lies above D^*, either because of the high value of the variable interest rate or because of large amounts of D_0 initially given to the debtor (overlending), it is clear that any reduction in D will lead to a higher expected payoff for the lender. Reducing D from D_3 toward D^* will lead to an increase of the lender's expected payoff from $E[R_2]_3$ toward $E[R_2]_{max}$.

It is also interesting to note here that the market price at $t = 0$ of a unit of debt that promises to pay one dollar at $t = 2$ depends on the aggregate level of outstanding debt. Using equations (17.13) and (17.14), it is easy to verify that $d_0 = D_0/D$ is always decreasing in D. The intuition is clear: A larger D more often implies debt renegotiation, and this decreases the expected return on each dollar of face value.

At this point the explicit correlation between the size of the debt D_0 and the probability of renegotiation is derived. Assume that $i(s)$ is distributed uniformly in the interval $[0, i^*]$ with $i^* = i_2$. From equation (17.15) $D_0 = D/(1 + R)$. Using table 17.1 and equation (17.13), the following results are derived: For $D_0 < aQ_1/(1 + R)$, $R = D$ at all states of the world, and the probability of renegotiation is zero. For $aQ_1/(1 + R) < D_0 < D_2/(1 + R)$, the probability of renegotiation is $pr[R_2 = aQ_1] = d/i^* + (D - aQ_1)/i^*I_M$.

For $D_0 > D_2/(1 + R)$, we have two cases where renegotiation takes place: $pr[R_2 = aQ_1] = d/(1 - a)i^*$, and $pr[R_2 = aQ_2] = 1 - d/(1 - a)i^*$. Therefore, the probability

Figure 17.3
Lender's Expected Payoff and the Level of Required Repayment

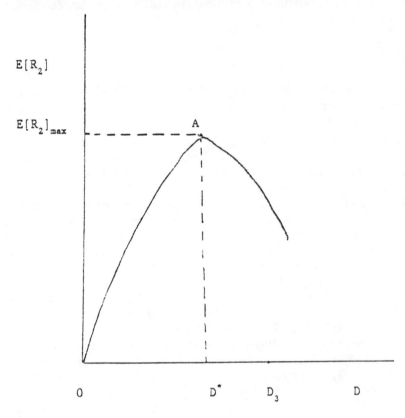

for renegotiation when $i = [0, i^* = i_2]$ is equal to one. Only if we allow for very good states to occur for $i > i_2$ do we not have renegotiation, and $R_2 = D$.

CONCLUSIONS AND POSSIBLE EXTENSIONS

The analysis presented in this chapter examines the investment incentives of a country that borrows from abroad. It is demonstrated that disincentives to investment arise when the level of debt-service requirements is high. This is primarily the result of the inability of the country to precommit its investment level at the time the loan agreement is signed. The possibility of renegotiation of the international loan contract, which exists because of the presence of sovereign risk in international lending, generates an ex post payoff function for the debtor that deteriorates further the incentives for investment. Nonprecommitment to the level of investment, together with sovereign risk, leads to lower levels of economic growth in the debtor countries with adverse consequences for the timely repayment of debts.

The management of the debt crisis is modelled as a renegotiation process between the lender (a cartel of commercial banks) and the borrower (a country's government). An implicit debt contract is derived as the cooperative outcome from renegotiation. The analysis is carried out under the assumption of no uncertainty concerning the cost of default. Uncertainty exists, in this model, only in the productivity of investment when the loan is made. This productivity is revealed to the borrower before the investment decision is taken. The model could be extended by allowing uncertainty in terms of the cost of default. By the renegotiation process, a new implicit debt contract would be derived, where the expected payoff to the lender would be a function of the uncertain extent of the cost of default. This in turn could reduce the incentives for investment. If uncertainty of the final output Q_2 is introduced in the analysis, both the results from the renegotiation process and the investment decision will be altered. In such a context with output uncertainty, some risk-sharing characteristics of loan contracts, along with the contract's incentive properties, could be examined.

As pointed out in the introduction of this chapter, an extension into a two-period investment decision model could solve some of the underinvestment problem. In such a repeated setting, reputation and exogenous cost of default give rise to self-enforceability of international debt contracts and ameliorate the underinvestment problem. By introducing some uncertainty as to the identity ("type") of the players, we can derive equilibria in which the subgame strategies of players might take a cooperative flavor.[5] Reputation could provide the link between the first and the second play of the game. It is this link that produces strategic and market behaviors that are different from those predicted from the analysis of independent games.

The behavior of the debtor in terms of its investment decision is affected by the form of the loan contract. In this chapter we examined the case of a debt contract that is renegotiable when difficulties in repayment arise. This renegotiation possibility leads to an implicit form of this debt contract of the form $R_2 = \text{Min}[D, aQ_1]$. This is taken as a constraint in the debtor's utility-maximization problem. If we substitute the implicit debt contract with an equity contract of the form $R_2 = eQ_2$, the investment incentives could get worse. On the other hand, we could expect that in a model with uncertainty in terms of output Q_2, the risk-sharing properties of such an equity contract will be better than those of its counterpart debt contract.

APPENDIX
Comparisons of Debtor's Utility Levels under Different Values of *D* and *i*(*s*)

As the level of *D* changes, and for different realizations of the state of the world, the debtor compares the payoffs of the following four actions:

1. $I = I^M$, $R_2 = D$

2. $I = I^M$, $R_2 = aQ_2$

3. $I = 0$, $R_2 = D$

4. $I = 0$, $R_2 = aQ_1$

Then it chooses the action that maximizes its utility. The payoffs corresponding to actions 1 to 4 are

1. $Q_1 + D_0 - I^M + [Q_1 + i(s)I^M - D]/d$

2. $Q_1 + D_0 - I^M + [Q_1 + i(s)I^M - aQ]/d$

3. $Q_1 + D_0 + (Q_1 - D)/d$

4. $Q_1 + D_0 + (Q_1 - aQ_1)/d$

Suppose that $D \leq aQ_1$. For values of D below aQ_1 the debtor never chooses to renegotiate, and it always pays the lender D. By comparing payoffs 1 and 3, we find that investment will switch from zero to I^M when $i > d$. (To simplify the notation, we drop s.)

Suppose that $D > aQ_1$. When $I = I^M$ and when the payoff from action 1 is less than the payoff from action 2, the debtor will pay D. To find this level of D, which we call D_2, it is necessary that

$$Q_1 + D_0 - I^M + [Q_1 + i(s)I^M - D_2]/d \leq Q_1 + D_0 - I^M + [Q_1 + i(s)I^M - aQ_2]/d,$$

which implies that

$$D_2 \leq aQ_1 + (adI^M)/(1 - a). \tag{17.19}$$

When $I = 0$, the debtor always chooses to renegotiate and pay aQ_1. When $I = I^M$ and the debtor produces Q_2, then it compares aQ_2 and D to decide whether $R_2 = D$ or $R_2 = aQ_2$:

$R_2 = D$ when $aQ_2 > D$,

$R_2 = aQ_2$ when $aQ_2 < D$.

For $aQ_1 < D \leq D_2$ we find the value of i for which investment will switch from zero to I^M by comparing the resulting payoffs from actions 1 and 4. (Notice that when $I = 0$ and for $D > aQ_1$, the debtor by comparing the payoffs under actions 2 and 4 will choose action 4.) The value of i, which we call i_1, at which investment switches from zero to I^M is calculated by setting

$$Q_1 + D_0 + (Q_1 - aQ_1)/d \leq Q_1 + D_0 - I^M + [Q_1 + i(s)I^M - D]/d,$$

which holds for

$$i_1 \geq d + (D - aQ_1)/I^M. \tag{17.20}$$

Suppose that $D > D_2$. For low states the debtor will choose to set investment equal to zero, renegotiate, and pay $R_2 = aQ_1$. For sufficiently high states investment switches to I^M, and the debtor starts to pay aQ_2. To find the level of i where the switch of actions takes place, we require that

$$Q_1 + D_0 + (Q_1 - aQ_1)/d \leq Q_1 + D_0 - I^M + [Q_1 + i(s)I^M - aQ_2]/d.$$

This holds for

$$i \geq d/(1 - a). \tag{17.21}$$

Now we observe that for Q_2 sufficiently large the debtor will choose to pay D instead of aQ_2. We calculate the level of i, which we call i_2, above which the debtor, instead of renegotiating it, pays D by setting

$$Q_i + D_0 - I^M + [Q_1 + i(s)I^M - D]/d \leq Q_1 + D_0 - I^M + [Q_1 + i(s)I^M - aQ_2]/d.$$

This holds for

$$i_2 \geq (D - aQ_1)/aI^M. \tag{17.22}$$

NOTES

I gratefully acknowledge the advice of Professors Pentti J. K. Kouri, Clive Bull, and Roy Radner. This paper benefitted from discussion with Professor Ishac Diwan and from comments by Jaime De Pinies. Their help is greatly appreciated.

1. This general formulation of the cost of default is used in the sovereign risk literature by Eaton and Gersovitz (1981a), and Sachs and Cohen (1982).

2. This solution to the bargaining problem was introduced by Nash (1950) in its symmetric form. The asymmetric form was developed by Kalai (1977).

3. London interbank offered rate. Loans to LDCs were made with a variable interest rate, with a spread or margin over LIBOR.

4. The debt-forgiveness or debt–write-off literature has grown recently. Sachs (1986a, 1986b) and Krugman (1987) considered various effects on lenders and borrowers from debt write-offs.

5. John and Nachman (1985) applied the Kreps and Wilson (1982) sequential equilibrium concept to show that endogenous reputation results in a partial resolution of the classic agency problem of underinvestment in corporate finance.

REFERENCES

Barnea, A., R. A. Haugen, and L. W. Senbet. (1985). *Agency Problems and Financial Contracting*. Englewood Cliffs, N.J.: Prentice-Hall.

Bulow, Jeremy I., and Kenneth Rogoff. (1986). "A Constant Recontracting Model of Sovereign Debt." Hoover Institution Working Paper no. P-86-6, December.

Eaton, Jonathan. (1986). "Lending with Costly Enforcement of Repayment and Potential Fraud." *Journal of Banking and Finance* 10: 281–293.

Eaton, J., and M. Gersovitz. (1986). "Country Risk and the Organization of International Capital Transfer." Paper presented at the Conference on Debt, Stabilization, and Development, Helsinki, Finland, August.

Gersovitz, Mark, and Jonathan Eaton. (1981). "Debt with Potential Repudiation: Theoretical and Empirical Analysis." *Review of Economic Studies* 48: 289–309.

Heffernan, Shelagh A. (1986). *Sovereign Risk Analysis*. London: Allen and Unwin.

John, Kose, and David C. Nachman. (1985). "Risky Debt, Investment Incentives, and Reputation in a Sequential Equilibrium." *Journal of Finance* 40, no. 3 (July): 863–880.

Kalai, E. (1977). "Nonsymmetric Nash Solutions and Replications of 2-Person Bargaining." *International Journal of Game Theory* 6, no. 3: 129–133.

Kreps, D., and R. Wilson. (1982). "Reputation and Imperfect Information." *Journal of Economic Theory* 27: 253–279.

Krugman, Paul. (1989). "Financing vs Forgiving a Debt Overhang." *Journal of Development Economics* 29: 253–268.

Myers, Stewart C. (1977). "Determinants of Corporate Borrowing." *Journal of Financial Economics* 5 (November): 147–175.

Nash, F. J. (1950). "The Bargaining Problem." *Econometrica* 18: 155–162.

Ozler, Sule. (1986). "The Motives for International Bank Rescheduling, 1978–1983: Theory and Evidence." UCLA Working Paper 401, May.

Sachs, Jeffrey. (1984). *Theoretical Issues in International Borrowing*. Princeton Studies in International Finance, Princeton: Princeton University, no. 54, July.

———. (1986a). "The Debt Overhang of Developing Countries." Paper presented at the conference on Debt, Stabilization, and Development, Helsinki, Finland, August.

———. (1987b). "Testimony to the Subcommittee on International Trade." Senate Finance Committee, Summary, May 13.

———. (1982). "LDC Debt in the 1980s: Risk and Reforms" in P. Wachtel, ed. *Crisis in the Economic and Financial Structure*. Lexington, Mass.: Lexington Books.

Sachs, J. D., and D. Cohen. (1982). "LDC Borrowing with Default Risk." NBER Working Paper 925 (July).

331- 34

F 34

ρ 315ᵗ Discussant: Ishac Diwan

O16

This chapter offers a nice summary of the debt-overhang arguments recently developed in Sachs (1989), Krugman (1989), Corden (1988), and many others. Using a simple stylized model, Anayiotos takes us through a guided tour of the main conceptual claims of this literature. In essence, high external debt acts as a tax on investment. A strategically minded central planner of a highly indebted country would thus reduce investment below its efficient level. This leads to a debt-relief Laffer curve: When external debt is too high, debt forgiveness is Pareto improving.

Is this argument valid in the real world? After all, banks have never been keen to forgive any debts, and the recent Brady initiative had to encourage the public sector to bribe private lenders in order to get some debt reduction. Building on recent literature, I will discuss two points: First, what is the empirical evidence? Second, are there serious additional constraints on debt reductions that are not modelled in the chapter?

EMPIRICAL EVIDENCE

It has often been argued that the disincentive effect cannot be large since debtors rarely pay out more than 2 to 5 percent of their GNP. However, since default sanctions are most likely trade related, it is more reasonable to focus on distortions in the tradable sector. Total debt service to exports is well above 20 percent for the highly indebted countries (HICs), and it is quite possible that the implicit marginal tax rate is much higher than this average tax rate. Moreover, efficiency losses associated with a small disincentive effect can be quite large. Assuming, for instance, that 1 percent of the drop in growth rates for the HICs over 1982–87 was caused by the debt overhang, raising growth rates from 1.5 percent to 2.5 percent would represent an increase in the debtor country's wealth that was 10 times larger than outstanding debt (Claessens and Diwan 1989).

The decapitalization of the HICs is apparent in statistics showing a remarkable drop in their aggregate investment, a drop larger than the increase in external transfers. This suggests that incentive effects must be at work. In a recent analysis of investment and growth in the HICs before and after the debt crisis, the International Monetary Fund (IMF) found that (1) investment/GDP ratios were 10 percentage points lower in 1987 than in the 1975–79 period; and (2) the annual rate of real GDP growth for the HICs averaged 4.6 percent per year over 1975–81 but declined to 1.5 percent per year during 1982–87. The report analyzed different reasons for the decline in investment and concluded: "The evidence suggests that the poor performance of investment in countries with debt-servicing problems is generally consistent with the presence of debt overhang incentives" (IMF 1989, p. 65).

While these analyses are not full-fledged, empirical estimations of the exact magnitude of the disincentive effect, they do suggest that reducing debt would increase investment. But to determine whether, in addition, debt reduction is in the interest of the creditors, debt repayments need to be linked to investment, and output levels to growth. Unfortunately, both relationships are not easily identifiable.

Another set of studies relies on relationships between the volume and the secondary market price of debt.[1] These cross-sectional regressions relate the market price to creditworthiness indicators and are used to derive an individual country's debt Laffer curves based on market perceptions (Claessens 1988; Cohen 1989).[2] The level of debt for which the market value of debt is maximized can then be compared to outstanding debt. This line of work finds that the market value of debt declines when the face value of debt increases in only a few countries.[3] But incentive effects may well be entirely separable from market perceptions. Overall, the evidence is not conclusive, but does suggest the existence of a debt overhang, at least for some debtors.

CONSTRAINTS ON DEBT REDUCTION

If commercial banks can gain by providing it, why has there been so little debt reduction to date? The answer must be related to collective action and coordination problems. Debt reduction may well benefit the whole creditor group, but each party in the crisis has incentives to enjoy the rewards without supporting the cost, resulting in an inferior equilibrium without relief. One major stumbling block to a large debt reduction is the collective-action problem within the commercial creditor group, embodied in the inevitable tendency of small banks to wait for others to grant relief. Another is the tendency of banks as a group to wait for official bailouts, given the continuing signal that public money will come to the rescue of the faltering negotiation process (Bulow and Rogoff 1988).

Tax, regulatory, and accounting practices in the various creditor countries also discourage debt reduction, but we should not expect speedy regulatory changes as individual creditor governments wait for other governments to pick up the bill (Bouchet and Hay 1989). First, book-value accounting distorts the incentives of money market banks that dominate the steering committees. These banks are resistant to debt reduction—even when it can raise the market value of their claims—because they cannot afford the required book losses given their large exposure and weak financial position.[4] Second, when banks are able to realize their tax benefits upon provisioning, there are limited tax incentives to recognize losses. Partial deductibility of loan-loss reserves for corporate income-tax purposes is allowed in all the major creditor nations (Canada, France, Germany, Switzerland, and the United Kingdom) except the United States, where general provisioning is not tax deductible. Third, some countries allow their commercial banks to include loan-loss provisions in capital (United States, France, and Japan). This also creates disincentives to formally recognize losses on LDC debt. Finally, valuable subsidies are available to banks—such as mispriced-deposit insurance and forbearance over capital-adequacy rules—that have increased in value as the debt crisis has worsened. With taxpayers underwriting a lower bound on stock prices, the incentives for banks to undertake actions that save taxpayers' resources, rather than their own, are reduced.

Mistrust between creditors and debtors also constrains debt reduction (Claessens and Diwan 1989; Cohen 1989). Because of the intertemporal nature of the credit relation, efficient solutions have to involve promises by both parties to undertake future actions. The banks cannot credibly promise to debtors that they would extract a small share of future resources if the debtor imposes austerity and increases investment, and the debtor cannot credibly promise to invest new loans if they were forthcoming. This mutual lack of confidence is akin to the bad equilibrium in a prisoner's dilemma. Coordinated action can increase the available resources that will have to be shared, but it will not occur in the absence of a commitment mechanism. While such a mechanism is available to debtors in the form of the multilateral institution's conditionality, complex financial contracts would be needed for the banks to commit to low resource extraction in bad times without creating serious moral hazard (Krugman 1989; Cohen 1989).

The debt-overhang argument has proven to be extremely important in policy debate. However, it should not obstruct the fact that for the HICs, bargaining remains the main determinant of capital flows. More empirical research is needed to make the overhang argument operational, and public policy should try to alleviate the constraints to debt reduction.

NOTES

I would like to thank S. Claessens for his comments. The views expressed in this discussion should not be attributed to the World Bank.

1. Examples of this are Sachs and Huizinga (1987), Purcell and Orlanski (1988), and Cohen (1989).

2. A typical equation would be the one reported by Sachs and Huizinga (1987) where the secondary market price is a function (with the sign of the parameter in parentheses) of the debt/GNP ratio (–), average GNP growth (+), a dummy indicating whether the country has ever suspended debt-service repayments (N), and a dummy indicating whether regulators have required an allocated reserve (N).

3. Claessens (1988) found only Bolivia, Zambia, Sudan, Peru, and Côte d'Ivoire. See also Cohen (1989).

4. While the ratio of net Latin American exposure to equity of the world's top 100 banks declined from 125 percent in 1982 to 57 percent in 1987, the money-center banks' net exposure to equity ratios remains high at 84 percent.

REFERENCES

Bouchet, Michel, and Jonathan Hay. (1989). "The Rise of the Market Based Menu Approach and Its Limitations." In *Dealing with the Debt Crisis*, ed. I. Husain and I. Diwan. Washington, D.C.: World Bank.

Bulow, Jeremy, and Kenneth Rogoff. (1988). *Multilateral Developing-Country Debt Rescheduling Negotiations*. IMF Working Paper 88/35. Washington, D.C.: International Monetary Fund.

Claessens, Stijn. (1988). "The Debt Laffer-Curve: Some Estimates." International Economics Department, World Bank, Washington, D.C.

Claessens, Stijn, and Ishac Diwan. (1989). "Liquidity, Debt Relief, and Conditionality." In *Dealing with the Debt Crisis*, ed. I. Husain and I. Diwan. Washington, D.C.: World Bank.

Cohen, Daniel. (1989). "How to Deal with a Debt Overhang: Cut Flows Rather Than Stocks." In *Dealing with the Debt Crisis*, ed. I. Husain and I. Diwan. Washington, D.C.: World Bank.

Corden, Max. (1988). *Is Debt Relief in the Interest of the Creditors?* IMF Working Paper 88/72. Washington, D.C.: International Monetary Funds.

International Monetary Fund. (1989). *World Economic Outlook*. April.

Krugman, Paul. (1989). "Financing versus Forgiving a Debt Overhang." *Journal of Development Economics* 29 253–268.

Purcell, J., and D. Orlanski. (1988). "Developing Country Loans: A New Valuation Model for Secondary Market Trading." Salomon Brothers, Corporate Bond Research, International Loan and Trading Analysis, New York.

Sachs, Jeffrey. (1989). "The Debt Overhang of Developing Countries." In *Debt, Stabilization, and Development: Essays in Memory of Carlos Diaz-Alejandro*, ed. G. Calvo et al. Oxford: Blackwell.

Sachs, Jeffrey, and Harry Huizinga. (1987). "U.S. Commercial Banks and the Developing-Country Debt Crisis." *Brookings Papers* 2: 555–606.

Uruguay

18

Expectations of Devaluation, the Real Rate of Interest, and the Private Sector in a Dual-Currency Economy

GRACIANA DEL CASTILLO

The economy of Uruguay presents itself as an interesting different case for analysis, both from a theoretical and a policy-oriented point of view. The economic perform-ance is paradoxical to a casual observer: The country stagnated and had recurrent balance-of-payments crises from the mid-1950s to the mid-1970s when the rest of the world was in an economic boom; it started growing at a high real rate in 1974 and showed large balance-of-payments surpluses at a time of the oil shocks and economic decline in the rest of the world (particularly in other nonoil developing countries).[1]

After the 1973 coup d'état the military regime in power adopted several innovative and bold economic measures. The most visible was the adoption of a managed rate of exchange in October 1978—which became known as the tablita[2]—where the future daily path of the exchange rate was preannounced for the next several months.[3] During this period Uruguay became an atypical case: an economy fully integrated internationally through the capital account (with no restrictions whatsoever) and with important restrictions (mainly in the form of high tariffs) in the current account. In the second half of the 1970s Uruguay became one of the least restricted financial markets in the world.[4]

One of the most interesting theoretical issues that arises from the analysis of the tablita period in the Southern Cone economies—Argentina, Chile, and Uruguay— is the interpretation of why nominal domestic interest rates were much higher than the dollar rate adjusted for devaluation of the domestic currency, even though the rate of devaluation was set by the monetary authorities six months in advance. The purpose of this chapter is to explain the high spread between interest rates in domestic currency and interest rates in foreign currency in a dual-currency, inflationary economy with an active crawling peg system but in which there was uncertainty about the continuation of the exchange-rate policy. A second objective of the chapter is to determine in what sense real interest rates were high during the period and discuss how they affected the private sector.

The remainder of the chapter is divided into three sections. In the first section we briefly present some of the economic measures adopted in the mid-1970s. We also discuss the economic scenario that eventually led to the adoption of the *tablita* system in 1978 as well as the internal and external factors that contributed to the decision to drop the *tablita* in 1982. In the second section we present the model and provide empirical evidence in support of it. We also illustrate the situation with regard to real interest rates and discuss their impact on the economic performance of the economy. Conclusions follow in the third section.

ECONOMIC REFORM

The new economic team that assumed power in 1974 had to face the following scenario: (1) productive stagnation and balance-of-payments disequilibria, (2) internal disequilibria (inflation and fiscal deficits), and (3) dramatic changes in the international market for energy.[5] The new authorities believed that the economic stagnation and the recurrent balance-of-payments crises of the previous 20 years had been in large part due to the progressive closing up of the Uruguayan economy. This took the form of import substitution behind high tariff protection and import restrictions (quotas) in the commercial area and different types of restrictions on private flows of capital in the financial area.

The new team's top priority was to improve the allocation of resources through increased reliance on market forces. Due to government intervention and the existence of various monopolies, the price system was not operating so as to optimize resource utilization. The improvement in the allocation of resources was to be achieved by integrating the domestic economy into the world economy, both in the real and in the financial sense. Liberalization took the form of elimination of price controls and import quotas and the reduction of redundant protection for different goods; tariff reform; liberalization of exchange-rate transactions and holdings of international assets; and liberalization and opening up of capital markets (including liberalization of interest rates and elimination of credit selectivity, rediscount facilities, subsidized credit, and bank-reserve requirements).

As financial liberalization was progressing, the Central Bank's instruments were being restricted up to a point where the only instruments under its control were the rate of devaluation as specified in the *tablita* and the level of net domestic assets of the Central Bank.[6] From March 2, 1972, to October 17, 1978, two exchange markets coexisted. The (controlled) commercial market operating at the Central Bank was used for all import and export transactions, including the service of the external public debt. The (free) financial market operating at the commercial banks was used for all other transactions. On September 24, 1974, the financial exchange market was liberalized, and the Uruguayan peso became fully convertible for private capital transactions. On October 17, 1978, the Central Bank announced a devaluation of the peso while at the same time announcing its willingness to buy and sell any amount of domestic and foreign exchange desired. This action de facto unified the two foreign exchange markets.

At the same time, to assist in bringing domestic inflation in line with world inflation, the monetary authorities modified the passive crawling peg system operating since 1972 and adopted their boldest measure, namely, the policy of preannouncing the future path of the exchange rate (with a declining rate of devaluation). The advantage of the *tablita* system over a fixed exchange rate was that a positive rate of devaluation allowed the government to benefit from inflationary finance.[7] The foreign exchange system was to be combined with fiscal discipline and strict limitation on domestic credit creation. If the government had to monetize a fiscal deficit, the *tablita* system would become unsustainable.[8]

In November 1982 the military regime in power decided to abandon the exchange-rate system, the *tablita*, in spite of opposition from the economic team and soon after the president himself had given strong assurances to the public that the exchange-rate policy was going to be maintained. Many internal and external factors contributed to this decision, but let us briefly describe the economic performance of the country during the *tablita* period before we discuss the reasons for the change in exchange-rate policy in 1982.[9]

External factors were favorable to Uruguay during the early years of the *tablita* system. At the time of the second oil shock in 1979, the boom in Uruguay was at its peak, in large part as a result of the spillover from what R. A. Mundell has referred to as the "Afghan effect." When the USSR invaded Afghanistan and the United States imposed a grain embargo on the USSR, the latter diverted part of its grain purchases to Argentina. International bank lending to Argentina also increased significantly during this period. The large increase in international reserves in Argentina led to expansion and investment, a large part of which spilled over to Uruguay. As a result of the *tablita* adopted in Argentina in January 1979, and because prices adjust with a lag, the Argentinian peso became increasingly overvalued vis-à-vis the U.S. dollar and the Uruguayan peso. In the 1979–81 period Uruguay was "cheap" to the Argentinians who shopped and invested in real estate in Uruguay, boosting many domestic industries.[10]

Most economic indicators improved up to the beginning of the world recession in 1981. A very important external factor responsible for the recession at the beginning of the 1980s was the U.S. Federal Reserve change in monetary policy in October 1979. Interest rates in international capital markets, which were negative in real terms in 1979–80, became highly positive in 1981–82. This had a devastating effect in small developing economies, particularly the highly indebted ones. Other external factors that contributed to the crisis in early 1982 were the fall in the unit price of exports, recession in the developed market economies in 1981–82, the very heavy reduction in international bank credit to Latin America, and the appreciation of the U.S. dollar (to which the peso was pegged from October 1978 until November 1982). These factors had a notorious deleterious effect on Uruguay's export performance in the early 1980s. Economic and political events in Argentina (the end of the "Afghan effect" and the Malvinas/Falklands War in March 1982), high interest rates abroad, and the confiscation of dollar assets in Mexico in August 1982 contributed to large capital flight.

By 1982 the economy was in a deep recession, and the government budget deficit was increasing rapidly.[11] The most obvious internal cause of the recession (which started in 1981) was the high domestic rate of interest. High rates of interest in Uruguay were the result of foreign developments (high international real rates of interest) and uncertainty about government policy, as we shall discuss later. Recession had a devastating effect on government finances.[12]

As we pointed out earlier, a fiscal imbalance that needed to be monetized was incompatible with the existing foreign exchange regime. Thus the most important domestic factor responsible for the change in exchange-rate policy was the large deficit in the government budget. Two main factors contributed to the deficit: (1) the fact that the tax system was very sensitive to changes in current output, and (2) the mechanism of fixing wages. Wages were fixed by the government with some degree of indexation. The government had approved a bill linking social security payments to changes in nominal wages. When the rate of inflation decreased significantly in 1981, wages and social security payments increased in real terms, aggravating the budget situation. Among the foreign factors that put pressure on the balance of payments[13] and caused the change in exchange-rate policy were the recession and rising protectionism in the developed world, the high real rates of interest in international capital markets, the drastic reduction in the flow of external financing to Latin America (particularly from international banks), the fall in commodity prices, the appreciation of the U.S. dollar, and the policy adjustments in Argentina and Brazil.

INTEREST-RATE DETERMINATION: A MODEL

As Edwards and Khan (1985a, 1985b) have pointed out, as more countries liberalize their financial systems, research efforts have been shifting from the effects of liberalization per se to how interest rates are in fact determined once liberalization has taken place. They asserted that two main factors have increased interest in this particular issue, namely, the extraordinarily high interest rates following financial liberalization in the Southern Cone economies in the 1970s and the empirical evidence suggesting that high and volatile interest rates in the international capital markets have been at least partially transmitted to the developing countries.

In the mid-1980s several models of interest-rate determination did not take into account uncertainty about the foreign exchange policy in modelling expectations of exchange-rate changes. We argue that during the *tablita* period it was not possible to model expectations of exchange-rate devaluation using conventional models. Both adaptive and perfect-foresight models would not pick up the effect of the change in expectations as the probability of a change in exchange-rate regime—and therefore the spread between peso and dollar rates—increased greatly in the latter part of the *tablita* period. A perfect-foresight model would grossly underestimate expectations of exchange-rate changes since the actual rate of devaluation as scheduled in the *tablita* was very much lower (particularly in the latter part of the period) than what economic agents expected the rate of change in the exchange rate to be.

The analysis of interest rates in an inflationary situation in which there is uncertainty about the foreign exchange policy can be illustrated with the following model:

$$r_t = i_t^p - \pi_t^e ,$$
(18.1)

$$i_t^p - i_t^d = \delta_t^e .$$
(18.2)

Equation (18.1) is the ex ante Fisher equation stating that the real rate of interest equals the nominal rate of interest minus the expected rate of inflation. Equation (18.2) states that the spread, that is, the difference between domestic and foreign-currency-denominated interest rates in the home economy, is equal to the expected rate of devaluation of the domestic currency vis-à-vis the foreign currency.

The model differs from other models of this kind in the way we shall model the expected rate of devaluation of the domestic currency. To explain the interest-rate puzzle during the *tablita* period, it is important to separate the expected rate of devaluation into three parts: what I shall call the "*tablita* factor," that is, the actual devaluation of the peso as preannounced in the *tablita* schedule (δ_t^t); a "policy risk factor" (δ_t^r); and an error term (ε_t) representing not only political risks that cannot be modelled but all external shocks that are stochastic. Expectations of devaluation are thus formulated as

$$\delta_t^e = \delta_t^t + \delta_t^r + \varepsilon_t.$$
(18.3)

In spite of the *tablita*, expectations of devaluation in the Southern Cone economies during the period in which the rate of devaluation was preannounced were much higher than the rate determined by the schedule. Looming in the background was the fact that the government could change the existing exchange-rate regime, either by changing the base of the *tablita*, by wiping out the *tablita* altogether, or by imposing exchange controls. Equally important was the risk that economic policies would change either as a result of a change in government or as a result of a change in the economic team. There was no explicit contract throughout the period to cover for the foreign exchange risk.[14] The policy-risk factor was the measure of the mathematical expectation of the probability of a devaluation, that is, the mistrust in the foreign exchange policy.

The spread between domestic and foreign-denominated interest rates in Uruguay (equation 18.2) may be rewritten as

$$\sigma_t = \delta_t^t + \delta_t^r + \varepsilon_t ,$$
(18.4)

where $\sigma_t = i_t^p - i_t^d$. Letting δ_t^a be the ex post rate of devaluation, we will posit that in the absence of a *tablita* δ_t^a is a good descriptor of expectations of devaluation. To show this, we estimated equation (18.4) using data of Uruguay for the period before and after the *tablita*: March 1977 to September 1978 and December 1982 to December 1984 (44 observations). Although data and data sources are detailed in the appendix to this chapter, we need to point out that peso and dollar interest rates are measured by bank lending rates in Uruguay. The rates i_t^p and i_t^d are the annualized lending rates on short-term loans. Since there is no information on the distribution of loans of different maturities, we arbitrarily assumed that they were one-year loans and calculated the actual monthly ex post rate of depreciation (δ_t^a) as the percentage change in the exchange rate in the next 12 months. The following results were obtained (t-statistics are in parentheses, and a second-order auto-regressive error specification used to correct for serial correlation is indicated as AR = 2):

$$\sigma_t = 20.82 + 0.52\delta_t^a , \tag{18.5}$$
$$(1.60) \quad (8.01)$$

where $R^2 = 0.96$, D.W. = 2.04, F = 715.09, and AR = 2.

In the absence of a *tablita*, then, a perfect-foresight model in which expectations of devaluation (δ_t^e) are proxied by the actual rate δ_t^a) is supported by empirical evidence. The coefficient is significantly lower than 1, which is expected, given the fact that assets in the domestic economy are hardly perfect substitutes for assets abroad and that many other factors interfered with perfect arbitrage.

While the *tablita* was in operation, however, the actual rate of devaluation ($\delta_t^a = \delta_t^t$) was an inadequate descriptor of expectations. We estimated equation (18.5) for the period October 1978 to November 1981, and the following results were obtained:[15]

$$\sigma_t = 39.48 + 0.05\delta_t^t , \tag{18.6}$$
$$(4.79) \quad (1.10)$$

where $R^2 = 0.93$, D.W. = 2.05, F = 151.78, and AR = 2.

Moving terms in equation (18.4), we define the currency-adjusted spread as

$$\Delta_t = \delta_t^r + \mu_t , \tag{18.7}$$

where $\Delta_t = i_t^p - i_t^d - \delta_t^t = \sigma_t - \delta_t^t$. Although the policy-risk factor δ_t^r is not an observable variable, we argue that it can be modelled as a function of monetary and fiscal variables that are not consistent with the sustainability of the *tablita*. During the *tablita* period economic agents had the choice of borrowing in pesos or getting dollar-denominated loans, and the way they decided for one or the other was determined by their expectations of exchange-rate devaluation. If they thought that economic policy was inconsistent with the exchange-rate parity set forth in the *tablita*, their expectations of devaluation would be higher than the ex ante *tablita* rate.

We will model δ_t^e as a function of fiscal and monetary variables that economic agents take into account when they are forming their expectations about the continuity of government policy. By analyzing the spread in terms of banks' lending rates (rather than their deposit rates), we abstract from the risk faced by economic agents that their dollar deposits may be converted into pesos, as happened in Mexico in August 1982.

Thus, while we stated that the formation of expectations during the *tablita* period was not consistent with assumptions of perfect foresight, our model is consistent with rational expectations since we assume that economic agents have full information and make use of the economic model in forming their expectations. In particular, we postulate that δ_t^e, that is, the systematic component of expectations that is not represented in δ_t^e, is basically a function of what is happening to the government budget deficit in relation to GDP (G_t) and to international reserves of the Uruguayan banking system (TRU_t). Given the fact that the Uruguayan economy is very much dependent on and integrated to that of Argentina,[16] we postulate that δ_t^e is also a function of international reserves in Argentina (TRA_t) since expectations in Uruguay are highly dependent on political and economic events in Argentina. Thus

$$\delta_t^e = f[G_t, TRU_t, TRA_t]. \tag{18.8}$$

After substituting for δ_t^e in equation (18.7), we estimated this equation for the *tablita* period (October 1978 to November 1982) with variables expressed as a three-month moving average; G_t was the share of the budget deficit to GDP, and $DLTRU_t$ and $DLTRA_t$ were percentage changes in total international reserves in Uruguay and Argentina, respectively. OLS results were as follows:

$$\Delta_t = 15.49 + 0.55G_t - 0.18DLTRU_t - 0.18DLTRA_t, \tag{18.9}$$
$$\quad (0.71) \quad (3.27) \quad (-1.99) \quad\quad (-2.26)$$

where $R^2 = 0.99$, D.W. $= 1.68$, F $= 715.38$, and AR $= 3$. Δ_t is the ex post currency-adjusted spread because the adjustment was made with δ_t^e given by the ex post actual depreciation of the peso. All coefficients have the predicted signs. An increase in the budget deficit in relation to GDP increases the ex post currency-adjusted spread in the same way as a fall in international reserves, not only in Uruguay but in Argentina as well. We found that while the G_t coefficient was significant at the 1 percent level, the other two coefficients were significant at the 5 percent level.

These results show that fiscal and monetary variables are successful in explaining the ex post currency-adjusted spread. This means that the growing fiscal deficit and the fall in international reserves both in Uruguay and Argentina explain the ex post devaluation of the peso in 1982. On the other hand, these variables could not explain the ex ante currency-adjusted spread when the *tablita* factor (δ_t^t) was given by the devaluation of the peso as preannounced in the *tablita* schedule. The reason is that fiscal and monetary variables were inconsistent with the maintenance of the *tablita* schedule during the latter part of the period.

But in what sense were real interest rates high during this period? Real rates are not observable, but since real rates are equal to nominal rates minus the expected rate of deviation of the domestic currency, from equations (18.1) and (18.2)

$$r_t = i_t^d + \delta_t^e - \pi_t^e . \tag{18.10}$$

From regression equation (18.9) we can get the estimator of the policy-risk factor, which we call $\hat{\delta}_t^r$. We will use this estimator to proxy expectations of devaluation as

$$\hat{\delta}_t^e = \delta_t^t + \hat{\delta}_t^r , \tag{18.11}$$

where $\hat{\delta}_t^e$ explains the systematic component of the difference between domestic and foreign-currency-denominated interest rates.

Letting $\pi_t^e = \pi_t$, measuring ex post inflation by the percentage change in the wholesale price index (WPI) during the previous year,[17] and using equation (18.11) to proxy expectations of devaluation, we calculated the ex post real rate of interest as

$$r_t = i_t^d + \delta_t^t + \hat{\delta}_t^r - \pi . \tag{18.12}$$

The quantity r_t is the ex post real rate of interest because we used the ex post rate of inflation and the ex post actual depreciation of the peso.[18] The latter was included not only in the *tablita* factor (δ_t^t) but was also used to calculate the estimator of the policy risk factor ($\hat{\delta}_t^r$). As is clear from figure 18.1, the perceived risk-adjusted real rate of interest was negative from April 1979 to April 1980. This coincided with the peak of the investment boom in Uruguay and with negative real interest rates in international capital markets (proxied by U.S. rates). The real rate of interest started increasing at a very high rate starting in mid-1981, which coincided with the downturn in economic activity. The real rate was spectacularly high in 1982, both as a result of the large ex post depreciation of the currency and the fall in the inflation rate. This explains the 10 percent fall in GDP after years of rapid growth.

This formulation of the real rate of interest points to the fact that even though the real rate in Uruguay was affected by the increase in real interest rates in international capital markets in 1980–82 (incorporated in the i_t^d term), policy

Figure 18.1
Real Interest Rates: United States versus Uruguay

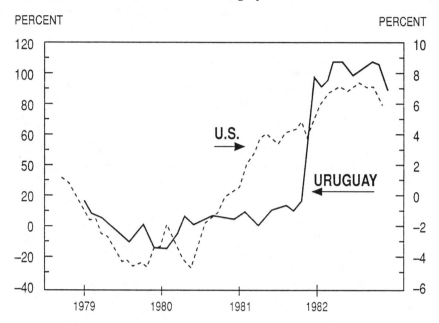

Source: Equation (8.12) for the *ex post* real rate of interest in Uruguay and IMF, *International Financial Statistics* data to calculate the real rate in the United States (see the Appendix for definition of vaiables and other data shources).

variables not consistent with the *tablita* had a systematic impact on expectations and therefore on the real rate of interest in Uruguay. In other words, ex ante expectations of devaluation exceeded the rate set forth by the *tablita* schedule. This is a particularly relevant point since Fisher's equation relies on ex ante expectations of devaluation to calculate the real rate of interest. Thus the ex ante real rate of interest, calculated as

$$r_t = i_t^d + \delta_t^t - \pi_t^e ,\tag{18.13}$$

would be a poor indicator of the cost of borrowing in real terms during this period.

To lower the policy-risk factor (and therefore what was perceived as real rates of interest) to a more desirable range (particularly in the latter period of the *tablita*), it would have been necessary to increase people's trust in the government policy of prefixing the rate of exchange, which was indeed low in view of developments in Argentina, starting with the collapse in its exchange-rate policy in 1981 and culminating with the Malvinas/Falklands War in March 1982. The fact that the Central Bank offered implicit exchange guarantees for a short period and then suspended them, and the fact that the Banco de la República sold future guarantees also for a short period did not by any means help to increase confidence in the government policy. Confidence in government policy could have been increased through the establishment of future markets or with the Central Bank guaranteeing the *tablita* rate on a more permanent basis. Failure to do so resulted in the fact that many borrowers—a large number of which were in key productive and exporting activities—got the worst of two worlds. During he *tablita* period they paid very high rates of interest on peso loans so that creditors could cover themselves for the policy-risk factor. Creditors had to charge a premium on the money they lent to allow for the fact that if they borrowed abroad and if the *tablita* was not changed, they would have to pay the world rate of interest plus the devaluation as scheduled in the *tablita* (ex ante δ_t^e), but if the exchange rate was devalued, they would have to pay an additional amount dependent upon what was devalued over and above what was determined by the *tablita* schedule (ex post δ_t^p). As it happened, some borrowers eventually began believing in the *tablita* and switched into dollar debt. Those who did so were badly hurt by the November 1982 devaluation.[19]

The ex post currency-adjusted spread (Δ_t) is shown in figure 18.2. Up to November 1981 the ex ante and ex post currency-adjusted spreads were equal.

Figure 18.2
Currency-adjusted Spread

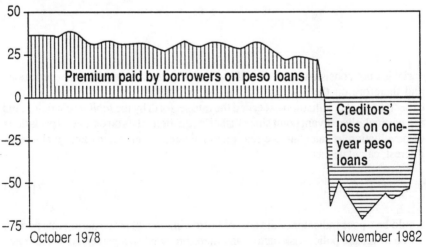

October 1978   November 1982

Source: See the Appendix to this chapter for a description of variables and data sources.

Since we used monthly rates annualized 12 months ahead, starting a year earlier, the ex post δ_t' included the actual devaluation of the peso (resulting from the change in exchange-rate policy) over and above what was specified in the *tablita* schedule. Figure 18.2 illustrates the extent to which economic agents benefitted or not from peso loans during the *tablita* period. As we said before, during this period economic agents had the clear choice of borrowing pesos or dollars, and they did the former or the latter depending on their expectations of devaluation. The ex ante currency-adjusted spread should be interpreted to represent the premium borrowers were willing to pay on the expectation that the exchange-rate policy would be changed and they would be able to pay their loans in depreciated currency. The premium was indeed high up to November 1981. Those who borrowed in pesos for one year after November 1981 (and before the peso was floated in November 1982) benefited from the change in exchange-rate policy and the fact that the ex post δ_t' was significantly higher than the ex ante δ_t'. Conversely, the ex post currency-adjusted spread shows how much creditors benefitted or not from lending pesos. During the year before the floating of the peso, creditors could not cover themselves for the devaluation of the peso. The fact that creditors lost so much on one-year loans made after November 1981 contributed to widespread difficulties in the banking system. Due to a large extent to poor performance during this period, domestic banks had to be rescued by the government, as a result of which there were, at the time this research was done, no private domestic commercial banks in Uruguay.

CONCLUSIONS

We have shown that while the *tablita* exchange-rate system was in operation in Uruguay, the rate of devaluation as scheduled in the *tablita* was an inadequate descriptor of expectations of devaluation. A second systematic component of expectations of devaluation was what we called the policy-risk factor and modelled as a function of the fiscal imbalance and international reserves both in Uruguay and Argentina. These fiscal and monetary variables were found to be successful in explaining the ex post but not the ex ante currency-adjusted spread between peso and dollar rates of interest. In other words, the fiscal imbalance and the fall in international reserves both in Uruguay and Argentina during the last period of the *tablita* were inconsistent with the ex ante *tablita* rate but were able to explain the ex post rate, which incorporated the large November 1982 devaluation of the peso.

By analyzing the ex post currency-adjusted spread, we have also shown that the cost of imposing monetary discipline through a managed exchange-rate system was high due to the fact that people did not expect the monetary authorities to stick to the new policy. As a result, the impact of expectations of devaluation (above the *tablita* rate) on real interest rates was extremely negative. The benefits in terms of increased stability, investment, employment, and capital inflows and reduced inflation were lost with the peso float of November 1982. The large fiscal imbalance starting in mid-1981 was incompatible with the foreign exchange policy. If the government had to monetize a large fiscal deficit, the *tablita* would become unsustainable. This indeed happened in 1982. The policy of managing the exchange rate was implemented at a very high initial cost, and many of the benefits were lost when the policy was discontinued.

Appendix
Glossary of Variables and Data Sources

i_t^p is the nominal interest rate in Uruguay, proxied by commercial banks' (average) annualized lending rate on ordinary domestic currency loans with a maturity not exceeding six months (Central Bank data bank).

i_t^d is the dollar interest rate in Uruguay, proxied by commercial banks' (average) lending rates on ordinary foreign currency loans with a maturity not exceeding six months (Central Bank data bank).

σ_t is the spread calculated as $i_t^p - i_t^d$.

δ_t^t is the actual depreciation of the exchange rate as scheduled in the *tablita*. It measures percentage changes in the exchange rate (expressed in pesos per U.S. dollar, implicit/market rate, period average taken from the International Monetary Fund [IMF], *International Financial Statistics [IFS]* line rf). Since δ_t^t is calculated as (log e_{t+12} – log e_t), ex ante and ex post δ_t^t are equal up to December 1981.

Δ_t is the currency-adjusted spread calculated as $\sigma_t - \delta_t^t$.

δ_t^a is the actual depreciation of the exchange rate when exchange parity is not preannounced.

$\hat{\delta_t^r}$ is the policy-risk component in economic agents' expectations of devaluation.

δ_t^r is the estimator of δ_t^r calculated from equation (18.9).

δ_t^e is the expected rate of devaluation. The rate δ_t^e can be proxied by δ_t^a when exchange parity is not preannounced but should be proxied by $\hat{\delta_t^e} = \delta_t^t + \hat{\delta_t^r} + \varepsilon_t$ during the *tablita* period.

π_t is the annualized rate of inflation calculated as (log WPI_t – log WPI_{t-12}).

G_t is the ratio of government deficit (IMF, *IFS*, line 80, multiplied by –1 so that a + indicates a deficit) as a ratio of GDP. Since there are no available monthly or quarterly data for GDP, it had to be interpolated from yearly figures (IMF, *IFS*, line 99b).

$DLTRU_t$ is the percentage changes (*d* log) in total reserves of Uruguay (total reserves minus gold plus gold at national valuation expressed in millions of Special Drawing Rights [SDRs]) taken from the IMF, *Supplement on International Reserves*, no. 6, 1983.

$DLTRA_t$ is defined as in *DLTRU_t* for Argentina.

NOTES

I thank R. A. Mundell, M. I. Blejer, S. Dell, J. Gil Diaz, A. Giovannini, P. Malan, C. Reinhart, A. Rodriguez, and an anonymous referee and the participants in the International Symposium on Business Finance in Less Developed Capital Markets for many useful comments.

1. The quadrupling of the international price of oil from 1972 to 1974 had a significant impact in raising the price of Uruguay's imports since petroleum accounted for about one-fourth of total imports and imports supplied about 60 percent of its total energy requirements. The oil crises affected Uruguay's exports as well: Recession in the developed world brewed protectionism, and the imposition of restrictive measures became widespread. Uruguay was particularly affected by the closing of the European Economic Community (EEC) markets to meat imports from third-world countries. As a result, the terms of trade deteriorated by about 50 percent in 1974 and by a further 20 percent in 1975.

2. The exchange-rate regime was called the *tablita* since the government published a "table" with the daily exchange parities.

3. This foreign exchange regime had been adopted by Chile in February 1978 and was subsequently adopted by Argentina in December 1978.

4. While Uruguay completely liberalized its financial sector first and was never able to make great progress in the area of trade liberalization, Chile followed the opposite path by thoroughly liberalizing trade flows and maintaining controls on short-term capital flows. Argentina followed a path somewhere in between by removing most (but not all) restrictions on short-term capital flows before implementing a tariff reform (for details see Corbo, de Melo, and Tybout 1986).

5. For an analysis of the 1974–82 period, see del Castillo (1986).

6. In a fixed exchange-rate system, the exchange rate is determined by the monetary authorities, and all other variables adjust to it. To fix the exchange rate implies that (1) equilibrium in the foreign exchange market is achieved by the monetary authorities buying and selling foreign exchange; (2) the nominal amount of money in the economy is determined by the public through the balance of payments, a surplus increasing the nominal amount of money and a deficit decreasing it; and (3) the monetary authorities have control only over domestic credit creation (in fact they have control only over their own credit operations), and the level of international reserves of the monetary authorities depends on their domestic credit policies.

7. Corbo, de Melo, and Tybout (1986, pp. 613–619) pointed out that in all three countries of the Southern Cone stabilization programs were implemented in two identifiable phases. In phase 1, anti-inflationary policy was based on major reductions in monetary growth and fiscal deficits under a passive crawling peg regime. They pointed out that the persistence of inflation motivated a major shift of stabilization tactics toward phase 2, in which the exchange rate was used as an anti-inflationary tool.

8. This is why the probability of collapse of the *tablita* was very high in Argentina from its inception and in Uruguay starting in late 1981.

9. An analysis of the exchange-rate policy followed after the ending of the *tablita* system is beyond the scope of this chapter.

10. Although empirical evidence seems to validate purchasing-power parity in the long

run, significant deviations from it seem to exist in the short run (see del Castillo (1986, pp. 159–161).

11. In 1978 the budget deficit was less than 1 percent of GDP. Fiscal balance was attained in 1979, and there was a small surplus in 1980. In 1981 the deficit was still below 1.5 percent of GDP, but it soared to over 9 percent in 1982.

12. In 1982 the deficit amounted to over 40 percent of total government revenue. This was due to the large fall in GDP (of over 9 percent) in 1982 since revenues as a percentage of GDP increased slightly from the previous year.

13. After an unprecedentedly large accumulation of international reserves from 1976 to 1981, the fall in reserves resulting from the balance-of-payments deficit in 1982 amounted to half a billion dollars.

14. The Central Bank actually did so from February to September 1981 by offering implicit exchange guarantees. During the first half of 1982 it was the Banco de la República (the state commercial bank) that sold future guarantees.

15. Given the way we define the actual depreciation of the peso, monthly observations of δ_t^f starting in November 1981 are different ex ante and ex post since by representing the rate of devaluation in the following 12 months they pick up the effect of the November 1982 devaluation that ended the *tablita* system. For this reason, to show our point that the devaluation as scheduled in the *tablita* was a poor indicator of expectations, it was better to estimate just up to November 1981.

16. For evidence on the integration hypothesis, see del Castillo (1987).

17. D. R. Khatkhate (1986) pointed out that the CPI gives too much weight to services and that the GDP deflator is a better measure of inflation to measure real interest rates since it gives more weight to capital goods and other long-lived assets. Since the GDP deflator is not available on a monthly or even a quarterly basis, we used the WPI since we found that it is highly correlated with the CPI and GDP deflator in estimations using annual data.

18. The best predictor of inflation this period is last period's inflation, given the persistence of shocks. Nevertheless, two other measures of inflation were used: (1) the annualized rate of the past six months and (2) the rate of the past six and future six months. The overall pattern of real rates did not change significantly.

19. The spread, however, was largest in 1982, indicating that a larger percentage of borrowers believed that they were better off borrowing in pesos.

REFERENCES

Blejer, M. I. (1982). "Interest Rate Differentials and exchange Risk: Recent Argentine Experience." *IMF Staff Papers* 29 (June): 270–279.

Blejer, M. I., and J. Gil Diaz. (1986). "Domestic and External Factors in the Determination of the Real Interest Rate: The Case of Uruguay." *Economic Development and Cultural Change* 34 (April): 589–606.

Calvo, G. (1986). "Fractured Liberalism: Argentina under Martinez de Hoz." *Economic Development and Cultural Change* 34 (April): 511–533.

Corbo, F., J. de Melo, and J. Tybout. (1986). "What Went Wrong with the Recent Reforms in the Southern Cone?" *Economic Development and Cultural Change* 34 (April): 607–640.

del Castillo, G. (1981). "Efecto del Riesgo de Cambio Sobre las Tasa de Interés Real." Paper presented at the conference on "The Southern Cone Economies and the World Monetary Context," Montevideo, Uruguay, December 16–19.

————. (1986). "Balance of Payments Analysis: An Econometric Test of Uruguay." Ph.D. diss., Columbia University, May.

————. (1987). "The MGRC Model: A Test of the Gulliver Effect." In *7th Latin American Meeting of the Econometric Society: Abstracts and Papers*, 1: 425–452. São Paulo, Brazil, August.

Edwards, S., and M. Khan. (1985a). "Interest Rate Determination in Developing Countries: A Conceptual Framework." *IMF Staff Papers* 32 (September): 377–403.

————. (1985b). "Interest Rates in Developing Countries: The Role of Domestic and External Influences in Determining Interest Rates." *Finance and Development*, June, 28–31.

Hanson, J., and J. de Melo. (1985). "External Shocks, Financial Reforms, and Stabilization Attempts in Uruguay, 1974–83," *World Development* 13 (August): 917–939.

Khatkhate, D. R. (1986). "Estimating Real Interest Rates in LDCs." *Finance and Development*, June, 45–58.

Mundell, R. A. (1973). "Inflation and Real Interest." *Journal of Political Economy* 71 (June): 280–283.

Discussant: Sarath Abeysekera

This chapter addresses some interesting issues associated with a dual-currency economy. The author sets out to achieve two major goals: first, to explain the high interest-rate spread between the domestic and the foreign currency (the dollar); second, to determine the magnitude of the real interest rates and its impact on the private sector of the Uruguayan economy.

The model used to explain the interest-rate spread is based on the well-known Fisher effect and the interest-rate-parity theory (IRPT). The equation (18.5) clearly shows that the IRPT has not been holding outside the *tablita* period. Given the situation of Uruguay at the time, this result is not surprising. The author's claim, however, that the results support a perfect-foresight model, where actual devaluations are used as the independent variable, is a little far-fetched. What the results indicate is that the actual ex post devaluation rates have limited economic significance and that the peso interest rates incorporate a large premium, as shown by the size of the intercept term. This premium almost doubled during the *tablita* period, as shown by equation (18.6), with a higher level of statistical significance. In addition, the coefficient associated with the *tablita* devaluation indicates much lower economic significance in explaining the interest differential. It would be interesting to take a closer look at the results from estimating the two models. In this regard, a closer look at the statistical characteristics of the time series also could improve the validity of the conclusions.

The chapter fails to discuss the relationship of the dollar interest rates in the international capital markets to the dollar interest rates in Uruguay. It is conceivable that these two rates are not the same. To the extent that the domestic and international dollar interest rates are unequal, it is not possible to relate the interest differential (peso and domestic dollar) to the changes in the exchange rates. It would be interesting to see how this issue impacts the results provided in the chapter.

It would have been appropriate for the author to provide both the models, ex post and ex ante, explaining currency-adjusted spread. While the author shows that the fiscal and monetary variables are successful in explaining the ex post currency-adjusted spread, she does not show how a similar relationship works with ex ante currency-adjusted spread. Inclusion of this will support the statement made in the body as well as in the conclusion of the chapter.

Some clarification is necessary in figure 18.2 as to what percentages (axes) apply to which country. If one assumes that the right-hand-side axis represents the United States and the left-hand-side axis represents Uruguay, then the real rates that are being discussed there, in the context of comparing those in the United States and Uruguay, appear to confound the general relationship given by the Fisher effect. The real rates associated with Uruguay are extremely high in U.S. standards. Perhaps if one defines these real rates as "effective" rates, then it is possible to view these effective rates as a combination of real rates (in the normal sense, accounting for the time value of money) plus a risk premium for policy and other risks. Then the nominal rate in Uruguay would be this "effective" rate plus the inflation rate. For all practical purposes the "effective" rate in the United States will be the real rate. In order to be clear, some kind of distinction between the rates compared in figure 18.2 will be extremely helpful.

In summary, the author has been fairly successful in identifying and modelling the interest-rate spread between the local and foreign currencies. The handling of the second issue, the impact of high real interest rates on the private sector, however, needs a more thorough analysis for us to come to the same conclusions.

Part VII

Research Directions

19

Research in Business Finance: A Mexican Perspective

EDGAR ORTIZ

RESTRICTIONS ON FINANCIAL RESEARCH

Research in business finance is in its infancy in Mexico and Latin America (LA). Thus we must identify priority topics that should be pursued now and in the near future. For this purpose, we should first pinpoint the main sources of boundaries on research and their impacts on this endeavor. Currently, three important, inter-related problems restrict research in finance: (1) distorted development of financial institutions; (2) weak academic development in business administration, particularly in the area of finance; and (3) the debt crisis.

Distorted Development of Financial Institutions

Full-fledged modernization of Mexico and all Latin American countries began after World War II. Then, these nations basically adopted import-substitution models to promote economic growth and welfare. Two major schools of thought supported public policy making: Keynesianism and structuralism, Latin America's contribution to world economic thought.[1] Both supported strong state intervention in the economy. Rival paradigms had a limited role. Monetarism gathered some influence among central banks and some state financial institutions, but it only played a major role when balance-of-payments disequilibria forced these nations to adopt adjustment measures. Marxism and neo-Marxist thinking, particularly dependency theory, where again many Latin Americans have made fine contributions, had little direct influence in policy making. However, serious research and criticisms from their supporters did lead the state to strengthen its role in the economy, often adopting "populist" postures.[2]

As a result, public enterprises and public banking institutions were created to support economic development. Many contributions can be attributed to these organizations. However, they had many failures, too.[3] Particularly, rather than "complementing" the market mechanism, in the long run they became an obstacle for its growth and for economic development as well. This was most accentuated in the financial sector. Financial repression, concerning mainly monetary and banking policies, led to continuous disequilibria, mainly manifested in recursive high inflation rates and regulated interest and exchange rates that led to severe devaluations and harsh adjustment policies. Moreover, market development was hindered by emphasis on the creation of banking institutions, particularly development banks. In addition, the financial sector was weakly structured and lacked regional integration. Other state and private institutions proliferated. Commercial banks did not have their functions clearly defined, and concentration of assets and liabilities in a few institutions took place, often creating oligopolistic behavior and political clashes with the state. Although these institutions channelled funds to corporate investments, their ill-defined role hindered capital markets' development, promoted excessive foreign debt acquisition, and promoted weak corporate management.

In sum, securities markets were substituted by other forms of intermediation. Their growth was mainly limited to short-term instruments, mostly government issued. Thus corporations had restricted possibilities for issuing equity and long-term financing in these markets. Furthermore, it was to their advantage to keep corporate control tight and get debt financing from public development institutions at preferential interest rates. In addition, to overcome market limitations, many corporations kept close ownership and control ties with private banking institutions.

Strong state regulation and intervention through financial institutions is also one of the origins of the Latin American debt crisis. In turn, this also became another form of repressing growth of the domestic capital markets. In lieu of supporting balanced budgets, sound tax reforms, and strong institutions to promote local financial intermediation, governments resorted to increased foreign debt acquisitions. Indeed, sharp disequilibria were deferred into the future: today's foreign debt crisis. A large share of this debt was made by both development banks and private commercial banks to support public and private investments, often evaluated inappropriately.

Imperfect markets naturally lead to imperfect decisions. In this respect, weak capital markets in LA also promoted weak corporate decision making. Many corporations showed low productivity and poor financial performance, not only due to high protectionism, erratic subsidies and other ill-conceived fiscal incentives, and imperfections in the real markets, but also because market discipline could not become enforced through valuation of the firm in the capital markets. In the absence of capital market indicators, firms often opted for inconsistent or unreachable goals in the management of their assets. Also, they often restricted their use of financial tools to simplistic or outdated techniques.

All these facts have had a profound impact on financial research. First, all financial research in LA has concentrated on macro issues concerning mainly money and credit, foreign exchange rates, inflation, and development financing. Second, research has been mainly carried out by economists, this being extensive in the case of researchers from developed countries interested in Latin American issues. Finally, demand for research in business finance has remained low and limited, again, to monitoring macro events. Research on corporate finance and capital markets has been restricted and mainly descriptive.

Nevertheless, many important contributions have been made in Latin America regarding macro financial issues. The studies by Navarrete and Noyola on inflation, written along structuralist thought and also influenced by Kalecki's works in the case of the latter,[4] and the research by Guzman, who takes a more radical approach, must be mentioned among Mexican authors.[5]

Weak Academic Development in Business

The number of business schools in LA has skyrocketed in the last three decades. Indeed, some U.S. universities like Harvard, Stanford, the University of Houston, the American Graduate School of International Management, and many others have established, independently or as joint projects with local institutions, some graduate programs there. There has also been an important adoption of modern financial thought and tools. For instance, in Mexico basic corporate finance is increasingly taught using translations of texts commonly used in the United States, for example, Block and Hirt, Brealey and Clark, Gitman, Philippatos, Van Horne, and Weston and Brigham. However, teaching has not been supported with findings from research dealing with local institutions and financial corporate practices. In addition, teaching has concentrated on the managerial practical level, that is, the undergraduate and master's levels. In Mexico there are only two doctoral programs in business administration, but both are plagued with problems due to incomplete faculty staffing and the lack of resources.

Emphasis on macro financial issues, excessive state intervention in the economy, protectionism and bailout operations to rescue bankrupt firms, and repressed financial markets have contributed somewhat to this situation. Research on macro issues has meant that schools and departments of economics become the leading centers for this type of work. However, it is worth noting that in most higher-education institutions in LA radical economic thought that has hindered contributions from other paradigms still predominates. With increased schooling of Latin Americans in the United States this is changing rapidly. In Mexico there is a rather significant number of economists holding doctorate degrees from U.S. universities. However, many are turning to politics as an alternative to professional development in Mexico.

Excessive state intervention in the economy, which contributed to the creation of imperfect markets, and exaggerated protective measures have favored informal and uncareful business management. Managers are aware of risks associated with business operations, but decisions are bounded by imperfect market indicators that have been cushioned with artificial hedging measures instrumented by the state.

This has induced firms to become inefficient in the allocation of their resources, and this inefficiency manifests itself mainly in low productivity and erratic financial performance. Firms have shown interest in following macroeconomic financial trends to adjust to them, but have demanded little hard-core research concerning financial management. Decisions have often been supported with outdated and uncomplicated tools, as pointed out earlier. All these facts have affected business curriculum and research development, limiting their scope.

Highly related to these issues is financial repression. In terms of business finance, among other things, this has meant a false security to get long-term debt financing from private or state financial intermediaries. But above all it has meant that financial markets remain underdeveloped. Particularly, capital markets have played a rather insignificant role in funding firms. Their underdevelopment is also one of the reasons why firms err in their financial decisions. Since securities markets are thin and limited to few firms, and information is scant, overall, corporations have lacked valuation measures to plan their decisions. Few firms are aware that maximizing the stockholder's wealth is the goal of the modern corporation. Furthermore, maximizing profits is rather sought with a short-term vision. For teaching and research this has meant that capital markets theory has been badly neglected and that managerial issues lag behind all important contributions developed in the last three decades.

An important outcome of all these facts is that the scope of business finance is still ill defined in all Latin American countries. This area is still strongly identified with accounting. Thus teaching and research in finance have been highly conditioned by this view. Although some important answers have been attained in this way, the results are not satisfactory. Similarly, most research has remained descriptive and normative.[6]

Debt Crisis

All Latin American countries are currently undergoing the most severe crisis of this century. Its graveness cannot be contested. However, there has been an excessive concentration on short-term adjustment. Governments have neglected development planning, and firms have largely ignored strategic planning. For financial research this has implied three things: Research has concentrated on debt and adjustment issues; funds have been severely curtailed to institutions of higher education; and corporations have been mainly concerned with current assets management, particularly liquidity issues. Since balancing public deficit and servicing the debt has led to increases in taxes and in their regulation, corporations have also been concerned with taxation. In both cases an accounting perspective has been taken.

However, Mexican economists have made outstanding contributions regarding the debt, adjustment, and other related problems. Some recent works that should be followed by researchers in finance are those by Aspe-Armella, Dornbusch, and Obstfeld; Blanco and Graver; Carrada-Bravo; Green; Ize and Ortiz; Ortiz; Ros and

Lustig; and Solis and Zedillo.[7] The works of these and other Mexican authors are also important because they affirm a positive tendency toward the creation of independent economic thought in Latin America. In addition, their models, findings, and recommendations will prove useful to other Latin American and developing nations.

RESEARCH PRIORITIES IN FINANCE

These considerations make it clear that research in business finance in Latin America is still an unexplored field and that it is badly needed to support sound policy making from governments, as well as sound corporate decision making. Moreover, the role of free markets and private enterprises in economic development has been reassessed, and research is needed to model the impacts of liberalization policies and ensure a successful application. Similarly, the relationship between equity and growth needs new conceptualizations, particularly in regard to development financing and the links between local fiscal policies and entrepreneurial activity. Thus topics abound. Their priority should be identified. Taking into account the landmark theoretical and instrumental advances that have been made in business finance in the last decades as well as recent trends of research in the area, four interrelated broad areas must be identified: capital markets development; corporate ownership and agent-principal relations; corporate financial structure; and managerial tools and practice.

Capital Markets Development

Besides defining risk and equilibrium and identifying market inefficiencies, research tasks must concentrate on modelling the relationships between macroeconomic policy, capital markets, and corporate activity. It is also imperative to create the right theoretical framework to support innovative financial intermediation in these markets. The nature and impact of imperfect information on market activity and development must be assessed. New institutions and new forms of securitization are needed. The links between local capital markets and the international capital markets must be established, too. The impact of financial repression and current financial deregulation and liberalization policies on these markets should also be examined. In all these cases country studies and comparative studies are needed to shed more light on the appropriate policies to promote capital markets and both to mobilize more internal savings toward investments and to make them attractive to international portfolio investors so that international resources are also mobilized to finance investments from private firms operating in Latin America. The links between domestic investments of local firms and of subsidiaries of multinational corporations and the local and international markets must be established. Finally, the nature of multinational corporate investments should be assessed in the context of financial liberalization and likely portfolio diversifications vis-à-vis corporate diversification in investments abroad.

Corporate Ownership and Agency Problems

Ownership of corporations in Latin American countries is usually held by small groups of investors. Many firms also diversify in unrelated lines of business. This problem has deep historical roots, but currently it is rather due to limitations of the capital markets. For that reason it is very important to model agency problems and corporate ownership under imperfect markets. Serious studies paralleling those currently under way in relation to developed capital markets are needed to promote corporate growth and investments. Models should determine conditions necessary for increased participation in both corporations and local portfolio investors in the capital markets. To benefit fully from the globalization of the economy, Latin America needs corporations that can take advantage of economies of scale and of local comparative advantages. An important extension of this line of studies comprises understanding the impact of capital markets in the socialization of corporate decisions. Another extension concerns state enterprises. These have double agency problems with potential contradictions among them. Managers should act on behalf of households—the owners of the firm. However, they act on behalf of higher public officials and often of a political party. This relationship should be examined particularly now that privatization programs are under way. Finally, the nature of multinational corporate ownership and governance should be studied to determine ways to strengthen further financing of these corporations in Latin America and other developing countries.

Corporate Financial Structure

The role of imperfect capital markets in corporate liquidity and financial structure and cost of capital of Latin American firms needs to be studied thoroughly. The impact of financial regulation and financial liberalization on the firm's investment decisions and capital structure must be analyzed. Related to this, a problem that needs to be studied is the impact of subsidized financing on the financial structure of the firm and in its investment decisions. The impact of operating and financial leverage on stock-market performance needs to be measured. The relationship between ownership, corporate growth, and equity versus debt financing needs careful analysis.

Managerial Tools and Practices

The managerial practices of Latin American corporations need to be investigated in order to determine their use of financial tools. Results should lead either to adapting existing tools already in use by corporations in the developed countries or else to creating new conceptual frameworks and tools appropriate for their case. As pointed out earlier, corporations in Latin America have made great strides in the adoption of existing financial technology in the last decades. However, a large number of tools and models remain ignored by many corporate decisions makers. In general, existing models and tools should be applicable to the case of Latin

American firms. In other cases, light adaptations may be necessary to make them suitable for the Latin American institutional system. Finally, in other cases, important contributions to the field of financial management will be advanced by studying Latin American corporate practices. This is also true for all the other studies previously suggested concerning business finance in Latin America.

In sum, research in business finance in Mexico, Latin America, and the developing nations is a challenge that must be fully embraced by all specialists from the area. Their efforts must be continued. Mexico offers a fine case to study. Data bases on capital markets and corporate activity are fairly well developed. Furthermore, in the last few years the government has carried out important reforms in its economic and financial systems that need careful research through local case studies or else through comparative studies with other developing capital markets like those of Korea, India, the Philippines, Turkey, Argentina, Brazil, Chile, and Colombia.

NOTES

1. Bibliographical references in this chapter are limited to financial research contributions from Mexican authors readily available to English readers. A few key works in Spanish are cited because there are no English translations. The works from schools of thought or English-speaking authors cited in this chapter are available at any data base in U.S. libraries.

2. Recently, this problem has been present in the management of the foreign debt. See Rudiger Dornbusch and Sebastian Edwards, *The Macroeconomics of Populism in Latin America*, Working Papers, Policy, Planning and Research, Country Studies Department (Washington, D.C.: World Bank, 1989).

3. M. D. Ramirez, *Development Banking in Mexico: The Case of the Nacional Financiera, S.A.* (New York: Praeger, 1986).

4. Kalecki's concern with business cycles, dynamic growth, and inflation influenced many Latin American economists, including Noyola, in the 1950s and 1960s. For an exhaustive review of Kalecki's works, see George R. Feiwel, *The Intellectual Capital of Michal Kalecki* (Knoxville: University of Tennessee Press, 1976).

5. M. L. Guzman-Ferrer, *La Inflacion y el Desarrollo en America Latina* (Mexico: Universidad Nacional Autonoma de Mexico, 1976); A. Navarrete, "Comparative Analysis of Public Instruments in Mexico's Experience," in *Inflation and Growth in Latin America*, ed. W. Baer and I. Kerstenetzky (Homewood, Ill.: Irwin, 1964); Carlos Bazdresch Parada, *El Pensamiento Economico de Juan F. Noyola* (Mexico: Fondo de Cultura Economica, 1988).

6. In the area of finance must be cited A. Bosch, *El Mercado de Capitales en Mexico* (Mexico: CEMLA, 1968); D. S. Brothers and L. Solis, *Mexican Financial Development* (Austin: University of Texas Press, 1966); T. Heyman, *La Inversion en Mexico* (Mexico: Diana, 1989); D. Ibarra, "Comments on the Mexican Financial System," in *Financial Liberalization and the Internal Structure of capital Markets in Asia and Latin America*, ed. Miguel Urrutia (Tokyo: United Nations University, 1988); Bernardo Paul, ed., *El Desarrollo Financiero de America Latina y el Caribe* (Caracas: Instituto Interamericano de Mercados de Capital, 1981).

7. P. Aspe-Armella, R. Dornbusch, and M. Obstfeld, *Financial Policies and the World*

Capital Market: The Problem of Latin American Countries (Chicago: University of Chicago Press, 1983); idem, "Mexico: Foreign Debt and Economic Growth," in *Mexico's Search for a New Development Strategy*, ed. D. S. Brothers and L. Solis M. (Boulder, Colo.: Westview Press, 1989); H. Blanco and P. Graver, "Recurrent Devaluation and Speculative Attacks on the Mexican Peso," *Journal of Political Economy* 94 (February 1986); F. Carrada-Bravo, *Oil, Money, and the Mexican Economy: A Macroeconometric Analysis* (Boulder, Colo.: Westview Press, 1982); R. Green, *Estado y Banca Transnacional en Mexico* (Mexico: CEESTEM/Nueva Imagen, 1981); idem, *La Deuda Publica Mexicana, 1973–1988* (Mexico: SRE/Siglo XXI, 1989); A. Ize and G. Ortiz, "Fiscal Rigidities, Public Debt, and Capital Flight," *IMF Staff Papers* 34, no. 2 (1987): 311–332; G. Ortiz, *Capital Accumulation and Economic Growth: A Financial Perspective on Mexico* (New York: Garland Pub., 1984); L. Solis and E. Zedillo, "The Foreign Debt of Mexico," in *International Debt and the Developing Countries*, ed. G. W. Smith and J. T. Cuddington (Washington, D.C.: World Bank, 1985); J. Ros and Nora Lusting, *Stabilization and Adjustment Programmes and Policies* (New York: WIDERUNU, 1986).

20

Research Directions:
A Theoretical Framework

LEMMA W. SENBET

One of the things that I have learned is that research in finance as it relates to less developed capital markets seems less developed as well. I am hoping, though, that there is no systematic relationship between research development and economic development; thus I am hoping that the research dimension will get the work done much faster than the development of those countries themselves.

I take the position that less developed capital markets are distinguishable from highly developed capital markets principally on the basis of market imperfections. I think that that is pretty obvious. Therefore, I view my topic of research in corporate finance as the impact that the market imperfections have on corporate finance in less developed capital markets. I view market imperfections broadly to include three categories, the first being incomplete markets and transaction costs. The second concerns agency conflicts and information. These agency conflicts may arise among parties within the private system, or they may arise between the private system and the public system. The third category is taxation. These are the issues that we have dealt with in corporate finance mostly in the context of highly developed capital markets. I warn that I outline these issues only because they are not readily doable. If they were, I would not be inclined to share them publicly. Thus these are issues that I think would be potentially doable by those who are highly initiated and highly motivated.

I first deal with the issue of agency conflicts and the design of securities. I started thinking about how these would be related to less developed capital markets. The chapter by Stavros Thomadakis shows that we can get good mileage out of an agency-theoretic framework. I may also add that in highly developed capital markets, the United States being an example, the agency-theoretic framework has been utilized to provide an economic rationale for the complex types of securities issued by the firm. For instance, why do firms issue debt with conversion privileges? Why are bonds that are simultaneously convertible and callable issued? These questions sound like they have simple answers, but if the questions are examined at a deeper level, there are no rationales for firms to issue such securities in perfect and well-functioning capital markets. The only rationale, as I understand it, would exist under market imperfections. For example, it used to be the case that people thought of callable debt as a means for firms to try to take advantage of declining interest rates. When interest rates declined, the firm holding an option on that bond could retire the bond and reissue it at lower rates of interest. The problem with this rationale is that the option would be fully priced in a callable bond versus a noncallable bond. There would be no marginal incentive for the firm to issue callable versus noncallable bonds. There has been work in the agency area that provides a rationale as to why firms will have an incentive to issue such securities. Essentially, to issue such securities would end up benefitting firms in the sense of reducing agency costs without harming bondholders. Since a call provision is an option held by equity holders of the firm written on an asset, which is a noncallable bond, every time firms do something to damage the interest of bondholders, they will end up damaging the option value. So it is possible to think of designing that call-provision contract so that the incentive problem is completely neutralized. Not by coincidence, we also see that these highly developed capital markets tend to have highly complex features in the securities issued by the firms.

One basic issue in less developed capital markets is actually a systematic examination of the nature of agency conflicts that arise in that setting. It is not immediately obvious that one could carry over various classes of agency problems that have been studied in finance directly into the setting of less developed capital markets. An example of that is that in those settings there exist financial institutions or large claim holders who have a large control of the firm so that there may not be much conflict within a private system. This is just one example that things do not always carry over. In fact, that is really the point in Thomadakis's chapter, although Thomadakis is focusing on the owner-manager, as opposed to a lending firm. Nevertheless, this gives an indication as to why there is actually a need for determining exactly what these conflicts are. It is important that we determine the nature of these conflicts, because without doing that, we will be unable to determine the nature of the contract that will resolve those conflicts.

The next issue really has to do with the design of contracts. What kind of contracts will emerge in the building up of the market setting? Again, I give an agency conflict as an example. The earlier example can emphasize the fact that there is a possibility of not observing major conflicts among financial claim holders within the private system, but there could be a significant conflict of interest between private financial claim holders and the public at large. The paper that I have done with Professor Kose John, which I mentioned in my discussion of the chapter by Thomadakis, provides a way of mitigating that conflict. It turns out that if there is a conflict between the private system and the public system, one way of mitigating that problem is to create mechanisms so that there will be conflict within the private system itself. One way of doing this would be to create incentives for firms to issue debt claims. This implies that if government policies are designed to focus on the development of markets, the policies should be targeted to the development of both the equity market and the bond markets. I think that debt claims could actually serve a useful self-enforcing mechanism in dealing with such conflicts in contrast to government regulation, which would unduly penalize or reward the actions of the agents (or the regulated).

The other implication has to do with the fact that the public might benefit by providing incentives for mergers. That may be a big issue in a less developed capital market. It might become an issue in the context of the Congress trying to attack outside raiders. Why is merger useful in that kind of conflict? It has to do with the fact that when a portfolio is worth less than the sum of the private values of the component options, part of the subsidy that the government provides will dissipate. If there are two assets that are identical in terms of their cash-flow patterns, one of which is already existing and the other is completely new, it seems to me that the government would benefit from encouraging expansion through existing assets, as opposed to acquiring a new asset. The reason is that a new asset would require new subsidies in the private sector. By the same token, what this suggests to me is that these conflicts provide an opportunity to examine the nature of the development capital that the less developed economies might attract, so as to minimize the unnecessary subsidy to outside agents. Much of what I am saying is without the benefit of detailed analysis. However I see here an opportunity for research in the area of direct foreign investment and the nature of development capital that countries can attract by virtue of the conflicts that exist between the private and the public sector.

Staying with the design of contracts, I feel strongly that the agency-based theoretic framework sheds some light on the design of alternative financial contracts between countries. I think that this point is particularly important concerning the debt crisis. I regard the debt crisis as resulting from the fact that debt has fixed obligations. Obligations would eventually imply the possibility for default. It is very hard for us to think of countries being bankrupt. The fundamental problem, though, is not the default per se. The problem is that we do not know what a default limit is. A default limit for these countries is not observable. For instance, if a firm that borrows goes under, it is possible for bondholders to take over the firm. It would be hard for the bankers in the United States to take over Mexico, but if the default limits had been established and were entirely observable, these bankruptcy proceedings could be done the same exact way as they would be done in the private sector. Perhaps one way to deal with this issue would be to think of alternative securities that would not imply, but that would counteract, this problem of the believability of the default limit. I happen to think that since the default limit is not observable, there might be a massive transfer of wealth from the borrower to the lender. It makes a lot of sense for the lender to stay put. It might just be possible to encroach upon all the future growth opportunities of the borrower if things are not readily observable. It has been said that the debt crisis actually has become an investment crisis. This is one of the things that I would expect in finance, that when there is a lot of outstanding debt, there is a disincentive for new investments. This is a classic underinvestment problem associated with debt financing. One way of thinking about these alternative securities would be to make them contingent on something. One way to make them contingent would be to use the foreign exchange reserves as a basis. However, it is possible for foreign exchange reserves to be manipulated, so it is necessary to think of factors that are mutually observable and verifiable. This is an interesting avenue for research in less developed capital markets.

There are a couple of other issues that I also regard as having a potential for research in this area. One is international taxation, and the other has to do with incomplete markets and transaction costs. This might be relevant to developed economies as well. I have written a paper with Jim Hodder (1990) that shows that differences in tax rates alone do not create a linkage between investment and financial decisions. If taxes are readily marketable, one can think of international corporate tax arbitrage, which would actually undo the imperfections that would arise from tax differences. This is an extension of the domestic tax model. An interesting implication is that the same forces we use in highly developed economies, such as agency costs, are required in developing optimal capital structure. Once we get into that, though, there is another dimension. Capital structure becomes a mechanism for corporate financial intermediation, especially in those countries whose capital markets are not well developed. One way that it could become a mechanism for financial intermediation is that in the process of optimizing the debt itself, the firm would not only engage in coming up to the level of optimal debt financing, but also in attaining the optimal currency composition of the debt.

The other issue has to do with incomplete markets and transaction costs. My friend Vihang Errunza and I have written a paper that deals with the theory of the multinational firm and the role that it has in completing international markets. That kind of research is still unsettled. It ought to be settled in such a way that it is communicated to those who are interested in finance. What I see in that kind of research is a very interesting policy implication, if we have a way of documenting it and a way that could get it communicated forcefully. There are financial benefits associated with direct foreign investment. That creates an incentive for firms in advanced economies to extend their development capital, not just because of their superior technologies, but by virtue of providing benefits of diversification, which are otherwise unavailable to their home-base investors. When I say benefits of diversification, I am not talking about diversification across stock exchanges. I think that one could access the London Stock Exchange or the Tokyo Stock Exchange easily. I think that the most important barrier to investment and other markets is the nontradability of some market components. A large segment of these markets is not traded, human capital being an example of this. What firms can do is to locate in various geographic areas and allow access to the nontraded segment. This view may be tested empirically. One way of doing that would be to use the arbitrage pricing theory, not because I am fond of it, but because people tend to use it a lot. One possibility would be to generate a regional arbitrage pricing—like Asian, European, or African. Then one could actually link the extent to which direct foreign investment attempts to undo this segmentation of arbitrage pricing across national boundaries.

Finally, I also think, with reference to incomplete markets, that corporate finance is a financial intermediation activity. When we think of financial intermediation services, we think of financial institutions. It may well be that capital markets or financial intermediation services could develop not from issuers of securities per se, but from firms that actually produce real goods and services. A very simple and primitive example of this would be to think of an all-equity economy, in which nothing else was available but people wanting to borrow or lend. The firm would have an incentive to split its equity into leveraged equity and debt and expand the investment opportunity. The firm could do it and would have a comparative advantage in providing these kinds of services rather than having a financial intermediary buying up the firm's securities and reissuing alternative securities. The chapter by Kumar and Tsetsekos shows the development phases of the financial markets. I think that what is missing is the possibility that some of these markets were not developed in the same fashion as in the United States, because there could have been substitute corporate financing intermediation services. You cannot simply link economic development with financial development and ignore corporate financing intermediation services.

REFERENCE

Hodder, James E., and Lemma W. Senbet. (1990). "International Capital Structure Equilibrium." *Journal of Finance* 45: 1495–1516.

F21 G₁₅³ 69-73

O16 F21

21

Research Directions: International Investments

VIHANG ERRUNZA

This chapter discusses investment issues in the emerging markets. I think that the best way to do this is to review what has been done in the past, to see where we are, and then to ponder the future. To this effect, I have prepared a bibliography. There are two basic problems with this list. First, it is heavily biased toward my research interests. Second, all the references are North American, which to some degree reflects my ignorance about other bibliographical sources. For example, I do know that there are quite a few Brazilian, Indian, and Hong Kong publications on the emerging markets. With the cooperation of authors who send me their published or working papers, I hope to be able to update the list appropriately.

DIVERSIFICATION BENEFITS

A number of studies have demonstrated gains from diversification into emerging markets. They include Levy and Sarnat (1970), the first study that included emerging markets (EMs); Lessard (1973), on four Latin American countries; Errunza (1977), on IMF data; and Errunza (1983), on the emerging markets data base. Since the results are well known and no surprises are expected, we can safely suggest that at present further work is not warranted.

ASSET PRICING MODELS

Perfect-market international asset pricing models (IAPMs) suggest that invest-ors should hold world market portfolios. However, we observe that relatively speaking, Americans hold more American stocks, Brazilians hold more Brazilian stocks, and so on. In an attempt to explain this divergence and to model a world market structure that is neither fully integrated nor completely segmented, researchers in recent years have developed IAPMs under barriers to free flow of capital. Some examples are Black (1974), Stulz (1981), and Cooper and Kaplanis (1986), on taxes on foreign investment; and Errunza and Losq (1985a), on unequal access and prohibitive taxes. These models suggest that investors will hold portfolios that are heavier in their home assets. Thus the newer models to some degree explain what we see in the real world as far as investor behavior is concerned. Let me give one example of an IAPM (one that is most appropriate for EMs). Losq and I developed a model under prohibitive capital-inflow barriers; otherwise, the market was assumed to be perfect. In a two-country setting, if we take the United States and Brazil to represent the two segments, the U.S. securities can be held by all investors, whereas only Brazilians are allowed to hold their home securities. Then the U.S. securities would be priced as though the markets were completely integrated, and the Brazilian securities would be priced with a national risk premium as well as a world risk premium. One of the major limitations of this paper (and other IAPMs under barriers to capital flows) is that they neglect exchange risk. If we view foreign exchange risk as purely an inflation risk, it would impact domestic as well as international asset pricing. Of course, the real exchange risk must be taken into account; see, for example, Senbet 1979).

Let us now turn to future research. To model the capital-flow controls, past researchers have used some form of tax. However, there are many different kinds of taxes, capital controls, and foreign exchange controls, as well as the differences in micro structure. The trading mechanisms are quite different across markets, and one should include these aspects in a real-world model. Finally, these newer models will create substantial problems in testing their implications. That is, they will not easily lend themselves to empirical tests.

EMPIRICAL TESTS

Market Efficiency

A number of tests of market efficiency have appeared in the literature. Some examples are: Niarchos (1972), Greece; Solnik (1973), European markets; Jennergren (1975), Sweden; Jennergren and Korsvold (1975), Norway and Sweden; Palacios (1975), Spain; Sharma and Kennedy (1977), India; Errunza (1979), Brazil; and Errunza and Losq (1985b), emerging markets. Most of these tests are of the weak form and suggest that EMs are reasonably efficient. Further tests on unexplored markets and semistrong tests based on reliable data would be welcome.

Asset Pricing

Some examples of tests of asset pricing models that include emerging markets are Niarchos (1972), Greece; Pogue and Solnik (1974), European markets; Palacios (1975), Spain; and Errunza and Losq (1985a), multicountry EM test. By and large, EMs appear to be neither fully integrated nor completely segmented. Further tests on unexplored markets, keeping in mind problems of Capital Asset Pricing Model (CAPM) and data reliability, would be very interesting.

EM PERSPECTIVE

There are two basic questions:

1. Benefits of developing local capital markets
2. Benefits of foreign portfolio investments

Developmental Effect of Capital Markets

A number of researchers have dealt with financial liberalization issues. Among them are Goldsmith (1969), Shaw (1973), and McKinnon (1973), financial markets; and Errunza (1974, 1979) and van Agtmael (1984), capital markets. A number of issues need further attention. For example, one can analyze the country-specific benefits of capital market development, optimal ways to develop local markets, and lessons from today's developed markets.

Impact of FPI Liberalization

In recent years a number of EMs have embarked upon ways to attract foreign portfolio investments (FPIs), for example, the National Index Funds from Brazil, India, Korea, and Mexico. At the theoretical level, attempts have been made to address the issues related to FPI liberalization, market integration, and welfare gains. Some examples are Subrahmanyam (1977), market integration; Errunza (1986), FPI liberalization; and Errunza and Losq (1988), welfare effects. Further research that documents gains from recent FPI liberalization efforts would be most welcome.

GENERAL OBSERVATIONS ON EM RESEARCH

When we research emerging markets, at times we have to question the basics that we take for granted in North America. We also encounter a number of myths that fortunately are slowly disappearing. For example, if one asked an investor five years ago whether the emerging markets were risky, the answer would have been yes, very risky. However, now the situation has changed. There is persuasive evidence that there is not that much difference in riskiness between emerging markets (on the average) and most European markets except London.

We also have to be bold and innovative. Journal referees are not very sympathetic, and in many instances rightly so. This is because there is generally a problem with data in terms of reliability and accuracy. It might also be fruitful to think differently. If we think in a North American finance context and tailor our research in the same vein, the gains in our understanding of EMs would be limited. It might be more useful to use EMs to resolve some of the puzzles in finance literature and to enrich the data banks and bring a fresh perspective.

SELECTED REFERENCES ON INVESTMENT ISSUES IN EMERGING MARKETS

Diversification Benefits

Errunza, V. (1977). "Gains from Portfolio Diversification into Less Developed Countries' Securities." *Journal of International Business Studies*, Fall/Winter, 83–99.
———. (1978). "Gains from Portfolio Diversification into Less Developed Countries' Securities: A Reply." *Journal of International Business Studies*, Spring/Summer, 117–123.
———. (1983). "Emerging Markets—A New Opportunity for Improving Global Portfolio Performance." *Financial Analysts Journal* 39, no. 5: 51–58.
Errunza, V., and P. Padmanabhan. (1988). "On Benefits of Portfolio Investments in Emerging Markets." *Financial Analysts Journal* 44, no. 4: 76–78.
Lessard, D. (1973). "International Portfolio Diversification: A Multivariate Analysis for a Group of Latin American Countries." *Journal of Finance*, 619–633.
Levy, H., and M. Sarnat. (1970). "International Diversification of Investment Portfolios." *American Economic Review*, September, 668–675.
van Agtmael, A., and V. Errunza. (1982). "Foreign Portfolio Investment in Emerging Securities Markets." *Columbia Journal of World Business*, Summer, 58–63.

Asset Pricing Models

Black, F. (1974). "International Capital Market Equilibrium with Investment Barriers." *Journal of Financial Economics* 1: 337–352.
Cooper, I., and C. Kaplanis. (1986). "Costs to Crossborder Investment and International Equity Market Equilibrium." In *Recent Developments in Corporate Finance*, ed. J. Edwards, J Franks, C. Mayer, and S. Schaefer. New York: Cambridge University Press.
Errunza, V., and E. Losq. (1985a). "International Asset Pricing under Mild Segmentation— Theory and Test." *Journal of Finance* 40 (March): 105–124.
Lessard, D., T. Bollier, R. Eckans, and R. Kahn. (1983). "Country Risk, Capital Market Integration, and Project Evaluation: A Canadian Perspective." Sloan School of Management, M.I.T. Mimeographed.
Senbet, L. (1979). "International Capital Market Equilibrium and the Multinational Firm Financing and Investment Policies." *Journal of Financial and Quantitative Analysis*, 455–480.
Stulz, R. (1981). "On the Effects of Barriers to International Investment." *Journal of Finance* 36 (September): 923–934.

Empirical Tests

Errunza, V. (1979). "Efficiency and the Programs to Develop Capital Markets: The Brazilian Experience." *Journal of Banking and Finance*, 355–382.

Errunza, V., and E. Losq. (1985b). "The Behavior of Stock Prices of LDC Markets." *Journal of Banking and Finance* 9: 561–575.

———. (1987). "On Riskiness of Emerging Markets: Myths and Perceptions versus Theory and Evidence." *Journal of Portfolio Management*, Fall, 62–67.

Errunza, V., and R. Roseberg. (1982). "Investment Risk in Developed and Less Developed Countries." *Journal of Financial and Quantitative Analysis* 17: 741–762.

Errunza, V., E. Losq, and P. Padmanabhan. (1987). "A Test of Integration, Mild Segmentation, and Segmentation Hypotheses." Working paper, McGill University, Montreal, Canada.

Jennergren, P. (1975). "Filter Test of Swedish Share Prices." In *International Capital Markets*, ed. E. J. Elton and M. J. Gruber. Amsterdam: North-Holland.

Jennergren, L. P., and P. Korsvold. (1975). "The Non-random Character of Norwegian and Swedish Stock Market Prices." In *International Capital Markets*, ed. E. J. Elton and M. J. Gruber. Amsterdam: North-Holland.

Niarchos, N. (1972). "The Stock Market in Greece." In *Mathematical Methods in Investment and Finance*, ed. G. Szego and K. Shell. Amsterdam: North-Holland.

Palacios, J. (1975). "The Stock Market in Spain: Tests of Efficiency and Capital Market Theory." In *International Capital Markets*, ed. E. J. Elton and M. J. Gruber. Amsterdam: North-Holland.

Pogue, G., and B. Solnik. (1974). "The Market Model Applied to European Common Stocks: Some Empirical Results." *Journal of Financial and Quantitative Analysis*, December, 917–944.

Sharma, J., and R. Kennedy. (1977). "A Comparative Analysis of Stock Price Behavior on the Bombay, London, and New York Stock Exchanges." *Journal of Financial and Quantitative Analysis*, September, 391–414.

Solnik, B. (1973). "Note on the Validity of the Random Walk for European Stock Prices." *Journal of Finance*, December, 1151–1159.

EM Perspective

Errunza, V. (1974). "Optimal International Portfolio Investments and the Development Process." Ph.D. diss., Graduate School of Business Administration, University of California, Berkeley.

Errunza, V., and E. Losq. (1988). "Capital Flow Controls, International Asset Pricing, and Investors' Welfare: A Multicountry Framework." Working paper, McGill University, Montreal, Canada.

Goldsmith, R. (1969). *Financial Structure and Development*. New Have, Conn.: Yale University Press.

McKinnon, R. (1973). *Money and Capital in Economic Development*. Washington, D.C.: Brookings Institution.

Ness, W., Jr. (1974). "Financial Markets Innovation as a Development Strategy: Initial Results from the Brazilian Experience." *Economic Development and Cultural Change* 23 (April): 436–453.

Shaw, E. (1973). *Financial Deepening in Economic Development*. New York: Oxford University Press.

Subrahmanyam, M. (1975). "On the Optimality of International Capital Market Integration." *Journal of Financial Economics* 2: 3–28.

van Agtmael, A. (1984). *Emerging Securities Markets*. London: Euromoney Publications.

Index

About the Editors
and Contributors

Professor Sarath Abeysekera, Department of Accounting and Finance, University of Manitoba, Canada

Dr. George C. Anayiotos, Department of Economics, University of Colorado, United States

Professor Yaman Asikoglu, Department of Economics, City University of New York, United States

Mr. Taeho Bark, Korean Development Institute, Korea

Graciela Bueno, Facultad de Ciencias Politicas y Sociales, Universidad Autónoma de México, Mexico

Dr. Graciana del Castillo, Department of Economics, Columbia University, United States

Mr. Chingfu Chang, Department of Business Administration, National Central University, Taiwan

Dr. Philip Chang, Faculty of Management, University of Calgary, Canada

Dr. Uwe Corsepius, Kiel Institute of World Economics, Federal Republic of Germany

Dr. Mansoor Dailami, Development Research Department, The World Bank, Washington, D.C., United States

Dr. Ishac Diwan, Institute of Economics Department, The World Bank, Washington, D.C., United States

Dr. Vihang Errunza, Faculty of Management, McGill University, Canada

Dr. I. Özer Ertuna, School of Administration, Bogazici University, Turkey

Professor Klaus P. Fischer, Faculty of Administration Sciences, Université Laval, Canada

Mr. Everaldo Guedes Franca, Faculty of Economics, University of São Paulo, Brazil

Professor Mahendra R. Gujarathi, Department of Finance, Bentley College, United States

Mr. Hugh Haworth, Securities and Exchange Commission, Washington, D.C., United States

Mr. V. N. Hukku, Department of Finance, University of Jodhpur, India

Dr. G. Wenchi Kao, Department of Economics and Finance, University of Dayton, United States

Dr. Richard Kitchen, Project Planning Center, University of Bradford, England

Dr. P. C. Kumar, Department of Finance and Real Estate, American University, United States

Professor Sevil Kutay, Department of Finance, Queens University, Canada

Professor Martin Laurence, Department of Finance, William Paterson College, United States

Professor Cheng Few Lee, Department of Finance, Rutgers University, United States

Professor Esmeralda O. Lyn, Department of Banking and Finance, Hofstra University, United States

Professor Ade T. Ojo, Department of Finance, University of Lagos, Nigeria

Dr. Edgar Ortiz, Department of Finance, University of San Diego, United States

Dr. Asmo P. Palasvirta, Faculty of Business Administration, Memorial University of Newfoundland, Canada

Dr. George J. Papaioannou, Chairperson, Department of Banking and Finance, Hofstra University, United States

Professor Antonio Zoratto Sanvicente, Department of Administration, Faculty of Economics and Administration, University of São Paulo, Brazil

Professor Lemma W. Senbet, College of Business and Management, University of Maryland, United States

Dr. Marjorie T. Stanley, M. J. Neeley School of Business, Texas Christian University, United States

Dr. Stavros B. Thomadakis, Department of Economics and Finance, Baruch College, City University of New York, United States

Dr. George Tsetsekos, Department of Finance, Drexel University, United States

Dr. Frank Tuzzolino, Department of World Business, Thunderbird University, United States

Dr. James Tybout, Department of Economics, Georgetown University and the World Bank, United States

Dr. Daniel D. Tzang, Department of Finance, National Chung Cheng University, Taiwan

Dr. Ashok Vora, Department of Economics and Finance, Baruch College, City University of New York, United States

Professor Jeffrey Weiss, Department of Economics and Finance, Baruch College, City University of New York, United States

Dr. Gili Yen, Department of Business Administration, National Central University, Taiwan

Professor Demir Yener, Babson College, United States

Dr. Othman Yong, National University of Malaysia, Malaysia